THE GOSPEL OF JOHN

Chapters 1 to 21

Dedicated to

*all who have supported
me in prayer*

THE GOSPEL OF JOHN

Pastoral and Theological Studies

Ronald S. Wallace

Editor
David C Searle

Published by
Rutherford House

British Library Cataloguing in Publication Data

A catalogue record for this book is available from
The British Library

ISBN 1-904429-01-7

Typeset by David Searle, Edinburgh
and Printed by
T.J. International Ltd., Padstow, Cornwall

iv

Contents

Foreword
to this Volume (2004)

Over the years of my ministry, as I prepared the Word of God for my people, I sought not to neglect any part of the Bible. Yet I found it was the John's Gospel which impressed itself upon my mind more constantly than any other book, and almost invariably when I was asked to preach or lecture on special occasions I have found myself using aspects or parts of it as my texts.

Ten years after I retired, I felt I had enough worthwhile material on the reflections, signs, conversations with Jesus, and on his personal claims in the first eleven chapters of the book to publish what might be of help to others who were engaged in a preaching or teaching ministry, and also to the ordinary reader, and I gave it a limited circulation. This first volume was published by Scottish Academic Press in September 1991.

After much encouragement from friends who have read it, and after further study, I have been able to complete what I then began, with this second volume (incorporating the first volume). The citations from Brown, Hoskyns, Godet and Calvin reveal the commentaries I have in my restricted bookshelves' space since I retired, and those from Newbigin, Temple and Luthi indicate the books I recently borrowed to help me to write the present volume. My treatment of chapters 12 to 21 is not as comprehensive as for chapters 1 to 11 in the 1990 volume, because I am no longer engaged in writing sermons. However, I have gladly given my editor, David Searle, permission to add footnotes to deal with points of interest which I have myself may have passed over.

I have little to add to what I said in my former Introduction (p. xiii) except that I found myself, in working through chapters 12 to 21, adapting the habit of calling the final editor of the Gospel as we have it 'the evangelist' (who is often assumed to have been the author of the Johannine epistles). The text which he edited gave full and clear expression to the witness, written and spoken, of John the Apostle, who was the 'beloved disciple'.

It has been my chief aim, in writing and seeking to publish this material, to make what I have felt to be a worthwhile contribution from another quite personal viewpoint to the unfolding of the unsearchable richness of the witness of the Gospel to Christ.

RSW

ACKNOWLEDGEMENTS

Once again I am indebted to my good friend Dr R.B.W. Walker for typing out my original script on John chapters 12 to 21. I am also most grateful to David Searle for editing the overall text and preparing the first volume to be combined with my manuscript on the remaining chapters for publication as an entire commentary on The Gospel of John. He has also added occasional footnotes to the text of the first eleven chapters, and improved the usefulness of chapters 12 to 21 by including further footnotes on points of particular interest on which I myself have not commented.

Ronald S Wallace

Edinburgh, July 2004

EDITOR'S FOREWORD

I want to express my deep appreciation to Dr Wallace both for affording me the privilege of preparing this volume for publication and for the freedom he has given me to fill out the text of chapters 12 to 21 with occasional footnotes. Readers must understand that his commentary on these chapters has largely been written after Dr Wallace reached the age of 90 years—surely an immense achievement. There cannot be many works written by authors of such a great age which match the high standards attained here.

The first volume covering chapters 1 to 11 (published in 1991) was based on the text of the Revised Standard Version. However, since chapters 12 to 21 are based on the New Revised Standard Version, for the sake of consistency I have adapted the material from the first volume to the NRSV also. Throughout the book, references to John's Gospel are referred to simply by chapter and verse, e.g. (10:15), without stating 'John' is being quoted.

I am grateful to the Revd David Easton, a parish minister who has found immense benefit in using the first volume in sermon preparation, for writing the Preface. I am also grateful to Mrs Alison Carter who has proof-read for me the whole revised text.

David C Searle

Edinburgh, 2004

Preface

It is thirteen years since Dr. Wallace's commentary on the first eleven chapters of *The Gospel of John, Pastoral and Theological Studies,* was published. All whose understanding of 'the spiritual gospel' has been deepened by his insights will welcome the publication of this second edition of the first volume of the together with chapters 12 to 21, thus forming a commentary on the whole book.

The reflective nature of the Gospel is mirrored in Dr. Wallace's commentary which is the fruit of many years of study and thought. (He had reached the great age of 92 when he completed the remaining ten chapters!) The concerns of the academic, the preacher and the pastor come together in a flow of thought which succeeds in engaging with the text at different levels. Scholarly comment, devotional reflection, pastoral application and topical relevance seamlessly combine. Insights abound.

Those who preach will find in his reflections the seminal thoughts from which sermons grow. For the ordinary reader, there is also much to nourish the faith, stimulate the mind and warm the heart.

But more than that, the commentary is faithful to John's purpose in writing his Gospel: *so that you may come to believe that Jesus is the Messiah, the Son of God, and that through believing you may have life in his name* (20:31). The exposition is punctuated with the earnest pleas of the preacher to believe, as Dr. Wallace presents to us not only who Jesus was when he lived among us, but also what the risen and ascended Christ would do for us today by his Spirit. In his own words: 'Christ is still opening blind eyes, making the lame to walk, the deaf to hear, enabling those who have been dumb to witness his glory. Indeed, the Gospels now appear to be not only about what he once did, but about what he wants to do in our midst today especially through the word preached within our churches.' Both the humanity and deity of Jesus Christ are faithfully portrayed.

All who study the Gospel of John will find in Dr. Wallace a wise and devout guide. I warmly commend his commentary.

David Easton
Minister of Burnside Blairbeth Church of Scotland, Glasgow

Foreword

to the first Volume (1991)

For over fifty years, ministering to various congregations, I have often preached from the Gospel of John, given it a place in my bible class teaching, studied it with fellow parish ministers, and lectured on it to lay people. I have taught it as a class subject in theological seminary. This book has been written to share with pastors and others who are concerned to study the Bible, some of the insights into the text that have, come to me in the course of such a ministry. My custom in preaching or teaching was to divide the text into sections which appeared to have some unity, and to go through it, section by section, story by story, incident by incident, concentrating mainly on the dynamic movement of the incident or the thought. Through this procedure I tried to bring out the meaning of words and sentences and thus the important theological and consequent practical lessons which might help my hearers to see what I saw, and to hear what I myself had already heard as I worked with each passage.

As a pastor I was always chiefly concerned to find what the Spirit is saying to the church today through the text as we have it before us. I often felt in my ministry that I discovered the meaning of a passage most clearly as I found it applying itself directly to the pastoral situation which I faced among those who were to listen to me. In writing this book, moreover, I have found that I could best convey the meaning of the passage before me if I kept the rhetorical form in which its meaning came to me in the course of my work. The reader will therefore find that while certain sections of the book reflect how I treated the passage under review in bible class studies or lectures, more often the comments indicate what I said in the pulpit, and sometimes have been shaped by the form of a sermon I preached.

Some time ago I attended a seminar for post-graduate students led by a visiting scholar of international reputation. The passage under discussion was the ministry of the Baptist as it is related in the first chapter of John. Some new background material of which I had not been fully aware was brought to light, and an interpretation was given which raised questions in my mind as to whether the approach I had previously made to the passage was justifiable. A student present, however, remarked that from these and other studies he had engaged in, he had come to wonder whether anyone today, having listened to such background purported 'revelations' about John's Gospel could now really preach from it at all. In reply the lecturer graciously conceded, however, that a preacher could legitimately take liberties with the text which were not open to himself as a scholar. Such a reply emboldened me not to alter what I had already written on John chapter 1. Indeed, I was relieved to feel there might be a place, even on the shelves of a New Testament student's library, for a book showing how a preacher took this liberty allowed to him in his task.

Only here and there in the book have I been able acknowledge my indebtedness to the many commentaries, academic essays, and sermons I have read on the Gospel, over the years. (I have lost all the other references I may have had.) Of course I read everything I could, and latterly I lived near a well-stocked theological library. I liked Hoskyn's commentary best of all, and I must record my admiration for Raymond Brown's more recent work.

My dear wife was my closest companion and collaborator throughout the whole ministry during which this book took shape. She was nearly always there when I preached, and often when I taught. Up until now she always read, and improved what I wrote. I have not felt I wanted to consult anyone in her place. This is why there may be infelicities in the text, which her acute mind would have corrected. I have to thank Dr Douglas Grant for the encouragement he has given me to produce this volume, and I am grateful to Rev Dr. R. B. W. Walker for careful proof reading and helpful suggestions.

As I was preparing its final draft, I had the opportunity of preaching some of it in 'series' to the congregations of Juniper Green Church, Edinburgh and St Paul's, Galashiels. It encouraged me that my hearers were so warmly appreciative. Then I was invited to go to Talladega, Alabama, for three months during the winter of 1988–89 to teach John's Gospel to the 'Caravan Bible Class'. I am most grateful for their warm hospitality and friendship, and for the extraordinary helpful and inspiring opportunity it gave me to teach such a large, eager and intelligent gathering of adults while I was preparing the book.

Of course in preaching and teaching I have become aware of the assumptions I have had to make about the purpose and authority of the 'writer' of the Gospel. For the sake of the early reader I have occasionally given in the text a reason for the interpretation I have made (see e.g. pp. 17ff. and 95f.) and I have clarified the presuppositions of my own personal approach in an introductory article.

Ronald S. Wallace
Edinburgh, September, 1991

Introduction

to the first Volume (1991)

An Approach to the Gospel

H.R Mackintosh, teaching us theology in the 1930's, advised us, in facing the doubts and problems we might have, to 'get into the presence of Jesus' and to allow him to make God's own presence and power real to us. He was appealing to us to turn to the Gospel accounts of Jesus, and to read them with devoted and receptive minds. Mackintosh believed that the Gospels were there to give us access to the living Christ today, and to enable us to enter a fellowship with him no less influential than that enjoyed by the Apostles themselves, and many other contemporaries, in his earthly presence. Such fellowship with Jesus in the days of his flesh inevitably brought the early disciples to a profound experience of repentance, accompanied by the immediate and complete assurance that their sins were forgiven. It was Mackintosh's concern that by our own recourse to the Gospel story we ourselves should first of all experience in some way the forgiving love of Christ.

He was confident, moreover, that the forgiving love thus experienced would help to confirm our faith in the divinity of Jesus himself, justify to our minds the authority that rings through all his teaching about God and life, and bring our lives under the constraint of his call to surrender our self-will and to follow him, even laying down our lives for his sake. A continuing openness to his influence would indeed ultimately lead us to give him the highest place in the universe. The logic of the experience would be inescapable: 'Only God can forgive, yet Jesus has forgiven us, only God has a right to demand the complete sacrifice of another for his own sake, yet the Jesus we know and hear through the Gospels makes such a demand upon us!' We must immediately confess that he is Lord, and cannot doubt that since he has enabled us to overcome sin, he has the power to see through every other difficulty which life, either in this world or beyond, can put in our way.

Of course Mackintosh in his theology also took us to the heart of every important aspect of the teaching of the Pauline Epistles. He directed our thought, faith and devotion to the exalted Christ.

He gave us a full understanding of the meaning of the Cross as it developed in the thought of the growing Church. Nevertheless, like Luther and Calvin he always saw the seeds of such a fuller development of the faith already there in what the earliest disciples experienced, apprehended and began to understand when they were with him in the flesh. Moreover, like the reformers he always stressed our need to return again and again to the One presented to us in the Gospels, in order to maintain our grasp of the faith in its fullness.

In our New Testament studies at the time I am referring to, the Gospel of John was sometimes set apart from the other synoptic accounts as being of lesser historical value. Matthew, Mark and Luke alone were accepted as intended to present us with reliable historical information about the human Jesus as he was actually seen and experienced by his disciples in 'the days of his flesh'. The Gospel of John, however, was regarded as a carefully drawn picture of the God-Man as he was seen within the faith of the early church by a writer who was concerned not to relate historical fact, but rather to give us a 'spiritual' Gospel. It was also held that its writer, in the picture he gave us of Jesus, was especially concerned to relate his person, work, and teaching to those who belonged to the contemporary Greek world of culture and thought.

It seems important, however, that in our modern 'quest for the historical Jesus' we should not in any way neglect the fourth Gospel. I myself have come to think of it as written under the guidance and close supervision of the Apostle John. He knew the tradition circulated through the other Gospels. He did not wish to repeat this in his own Gospel though he confirmed it where he could. He had, however, other things to say than had been already said. He himself had been differently impressed than were his fellow Apostles by some of the events which had taken place, and had been more sensitive to certain aspects of the person, teaching, and life-work of Jesus when he had been with them. It was his mission to give this witness in his own independent way in the midst of circumstances surrounding him.

While all the Gospel accounts of Jesus continually stress his real humanity and his close identification with us in our human weakness and need, a fuller picture is given in John's Gospel than in the others of the difference, indeed of the apartness, between himself and us. We find in the fourth Gospel much that isolates him from us, and exalts him in character far above anything that can normally be defined as 'human'. His personal sinlessness and holiness seem to put him at a distance from us. Moreover, even while he is so much at home with us in this world, he seems to belong to another world, one which he uniquely shares with his Father in Heaven. John obviously threw such aspects of Jesus' person into strong relief because he believed that it was important for the church to have them in mind in its devotion and preaching. His holiness and majesty do not repel but attract us to him. In his sheer apartness he is near to our need. He is able to save us not only because he is like us, but also because he is different from us. The isolation into which he was 'lifted up' not only on his cross but also even in his exaltation draws us to himself (John 12:32).

We need not imagine that John's presentation of Jesus is in any way an artificially drawn portrait designed to emphasise a theological point. His account is what he remembered from his fellowship with the Lord. That a Gospel was given its final form even many years after the occurrence of the events it relates need not imply that its witness is any less reliable, historically or otherwise, than any writing more immediately composed. We suggest that John was able to penetrate the history which he remembered and probe its meaning all the more accurately, because of the greater historical distance between himself and the events which it was his purpose to relate. On such late reflection, under the influence of the Spirit, he was possibly able to see what had really been there when his mind was not so acute and sensitive to the realities which Jesus presented to those around him through the years of his early ministry. We can well imagine, moreover, that as the years passed it would become impossible for the Apostle to distinguish between what had been there in the earlier layers of memory and what came to clarification through later reflection and insight.

I have found helpful the suggestion that there was a Johannine circle of disciples who were active in preaching and in teaching the Gospel under the Apostle's leadership. Such preaching involved the continual re-telling and re-consideration of the incidents and stories within the presentation of the whole proclamation and its purpose would be to open to the hearer the same possibilities of seeing the glory of the 'Word made flesh', and of receiving 'from his fullness', as had been open to the contemporaries of Jesus when he was himself living and working among them.

There is no doubt that to all the Gospel writers everything that Jesus did was full of significance. His miracles, for example, as well as being revelations of his compassionate humanity and unique demonstrations of his power, are also signs pointing to his Messiah-ship and revealing the place he has come to fulfil in the life of the people of God. The Apostle John, however was especially sensitive to the fact that every deed of the Word was uniquely and inevitably itself a Word of God. When he was with Jesus as a disciple he had found that certain events which he had been involved in, or had witnessed, had especially impressed his mind. They had clarified his vision of who Jesus was, and had deepened his understanding of what he had come to do. As he had thought over such events and spoken of them in his later ministry he had come to regard them as signs of the 'glory as of the only Son from the Father' (John 1:14 RSV), that was always there in Jesus seeking expression in his activity. He believed, too, that in the ministry he fulfilled amongst people during his earthly life, Jesus was continually giving signs of the kind of ministry he was going to fulfil through his Apostles, after he sent them out to continue his work in his name. We have often discovered what we believe to have been an intended meaning in the text, when we have regarded it as bearing witness not simply to one historic event but to 'Jesus Christ... the same yesterday and today and forever' (see pp 17ff.).

For the purpose of handing on his own unique testimony in one Gospel, John selected certain of these signs and encounters which had especially impressed themselves on his mind and which he treasured in his memory. He put them within a more convincing historical framework than is found by only to the Synoptic Gospels. Though it is not impossible to harmonize the first three Gospels with that of John, it seems indeed that John was more concerned than the other writers to be 'historical'. Yet he also indicates the wealth of meaning which he found in much of what Jesus had done by bringing into his narrative frequent allegorical suggestions. Such allegorical elements are to be regarded not as artificially contrived, but as embedded deeply within the unique history itself. They are pointers through which he is inviting us to 'see through a glass darkly' into the Kingdom of God which has brought into our midst in Jesus.

Although he had such concern to bear faithful testimony to the 'Word... made flesh', John made no attempt to reproduce for us many of the sayings, parables and sermons with which the hearers of the other Gospels would be familiar. There was no need for this in the Church of his day. He himself may have been more sensitive, however, than other disciples to certain aspects of Jesus' teaching of which they give us less clear indications than John would have wished. He had possibly in private asked questions of Jesus and discussed with him the themes on which he had such intense interest. He does not seek to cast what he remembers in a style directly recognisable by those already familiar with the other Gospels. Indeed, in John's Gospel, Jesus expresses himself in a language and style only occasionally used by him in the Synoptics, but used freely by John himself in the Epistles which he wrote later to the churches.

We must not set too narrow limits to the language and phraseology Jesus could have used during his earthly ministry. Might he not have used the kind of language John presents to us, on sufficiently many occasions for it to take a firm grip on the minds of some of his hearers to whom he knew it was especially relevant and appealing? It may be that as the corpus of Jesus' teaching had been stored in John's mind over many years, and dominated all his thought, it had both affected, and been affected by, his own way of thinking and style of speaking, without any contamination of its own true force and meaning. It is remarkable that when reading the New Testament, we turn from hearing the spoken words of Jesus, as they are brought to us in the Synoptic Gospels, to the discourses quoted to us in John, we know ourselves to be still listening to his one authentic voice.

RSW

CHAPTER 1

THE PROLOGUE

John 1:1-18

1 In the beginning was the Word, and the Word was with God, and the Word was God. [2]He was in the beginning with God. [3]All things came into being through him, and without him not one thing came into being. What has come into being [4]in him was life, and the life was the light of all people. [5]The light shines in the darkness, and the darkness did not overcome it.

6 There was a man sent from God, whose name was John. [7]He came as a witness, to testify to the light, so that all might believe through him. [8]He himself was not the light, but he came to testify to the light. [9]The true light, which enlightens everyone, was coming into the world.

10 He was in the world, and the world came into being through him; yet the world did not know him. [11]He came to what was his own, and his own people did not accept him. [12]But to all who received him, who believed in his name, he gave power to become children of God, [13]who were born, not of blood or of the will of the flesh or of the will of man, but of God.

14 And the Word became flesh and lived among us, and we have seen his glory, the glory as of a father's only son, full of grace and truth. [15](John testified to him and cried out, 'This was he of whom I said, "He who comes after me ranks ahead of me because he was before me."') [16]From his fullness we have all received, grace upon grace. [17]The law indeed was given through Moses; grace and truth came through Jesus Christ. [18]No one has ever seen God. It is God the only Son, who is close to the Father's heart, who has made him known.

The Prologue to the Gospel reads like a hymn in praise of Christ—a doxology in which the author expresses his devotion to the One who has brought light, life and hope into a lost and perishing world. In it he gives his testimony to the glory which he saw in Jesus, and the eternal life which he received from him as he lived with him on earth. He gives us a summary of the faith and experience into which he hopes the reading of the Gospel will introduce us.

We need not spend much time in the study of the verbal detail of the Prologue before we proceed to the Gospel. What it is meant to tell us is best appreciated if its contents are remembered and referred to often as we read the book itself. It is intended, indeed, to direct us to a better appreciation of the witness of the Gospel itself to Jesus. It is in this way simply a key to the understanding of what follows.

The Word and creation

The poem before us will remind us, as we turn to the Gospel, that the Word spoken in the life, death, and resurrection of Jesus is the true and full expression of what God is, and of what he ever was, in the mystery of his own being—even before creation. God uttered himself when he uttered the Word spoken in Jesus.

Jesus brought into this world the life as well as the light of God. These two are inseparable. *In him was life, and the life was the light of all people.* In seeing what he has come to reveal to us we have seen the eternal light that was there in the beginning with God. In our fellowship with him we have tasted the eternal fellowship which God from the beginning desired to share with humankind.

Moreover we have begun also to understand the meaning and purpose of creation itself, for the Word spoken in Jesus is the 'Wisdom' by which God made the world, and which he expressed in its making. Here, in and through him, we find a clear answer to the questions: 'Who am I, and what am I here for?' Here in him, we are in touch with the One who holds everything in the universe together, and who alone can keep it healthy and in order till its final purpose is fulfilled.

The Word and the darkness

The Gospel before us is the story not only of what is revealed and given in Jesus, but also of what was overcome by Jesus. It is the story of a long, relentless conflict. He has come to rescue the world from bondage, and to put right what has absurdly and tragically gone wrong with it. Yet at every step of his way he is

2

opposed. Those in charge of human affairs react to him with deadly hatred. His crucifixion at their hands is a central theme of the unfolding story. The light shines in the darkness, a darkness that seeks to overcome it.[1] The greater and clearer the light, the more intense and forceful the darkness.

The common people around him are in the end no better than their leaders. They welcome him for a while but eventually despise and reject him. Their decision is all the more absurd and tragic because they were his own people. They had been chosen by the Father to receive him, to prepare a place where he would find a welcome and nurture when he came. They had been trained for centuries to understand the message he would bring, the mission he would accomplish, and to give him devotion, service and honour as their Prophet, Priest and King. The appeals he made were irresistible and yet they resisted. The signs he gave them were irrefutable, and yet they argued that he was an impostor. He will offer them their liberty, they will prefer bondage.

Yet his victory was all the more complete because of their very efforts to destroy him. The humiliation to which they subjected him manifested clearly his glory. Each step they took to destroy him fulfilled the plan made by God his Father from all eternity (Eph. 1:4; Rev. 13:8) to manifest his redeeming power and love. In lifting him up to die they set him on the throne from which he has ever since won and ruled the hearts of generations who were now to become his own.

The writer of the prologue links up the darkness which Jesus confronted among his own people in Galilee and Jerusalem with a darkness that seems to have arisen there, 'in the beginning' when God uttered his creative Word and the world came into being. Even then the same darkness sought to overcome the same light. The Prologue thus reminds us at this point that the conflict which we will see Jesus entering when he came to earth was primordial in its origin, age-long in its implications and that his victory was

---

[1] The Greek verb translated by NRSV 'overcome' (v. 5, with GNB, ESV, Jerusalem Bible, etc.) can properly be translated 'understood' (NIV, NKJ, etc.). John may have wanted both meanings as he often appears deliberately to use words ambiguously. (Cf. the verb 'lived', v. 14 below.) Verse 5 would then carry the double meaning that the 'light' of Christ in men and women — 'conscience', or the (marred) image of God — cannot ever be completely extinguished by the darkness, but neither can that residual 'light', without Christ, penetrate the darkness sufficiently to comprehend the love of God.

cosmic in its issues and effects. The challenge which he takes up to settle once for all as he goes to Golgotha was the challenge presented by the powers of darkness to God's sovereignty and love at the very moment of creation. He has come to destroy the works of the devil (1 John 3:8).

The Word became flesh and lived among us

This affirmation expresses the faith of his disciples as they looked back over his life with them on earth.

He was flesh as we are flesh—a truly human being with all our natural affections. They knew his mother and his brothers. They knew that he had been trained as a carpenter. They knew he felt as they themselves felt in many of the common situations and problems that vex us all on our way through life. Under the varied circumstances of his ministry they knew how human his reactions were. They had seen his tears. They had noticed his surprise, wonder and thankfulness in success, his disappointment and frustration in failure, his tiredness under the strain of over-exertion, his occasional weariness, his sensitivity to insult. They knew that in his sheer physical weakness at times he had to find consolation and strength in desperate prayer. Flesh is that which, like everything human, fades and perishes with the passing of time (Isa. 40:6-8) It is prone, they believed, to disease and death.

Yet he rose from the dead, and his resurrection confirmed and explained many other thoughts and experiences which had come to them in his fellowship. At times they had heard him pray and speak to God as if he himself were already in heaven. At times he had made pronouncements about God, life and the future as if he had a clarity of vision, fullness of understanding, and absolute certainty on matters entirely beyond the range of any human mind. To listen to him simply unfolding his own mind had been to listen to the Word and Wisdom of God. Had he not forgiven sins in his own name and on his own authority? Had he not called on people to lay down their lives for his own sake? They had themselves felt that from the moment he called them, it was eternal gain to go on with him, eternal loss to reject his way and offer. The confession made first by Thomas reflected the faith that each one of them finally came to: 'My Lord and my God' (John 20:28). Such thoughts and questions about the mystery of Jesus' personal life led to questions and thoughts about his birth. John did not need to repeat the story of the virgin birth, though there is evidence in his Gospel that he accepted the tradition. He expresses the whole matter much more briefly: *The Word became flesh and lived among us.* There was an incarnation. God did not merely choose this child of Mary, and condescend to express his divine character in the way he lived and died and triumphed. In this man, rather he gave us his own presence, 'his very self and essence all-divine' dwelling *among us.* The testimony of the whole Gospel is that while he dwelt with us in the flesh he was also no less truly dwelling with God.[2]

We have seen… we have all received

As there was in the coming of Jesus into the world an incarnation, so there was also concealment. No one has expressed this mystery better than Charles Wesley:

> Veiled in flesh the Godhead see;
> Hail the Incarnate Deity.

Eternal God—a babe in a manger—ruling the universe!

There are traces in the Old Testament of how God practised such concealment when he dealt with Israel, his people. We are shown how often he went to work most powerfully where there was little outward sign of his activity and how he could hide his glory when he was about to reveal it.

'Truly you are a God who hides himself, O God of Israel, the Saviour' wrote one of the great prophets (Isa. 45:15, AV). He may have been thinking of such events as the destruction of Pharoah's power in Egypt, when instead of launching the battleships of a mighty enemy on the Nile, God launched a little helpless male child in a fragile basket of bulrushes to be pitied and picked up by Pharoah's daughter.

Or he may have remembered that when God wanted to 'visit' and have personal encounter with certain people in the earlier history of

---

[2] The verb translated by NRSV 'lived' is sometimes accurately rendered 'pitched his tent' with the meaning 'lived [among us] for a short time'. This may be another example of John's use of words with two possible meanings. On the one hand, the verb suggests the temporary life of Christ on earth. On the other hand, the same verb is used elsewhere in the NT of the eternal home of the Father. See Revelation 12:12.

Israel, he chose to come and show himself present to them in the humble form of an angel or even of a human-like visitor. We do not wonder that in such aspects of God's work in former times, our forefathers in the faith saw analogies of how he was going to set about his redeeming work in the days to come.

Another Old Testament text from the same prophet foreshadows with even more fitting detail the concealment that was to take place during the early (sometimes called 'hidden') years of Jesus' life, 'For he grew up before him like a young plant, and like a root out of dry ground; he had no form or majesty that we should look at him, and nothing in his appearance that we should desire him' (Isa. 53:2).

The hidden-ness referred to by the prophet was sustained and complete during these early years. People around Jesus of Nazareth heard nothing from him, and saw nothing in him that could lead · them towards discipleship. It was only when he began his earthly ministry declaring himself to be the Messiah that they began to hear and to see. The Baptist himself was the first to see his glory and truth, and he saw it with a clarity and fullness excelled in Jesus' lifetime by no other witness who followed him. *There was a man sent from God, whose name was John. He came as a witness to testify to the light, so that all might believe through him* (v. 6f.).

Central to the story in John's Gospel (as in the others too) is the account of a chosen group of witnesses—the twelve. It is their testimony that is echoed in the prologue and given in the Gospel. *We have seen.... we have all received.* That they should have been chosen to hear and receive was to them miraculously due to the grace of God who had not only revealed himself to them in Jesus, but had given them the inward illumination and disposition to see and believe. They recognized in him what no merely human eye could see. They describe what they saw as his *glory.* They speak of what they received as a sharing of his *fullness* and they add their testimony to its abundance: *grace upon grace.*[3] There was no end to it. This is why they preached and why the Gospel was written.

---

[3] The Greek phrase translated 'grace upon grace' is better translated, 'a grace in place of another grace' (the pronoun is not *epi,* 'upon' but '*anti,* 'instead of'). The meaning therefore is that the grace of the Old Covenant—through Moses—has now been replaced by the grace that has come through Jesus Christ. The Old Covenant was prophetic of the New Covenant for *both* were covenants of grace. For a discussion of the way in which this section of the *Prologue* reflects a section from the book of Exodus, see Morris, p. 103, note 87.

Their witness is handed down to us so that we too, reading and listening, may see, believe and receive as they did.

The poem ends as it began, with praise. What is seen and given in Jesus puts everything else into the shade! Even the Law, which in its day brought light and life to those who loved it, is now seen to be outdated and powerless, for it demands and threatens before it gives: *The law indeed was given through Moses; grace and truth came through Jesus Christ* (v. 17).

He sums up: *No one has ever seen God. It is God the only Son, who is close to the Father's heart, who has made him known.* He is not here giving the result of any careful research he had made either into the other religions of his day or into current philosophical thought. He is simply expressing his wonder at the grace he has encountered and the glory he has seen in Jesus. What is given and seen here can be found only in him and nowhere else. He is giving expression also to its finality. H. R. Mackintosh put it simply and clearly for us in one of his lectures: 'Never in any experience of God here or hereafter will you or I ever find anything that is not already there for us in Jesus Christ, the Word become flesh.'

The Baptist under questioning

John 1:19-28

1 This is the testimony given by John when the Jews sent priests and Levites from Jerusalem to ask him, 'Who are you?' [20]He confessed and did not deny it, but confessed, 'I am not the Messiah.' [21]And they asked him, 'What then? Are you Elijah?' He said, 'I am not.' 'Are you the prophet?' He answered, 'No.' [22]Then they said to him, 'Who are you? Let us have an answer for those who sent us. What do you say about yourself?' [23]He said, 'I am the voice of one crying out in the wilderness, "Make straight the way of the Lord,"' as the prophet Isaiah said.

24 Now they had been sent from the Pharisees. [25]They asked him, 'Why then are you baptizing if you are neither the Messiah, nor Elijah, nor the prophet?' [26]John answered them, 'I baptize with water. Among

you stands one whom you do not know, [27]the one who is coming after me; I am not worthy to untie the thong of his sandal.' [28]This took place in Bethany across the Jordan where John was baptizing.

The last and greatest of the prophets

John the Baptist, in his early preaching, re-echoed the message of all the great Old Testament prophets. He proclaimed a new and better age for the oppressed and the righteous. He spoke of a Messiah who was to usher in the Kingdom of God. He would bring blessing to those prepared to welcome him. He would baptize with the Holy Spirit. He would cleanse public life. What he rejected would be consumed with unquenchable fire. John's central theme was repentance. Each must forsake his sordid aims and lusts, begin to deal righteously with his neighbour, and share with the needy. The rulers of this present world must tremble. The axe was now laid to the root of every corrupt and proud tree. (See Matt. 3:7-12.)

The crowds who flocked to hear him compared John to men like Moses, Elijah, Isaiah and Jeremiah. At last, after 300 years of silence, they believed God was speaking again a living, prophetic word to their nation, and was about to intervene decisively in its historical destiny.

There was one striking difference between John and his predecessors. When the great prophets of Israel had spoken about the coming of the Messiah's kingdom, their timing had been vague. They had spoken much of the 'latter days' or 'days to come' when most of their prophecies would find fulfilment. John's message to his generation, however, was that the 'latter days' so often promised as future, were here and now. The kingdom of God was 'at hand' and ready to break into this present world in its fullness. Israel's Messiah, moreover, John declared dramatically, was present already in the world. Somewhere in their midst, at present unrecognized, God was preparing him for his life's work, and soon, at the decisive great moment, his glory and his kingdom would be revealed and discovered. John believed he had authority from God to prepare a group of representative people who themselves would search for and serve this hidden One when he chose to appear. Moreover he offered to baptize with water in the Jordan everyone who believed and was willing to enter the kingdom which had already so quietly and wonderfully begun. Their baptism by water

8

was a pledge that the Messiah himself would bring about their re-birth by the Holy Spirit. Many in the crowds responded to his call to receive baptism in the name of the coming One, and thus gave the sign that in heart and mind they were willing to forsake the ways of the present corrupt age, and desired the promised new life.

Simplicity and wisdom

The Baptist was for a time successful and popular. The great crowds from all over the country who gathered to listen were impressed by his fearlessness, by the urgency of his message, and the passionate conviction with which he gave it. People began to think, to study the Scriptures and to change their ways. Even some of the Pharisees, as Jesus later pointed out, 'were willing to rejoice for a while in his light' (5:35).

As his popularity grew, however, the leaders of the Jewish establishment in Jerusalem began to suspect that John might be one of those crazy people who from time to time disturbed the peace and led crowds astray by claiming falsely to be themselves the Messiah, the Christ. They sent messages to ask him if he made such a claim. John immediately denied the suggestion.

A series of other questions, however, followed. Moses, looking into the future, had promised that God would one day raise up from among his people a prophet, a second Moses, whom his people were to heed (Deut. 18:15)—did John ever think of himself as fitting into such a prophecy? Or did he claim to be Elijah? Malachi, the last of the great prophets, at the end of his book had uttered the promise: 'Lo, I will send you the prophet Elijah before the great and terrible day of the LORD comes (Mal. 4:5). Did John, in launching on his ministry and deciding his message, think of himself as called to fulfil this remarkable promise?

John may have felt himself challenged by such questions. He must have asked himself if the texts they referred to really did describe the part and place given to him by God in the events leading up to the coming of the Messiah. The dress he adopted and the food he ate were reminiscent of Elijah (cf. Mk. 1:6) and his location in the desert (like a second Moses) were signs that in beginning his ministry his thought had moved in this direction. Moreover, we know that Jesus, later on, looking over the events that led to his own baptism, taught that John was indeed the Elijah

(Matt. 11:14) who was to be the forerunner of the true Messiah (Mal. 3:1).

The unexpected answer which he now gave to his questioners, therefore, casts some light for us on the kind of man he was and on his attitude in his ministry. Even though he had given some thought to such questions, he had refused to allow his mind to dwell on them because to him they had become superficial and purely speculative. He had concerned himself completely with doing faithfully the one central task he knew himself called to do in the service of God—proclaiming the kingdom and the coming One. He wanted nothing that might divert him from this, or tempt him to become too concerned to play up to an expected role. He wanted his hearers and questioners not to speculate over his identity and character as a preacher, but to repent. He therefore gave an answer which he hoped would draw attention away from his style and manner of preaching to the urgency and content of his message. He refused to be drawn into the discussion they were seeking. He wanted his would-be examiners to forget the preacher and to think about the word.

We can recognize the trap that John was seeking to avoid, and can appreciate the sheer wisdom and singleness of purpose which shone out in his attitude before his questioners. Too often in this respect we fail. Those of us who are called to a ministry within the church can become so concerned to conform ourselves to the traditional role which we feel is expected of us that we neglect what is more essential to our task. Even in the conduct of the evangelistic service the preacher can indulge in role-playing at the cost of true effectiveness. Hearers sometimes decide the worth of the message by evaluating the personality, style or way of life of the one who brings it.

Realism and faith

In reply to further interrogation from his persistent questioners, *'Who are you?'*, John quoted the well known text: *'I am the voice of one crying out in the wilderness, "Make straight the way of the Lord"', as the prophet Isaiah said.*

When the prophet to whom he was referring originally spoke these words he was calling on the people of God after seventy years in exile in Babylon to prepare themselves for a great miracle to happen in their wilderness surroundings.

Far away in a kingdom remote from them, Cyrus, the King of Persia, was meanwhile setting out on a campaign that was to bring about the complete destruction of the Babylonian emperor and lead to their liberation.

Long before there was any evidence that such a deliverance was to happen, God gave the prophet the task of announcing it. He used poetical language. God, he said, was going to come and reveal his glory, preparing a way for them in the wilderness, leveling every mountain and exalting every valley, so that they could soon go back to their own homeland over the deserts to start again in the service of God.

The people in Babylon when they heard his 'good news' easily dismissed it from their minds. How could such a way be opened up? How could they ever expect the glory of God to be revealed in their dreadful and despondent situation? Facing their unbelief the prophet himself felt all the more how indefensible was his message, how frail his voice, how weak his cry, dying out so soon in the vast wilderness spaces!

Yet within a few months they were to find that the voice that had seemed to create nothing more than an empty echo in the wasteland around them was going to prove itself the very word of God, going forth with power into history to effect one of God's great redemptive purposes!

The Baptist, in his choice of this text to describe himself and his situation to his questioners, showed that he was taking a sober and entirely realistic view of his ministry and its limitations. He knew that, like Isaiah, he himself could be suspected of merely throwing into the wilderness empty words that could effect nothing. He himself, too, in despondent moments may have been tempted to share this view of his preaching. After all, what evidence had he that anything more was at issue? The same realistic admission of the apparent limitation of everything he was doing comes out in his further reply to their question put to him about his baptism: '*I baptize with water*'.

Mere *voice*! Mere *water*! He claims nothing more. Possibly he was too acutely conscious of his own personal unworthiness to do so. Certainly he did not boast (though a more foolish man might have done so) about the large numbers who were coming to the Jordan, their ardent enthusiasm, and the signs of genuine repentance that were evident.

He was only too aware that numbers can mean nothing, that human enthusiasm can soon fade, and that the signs of success can often be ambiguous. Yet the faith he expressed in these very utterances looked to the future with serene confidence. His own *voice... crying out in the wilderness* of Judaea would soon prove itself no less true and effective as a word of God than that which, uttered among the Babylonian wastes, brought about the re-birth of the people of God centuries before. From day to day he looked forward with increasing ardour to the appearance of One whom he knew would come to claim him, to take over his work, to baptize with the Holy Spirit, and to pronounce the only verdict worth listening to.

How little we ourselves sometimes have to show or speak about, when we face the world and its questioning: *a voice... water*—bread and wine! Even when there is a crowd around us to watch and listen, it is so obviously a mere crowd of ordinary people! But how much we have in the now hidden present and glorious future to be confident about, to rejoice and even to boast in!

No answer

We can trace an element of uneasiness in the pressure which John's questioners exert for definite information about himself, *'Let us have an answer for those who sent us'*. John has been deliberately enigmatic and his final answers simply deepen the mystery.

Here we are at the beginning of a conflict which runs through the whole of John's Gospel, and continually comes to the surface—the conflict caused by the reaction of the darkness prevailing in the world to the light which has come to take over in Jesus. The stage is set for the appearance of Jesus, and the chosen first witness is there ready to welcome and proclaim him. But before he even appears in public the opposition is also there, alert and determined even in its perplexity. The questioning of the Baptist is to be regarded as a form of inquisition, for suspicion and fear have been aroused.

Perhaps it is because he senses their hostility that John is so careful and indirect in his answers. It is fitting that in their anxiety the authorities should be shown up as unable to grasp what they are opposing, for they are doomed to be overwhelmed by something they are incapable of comprehending (cf. 1:5 and footnote 1 above). Here there is at work the wisdom of God which 'none of the rulers of this age understood', says Paul, 'for if they had, they would not have crucified the Lord of glory' (1 Cor. 2:8).

The Baptist and Jesus

John 1:29-38a

1 The next day he saw Jesus coming towards him and declared, 'Here is the Lamb of God who takes away the sin of the world! [30]This is he of whom I said, "After me comes a man who ranks ahead of me because he was before me." [31]I myself did not know him; but I came baptizing with water for this reason, that he might be revealed to Israel.' [32]And John testified, 'I saw the Spirit descending from heaven like a dove, and it remained on him. [33]I myself did not know him, but the one who sent me to baptize with water said to me, "He on whom you see the Spirit descend and remain is the one who baptizes with the Holy Spirit." [34]And I myself have seen and have testified that this is the Son of God.'

35 The next day John again was standing with two of his disciples, [36]and as he watched Jesus walk by, he exclaimed, 'Look, here is the Lamb of God!' [37]The two disciples heard him say this, and they followed Jesus. [38]When Jesus turned and saw them following....

The reorientation of a ministry

The crowd which gathered on one particular day to hear the Baptist must have been astonished at the sudden change in his message and tone. In place of the usual vivid descriptions of the catastrophic changes threatening history, there was the story of what he had heard and seen as he had baptized Jesus. Instead of the call, 'Repent and flee from the wrath to come', they heard the call to give the devotion of their minds and hearts to the one who had come to be their Messiah, there now walking in humility among them.

From the moment Jesus had approached him for baptism, John had sensed that he was on the verge of the revelation they had all for so long been waiting for. The hidden Messiah had now declared himself. John had felt awe in the presence of one of whom he said, *I am not worthy to untie the thong of his sandal* (v. 27). The vision that he had then had by the Jordan played a large part in determining his whole future prophetic ministry. Jesus had demanded baptism. John had obeyed him. The heavens had been opened, he had seen the Spirit descending like a dove on Jesus, and he had heard the voice of God declaring the very presence on earth, to begin his reign, of his beloved Son (Matt. 3:13-17). At that moment he had come to know with complete certainty why he had been raised up by God to be his prophet. He had to bear witness to what he had seen and heard in his encounter with Jesus. He had to plead with all around to look, to enter the fellowship offered in his presence, so that they too might hear and see for themselves that this is the Son of God.

Moreover, the sight of Jesus, the Son of God, submitting himself in such deep humility to a sinner's baptism transformed everything he now had to say about what God's Messiah had come into the world to do and achieve. In his preaching up to this moment he had drawn pictures of him as he had thought he found him in Scripture—of a Lord glorious in visible majesty, no one able to stand alongside him, compelling submission and obedience whenever he willed. But Jesus had now shown himself a Messiah humble, gentle, dedicated to self-sacrifice. By submitting himself to baptism alongside repentant sinners in all their need, he had recalled to John's mind how the coming One was described in other parts of Scripture—especially in the fifty-third chapter of Isaiah. He was to be the Servant of God who had come to number himself with the transgressors in identifying with them as their sin-bearer (Isa. 53:6b, 8c, 11c, 12). He had come to pour out his soul to death in intercession for those whose sins he had come thus to carry. He was going to allow himself to be 'led to the slaughter' as the Passover Lamb was slain so that it might set God's people free. *Here is the Lamb of God*, cried John, pointing to Jesus, *who takes away the sin of the world!* (cf. Isa. 53, Exod. 12:1-3).

Of course, as John continued to preach and baptize during the weeks or months that lay ahead, the other themes that had up till now been central to his ministry continued to reappear in what he said—the warnings of the approaching end of the world, the call to renounce the ways and aims of the present age, the demands for uprightness in heart and in personal dealings each with one's neighbour, the call to repent and be baptized. Indeed he preached on such things with all the more force and certainty than ever before, because Jesus himself had given such aspects of his former ministry wholehearted approval by coming to receive his baptism of repentance and to confirm the truth of his witness.

Yet there can be no doubt that on whatever aspect of life he preached, the Word of God was now for him the Word made flesh in Jesus of Nazareth the Son of God, who had come amongst us in his grace to take away the sin of the world. This now gave him a new central point for all his thought about his message and his mission. It also gave him a new motive in all his appeals for political reform, social justice and personal repentance. It was for the sake of this man that the world must now be purged of the evils that hindered the coming of his kingdom, and robbed him of his rightful rule over everything in the universe. It was only as they devoted themselves to the service and fellowship of this man, came under his influence, understood their indebtedness to him, that John now believed the world could be purged of its evils. Only as he was given his rightful personal place in the hearts and minds of men and women could the kingdom of God come, could people begin to understand themselves, the true meaning of life, and the true nature of God.

Take, over and surrender

Amongst the crowds who came to hear John, there were those especially close to him who had come most deeply under his influence—his 'disciples'. Jesus is pictured here as deliberately drawing into his own service two of these men. John himself is shown as not only freely surrendering them, but also as initiating the movement that was to deprive himself of them.

Pastoral conversation between the preacher and his hearers is often a valuable part of church life. It is sometimes required to clarify impressions that are too hazy, and to clinch the message. Such a conversation was taking place. John was re-telling what he had seen and heard. No doubt the two were asking questions. As they were speaking together, Jesus came again in view. He seemed, indeed, to bring himself within an engaging distance of them, and John could point to him as he had done in his sermon on the day before. *Look, here is the Lamb of God!* John said (vv. 29, 36). This time he makes no direct reference to the way Jesus has chosen to meet the sin of the world. He is dwelling at this particular point in the conversation not primarily on the sacrifice that is finally to prove and seal God's love, but on what has impressed him about the man Jesus himself—the one whom God has sent.

We cannot of course separate Jesus from his cross. But the 'Lamb' himself, and purely for his own sake, is as worthy of open-hearted contemplation and adoration as the cross for which he is destined. 'Here is the Lamb without blemish!' (cf. Exod. 12:5), the Baptist is saying. He had known him from childhood, and had admired him as a person—a man pure, true, humble, untainted in character and aim by the vicious devouring world, a leader worthy of complete devotion and trust! There is a truth enshrined in hymns like 'Fairest Lord Jesus'[4] that makes them of great value in our worship.

The two disciples, as they looked, felt drawn to the man there within their view. They yielded, and the transfer from one leader to another took place quietly and without fuss.[5] No formal farewell or acknowledgement of debt to John is recorded: *The two disciples heard him say this, and they followed Jesus* (v. 37). What happened at this moment was John's greatest achievement, the climax of his ministry. The two friends to whom he spoke found at last everything they had hoped that life would give them. Jesus found his first disciples. The Christian church began to take shape. No doubt there were other memorable days when the crowds around John were very great, the word seemed especially inspired, and the response astonished observers. But did anything greater happen because of the Baptist's witness than here, so quietly, unnoticed by anyone else, when the two disciples heard John speak and they followed the One of whom he spoke? The kingdom of God, said Jesus, comes not with careful observation (Luke 17:20). Later observers, looking back on the whole ministry of the Baptist made the comment: 'John performed no sign, but everything that John said about this man was true' (10:41).

It was an act of deliberate and costly self-denial on John's part to open up to Jesus in this way the whole sphere in which he had been

---

[4] No. 375, *The Church Hymnary*, Third Edition, OUP, London, 1973.

[5] It is evident from the Gospel account that John made a complete transfer of loyalty and trust from the Baptist's discipleship to the discipleship of Jesus, for in every single reference to John the Baptist, John the Evangelist is 'playing down' the Baptist and lifting up Jesus.

the leading and guiding light and influence. John well knew that even the part he had played in introducing his disciples to Jesus would soon be forgotten, and they would begin to talk as if they by themselves had found what he had introduced to them (cf. 1:41). It is not easy to find those we have toiled to care for and educate, on whom perhaps we have learned to some extent to depend, beginning to grow careless towards us because they have found something that can give them more satisfaction in life, and a better direction, than we ourselves could ever have offered had they stayed with us. John was content, as long as what happened bore witness to the light that had come into the world in Jesus.

Jesus Christ is the same yesterday, today and forever

Though we are meant to admire the self-effacement and faithful witnessing of John, we are meant to note especially in the latter part of this incident the decisive part played by Jesus himself. He is about to begin his own ministry. He needs disciples. He wants to start with these two men. He is aware that he is being talked about, and is sensitive to their thoughts and inclinations as they listen to John. He watches for the response and anticipates their approach to him, by himself turning from his way so that he and they can meet face to face.

At this point we can begin to notice also how directly relevant the Gospel story is to our present-day, and how easy it is to move in thought from Jesus and his disciples in that world of past history, to the presence of the living and risen Jesus in the church world of today. We need not doubt that all these things we have been reading about happened as history when Jesus Christ was here on earth physically. Yet what we have read seems at times intentionally designed to tell us not only about what once happened there and then, but also about what is happening, and can happen here and now, between Jesus and ourselves.

One recent scholar has strongly affirmed his belief that in some incidents, the narrative in John's Gospel was deliberately constructed to describe the action of the risen Christ during eucharistic worship in the early church. However this may be, it is certainly true that many of the Gospel stories here and elsewhere are about 'Jesus Christ... the same yesterday and today and forever' (Heb. 13:8). Indeed Jesus later remarked that what he did to the disciples when he washed their feet in the upper room would only be fully understood by them when he came back to have dealings with them after his resurrection (John 13:7). Are there not other incidents in the Gospel story whose meaning we can best uncover in what Jesus himself is doing in our midst today? We can therefore allow this incident to bring before our minds the later promise of Jesus: 'For where two or three are gathered in my name, I am there among them' (Matt. 18:20).

Where the preacher or teacher today seeks to give the same faithful witness as did the Baptist in his day, speaks of the Man, his sacrifice, his presence and what he demands and offers today, Jesus himself will come near as he came to these three at the Jordan. He has the same delicate sensitivity as he had then to every thought of a mind that is turning towards his light, and he will put himself within the reach of the least desire that is kindled in a longing heart by the promises of his presence and power. Is there not in this text the assurance that there can and will take place today in our midst, the eternally significant take-over: They heard him preach and they followed Jesus?

We need not confine our application of this incident to what takes place between pastor and congregation. Indeed, the fact that the group consisted only of three is an encouragement to apply it to the Sunday School teacher, or to the study leader in a church group, or to the pastoral counsellor, or to the mother in the home who may have only two, or perhaps only one little one, beside her, but who knows that it is vain for our children to have everything that life can give, if they do not have Christ. We can at least trust and pray that, whatever the circumstances, this quiet, binding encounter and commitment may go on continually within the life of the church.

Jesus and his first disciples

John 1:37–51

It is worthwhile, as we go through this passage, to note the different ways in which Jesus dealt with different disciples of John on his first introduction to them. In each case we can assume that there took place a quite decisive meeting, bringing sudden and deep commitment to Jesus and his service. Yet the level and type of immediate experience, the degree of spiritual insight, and the confession of faith arising out of the experience, vary. Each individual has a unique temperament and character, and Jesus himself has his own special way with each one he meets.

John 1:37-39

1 The two disciples heard him say this, and they followed Jesus. [38]When Jesus turned and saw them following, he said to them, 'What are you looking for?' They said to him, 'Rabbi' (which translated means Teacher), 'where are you staying?' [39]He said to them, 'Come and see.' They came and saw where he was staying, and they remained with him that day. It was about four o'clock in the afternoon.

Jesus, Andrew and John

As the two disciples caught up with Jesus, he faced them with a question meant to be all the more searching and disturbing because it was put so abruptly and seriously: *What are you looking for*?

It was a question about the strength and purity of their motives for seeking to enter his service. Obviously they had become attracted to his person. They were also deeply interested in his cause and the way he was going to take to fulfil it. But what did they really expect to find in it? How far indeed will they let themselves be led on when the cost involves persecution and the difficulties seem overwhelming? He does not want to steal loyalty by false pretence, nor to trap people into his service by delusive, superficial charm.

Jesus had not yet spoken of the cost of becoming a disciple, or of the purity of heart, the singleness of purpose and the utter carelessness of self-interest which he expected his followers to seek under his influence. Nor had he yet described the great and thrilling rewards they would receive. Yet in his presence even at this early stage in his ministry they must have felt to some extent the issues and constraints that later became explicit in his teaching. They were disturbed by the questions of conscience and the sense of unworthiness which is felt in all genuine human encounter with

Jesus (cf. Luke 5:8). His presence itself was searching. They felt that deceit or reserve were impossible.

The answer which Jesus' abrupt question evoked is striking: *Rabbi... where are you staying?* It is an answer that he himself inspires. In his presence they find themselves accepted, and drawn on. They do not shrink from the light in which they have had to begin uncomfortably to question themselves. They want more of it. They want to go on with him and to know him better. They make no attempt at self-assessment or even confession, for they want *him* to tell them who and what they are.

Moreover, the Baptist, by his description of what happened to him with Jesus at the Jordan when 'the heaven was opened' (vv. 32-34) had aroused in them a desire also to see. Might they too in their encounter here with Jesus not be on the threshold of the kind of vision and experience which had so transformed the life and ministry of their friend John? They want to probe further.

In the way they worded their reply, a healthy desire is expressed for what is down-to-earth and permanent. Their first aim is not some once-for-all mystical encounter with heavenly reality which leaves them momentarily excited and impressed, and even perhaps suddenly changed. Rather, they know themselves to be entering a lasting friendship with a person at whose 'address' they can find him again and again. They call him *Rabbi (which translated means Teacher)*, for they believe he has a store of wisdom from which they will gradually learn. They will surrender to him the mind, as well as the will and the heart.

Jesus, having inspired their manifold prayer, immediately said to them, *'Come and see.' They came and saw where he was staying, and they remained with him that day* (v. 39).

We must of course, interpret this in the first place on a quite mundane level. He took them to his lodgings and they spent the rest of the day with him. They now had his 'home address', the promise of easy access when they want to find him. There was too, in this gesture, the promise of personal friendship. If they have questions and problems, his mind and heart will be as open to them as his lodgings were.

Reading this incident in the context of the whole of John's Gospel, however, it is natural that our thoughts should move to a level of meaning which the writer often had in mind. When Jesus said, *Come and see*, was he not seeking to answer the desire which John the Baptist's testimony to the 'Son' and 'Lamb' of God had raised in their minds and hearts? Was he not hoping and praying that having stepped over the threshold of his earthly lodgings they might come also to step over another threshold to share something of the vision and insight of their former leader?

When I was a divinity student in Edinburgh, it was a coincidence that on two occasions on our 'retreats' members of the faculty chose this passage from John's Gospel as the basis of their talk to us about our ministry. Both of them pointed out that it was unusual for John to mention the exact time of day in relation to any incident, yet here we had it: *it was about four in the afternoon* (NEB). Their explanation was that for John what happened as he came to know Jesus on that visit was so memorable and of such lasting significance he could not forbear to mention significantly in the Gospel that exact time of the day. It was the hour when *they came and saw where he was staying.* Might there not have been there and then indeed a moment of new and unforgettable insight into who Jesus really was and where he really belonged? From this hour on they began to see that this man Jesus lived not only in these lodgings, but was also, as he later describes himself, 'the Son of Man whose home is in heaven' (3:13 NEB). In Scotland they used to speak of certain godly men or women as being 'far ben with God'. In a quite unique and realistic way this was where Jesus was, and this was what they 'saw'.

There are further suggestive overtones in this remarkable account as we have it. Throughout the text, and in the comment, *they remained with him that day,* one Greek verb is used which as well as being translated 'remain' can be translated 'dwell' or 'abide'. The same word is later used in the Gospel to refer to our indwelling or abiding in Christ (15:4, etc.). As one recent commentator says: 'The abiding of the disciples with Jesus anticipates their abiding in Him even as He abides in the Father.' This aspect of the text further underlines the permanence and stability of the relationship which Jesus comes to set up between ourselves and him, and thus between ourselves and God.

It was one of the vexations felt by people in Old Testament times that their visitations by God and their experiences of confident faith were at times so transitory—even though they had their temple services through which to find him, and the Law and Prophets through which to hear his voice. Jeremiah once put the complaint this way:

O hope of Israel,
its saviour in time of trouble,
why should you be like a stranger in the land,
like a traveller turning aside for the night? (14:8).

It is true that even in the fellowship which we have with the risen
Christ under the new covenant, there still remains an element of the
same transitoriness (cf. Luke 24:31). We can never localize God or
try to hold his presence down anywhere or anyhow. But when
Jesus said, 'search, and you will find; knock, and the door will be
opened for you' (Matt. 7:7), he is reminding us that now there is an
address, a door through knocking at which we have a more sure
promise of finding him present with us today than ever anyone had
before. He sets before us today the Gospel story, and the witness of
all the apostles to what they have seen and heard, and the
sacraments, his special extra gifts to the believing church. Here is
his address. Here is the door. Here he invites us to seek, to knock,
to ask and wait and to enter so that we can continually abide in
him, as he seeks to abide in us.

John 1:40-42

1   One of the two who heard John speak and followed him was
Andrew, Simon Peter's brother. [41]He first found his brother Simon and
said to him, 'We have found the Messiah' (which is translated
Anointed). [42]He brought Simon to Jesus, who looked at him and said,
'You are Simon son of John. You are to be called Cephas' (which is
translated Peter).

Jesus and Peter

Of course Andrew, as soon as he could, told the news of this
meeting with Jesus to his brother Simon, and lost no time in
bringing him to Jesus. He must have been disappointed that with
Peter, Jesus did not take the same approach or make the same
immediate effort as he had with himself and John. Little time was
taken there and then, no questions were asked, and Jesus was
content to dismiss him, with simply one word, 'You are Simon son
of John. You are to be called Cephas' (which is translated Peter).
Peter himself possibly had come with greater expectations.

Yet the word spoken by Jesus was a word of God: 'it shall not return to me empty, but it shall accomplish that which I purpose, and succeed in the thing for which I sent it' (Isa. 55:11). We can read of its magnificent fulfilment in the great moment of vision, discovery and public confession of Jesus as the Christ, the Son of the living God, at Caesarea Philippi, when Jesus himself was thrilled at the faith and gift of leadership which his Father had given to this elect disciple (Matt. 16:13-20). We can read, too, of the long struggle between the old Simon and the new Peter in this one man as he followed Jesus. It was a struggle which went on even till the time of his final denial of Jesus (John 18:25), and his final re-affirmation of his loyalty and his restoration by Jesus at the lakeside (John 21:15-19).

Nothing of what was to happen was known when the word that brought it about was first spoken. It is an encouragement to all of us who cannot tell, as others seem to be able to do, any dramatic story of what we saw and experienced as the beginning of our Christian life. All that may have come to us at that period was simply the impression, from what we had heard or read of Jesus and his words that in him we were faced with the truth—an impression confirmed by the testimonies we heard from friends and relatives whom we respect and trust. Even now we may have nothing much more to grasp than the many promises and assuring words which have come home to us through the Word of God which holds us to our faith in him and in what he has done for us. Within us there may be simply a steady and growing conviction that in following and trusting we have a future, a destiny, and that the world, too, has its destiny only in him. 'We walk by faith, not by sight' wrote Paul (2 Cor. 5:7). It is on Christ's decision, Christ's word, and not on the experience he grants us, that the future depends. Experience is his gift and he does not fail to bring comfort when his people need it. In the working out of our Christian way, long-term perseverance is of more importance than great moments of initial excitement.

John 1:43-46

1 The next day Jesus decided to go to Galilee. He found Philip and said to him, 'Follow me.' ⁴⁴Now Philip was from Bethsaida, the city of Andrew and Peter. ⁴⁵Philip found Nathanael and said to him, 'We have found him about whom Moses in the law and also the prophets wrote, Jesus son of Joseph from Nazareth.' ⁴⁶Nathanael said to him, 'Can anything good come out of Nazareth?' Philip said to him, 'Come and see.'

Jesus and Philip

Philip began enthusiastically and did well. He was keen to share what he had seen and found, even in that first short personal encounter when Jesus came seeking him. *Come and see*, he said to Nathanael. Later on it was he who contacted the Greeks who wanted to see Jesus (12:21, 22).

Jesus seemed to be on familiar terms and free in his conversation with him (6:4-7). Of course he was there with the others in the upper room at the Last Supper, and along with Thomas was disarmingly frank in expressing the difficulties he had in understanding what Jesus was talking about. It was at that crucial moment, however, that Jesus expressed disappointment that Philip still remained unaware of much that Jesus had hoped he would have learned and seen: 'Have I been with you all this time, Philip, and you still do not know me?' (14:9)

It is certainly hazardous to try to guess what it was that, during this first encounter, fascinated Philip, and made him say, *Come and see*, yet it is possible that he found so much attractive and great simply in Jesus as a man, that he settled down with it, and made no great effort even to ask if there was more to discover. He had been looking for no more than could be found on a human level, and he may well have been too soon satisfied. The lack of understanding which he confessed to have concerning Jesus' talk about the Father, even in the upper room, seems to confirm this.

However satisfying our new-found faith, however deep our new insights may seem to be, the beginning is always meant to be simply a beginning. However much we might have already seen, there is more to see, and what we have seen has to be allowed to unfold itself through time, so that we can understand it more clearly, and it comes to have all the greater effect on our temperament and our way of life.

It is interesting to reflect on John's subtle statements that, on the one hand, Jesus found Philip (v. 43), whereas on the other hand, Philip said to Nathaniel, *We have found him...* (v. 45). Of course both statements are true. But John's order is important. Jesus first found Philip!

John 1:45-49

1   Philip found Nathanael and said to him, 'We have found him about whom Moses in the law and also the prophets wrote, Jesus son of Joseph from Nazareth.' [46]Nathanael said to him, 'Can anything good come out of Nazareth?' Philip said to him, 'Come and see.' [47]When Jesus saw Nathanael coming towards him, he said of him, 'Here is truly an Israelite in whom there is no deceit!' [48]Nathanael asked him, 'Where did you come to know me?' Jesus answered, 'I saw you under the fig tree before Philip called you.' [49]Nathanael replied, 'Rabbi, you are the Son of God! You are the King of Israel!'

Jesus and Nathanael

Jesus' first words to Nathanael must have seemed to an onlooker like Philip completely enigmatic: *'Here is truly an Israelite in whom there is no deceit!'*

From Nathanael himself, however, it brought a cry of astonished wonder. Here was someone who, before he had even talked to him, seemed already to have read his heart, heard his secret and ardent prayer, and had an answer to it! One of the Psalmists in the Old Testament one day suddenly found himself overwhelmed by the realization of the intimate knowledge the all-seeing and all-knowing God had of him, of how close and personal he was, how inescapable and holy: 'O LORD, you have searched me and known me. You know when I sit down and when I rise up; you discern my thoughts from far away' (139:1, 2). As Nathanael, perhaps gradually, took in the full meaning of Jesus' word to him, he expressed his feelings in a phrase that echoed something of the Psalmist's wonder before the all-seeing God. How was it that this man had come to such a perfect understanding of the whole tenor of his inner desire and thought?

The exact way in which Jesus' strange remark proved that he had this intimate knowledge of the thoughts of Nathanael's mind and the desires of his heart, is not explained here in detail, but clear hints are given throughout the whole conversation of the points at which Nathanael felt himself deeply and sensitively touched.

We must assume that Nathanael was a sincere and ardent student of the Word of God who read it in depth and allowed the full searching challenge of its teaching to penetrate his heart and to dominate his personal life in all its aspects. Jesus' remark, *'Here is truly an Israelite in whom there is no deceit!'* was made with the clear implication that Nathanael had been thinking about Jacob, the story of whom is *the* story of deliverance from the guilt and power of guile. It was also made with the implication that one of the blessings Nathanael ardently sought was that promised in Psalm 32: 'Happy are those to whom the LORD imputes no iniquity, and in whose spirit there is no deceit' (32:2). Had this been Nathanael's deepest problem as he had tried sincerely to serve God and to prepare himself to meet the Messiah? And had it surfaced strongly and perhaps was tormenting his mind at the moment of his encounter with Jesus? That may well have been so. Now here was Jesus revealing that he understood, as only God can understand, the innermost drift of the secret thoughts of the man before him.

The word spoken by Jesus was intended not simply to uncover Nathanael's personal problem, but to solve it. It was apparently heard by Nathanael as a word of assurance and grace. His problem had been a burden on his conscience. Jesus had come to lift it. We can remember how later on, the word of Jesus to the leper, 'Be clean' brought immediate cleansing and wholeness. In the same powerful way, the word of Jesus, *'Here is truly an Israelite in whom there is no deceit!'* came to Nathanael as a declaration of forgiveness and liberty which appears to have brought immediate inner release, and an answer to years of prayer.

The awe which Nathanael felt in the presence of Jesus was deepened by a second remark in reply to his first expression of astonishment. There was a current tradition that the ideal Israelite in the Messianic age would go at times to meditate, 'each under his fig tree' (cf. Mic. 4:4; Zech. 3:10). There may have been a fig tree somewhere in his garden where Nathanael had just been seeking to prepare himself in prayer for the coming new age, or it may have been that just before the time of Jesus' approach with Philip, Nathanael had in imagination thought of himself in that setting. Jesus said to him: *I saw you under the fig tree before Philip called you* (v. 48).

Nathanael tried to express his continuing wonder at what has happened in a confession of faith: *Rabbi, you are the Son of God! You are the King of Israel!* Commentators warn us not to read too

26

much theology into his confession. Nathanael, they warn us, is here addressing Jesus as 'Teacher', and in the titles *Son of God* and *King of Israel* he is simply acknowledging that he is the Messiah. Yet, even though the confession may be read in this superficial way there can be no doubt that Nathanael believes that in Jesus the eternal God himself has come close to him with redeeming power, and the flow of the text, following as it does from the Prologue, appears to indicate John intends us to understand Nathaniel is seeking to give an adequate confession of this faith.

We are meant to notice, in passing, the initial mental barrier which Nathanael raised when Philip first spoke of Jesus. *Can anything good come out of Nazareth?* It was a piece of local prejudice that made life occasionally difficult for those who came from the place. Of course it would indicate to us a rather sad initial defect in the character of Nathanael. Such cultural snobbery seems incompatible with genuine personal piety. Indeed, it is such cultural prejudice, void of any rational basis, that is the origin of racism with its devastating modern effects. We ourselves are therefore apt to judge those who harbour even a suspicion of it more harshly than they themselves judge the victims of their own minds. Yet in Nathanael's case Jesus showed no reverse prejudice against the prejudice!

In some cases the heart can be genuine even though the outlook is warped! He looked at the heart and was able to see beyond this defect and no doubt many other defects also. Where he finds faith and an earnest desire for communion with himself he is prepared to enter that close relationship with people which can ultimately melt away everything that cuts us off from each other.

John 1:50-51

1 Jesus answered, 'Do you believe because I told you that I saw you under the fig tree? You will see greater things than these.' [51]And he said to him, 'Very truly, I tell you, you will see heaven opened and the angels of God ascending and descending upon the Son of Man.'

A final word

Jesus' final word in this chapter was, of course, especially to Nathanael. He is referring him again to the story of Jacob, the man who ultimately, delivered from guile, became the true Israel. Jacob even early in his career was granted the great vision of a ladder stretched from heaven to earth and the angels of God ascending and descending on it. Nathanael is being challenged not to be content till, through his fellowship with Jesus, such a vision is granted to him also. It is the same challenge which, the day before, Jesus had already given to Andrew and John with his invitation: *Come and see.*

John Calvin is correct in isolating this last verse from its immediate context and suggesting that it should be interpreted as a promise addressed by Jesus to all Christians who have begun each in his or her own way to follow Jesus. They should expect to happen to them what happened to Jacob at Bethel, what happened also to John the Baptist by the Jordan. Calvin is not suggesting that we should seek for the fulfilment of this promise in some kind of dream or visionary experience in which the pictorial detail of those former experiences is reproduced before our minds. The promise is, rather, a plea to us not to remain content with limited and low-level views of the significance of Jesus himself, but to seek the same kind of insight as made these early disciples worship him, and strain their language to find an adequate confession of who he is, and where he really belongs. In this word he is giving all of us the same challenge and the same promise as he had already given to Andrew and John: *Come and see.*

CHAPTER 2

THE WEDDING AT CANA

(The 1ˢᵗ Sign)

John 2:1-11

2 On the third day there was a wedding in Cana of Galilee, and the mother of Jesus was there. ²Jesus and his disciples had also been invited to the wedding. ³When the wine gave out, the mother of Jesus said to him, 'They have no wine.' ⁴And Jesus said to her, 'Woman, what concern is that to you and to me? My hour has not yet come.' ⁵His mother said to the servants, 'Do whatever he tells you.' ⁶Now standing there were six stone water-jars for the Jewish rites of purification, each holding twenty or thirty gallons. ⁷Jesus said to them, 'Fill the jars with water.' And they filled them up to the brim. ⁸He said to them, 'Now draw some out, and take it to the chief-steward.' So they took it. ⁹When the steward tasted the water that had become wine, and did not know where it came from (though the servants who had drawn the water knew), the steward called the bridegroom ¹⁰and said to him, 'Everyone serves the good wine first, and then the inferior wine after the guests have become drunk. But you have kept the good wine until now.' ¹¹Jesus did this, the first of his signs, in Cana of Galilee, and revealed his glory; and his disciples believed in him.

Invitation to local celebration

The writer wants us to notice the contrast which suddenly appears here. In the first chapter of this Gospel we were introduced to Jesus as the one inspiring reverence, majestic in his bearing and his talk—the only Son and Word of the Father. Here in this chapter we are reminded that he was indeed also the son of Mary, the carpenter of Nazareth, our brother man in our humanity. We are shown how he loved his involvement in the social and family life of the towns and villages around Galilee: *there was a wedding in Cana of Galilee, and the mother of Jesus was there. Jesus and his disciples had also been invited to the wedding.*

That he accepted this invitation, given because he was a member of a family circle, reminds us of one of the features of the gospel that should continually fill us with wonder and gratitude: that God has entered our human life in an intimate way. He has become like one of our family relatives. He can be easily known and approached by us if we want him. He can he given an invitation to come and celebrate with us on happy family occasions. One of Augustine's prayers runs thus: 'O God, you have set yourself at but an hand's breadth from us, that we might seek you with a whole heart; and seeking you, find you.'

There is a further contrast, of which we are meant to become increasingly aware as we read through this incident. In the first chapter of the Gospel, Jesus is pointed to as *the Lamb of God who takes away the sin of the world.* He knows himself called to a ministry characterized by self-denial, suffering and prayer. He has identified himself closely with John the Baptist, with his proclamation of the end of the world and the coming of the kingdom of God, and his call to renounce the present age with its pride, ambitions and sought-after pleasures. In this chapter, however, what he does at the wedding underlines his care for the immediate happiness of people around him who have little concern for his religious programme, and who are out simply for the pleasure it gives them to be at one of the happiest social occasions of the year. We see them here taking part not in the religious ceremony but in the feasting—the secular part of the occasion which ordinary people in the world can appreciate and enjoy whether they are religious or not. He seems glad to be there, though for the most of the time he is entirely in the background, apparently not needed. Yet when he *is* called on, he is there to give marvellous help.

It is good that we should pause for a moment to take in the full significance of the central point we want to make in our approach to this passage. The Bible, in its stories about our beginnings, tells us that after Adam and Eve fell and were expelled from the Garden, they were treated with tender consideration. God was gracious even to the family of Cain, the most disobedient son of Adam. It was to members of this family that were given special skills in music, the arts and sciences. God indeed wanted to make life not only bearable but happy and rich for them while he waited in his redemptive purpose to send his Son into the world to save them. Therefore even while they lived at enmity against God, he nevertheless gave them all the gifts they required to enable them, if they wanted to, to develop a good human secular culture and civilization.

The ancient Genesis account is there to show us in simple and vivid pictures how we are to think about our contemporary human situation. Today through innumerable signs, God shows his goodness not only to those who believe in him, but also to the whole human race. We know that whether we are Christians or not we can enjoy and find use for many good secular gifts in such things as music, the arts and sciences. We are to be thankful for such gifts to humanity, even though we often abuse them. Jesus means us to recognize this when he reminded us that the heavenly Father makes his sun rise on the evil and the good, and sends rain on the righteous and on the unrighteous (Matt. 5:45).

Of all the good gifts God wants all humankind to enjoy while they live on earth—whether they believe in him or not—one of the greatest and most to be prized is the gift of marriage. Where on earth, within the vast range of interesting and joyful occasions which occur for celebration in our everyday lives, can there be any human joy so great and good as that in which we share by being present, as a wedding reception? Can we have any clearer proof that anyone has become plain foolish, if not inhuman, than to find him (or her) refusing the invitation to a wedding because he wants to go to a football match or she prefers to attend a symphony concert? Surely the height of social privilege is to be invited to a wedding. The height of social joy is to be there as a welcome guest—and there was Jesus Christ, in quite secular company.

An ever,recurring human situation

It starts off well with the dancing, clapping, feasting, and laughing. Jeremiah, thinking back to the good days of his youth, remembered at weddings 'the voice of mirth and the voice of gladness, the voice of the bridegroom and the voice of the bride' (Jer. 16:9; 25:10). It is all the more spontaneous within any community where the guests know each other well. The pace of the festivities is mounting and everything that is happening promises so much!

Yet a flaw appeared and a threat occurred—the wine began to fail! It was very strange that this should happen at an occasion so carefully planned. Had some of the jars been cracked or faulty? Could those responsible for the catering have badly miscalculated? (Some commentators conjecture that the guests themselves were expected to provide the wine by bringing gifts with them, and that perhaps people like Jesus had let them down!)

Whatever our minds suggest as the immediate cause of the shortage we are meant to recognize the seriousness of the situation which arose as a result. The wine at this wedding had great importance in the minds of those concerned, and its failure was bound to have deep significance. These were superstitious days and this was a very ordinary crowd of people. The failure of the wine if it had taken place would not only have been a ridiculous anti-climax, a sad and embarrassing ending to the great day, and a kind of family disgrace, it would have been interpreted as a portent, a shadow hanging over the couple all their days. The situation was one of real crisis, possibly a portent of future marital failure.

Moreover the situation was made all the more tragic and absurd by the fact that the wine began to fail quite suddenly and unexpectedly at the high point of the success of the party. They were having the time of their lives when suddenly with dismay and alarm, in deep anxiety and desperate frustration, those who were responsible went to Mary the mother of Jesus and spoke of the shadow that was about to fall on this great gathering, 'Can you believe it, Mary? The wine is running out!' They were evidently apprehensive for the future of the young couple.

Is the situation which occurred at this wedding not very familiar today to those of us who are able to enjoy life as we are meant to do in an affluent society? In what we have around us in our ordinary day to day lives within our families, our culture and society, we can find much that brings us joy. There is beauty and goodness in many aspects of our human relationships. We can admire what talented people with their God-given gifts can produce for our pleasure. They add colour to our lives. We sometimes say 'Life is sweet.' Moreover, in spite of all the threats and dangers which science brings, we have to be thankful for the progress it has brought in easing our drudgery, in spreading entertainment, in overcoming so much ill-health.

And yet, within such a situation, do we not at times come to the point of utter and pathetic crisis? The wine threatens to run out, and what has seemed so real and exciting appears to be empty, insipid and meaningless. Life with its sweetness and goodness suddenly reveals its vanity. The ground which we had felt secure suddenly gives way beneath us, and even we, too, of the 21st century, have our forebodings about what is to happen.

The crisis can indeed come suddenly upon us—like the coming of the thieves in Jesus' parable who without warning 'break in and steal' (Matt. 6:19). Illness can strike, disaster can happen, bereavement can come quickly and shatteringly. More often, however, we become aware of ourselves moving towards it gradually. The moth and rust consume! (Matt. 6:19) Strength ebbs, beauty fades and the mind grows feeble. The fact that the crisis at Cana took place at a wedding reception reminds us of how often such events happen today, suddenly or slowly, in our marriages. However great the early happiness, however binding the vows, so often, after few or many years, in a home bereft of everything they have hoped for, the man and the woman find they have to face each other and the situation: 'We have no wine!'

Perhaps there is something in the structure of life itself which makes us sense the approach of the crisis before it comes upon us. We remember the story of the little girl at the pantomime who was so thrilled at what she was enjoying that she suddenly clutched her mother's arm and said: 'It's not going to end soon, is it Mummy?' Solomon after all his efforts to ensure he was surrounded by everything that could guarantee his well-being and pleasure, made his confession: 'Then I considered all that my hands had done and the toil I had spent in doing it, and again all was vanity and a chasing after wind...' (Eccl. 2:11). As someone once put it, 'The word "enjoy" comes to have no strength in it.'

The world of politics is not exempt. Too often the hopes invested in radical change towards the right or the left are soon dashed, and it becomes a relief to disillusioned followers and voters that there is some other administration ready in the wings to take over. A recent review of books on the French Revolution remarked: 'There can be no doubt that the noble ideals which characterized its early stages were soon perverted.'

The Hidden Sign

Jesus, appealed to by his mother, answered her request and enabled the celebration to go on. It was a miracle done without fuss or ceremony, almost in secrecy. It is emphasized throughout the story that Jesus did not have any prominence at any time among the guests and even to the end remained only in the background. The praise for the wine therefore went to others. How unusual to serve such perfect wine towards the end of the feast, when people who had already drunk so much were all the less able to appreciate it! The steward of the feast complimented the bridegroom and the implication was that even the bridegroom, accepting the compliment no doubt gratefully, was unaware of what was happening around him.

At this moment, even when they were praising each other for the goodness and joy of it, they all depended for that goodness and joy on the miracle that was the work of a guest they hardly noticed. Only Mary and the few servants who obeyed her orders knew what had actually happened!

Jesus did this, the first of his signs, in Cana of Galilee, and revealed his glory; and his disciples believed in him (v. 11). When the disciples heard of it, saw clearly what had happened, and reflected on it, they saw in this miracle much more than water turned to wine. They saw in it a sign of his glory—of his power to bring new and glorious life into the heart of a universe where everything seems to be marked for death. They discerned here an indication of his power to bring a healing and stabilizing influence into some personal life-situation or family problem where things are moving beyond human control into depression, collapse and divorce. They recognized his power to bring purpose and joy into a world whose celebration tends too soon otherwise to move to a sad end, with people becoming bored, depressed and threatened.

Now we are in a position to understand why of all the miracles which Jesus did, John attached so much importance to this first one—a miracle which did not loom so large in the minds and memories of those who wrote the other Gospels. John saw clearly that the Word became flesh, lived among us, died and rose again, to do even more than simply to bring salvation, healing and blessing to individuals or to proclaim a noble ethic which demands social justice and warns of judgement to come. John also clearly saw that the risen Christ must in every generation continue to come into the midst of perplexing, critical and tragic human situations, with his power to work the kind of renewal of which this miracle was the 'sign'.[1] Are we not now in a position to recognize that this was indeed only *the first* of innumerable following signs?

The message preached unashamedly from church pulpits seventy years ago was that in spite of the Great War and the misery it had brought, in spite of the defects which were still so obvious in our social life, we could nevertheless call our society 'Christian', for there was much in our midst that was truly good, stable and worth struggling to preserve. Everything that was worthwhile, it was then asserted, we owed to the permeating influence through the centuries of the Christian gospel.

Undoubtedly Paul was thinking of the influence of Christ on our secular life when in the course of writing about him he drew up his list of those things worth holding on to: 'Finally, beloved, whatever is true, whatever is honourable, whatever is just, whatever is pure, whatever is pleasing, whatever is commendable, if there is any excellence and if there is anything worthy of praise, think about these things.' (Phil. 4:8) It is a reminder that if anywhere on earth there is to be found what is truly good it is owed to the redeeming work of him who at the beginning of his ministry turned the water into wine at Cana.

Yet today even in our own land most people do not know what they owe him: 'He was in the world, and the world came into being through him; yet the world did not know him' (1:10). He is still active in the world today saving, sustaining, renewing, as he was at the wedding. The world still depends on him for its goodness. Indeed it has had so much from his generosity that it becomes absorbed in what it has, and forgets the hidden Giver. P. T. Forsyth, speaking about this, quoted the saying current in the early church: 'Because of Jesus we do not seek Jesus.'

---

[1] John's use of the word 'sign' is significant and worthy of further study. Here it indicates a miracle of Jesus which strengthens and confirms a faith already there: 'and his *disciples* believed in him' (v. 11). Those who believed in Jesus only because they witnessed a sign appear to have had a shallow, fleeting faith. Those who demanded a sign before they would believe were denied. (See 2:18; 4:54; 6:30; 10:41; 12:18.)

THE GOSPEL OF JOHN

The turning point

Though the world around us is unaware of his grace, those of us who understand it should read this story as a call to action. If we are to recover today healthy marriage and family life, and find a stable basis for worthwhile progress towards creating the good society, we must seek it from the same source. We dare not take his work among us for granted. He did this miracle for the couple and the little community at Cana because a certain woman prayed, and a few humble and concerned people gave him obedient service.

The turning point was certainly the faith and prayer of Mary. She had known all her life that he was destined to do great things for the salvation of the world he had entered, and she had waited and watched, expecting him someday to reveal who he was. She had, no doubt, heard of the happening down by the Jordan and was full of anticipation. After years of living with him, she knew his concern for the little things in life which can weigh down the balance either on the side of happiness or misery. She knew that his care could reach out even to things as commonplace as wine at weddings. What better occasion than he was in now to launch out on the kind of ministry she must have dreamed of for him?

Jesus had to try to help her to understand both her own new situation and his own. For years she had commanded him and he had obeyed her. It was her right as his mother and his duty as a son. But now that his public ministry had begun, she must understand that his work was beyond her authority. His word to her was one of quiet and gentle disengagement: *Woman, what concern is that to you and me?*[2] Moreover he wants her to know even now that the work into which she is trying so earnestly to press him is going to be far more costly for her and himself than she yet dreams of. The *hour* (v. 4) in which he will indeed be able to reveal himself to the world will come only after months and years of toil, trial, and waiting. When she herself is torn in heart, agonized in spirit, then will she know that his hour is come![3]

Yet along with this word that humbled her heart and orientated her thoughts he gave her encouragement. She had the key to the

---

[2] Apparently without any linguistic warrant, NIV translates verse 4, '*Dear woman...*' (cf. also 19:26). The same expression in 4:21, 8:10, 20:15 is simply translated 'woman'.
[3] Cf. 7:6, 8, 30; 8:20; 12:23, 27; 13:1; 16:32; 17:1.

36

whole situation in her hand because she could go to him and pray—with confidence that he would answer.

We need to listen to Jesus' warnings about prayers that are too presumptuous, too familiar, too forgetful sometimes of what it costs God to save the world. Yet we need the encouragement and challenge which this simple incident brings to us. If we know Christ and understand how he hears and answers, we are the key people within our human situations. Around us there are friends, neighbours, relations, acquaintances facing some crisis in career or marriage, in personal stability or in choice of destiny. *They have no wine.* They need what Christ alone can give them. If we have his ear we are surely meant to ask!

Let us not forget the *servants* who in obedience and faith carried round the water that became wine. They were privy to what was happening. They were told by Mary: *Do whatever he tells you* (v. 5). There is nothing necessarily dramatic in what he so often wants us to do in the sphere of life within which he has set us. It is given its significance by the fact that he too wants to share his grace and reveal his glory through simple acts of obedient faith. 'Faith and the prayers of Christians', Luther once said, 'sustain the universe.'

The cleansing of the Temple

John 2:12-22

2 After this he went down to Capernaum with his mother, his brothers, and his disciples; and they remained there for a few days.

13 The Passover of the Jews was near, and Jesus went up to Jerusalem. [14]In the temple he found people selling cattle, sheep and doves, and the money-changers seated at their tables. [15]Making a whip of cords, he drove all of them out of the temple, both the sheep and the cattle. He also poured out the coins of the money-changers and overturned their tables. [16]He told those who were selling the doves, 'Take these things out of here! Stop making my Father's house a marketplace!' [17]His disciples remembered that it was written, 'Zeal for

your house will consume me.' [18]The Jews then said to him, 'What sign can you show us for doing this?' [19]Jesus answered them, 'Destroy this temple, and in three days I will raise it up.' [20]The Jews then said, 'This temple has been under construction for forty-six years, and will you raise it up in three days?' [21]But he was speaking of the temple of his body. [22]After he was raised from the dead, his disciples remembered that he had said this; and they believed the scripture and the word that Jesus had spoken.

From Galilee to Jerusalem

When they describe how Jesus began his ministry, the other three Gospels quite directly show him entering into the conflict with Satan in the wilderness. As man, he is the second Adam, and has come to live a life of perfect obedience to God, thus reversing the disobedience of the first Adam, the shameful surrender to evil which has brought death into the world. In his temptation, decisively, at the beginning of his life he defeats the enemy who from generation to generation has held humankind in bondage, and blighted our human happiness.

John in his Gospel assumes our knowledge of this story. He reminds us, however, that Jesus, immediately his ministry on earth began, challenged the evil he had come to destroy not only in the wilderness in the presence of the angels and wild beasts, but also in the one place on earth where it was most powerfully entrenched. Jesus' first exercise of his Messianic power, as we have seen, had taken place almost inadvertently at Cana. He retreated for a short time to think over what had happened and possibly to plan his way ahead (v. 12). Almost immediately he made the decision to go straight from Galilee to Jerusalem to begin his campaign where he knew his chief task really lay. His intention was deliberately to engage in a first dramatic and decisive encounter with the Jewish authorities in the Temple.

The Prophet Ezekiel once had the vision of a river which had its origin in a small stream of water flowing from below the threshold of a restored and cleansed Temple of God in Jerusalem. As it flowed downward and outward to other areas of the holy land around it, the volume and depth of its water increased, and its fruitfulness became more and more marvellous. Wherever it went everything teemed with new life and vegetation. Even when it entered the Dead Sea, the stagnant water became fresh. And of the trees which flourished on its banks on both sides, whose leaves had healing powers, it was written, 'Their leaves will not wither nor their fruit fail... because the water for them flows from the sanctuary' (Ezek. 47:12). This was the prophet's way of stating the truth, taught everywhere in the Bible, that what prevails in the life of a community, health or sickness, happiness or misery, justice or wrongdoing, corruption or progress, depends on what people can see and hear and experience as they worship in their sanctuary.

No doubt Jesus, meditating especially on the miraculous sign that God had given at Cana, and thinking of such passages of Scripture, had similar thoughts in his mind as he went on his way up to Jerusalem. Here was the place from which the river of renewal must flow outward and downward again for God's people. Here, then, was where cleansing first of all must begin.

It was the time of the Passover feast when he made this momentous journey. His mind must have dwelt on the Psalms which describe the joy of such pilgrimage as well as the thrill of arrival (Pss 121; 84). Here before him was the place where 'all the nations' were to be taught the law of God, and were to find inspiration to beat their swords into ploughshares and their spears into pruning hooks (Isa. 2:3-5). Everything here, Zechariah had said, would be holy to the Lord, and all trading would be banished (Zech. 14:20-21).

Even from a distance he must have heard the shouting of the merchants. He made his entry where the money-changers offering temple coinage for ordinary currency were at their business. His reaction was immediate and violent. He had no weapon, but the whip made out of cords was enough, since no one present dared to withstand him in his divinely inspired anger. There was a deliberate purpose behind the passionate indignation which inspired his action. The prophet Malachi, centuries before, had described the coming of the Messiah, in the latter days, to the Temple. His oracle was now in Jesus mind: 'the Lord whom you seek will suddenly come to his temple... But who can endure the day of his coming, and who can stand when he appears? For he is like a refiner's fire...' (Mal. 3:1-2). The authorities knew their Scriptures. Jesus had given them a sign (v. 18) which he hoped they would fully understand.

'Zeal for your house will consume me'

This was the disciples' first public appearance alongside their Master. Perhaps they were nervous. We can imagine their amazement to see him so recklessly challenge the authorities in the full publicity of the Temple area. As they watched him and tried to understand what was driving him on they found themselves thinking about some verses from Psalm 69 which seemed to describe the strength and source of his emotion and to reveal his motives.

The writer of this Psalm had lived at a time of communal apostasy and disobedience to God's law when the sanctity of the temple had been violated. He alone, refusing all compromise, had been ostracized, and even at home treated with contempt. Though he felt deep shame under the insults that were being heaped upon him because of his holy zeal, it came to him that he was being bated simply because the people around him hated God himself. 'It is zeal for your house that has consumed me; the insults of those who insult you have fallen on me' (Ps. 69:9).

From that moment on, the disciples began to understand how always at the heart of all Jesus' passion, love and anger, as the motive of all his activity, there lay this zeal for the glory of God his Father. They saw moreover that it was the key to understanding the conflict that arose between himself and his enemies. It was his pure zeal for God that provoked their anger as nothing else did. Perhaps the disciples sensed dimly and uncomfortably, even at this early stage in his ministry, that inevitably this zeal would literally 'consume' him. At least, looking back later, they saw that they should have seen his cross looming even then. The verse of the Psalm which gripped them at that time seemed to contain a hidden prophecy of his death: *His disciples remembered that it was written, 'Zeal for your house will consume me'* (v. 17).

In the view of the apostles, therefore, Jesus' attack on the Jewish authorities was primarily an attack on their attitude towards God. It was directed against the cold and calculating spirit that had taken over in the religious life. They were robbing God of his honour, of their own souls, and of his reign in the hearts of the people they were meant to lead to him. Jesus' enemies reacted with such intense hatred because they felt he took God and his Word too seriously. They felt condemned and threatened by one so patently and wholly devoted to the service they themselves were guilty of neglecting. They could not tolerate such exposure.

It has become a fashion of today to interpret in quite other terms the cause of the tension which arose between Jesus and the Jewish authorities. It is often claimed that Jesus was crucified because he stood for the rights of the poor and challenged an unjustly privileged and careless establishment by identifying himself completely with the oppressed. Undoubtedly the Bible in many of its passages shows us the prophet of God challenging the rulers of the day on social and economic issues. Jesus was a prophet and it is impossible to deny that there was such an element in his teaching and preaching, and that this also angered the authorities. Yet as we read this Gospel we find nowhere the suggestion that it was on this account that they went the length of crucifying him. The Jesus whom we hear and encounter in the New Testament would not have put social and economic issues before religious issues. We cannot faithfully reflect the witness of the New Testament by distorting its account of history.

An enigmatic utterance

As they looked back on that memorable first encounter alongside Jesus with the Temple authorities, the disciples remembered another of his utterances in the course of the conversation—a saying the meaning of which became clear to them only after Jesus' death and resurrection.

Sometimes when a prophet had spoken an oracle, God gave him miraculous signs to prove the truth of what had been spoken. After Isaiah had prophesied the recovery of King Hezekiah from a sickness, for example, we are told that the Lord made the shadow cast by the declining sun on a sundial in the palace turn back ten steps (Isa. 38:8). Now the authorities in the Temple, angered at what they regarded as a falsely assumed air of authority on the part of Jesus, raised the question: *What sign can you show...?* (v. 18). Of course Jesus had already given them all the proof of his authority that was needed. God had already allowed him miraculously to cleanse the Temple court before their very eyes! Yet in reply to their demand for a further sign he made an enigmatic utterance. He spoke a word which they could not possibly then have understood. Yet it was meant to haunt

41

their minds, and to become a prophecy and a warning to them as they remembered it. *Destroy this temple*, he said, *and in three days I will raise it up* (v. 19).

When Jesus said, *Destroy this temple*, it was both a forecast of his own violent death and also a challenge to his hearers to fulfil the intention they were already conceiving in their hearts and minds—the intention to destroy him. Reflecting on the whole gospel history, we can see that Jesus is here in a sovereign way actually provoking his own death at their hands just as, later on, he actually took command of Judas on his way to betray him (13:27). Of course he could not have expected even his disciples to have then understood anything of what he was saying. Yet it is printed here for us to be able to overhear it today as the utterance of a man giving up himself in extreme isolation of soul to the great cause which has brought him into the world. No one around him, no one but the Father, would understand his feelings. Yet he seemed to find relief in giving them this lonely utterance.

When they heard him speaking about raising up the Temple *in three days*, of course, his enemies had no alternative but to make the saying refer to the stone and lime of the building before them, and they poured ridicule on him—giving at the same time unconscious proof of how utterly unable they were to understand the events in which they were beginning to be involved.

In the case of the disciples of Jesus however, some time after his death and resurrection they actually began to see how profound and penetrating his thought had really been when he uttered this prophecy. Indeed in the account we have here of the incident, John gives us an important clue to what he then meant: *But he was speaking of the temple of his body* (v. 21), he writes. They had by this time begun to make one of the most wonderful discoveries which came to the followers of Jesus after his resurrection and ascension to heaven: the body of Jesus, his humanity now raised to heaven, had become the new meeting place between God and his people. The old Temple destroyed finally by the Romans in AD 70 was for them already replaced by the risen and ascended Jesus in his humanity. The phrase 'the body of Christ' is given as much prominence in the New Testament as the Jerusalem Temple is in the Old. What happens in and through it, is similar to what was designed to happen between God and his people in and through the Temple in former times. We are reconciled to him and to one another through his body (Eph. 2:16; Col. 1:22). We ourselves are baptized into his body (1 Cor. 12:13), become members of it (Rom. 12:4-5; 1 Cor. 12:12-13ff., 27ff.) and partake of what he offers us within it through the Lord's Supper (Matt. 26:26). Jesus himself led them towards such thoughts when he spoke of himself as the vine and of them as the branches (ch. 15). The 'Temple of his body' is for them now both on earth and in heaven. It is on earth where his people are gathered in his name to hear his Word and to receive him in the bread and wine. It is in heaven too, because he is there too. 'See the home of God is among mortals. He will dwell with them, and they will be his peoples, and God himself will be with them' (Rev. 21:3).

Zeal, cleansing and renewal

The disciples were not allowed by Jesus to remain mere spectators of his zeal to cleanse. As he continued to teach them, they were often faced personally with his zeal in his uncompromising calls for purity of heart. Towards the end of his life moreover, in the upper room, and before he gave them the Last Supper, after a solemn action he took a basin and went round the whole body of men washing the feet of each (John 13:1ff). It was a sign of his desire to cleanse them from all the defilement they had brought with them from the world which was going to crucify him, and apart from which he had drawn them. In the word he spoke to Peter, who seemed for a moment to misunderstand or resent his intention, he warned them not to resist what he was seeking to do: *'Unless I wash you, you have no share with me'* (13:8b). There could be no renewal without cleansing! The disciples knew themselves confronted directly both as individuals and as a body by the same zeal for holiness and cleansing as they had witnessed in his visit to the Temple.

It was a lesson they never forgot, and there was always a strong conviction in the early church that the health and vigour of the whole community depended on its allowing itself to be cleansed by hearing the Word and by community discipline. They were especially concerned that people who came to the Lord's Supper should first examine themselves (1 Cor. 11:27-32) and they prayed in their liturgy to be cleansed 'from all filthiness of the flesh and spirit'.

We ourselves are not meant to remain spectators looking over past history when we read of the cleansing of the Temple. Jesus, as well as giving us the Lord's Supper to remind us of his desire for our renewal, has also given us the sacrament of baptism continually to remind us that he seeks to cleanse us as we ourselves seek to come to know him better and to receive new life from him. The picture we have of his cleansing of the Temple with its vivid details surely raises questions about the pride, commercialism and bureaucracy which too often mars and obscures our corporate witness. The picture we have of his cleansing the disciples from the pollution of the world reminds us of his desire for each of us as individuals. The prayer of the leper can have a place in our devotions: 'Lord, if you choose, you can make me clean' (Matt. 8:2).

Descending to details of what can clutter up our lives, a generation or two ago we heard more than we do today within the church of the 'seven deadly sins' from which we require such cleansing. Alongside pride there was listed sloth, lust, avarice, envy, anger, gluttony. It could be a healthy exercise for us even to add such things as anxiety and gloom.

We must not, however, forget that our cleansing is the task which Christ himself undertakes when he enlists us in his service. It is the gift he seeks to bring to us along with the new life he promises. The secret of having both is to receive him in his fullness and continually to set him before us with devotion, confidence and gratitude.

CHAPTER 3

JESUS AND NICODEMUS (1)

John 2:23-25 – 3:1-12

2 When he was in Jerusalem during the Passover festival, many believed in his name because they saw the signs that he was doing. [24]But Jesus on his part would not entrust himself to them, because he knew all people [25]and needed no one to testify about anyone; for he himself knew what was in everyone.

3 Now there was a Pharisee named Nicodemus, a leader of the Jews. [2]He came to Jesus by night and said to him, 'Rabbi, we know that you are a teacher who has come from God; for no one can do these signs that you do apart from the presence of God.' [3]Jesus answered him, 'Very truly, I tell you, no one can see the kingdom of God without being born from above.' [4]Nicodemus said to him, 'How can anyone be born after having grown old? Can one enter a second time into the mother's womb and be born?' [5]Jesus answered, 'Very truly, I tell you, no one can enter the kingdom of God without being born of water and Spirit. [6]What is born of the flesh is flesh, and what is born of the Spirit is spirit. [7]Do not be astonished that I said to you, "You must be born from above." [8]The wind blows where it chooses, and you hear the sound of it, but you do not know where it comes from or where it goes. So it is with everyone who is born of the Spirit.' [9]Nicodemus said to him, 'How can these things be?' [10]Jesus answered him, 'Are you a teacher of Israel, and yet you do not understand these things? Very truly, I tell you, we speak of what we know, and testify to what we have seen; yet you do not receive our testimony. [12]If I have told you about earthly things and you do not believe, how can you believe if I tell you about heavenly things?

An unhappy encounter

This section contains one or two of the most memorable and often-repeated sayings of Jesus. We will not, however, attempt to isolate these and analyse them apart from their immediate context. Here, as elsewhere in John's Gospel, we find that we begin to understand the force and meaning of the words used as we try to enter the dynamics of the personal encounter that is taking place between the speakers. That encounter, in this case, was an unhappy one. Nicodemus reminds us of the rich young ruler who went so eagerly to Jesus with his question about eternal life. His hopes were shattered by the word he heard, and afterwards he went away sorrowful. Nicodemus, however, in this instance went away from Jesus impatient and possibly resentful. Some perceptive commentators point out that the mention of the 'night' as the physical setting of the interview is symbolic, and helps to explain the story itself. Nicodemus comes to Jesus in the night because he belongs to the night in heart and mind. Light then begins to shine from Jesus into the darkness of his mind. But he shuts out the light in order to retain the inner darkness. He is unwilling to hear Jesus out, cuts the interview short, and leaves without ceremony, possibly while Jesus is still speaking to him. It appears that at this point in time, Nicodemus returns to the moral and spiritual darkness from which earlier he had begun to turn.

It was a miracle of grace that many months later Nicodemus did change his mind and was prepared to testify openly to his faith in Jesus (cf. 7:50; 19:39). At this present stage, however, we are not given any sign of hope to relieve the tragedy of the immediate outcome.

The background

That Nicodemus was a man of the Pharisees[1] and a teacher of Israel indicates that he was of some importance in the city. The Pharisees were the up-to-date interpreters of Moses and the prophets. They gave people guidance, for example, on such questions as how to know God, and how to get into his kingdom, and about eternal life.

---

[1] The expression 'a man of the Pharisees' (Gk, and RSV, NIV, AV, ESV etc.) is unusual and occurs nowhere else in the NT. Its significance undoubtedly lies in its close proximity to 2:25 where John states that Jesus 'needed no one to bear witness of man; for he himself knew what was in man' (RSV), then at once continues, ''Now there was a man of the Pharisees...' Dr Wallace's interpretation of Nicodemus's darkness of heart and mind at this point of time is therefore most probably a correct understanding of John's intended meaning of the encounter.

That he was a *leader of the Jews* indicates that he was a member of the Sanhedrin, the highest ruling body of the day. He must have been associated with the Sadducees and the priests, the keepers of the Temple which Jesus had recently cleansed of racketeering.

A great 17th century Hebrew scholar commenting on the Nicodemus story quotes a legend current in early Jerusalem that a 'Nicodemus ben Gurion' once held 'that kind of office whose title was digger of wells, under whose peculiar care and charge was the provision of water for those who came up to the feast'. It would certainly fit well into our story if the Nicodemus who came to Jesus was indeed the city engineer of his own day, responsible for maintaining the huge and abnormal water supply required for all the baptisms and lustrations which took place within the crowded city at that Passover time. Thus, even before he came to Jesus, he may have been already deeply interested in questions about baptism, water and the Holy Spirit.

That Nicodemus was so closely bound up with such an establishment put him under great tension before he could make up his mind to visit Jesus with his questions. Nowhere did Jesus in his early ministry find such blindness to truth, or face such fierce personal opposition, as when he encountered these men to whom God had entrusted the leadership of his people. It seems that almost all of them had betrayed the trust God had put in them when he endowed them with their privileges. The Pharisees and scribes had set up a tradition of their own in place of the Word of God which had come to Israel through Moses and the Prophets. They had perverted the truth to make it conform to the lies of their own minds, and they had blindly persuaded themselves that every letter of this distorted teaching had in itself divine sanctity. The Sadducees had cultivated the worst type of priestcraft to draw honour and wealth to themselves instead of God. They had become cold and calculating, had entrenched themselves in social privileges, had become an aristocracy rather than a humble priesthood. As we shall see, living within such an environment gave Nicodemus a mind-set which, humanly speaking, created almost insuperable difficulty when he confronted Jesus.

The visit

Among so many inclined to be hostile to Jesus, what was it that impelled Nicodemus, alone as he was that night, to go to him seeking at least a friendly conversation? He may have been momentarily disturbed, indeed repelled, when he saw the fanaticism displayed by some of his colleagues in their irrational reaction to Jesus, and their immediate recourse to conspiracy against him. His own first impression of the man had been quite different from theirs. He had been struck by what he had heard of his teaching and especially of his extraordinary miracles which seemed to indicate that he had prophetic power and authority.

Moreover as he had listened to Jesus he had been struck by the contrast between what Jesus taught about the living God, so related to life and so powerful in his working, and the mass of dead doctrine associated with the schools to which he belonged. Possibly Nicodemus in this respect was dissatisfied with his own personal religious experience. No matter how faithfully he had observed the routine prescribed by the Pharisees, reality and life had been too often lacking. Might not a session with Jesus bring just that extra illumination and thrust to his own traditional teaching that would enable him to capture some of the dynamic and attractiveness of the religion of Jesus? He seemed to sense that Jesus might even help him to add to his Rabbinical store of wisdom, for he, too, obviously was a learned man.

Though he went to Jesus seeking such enrichment and counsel, he appears not to have been driven by any desperately felt need. Nicodemus was proud of his rabbinical status and attainments. His visit was made in a mood of self-confidence. What he wanted was chiefly discussion. When he sat down before Jesus, he opened the talk with a compliment—a word of encouragement from a fellow Rabbi to this *teacher who has come from God*! He expects to be encouraged in the kind of teaching he himself was giving on the matter he was going to bring up for discussion. Perhaps, too, he flattered himself that he could bring some enlightenment to Jesus on certain aspects of the truth. It was of special interest to him that Jesus loved to discuss the very subjects he himself had for years tried to teach his own pupils: subjects such as, How does one enter the kingdom of God and inherit eternal life?

The tension

We are meant ourselves to be arrested by the sheer bluntness which we can overhear in Jesus' opening words to his visitor. Often when he knew that people, coming to him for help, admitted or felt some

48

deep need, he overlooked differences and showed his unfailing compassion. We must assume therefore that he viewed Nicodemus, approaching him as he did, as a case for especially frank treatment. Jesus saw that there was such a gulf between himself and the man before him in attitude to God and life, that there could be no easy dialogue or pleasant, informative conversation between them.

He could not begin by hiding this from the man and deceiving him even for a short time about his position. His opening word to Nicodemus was therefore directed to shock him out of all self-confidence, and shatter all his illusions: *'Very trul,y I tell you, no one see the kingdom of God without being born from above'* (v. 3). Nicodemus was expected to recognize that this first word of Jesus was designed to crush out of his mind, there and then, many of the questions he had imagined himself asking as they settled down to talk.

This important word of Jesus to a man such as Nicodemus in this situation should make us uncomfortable. We may feel that it should not be given the special place among the words of Jesus which it is often accorded. We feel that our own way has been a way not of rebirth but of progress—more a journey than a crisis experience—and that we have had some success in following it. Like Nicodemus, we may feel that we, too, have already had some measure of valid religious experience now and then in our lives, without any radical conversion. Surely we cannot be so far out as to deserve a word like this!

Nicodemus himself had believed that as a result of the pilgrimage he had so far made, he must be already at least on the threshold of the great hoped-for reward of all his seeking and searching: the kingdom of God! He had known that he was not quite yet there. He had hoped that Jesus might have some encouragement to give, and some insight to share. Instead, he heard this word: 'You have not seen it, Nicodemus, far less have you come near it! Discussion teaching, insight, effort—they will not lead you there! Only being born again! For a man rooted as you are in this world's life and establishment, there is no other way from your darkness to light!'

This, then, was Jesus' shattering announcement to his visitor: that he was indeed a blind man groping in a dark world for a truth that is not to be found by his method of searching, that the light and life of God to which he had thought himself so near belong to another region entirely, and that the only way from the world to which he at present belonged into fellowship with Jesus was indeed by a new birth.

The closing of the mind

Nicodemus said to him, 'How can anyone be born after having grown old? Can one enter a second time into the mother's womb and be born?' (v. 4).

We are free to subject this question of Nicodemus to varied interpretations. If some readers tend to be sympathetic towards Nicodemus, for example, the question can be heard as expressing the wistful longing of a man who desired such rebirth but regarded it as an impossible dream.

Our own view here is that an offended Nicodemus is dismissing Jesus' solemn word as brusquely as he felt Jesus himself had dealt with his polite approach to him. He intended in his reply to make a caricature of Jesus' remark, to show how ridiculous the idea of re-birth appeared to his mind. There is a slightly cynical tone in the way he put it: 'How can an old man become like a foetus implanted in the womb?'

Hoskyns, in his commentary, puts the case well: 'By a strange paradox, the man who has come to converse about God, and who is sure that he knows what a divine mission is, turns out to be, in spite of his delicate perceptions, a complete materialist. He can conceive of no other truth than that which has made him what he is.'

An appeal for openness

Jesus, having effectively shocked Nicodemus, was now patient and appealing. He explained the kind of re-birth that had been in his mind. It was a complete inward renewal brought about by the Spirit of God. Nicodemus himself knew well the great Old Testament prophecy about the coming of new life to God's people which was to take place in the age to come—in the very kingdom of God of which they had been speaking. It was to be a re-birth brought about through the sprinkling of water as well as by the giving of the Spirit. Jesus was no doubt referring to this passage when he spoke of being *born of water and Spirit* (v. 5). It is possible that he quoted it to Nicodemus: 'I will sprinkle clean water upon you, and you shall be clean from all your uncleannesses.... A new heart I will give you, and a new spirit I will put within you;

and I will remove from your body the heart of stone and give you a heart of flesh. I will put my spirit within you, and make you follow in my statutes...' (Ezek. 36:25-7).

Then an event happened which allowed Jesus suddenly to turn the conversation from Scripture to life. They may have been talking on the rooftop in the cool of the evening, or they may have been in a room with windows open in the direction of the evening breeze. It came for a moment or two with some force. Jesus immediately said, 'Feel it Nicodemus! The wind! Think of how far beyond your control or understanding are its movements. Can you tell where it comes from and why it chooses to come this way? Yet it is powerfully felt even though its ways are beyond your ken. You cannot understand and yet you hear and feel it!' — *so it is with everyone who is born of the Spirit* (v. 8).

It was an appeal to the man before him for openness and honesty in face of all that was actually taking place in the religious world of his own day. What the wind was doing in the place where they were talking, the Spirit was doing in the hearts of men and women in contemporary Jerusalem and Judaea. We cannot doubt that Jesus had good ground for this appeal. Nicodemus had personally encountered here and there people who had come strongly under the renewing influence of the Spirit of God. The Baptist's disciples were moving around everywhere, and as well as John, Jesus' own disciples were now baptizing in Jesus' name and by his Spirit (4:1-2). In his words about the evening breeze, Jesus was indeed reminding Nicodemus forcibly of what he had already observed, and what he himself could experience if wished—the power of God's Spirit to bring re-birth into the lives of ordinary people. Though he could not understand it nor analyse its workings, *the wind blows where it chooses, and you hear the sound of it, but you do not know where it comes from or where it goes* (v. 8).

Perhaps in this challenge to Nicodemus to become *born of water and Spirit* there was a warning to him to throw off the fear of public opinion that had forced him to visit Jesus, unknown to others, in the night. Nothing is given or promised by Jesus to those who are ashamed to confess openly their interest or their faith, as an adult undergoing water baptism must do.

Closed mind and patient teacher

The conversation between the two of them comes gradually to an end. We have just seen how in reply to Nicodemus' scepticism about re-birth, Jesus had pointed him to the teaching of Scripture on the possibility of a marvellous renewal taking place inwardly through the Spirit for anyone who would open the heart to God; and also to the evidence of its taking place in the contemporary world. Was the last word John records from Nicodemus a flat rejection of both the argument and the evidence? *How can these things be?*

Jesus did not accept his plea of ignorance. His very position at the centre of public affairs in Jerusalem as *a teacher of Israel* made it impossible for him not to know what was going on in the city and its environment! He not only implied Nicodemus was failing to acknowledge the truth, but also expressed sorrow that, by refusing Jesus' testimony, Nicodemus was as good as saying he, Jesus, was not bearing faithful witness: *We speak what we know and testify to what we have seen, yet you do not receive our testimony* (v. 11).

At this point, knowing that Nicodemus was not receiving his message, Jesus appears to question whether he should continue the conversation. *If I have told you of earthly things and you do not believe, how can you believe if I tell you heavenly things?* (v. 12). He had much more to say. 'How far was it worthwhile continuing to speak to such a man?' Jesus seems to be saying.

We take the view that at this point there was an important development in the situation. Nicodemus had not only closed his mind, he signified that he was now ready to close the interview. He had had enough. He had given his final word, dismissing Jesus himself. He possibly began, even while Jesus was talking, to show signs of restlessness. The account of the incident may indicate that he even left without ceremony as Jesus was continuing to speak. Yet Jesus did not stop speaking. He continued to preach the gospel to this man who had given the clearest of signs that he did not want to hear more. He went on to speak in the most appealing, profound, simple and memorable way about his Father and his own cross. He went on in the hope that Nicodemus would overhear even as he pretended that he was otherwise engaged, and would ultimately remember what had been said. One wonders how such words as these from Jesus could ever fail to register in any mind?

We are reminded of an incidental feature in one of the Easter appearances recorded at the end of John's Gospel. The disciples in the upper room had shut the door for fear of the Jews, but Jesus came, stood in the midst and spoke. They shut him out unwillingly; Nicodemus did it knowingly. Deliberately he decided that there was no more he need listen to, and he closed up his mind. Yet Jesus stands at the door and knocks, speaking so that his voice can be heard! We cannot keep him shut out and in silence. No matter how fully we fold up our accounts with him to file them away, he comes to re-open everything, sometimes sooner than later. 'He will not grow faint or be crushed…' (Isa. 42:4). Even though we think we have finished with him, he may not yet be finished with us.

Jesus and Nicodemus (2)

John 3:11-21

3 'Very truly, I tell you, we speak of what we know and testify to what we have seen; yet you do not receive our testimony. [12]If I have told you about earthly things and you do not believe, how can you believe if I tell you about heavenly things? [13]No one has ascended into heaven except the one who descended from heaven, the Son of Man. [14]And just as Moses lifted up the serpent in the wilderness, so must the Son of Man be lifted up, [15]that whoever believes in him may have eternal life.

16 'For God so loved the world that he gave his only Son, so that everyone who believes in him may not perish but may have eternal life.

17 'Indeed, God did not sent the Son into the world to condemn the world, but in order that the world might be saved through him. [18]Those who believe in him are not condemned; but those who do not believe are condemned already, because they have not believed in the name of the only Son of God. [19]And this is the judgement, that the light has come into the world, and people loved darkness rather than light because their deeds were evil. [20]For all who do evil hate the

light and do not come to the light, so that their deeds may not be exposed. [21]But those who do what is true come to the light, so that it may be clearly seen that their deeds have been done in God.'

From 'earthly things' to 'heavenly things'

Nicodemus, as we have seen, had shown himself so tough in his denial of simple facts that on one level Jesus had misgivings about the worthwhileness of going on with the conversation. However, it seems he felt he had not yet spoken about what mattered most in the message he had come to deliver to people like this leader of the Jews. Therefore, in a comment which confronted Nicodemus with his unbelief, he announced his decision to go on speaking: *'If I have told you about earthly things and you do not believe, how can you believe if I tell you about heavenly things?'* (v. 12). What did Jesus mean when he divided what he had to speak about into 'earthly things' and 'heavenly things'? The meaning of these two terms, of course, becomes clear if we compare what he had already said to Nicodemus with what he actually now went on to say.

So far Jesus in his talk that night had dwelt on the evidences of the impact of the Spirit of God on the earthly lives of men and women, of the Spirit's power to bring about a radical change in heart, mind and attitude here and now. He had called this experience being 'born again'. He had even asked Nicodemus to feel the wind of the Spirit. He had deliberately taken this very down-to-earth approach because Nicodemus in making his visit had had in mind questions about such 'earthly things'. All this had been a good start, and Nicodemus should have responded to such an appeal to face the power of the Spirit working in his neighbourhood.

But if Jesus wanted now to go on to even better news, he had to speak about God himself, about his own relationship of love to the Father as his only Son, and about why he had come into the world. Now, before he allowed Nicodemus to go, he must be made even to overhear some word about these 'heavenly things'. Therefore, in spite of whether or not it was worth continuing, he went on speaking, and we have from him this word about God so loving the world as to give his only Son, about the eternal decision of love made in heaven when he himself was sent into the world, and of the quite unique heavenly nature that lay hidden in the heart of his own being even as he was speaking to this man before him.[2]

Today we have far greater evidence around us than Nicodemus could ever have had of the *earthly things*—of the Spirit's power to bring re-birth and new life from above. We live after Pentecost. The Spirit of God has proved time and again within the history of the church and in the lives of individual men and women that the gospel is the 'power of God for salvation to everyone who has faith' (Rom. 1:16). Large numbers of Christians today indeed give place at the centre of their church life to continual Pentecostal renewal, the cultivation of charismatic gifts, and divine healing. Therefore, while we can rejoice in what is thus seen and heard today of the work of the Spirit, we must pay heed to the fact that Jesus wants continually to move the attention of our faith upwards—to the things that lie beyond the range of our earthly experience and must be grasped by faith alone.

Often he wants to lift our minds to God, the Holy Trinity, the good news of the Father and the Son and their love in the Spirit. It is when our minds and hearts are gripped by the word and vision of such *heavenly things* that we have a more firm and steady basis for living the Christian life and proclaiming the Christian message. John Calvin said on this subject: 'Our hearts will never find calm repose till they rest on the unmerited love of God.'

Before he gives his final word to Nicodemus, Jesus first claims that on such matters he alone can speak with absolute certainty and authority: *'No one has ascended into heaven except the one who descended from heaven, the Son of Man'* (v. 13) Here we are beyond the ken of the most learned Rabbi, the greatest philosopher or the most practised mystic. As one commentator puts it: 'Jesus is the only one who has ever been in heaven because he comes down from heaven' (Brown). The Gospel writer himself in the Prologue has already underlined for us the sheer uniqueness of what he has to say to us on this matter: *'No one has ever seen God. It is God the only Son, who is close to the Father's heart, who has made him known'* (1:18).

---

[2] Dr Wallace here goes with those translations which punctuate verses 16-21 as continuing the words of Jesus (e.g. AV, NKJV, NRSV, ESV, etc.).

The earthly way to heavenly things

It is a remarkable fact that even that night, Jesus, in attempting to lift Nicodemus up in mind to the level at which he could convincingly speak to him about God, felt that he had to speak about his own death. If Nicodemus was ever to know God he had to be brought to see what the cross would reveal. It is true that at other times and on other occasions Jesus expressed his teaching about God in ways that seem more directly appealing to the human mind. We cannot forget his word to the crowd in Galilee about the heavenly Father and his care for the sparrows and the lilies, nor his parable about the Father who waited longingly and anxiously for the prodigal son to return, and then ran and embraced and kissed him. Yet here before Nicodemus he had no time for many such elaborate words. He knew, moreover, that only what was revealed in the cross would be adequate to break down the man's stubborn resistance to the truth, in order to enable him to see and believe.

That the cross had not yet happened did not prevent him from speaking about it there and then. It is sometimes assumed by those who interpret the Gospels that it was only late in his life that Jesus became aware that he would suffer death on the cross. The writer of this Gospel, however, as we have seen, had no doubt that at the beginning of his ministry Jesus knew what was going to happen to himself. He knew it was bound to happen. *So must the Son of Man*, he said, *be lifted up*. He knew, too, that Nicodemus was bound to be there in Jerusalem when it happened, and would be in a position to take it all in. If he could help this man to think about it properly and to see what it meant as it happened Nicodemus would indeed then be able to see through to the heart of it. He wanted to tell him about it now so that then he could believe and respond!

As Jesus read the Old Testament he found that many parts of it referred to himself, his coming, and the work he was to do when he came. 'You search the Scriptures, he said once to the Pharisees, because you think that in them you have eternal life; and it is they that testify on my behalf' (5:39). There was one remarkable story in the book of Numbers (Num. 21:4-9) which his visitor would know well, and Jesus reminded him of it, because it fitted in exactly with what he wanted to say to him about his crucifixion.

While the Israelites were passing through the wilderness, on more than one occasion they demonstrated unbelief and disobedience. They spoke bitterly against God and Moses. While they remained in this mood a plague of serpents harassed them in their camp. Their bite was deadly and many perished. In their distress the people turned to Moses and asked him to pray for mercy. In reply to his prayer Moses was instructed by God to make a bronze serpent and set it on a pole. The serpent of bronze was set up, and whenever anyone was bitten, if he looked on the bronze serpent hanging on the pole he was marvellously cured.

Through this story Jesus' own future on earth had become more clear to himself. He, too, was to be *lifted up*—condemned to a brutal death. Crucifixion was the kind of death reserved by the Romans for criminals of the worst sort—painful and lingering. He was to be insulted and ridiculed. He was to hang on a pole as if he himself were that serpent—mean, grovelling and spiteful. The crowd around him would be glad to see justice done, and even his friends would be tempted to imagine him a failure. He would be hanged there on that pole to bear the agony and shame alone. Often he had thought of the cry of the Psalmist out of the same kind of dereliction and isolation of the soul as he knew himself destined to face: 'My God, my God, why have you forsaken me?' (Ps. 22:1). No one else could indeed be there. A work had to be done that he alone could do. A burden had to be borne that he alone could bear, and no one was able even to stand beside him as he bore it.

As he had thought it over Jesus had found his mind arrested by another dark aspect of the story. He found that it described to him not only the kind of death that awaited him, but the kind of community that was going to inflict it on him. Already in Jerusalem he had faced the deadly and devilish antagonism of the kind of people who had this world's life under their leadership. He knew that as time passed he would experience the same falsehood, bitterness against God, and hatred of opposition everywhere. He knew that his death was going to be the scene of the worst and most shameful outbreak of malice and injustice the world had ever witnessed. At the beginning of his interview with Nicodemus he had dwelt on the blindness and darkness of our natural human condition—on our need for light and life. Now in speaking of this story he dwells on the deadly poison that has entered the human blood, on our viciousness of mind and heart, and on our need to be reconciled to the God we have rejected with such proud enmity.

However grim and dark its hints of our human condition, however, Jesus recalled the story so as to preach not condemnation but salvation. He underlined the power of his cross and the transformation it could bring wherever its influence was allowed to work freely. One believing look would bring healing to whomever turned towards it. Nothing else was demanded—nothing in the hand, no other sacrifice than what has been made by Jesus himself, only a look by a poor soul seeking mercy, and driven perhaps by sheer despair! One look in simple faith, and everything would be changed. There was hope, health, freedom and eternal life.

God so loved...

The cross is called the 'wondrous cross' because when people behold it they see God. Jesus could have spoken about what it cost himself to come into this bitter, poisoned, perishing world. We sing about it at Christmas:

> Sacred Infant, all Divine
> What a tender love was thine,
> Thus to come from highest bliss
> Down to such a world as this.

How greatly he loved us! Yet here he prefers to speak to us about how greatly the Father loved us in giving *his only Son*.

H. R. Mackintosh in one of his lectures had a story of the captain of an Aberdeen trawler who had his only son on the bridge of his boat in the North Sea when a completely unexpected enormous wave washed the deck and swept the boy away before his own eyes. Later on, still horror-struck and awed at what had happened, he told one of the leading pastors in the city that never till that moment had he had the faintest conception of what it cost God to send Christ into the world.

We can find in the writings of each New Testament apostle some new rich insight into the meaning and message of what happened at Calvary. Here we have the most important and essential thing said about that message, a word from Jesus himself about its revelation of a sacrifice that was made in heaven out of the fullness and uncalculating tenderness and grace of the Father's love.

Look at it! In comparison, our human love is hopelessly faint and poor, for it has so often to be kindled and stirred by the worth of what it goes out towards. Indeed we sometimes love only when we see something worth gaining. But here in this divine love (C. S.

Lewis has called it 'gift-love', to distinguish it from our human
'need-love') we see a fountain full in itself and flowing freely in
sheer, self-giving grace. No worth in us to kindle a spark of it!
Paul reminds us that it was 'while we still were sinners', indeed,
'while we were enemies' (Rom. 5:8, 10) that God sent his Son to
die for us.

There is no prior calculation of whether anything might be given
back in return. No cost too great! He pays without heed
everything it takes to deliver us and bring us back. He had only
one Son, and he sent him! When I read John 3:16, I cannot help
thinking of one Old Testament passage where God tells Abraham
to offer Isaac as a sacrifice on the mountain. 'Take your son, your
only son Isaac, whom you love… and offer him.' Where does it
come from, the tenderness of feeling that throbs through that word
to Abraham, if not from the heart that has faced up beforehand to
the cost of making such a sacrifice? He knows even then as he
seeks the foreshadowing of his own coming sacrifice, that Isaac
will he spared because his own dear One will be given.

It is sometimes imagined that the chief barrier against the
consummation of our forgiveness is in our own minds, alienated
from God, full of suspicion and bitterness. The cross is therefore
held to be simply a dramatic display aimed to demonstrate the
extent to which his love is prepared to go in order to win us back.
The barrier to our redemption, however, was in our whole situation.
We were perishing, helpless and doomed, as well as estranged in
mind and heart. We had become the victims of overwhelming
destructive power. In the cross, God offers the sacrifice. He
resigned himself to whatever it cost in pain and effort to rescue us.
He sent his Son to abandon himself to our state and fate, to rescue
us from our eternal doom.

And now the great inward miracle of reconciliation to God can
begin to happen within us. Strangely, when we read the story of
Christ's passion and cross we are constrained to feel our part in it,
and our own responsibility for it. Our own sin is truly uncovered.
We see what we ourselves have involved him in, with all our
waywardness, carelessness and vice. Whatever our sin may have
done to other men and women, now we see that it was directed also
at God himself in this Man who has so loved us! This is why,
when we really look and see what he has suffered from us, we
begin to change. We experience true repentance. The hatred which
we begin to see we have shown to God we find is now redirected at

ourselves—not to become an inwardly damaging repression, but a healing self-denial that can deliver us for ever, if we will to have it, from pride and sloth, from lust and unbelief, enabling us to walk in newness of life.

The Baptist—the final testimony

John 3:22-36

3 After this Jesus and his disciples went into the Judean countryside, and he spent some time there with them and baptized. [23]John also was baptizing at Aenon near Salim because water was abundant there; and people kept coming and were being baptized— [24]John, of course, had not yet been thrown into prison.

25 Now a discussion about purification arose between John's disciples and a Jew. [26]They came to John and said to him, 'Rabbi, the one who was with you across the Jordan, to whom you testified, here he is baptizing, and all are going to him.' [27]John answered, 'No one can receive anything except what has been given from heaven. [28]You yourselves are my witnesses that I said, "I am not the Messiah, but I have been sent ahead of him." [29]He who has the bride is the bridegroom. The friend of the bridegroom, who stands and hears him, rejoices greatly at the bridegroom's voice. For this reason my joy has been fulfilled. [30]He must increase, but I must decrease.'

31 The one who comes from above is above all; the one who is of the earth belongs to the earth and speaks about earthly things. The one who comes from heaven is above all. [32]He testifies to what he has seen and heard, yet no one accepts his testimony. [33]Whoever has accepted his testimony has certified this, that God is true. [34]He whom God has sent speaks the words of God, for he gives the Spirit without measure. [35]The Father loves the Son and has placed all things in his hands. [36]Whoever believes in the Son has eternal life; whoever disobeys the Son will not see life, but must endure God's wrath.

A prophet in eclipse

John the Baptist, after his experience at the baptism of Jesus, continued his ministry. The revelation that Jesus was the Messiah encouraged him to be all the more zealous in proclaiming that the kingdom was indeed 'at hand'. While he still demanded that as people repented they should be baptized with water, he also bore witness to Jesus as the one who would baptize with the Spirit.

For Jesus too the message was the same as John's: 'Repent, for the kingdom of heaven has come near' (Matt. 4:17). Like John, he recognized that baptism was a sign that could help people to renounce the present age and the self-life, and, in turning from their evil ways, to seek cleansing from their past. He taught his own disciples also to baptize as John did. Thus for some time before John was put in prison, an observer could find Jesus in one part of the country and John in another, both preaching what seemed to be a similar message, and both encouraging baptism.

Naturally, since other sects flourishing at the time had rites of purification which looked like baptism, there was much confusion in people's minds about such movements and rites. We do not wonder then that *a discussion about purification arose between John's disciples and a Jew* (v. 25). It was understandable also that comparisons should be made. It was obvious that the older man's ministry was on the wane, and someone brought to him the report that Jesus was not far away baptizing people and *all are going to him.*

There is not a trace of envy in John's reply: *'No one can receive anything except what has been given from heaven.'* It reveals him full of gratitude. He himself in his day has received so much to pass on to others! He is grateful for his call to preach, for the answers to his hopes and prayers, for the coming of the Messiah, for the new insights and visions given to him at the Jordan, for the gifts that have enabled him to make his witness clear to others. His ministry has so far been crowned with success. Facing his own inevitable decline his mood is of prayerful and confident resignation—especially since he is being eclipsed by Jesus for the sake of whose glory he has hitherto lived his whole life.

Luther, at this point in the Gospel, contrasted the attitude and ministry of John with that of the mediaeval clergy of his day, and he described this utterance of the Baptist as 'golden text'. The bishops and priests of Rome, he affirmed, taught, preached and exercised authority according to earthly tradition without ever seeking inspiration and guidance from heaven—from a living word of God. They did not seek their calling or position from above, but pushed, schemed or worked to obtain their offices. Luther pled for a ministry that looks upwards for its inspiration, gifts and preferments.

Of course much that we have to pass on to each other within the church we receive from below. Each of us in the laity has quite natural talents and abilities which we can put to good use in helping others within the body of Christ to enrich its community life and worship. Teachers and preachers in the ordained ministry can pass on the wisdom and understanding that has come to them through training, through good theological writing, and libraries of commentaries. All this from below! All this is good in its place.

The New Testament elsewhere encourages us to look where John the Baptist directed us. It is to the ascended Christ who, knowing what we need within the church, pours out upon us from above a multitude of different gifts so that one may help and encourage another by sharing what has thus been given, and so that in this way the church may be built up and its life enriched (cf. Eph. 4:8-13). He continually calls and equips some to be pastors, teachers and leaders. He seeks continually to open from above both the Scriptures and our human understanding, that a fresh and relevant word may continually be heard (Luke 24:27, 45). Moreover the love and the patience which can enable us to devote ourselves to the church, to each other and to the world around us, can be received only in the same way, as the greatest gift of all, coming to us continually from above.

The 'friend of the bridegroom'

We have already pointed out (see p.14) that his contact and conversation with Jesus brought to the mind of John the Baptist some aspects of the Old Testament message that he had hitherto missed in his preaching about the coming Messiah. It should not surprise us that John's final recorded words about Jesus show us that now Jesus had been revealed to John as *the Lamb of God*, he was able to discover even more fully what the Old Testament had said both about the Christ and about himself as the forerunner.

When the prophets described the relationship of God to his people they sometimes used the analogy of the love, hope and trust involved in betrothal and marriage. God was the husband who had loved and wooed his bride Israel. They likened the sin of Israel to the adultery of an unfaithful wife who soon after the happy first days of wedlock, gives herself up to playing the harlot. This does not alter the resolve of God's love. He goes through the agony of a great forgiveness, and with infinite patience waits and woos back his bride with an ardour even greater to our human understanding, because it is more costly, than that which won her in the first place.

With true prophetic insight, John saw that the Old Testament passages which referred to this aspect of God's love for his people were finding their real fulfilment in the ardour and faithfulness which he saw now being demonstrated by Jesus as he sought to draw people with his friendship. The Lord's approach to human souls was like that of a bridegroom seeking to win their complete confidence and trust so that they could now enter a relationship of love, warm, deep and inviolate. Jesus confirmed all the Baptist's thoughts of himself when he likened his offer of the kingdom to an invitation to a wedding feast.

In the light of such thoughts John had begun to understand in a new way the place he himself had been given in God's plan to win the world. He had been given the task of *the friend of the bridegroom* (v. 29). He had to act as a messenger for the bridegroom, to procure and prepare the bride for his coming, and of course it was his privilege to share even intimately in the thrill and joy of the moment when the voice of the bridegroom was heard announcing his arrival. John confesses here that he had shared that joy to the full as he had stood by and watched Jesus taking his own place at the centre of the movement he had initiated.

There is indeed a suggestion here that John himself had had opportunities of hearing Jesus' own preaching to the crowds around him and that he had had such joy confirmed by the very tone of Jesus' own voice as he had appealed to people to respond to himself: *the friend of the bridegroom… rejoices greatly at the bridegroom's voice* (v. 29).

For this reason my joy has been fulfilled, he could honestly say when his disciples came and told him that people were leaving him and going to Jesus. He had never imagined any other outcome of his ministry. The bride belonged to the bridegroom. He found joy in the fact that he was no longer needed. It is in this context that John uttered his memorable words: *He must increase, but I must decrease* (v. 30). We have admired the selflessness of this man. Here he takes us to the heart of it, and gives us the secret. It comes without being cultivated or thought about, to those who allow themselves to become absorbed as John did, in the glory and wonder of what is happening around us in the presence of the Christ.

A final testimony

The closing verses of this chapter are a tribute to Jesus. On first reading they seem to be a parenthesis in which the writer of the Gospel interrupts the narrative and gives us his own reflections. Some commentators suggest that the Gospel author is here reflecting on the contrast between Nicodemus and John the Baptist.

However, it is more likely that this whole passage is the continuation and the conclusion of the Baptist's own testimony to Jesus, and reflects his developing thought about his friend, the Messiah. When he made this utterance John had possibly overheard from others more about the teaching of Jesus and had seen more clearly the course his ministry was going to follow. The difficult phrase, *no one accepts his testimony* (v. 32), may simply express his perplexity over a growing opposition to Jesus appearing here and there at that time. He is appealing to his contemporaries no longer to listen to himself, for he had had only a limited measure of the Spirit, but now to listen to Jesus to whom God had given the total fullness of the Spirit, on whom had been set a final, divine seal and whose every word was therefore a living Word of God (v. 34). In closing he repeats what he has already said in the witness he gave at the baptism of Jesus concerning the Father's love for his one and only Son (v. 35), and his final sentence is an appeal to his (and every) generation to choose the *eternal life* offered through faith in him, in face of the certainty that otherwise they will remain under *God's wrath*.

CHAPTER 4

THE WOMAN OF SAMARIA (1)

John 4:1-26

4 Now when Jesus learned that the Pharisees had heard, 'Jesus is making and baptizing more disciples than John' — ²although it was not Jesus himself but his disciples who baptized — ³he left Judea and started back to Galilee. ⁴But he had to go through Samaria. ⁵So he came to a Samaritan city called Sychar, near the plot of ground that Jacob had given to his son Joseph. ⁶Jacob's well was there, and Jesus, tired out by his journey, was sitting by the well. It was about noon.

7 A Samaritan woman came to draw water, and Jesus said to her, 'Give me a drink.' ⁸(His disciples had gone to the city to buy food.) ⁹The Samaritan woman said to him, 'How is it that you, a Jew, ask a drink of me, a woman of Samaria?' (Jews do not share things in common with Samaritans.) ¹⁰Jesus answered her, 'If you knew the gift of God, and who it is that is saying to you, "Give me a drink", you would have asked him, and he would have given you living water.' ¹¹The woman said to him, 'Sir, you have no bucket, and the well is deep. Where do you get that living water? ¹²Are you greater than our ancestor Jacob, who gave us the well, and with his sons and his flocks drank from it?' ¹³Jesus said to her, 'Everyone who drinks of this water will be thirsty again, ¹⁴but those who drink of the water that I will give them will never be thirsty. The water that I will give will become in them a spring of water gushing up to eternal life.' ¹⁵The woman said to him, 'Sir, give me this water, so that I may never be thirsty or have to keep coming here to draw water.'

16 Jesus said to her, 'Go, call your husband, and come back.' ¹⁷The woman answered him, 'I have no husband.' Jesus said to her, 'You are right in saying, "I have no husband"; ¹⁸for you have had five husbands, and the one you have now is not your husband. What you have said is true!' ¹⁹The woman said to him, 'Sir, I see that you are a prophet. ²⁰Our ancestors worshipped on this mountain, but you say that the place where people must worship is in Jerusalem.' ²¹Jesus said to her, 'Woman, believe me, the hour is coming when you will worship the Father neither on this mountain nor in Jerusalem. ²²You

worship what you do not know; we worship what we know, for salvation is from the Jews. [23]But the hour is coming, and is now here, when the true worshippers will worship the Father in spirit and truth, for the Father seeks such as these to worship him. [24]God is spirit, and those who worship him must worship in spirit and truth.' [25]The woman said to him, 'I know that Messiah is coming' (who is called Christ). 'When he comes, he will proclaim all things to us.' [26]Jesus said to her, 'I am he, the one who is speaking to you.'

Encounter by the well

Weary, thirsty and hungry when he arrived at the well at Samaria in an intense heat, Jesus sent his disciples to the nearby village for food. He had originally intended to take another more usual way on his journey from Jerusalem to the North, but an inner impulse apparently had directed him to this longer and more tiring route: *He had to go through Samaria.*[1] When the woman arrived, he knew that his Father had providentially led him. He had to speak to her. What took place between Jesus and herself contrasts sharply with what we have just witnessed in the interview between Jesus and Nicodemus. The latter, coming by night and wanting to be friendly, took the initiative and approached Jesus confidently. She on the other hand, coming to him in the blazing noon daylight, was at the beginning full of suspicion, even hostility. The talking began on the initiative of Jesus, and only later did she open up and reveal herself.

She reveals herself to us engagingly as she talks on and on. We discover that she was highly intelligent and well educated in the history and tradition of her nation and village. She was interested in religion and was prepared quickly to take up a theological point and talk it through. She belonged to a religious community looking for a Messiah whom they believed their Scriptures promised them.

As the conversation developed, we gradually find out what Jesus began to discern as he talked with her. She was living in her village with a man who was not her husband. This accounted for her being there at the well when the heat was so intense that no one else was about. She had wanted to be there alone, for she

---

[1] Greek *'edei, had to,* can refer either to the route Jesus took, or to a providential leading of the Spirit, or to both.

had felt herself to be an outcast, embarrassed when she had to mix with people who might think her a bad influence, whisper to one another, and perhaps register their disapproval of her presence.

Though her approach and response contrasted so sharply with those of Nicodemus, Jesus' aim in speaking to both was the same, and his conversation followed the same pattern of thought. He began by talking of 'earthly things' (cf. 3:31) and then moved to 'heavenly things'. We find here in the case of this woman that his desire throughout is to present himself as the Messiah, the Son of God, who has sought her out and come to meet her where she is, at this well. He wanted to raise her mind finally to the spiritual nature of God the Father who, in response to his seeking love, wants her true and loving worship and devotion. But, as with Nicodemus, he first began through talk that was on a more earthly level. He showed his human understanding of the burden she was needlessly bearing, and of the dissatisfaction he knew she felt in the way she was living. He spoke of the marvellous change and renewal that can take place in those who receive what he can here and now give.

'Give me a drink'

Everything began unpromisingly. The etiquette of decency which prevailed in those days would have prevented a woman from opening up the conversation had she even desired to do so. It was therefore Jesus, more keen to open a dialogue than to obtain any favour from her, who broke the silence and said, *'Give me a drink'* (v. 7).

It was an opportunity for her to insult him, and she took it. Here was a Jew! Typical of most Samaritan women of those days she hated the Jews — and all the more so because she knew they despised Samaritans. Here, moreover, was a man! Her life experience had probably made her slightly bitter and cynical towards the opposite sex. That she had had five husbands before she lived with her present partner seems to indicate that she had been through more than one divorce. She felt that Jesus with his request, *'Give me a drink,'* had given her at least a moment of power over him, and she tried to wound him even as she made a show of helping him. Jesus, before he was offered a drink, was therefore given a taste of the backlash of years of anti-Jewish cultural training given in home and perhaps in school in Samaria, and he was made to feel the personal frustration of a very unhappy individual: *'How is it that you, a Jew, ask a drink of me, a woman of Samaria?'* (v. 9). Her voice rang with contempt — the Jewish male snob, condescending to take notice of her existence only because she happened to have a pitcher handy when he was desperately in need of it! She well knew that in Jerusalem she would not be given a place even among the beggars in the street.

Here we are forced to take notice of the deepening humiliation to which, as time passed, the Son of God was subjected when he dwelt amongst us in order to save us. Here, in the eyes of one he has come to save, he is regarded as belonging to a hated race of men. He sits at the side of a well and begs a drink of a passer-by. In the end we will be asked to behold the same man crying out, 'I am thirsty,' as exhausted and broken, scorned and ridiculed, he dies (19:28).

Look again and ask!

Jesus must have felt the intended insult and must therefore have been grieved at her aloofness. He was well used to such treatment. Many around him seemed to have neither the eye nor the ear for anything other than the superficial, and he had little of that to offer. Yet he had been sent to this village well by the Father to meet her, to reveal his love and to liberate her.

He expressed his hope that she would think again, as he appealed to her with a second request: *'If you knew the gift of God, and who it is that is saying to you, "Give me a drink", you would have asked him, and he would have given you living water'* (v. 10). Obviously his concern is to persuade her to ask for what he has come to give her. If only she could overcome the racism, the class distinction and sexism that were reinforcing her spiritual blindness; if only she were given the insight to penetrate behind his lowly Jewish appearance to see who it was there speaking to her; if only she would listen, look and believe, she would find herself beginning now to ask!

We have to note how skilfully he phrased his appeal, obviously choosing his words carefully. He offered her *living water*. Perhaps he intended this phrase at least be taken as an expression of his sympathy for her as she prepared to fill her already heavy jar with much heavier water. She was a clever and intelligent woman, and this was the task to which her place in life and especially her gender condemned her, day after day, this intolerable dead weight of stone and water! It may have seemed at times to be a symbol, too, of her domestic slavery in the kitchen in the service of a man not worth it. Perhaps here was a different type of man, now speaking to her, who really understood her mood and her lot in life?

Jesus had a further purpose in the phrase he chose for his offer to her. He knew that the woman to whom he was speaking was ready to respond to talk about God. No matter how far she had failed to live up to it, she knew well what the phrase *living water* meant in religious tradition, even in Samaria. It stood for the joyful and satisfying experience of refreshment and new life that the souls of sincere believers received when they entered communion with God, who was himself the 'fountain of living water'. He longed that his offer would awaken within her something of this thirst for the living God that she had heard about from the days of her youth.

She was certainly touched and attracted by his sympathy and understanding of her feelings, and indeed he seems also to have begun to awaken desires within her for a better way of life. She felt he would not be able to speak as convincingly as he did, unless there was something genuine behind his offer, yet she was obviously confused about what he was really offering to do for her. '*Sir,*' she said, '*you have no bucket, and the well is deep. Where do you get that living water? Are you greater than our ancestor Jacob, who gave us the well, and with his sons and his flocks drank from it?*' (v. 11f.). Two things are clear: she is interested in him, and in what he has to offer, and she wants now to remain in his company and hear more of what he has to say about himself.

The word reveals his glory

It is well known that the Gospel of John makes much of the seven miraculous signs which the evangelist especially selects to show how in and through them Jesus manifested his glory. Alongside such signs, the Gospel also at times give prominence to certain words uttered when Jesus becomes especially majestic in his speaking—words that are no less inspired or eloquent in revealing his serene power and divine self-confidence than any miracle could be. This woman now needs no further argument, nor does she need any sign. She is ready to listen, to ask and to receive; Jesus is inspired to put everything he has to say and give to her into such a spoken word.

As we ourselves listen to him speaking it, we are reminded of the great final appeal spoken in the name of God by a prophet to captive Israel in Babylon just as they were about to be released by God from their captivity. Though a great and exciting opportunity for freedom was before them, some of them were loath to take it. They had begun to settle down comfortably in their foreign homes, amidst the wealth and culture which Babylon now offered them. The prophet tried to expose the emptiness of it all compared with what God was now holding before them:

Ho, everyone who thirsts, come to the waters; and you that have no money, come, buy and eat! Come, buy wine and milk without money and without price. Why do you spend your money for that which is not bread, and your labour for that which does not satisfy? Listen carefully to me, and eat what is good, and delight yourselves in rich food (Isa. 55:1-2).

Jesus, as was often his custom, put himself both in the place of the prophet and in the place of God, and gave fresh expression to Isaiah's words as he talked with this poor, deluded, captive Samaritan woman: *'Everyone who drinks of this water will be thirsty again, but those who drink of the water that I will give them will never be thirsty. The water that I will give will become in them a spring of water gushing up to eternal life'* (v. 13f.).

Here alone is what satisfies and lasts while nothing else endures! Here is a treasure incomparable and irreplaceable! He promises to transform the way she lives and the attitudes she takes in life. He promises her a new task and a new sphere of influence. No longer will she remain the social drudge, in bondage to the house, the kitchen and the bed. She will now become the centre of a great renewing influence on other lives around her. His words glow with warmth as he speaks them, and she cannot but listen. He makes her want what he is promising, and certain of what he is offering—certain too that all he is waiting for is her own decision to ask. Therefore she begins to do so: *'Sir, give me this water, so that I may never be thirsty or have to keep coming here to draw water'* (v. 15). She is so certain of his power to put her *whole* life right, that in her prayer she makes him responsible for delivering her from her physical drudgery, as well as for responding to the intense longing of her thirsty soul for the living God.

Of course these unforgettable words of Jesus were intended not for the woman only, but for all of us today. They were meant to be re-echoed to awaken each generation to its need, to bring the grace they promise to whoever hears and asks in any age. They never seem to belong to the past, as we hear them again and again, and they will never do so. They are meant to make us, too, long for what he has to give. We are cold indeed, and distant from reality, if they do not reach and touch us deeply. They come to us as the perfect expression of who he is, and of what he has come to do for each and every one of us.

The moment of truth

Her prayer *'Sir, give me this water, so that I may never be thirsty or have to keep coming here to draw water,'* expressed sincerely the desire of her heart and mind, but it revealed that she was still confused about what he was really offering her. Her confusion was possibly due to her uncertainty about herself. She had one step more to go before things could become quite clear.

In the presence of Jesus she had become uncomfortably conscious that her life had been sinful as well as empty. But she had not yet been entirely honest and frank with him. There could be no possibility of her receiving new life without forgiveness, and that meant complete openness before him. The moment of truth had to come. He decided mercifully that he could bring it about better than she herself could, and in his grace he did it for her, quickly, abruptly and thoroughly: *'Go, call your husband, and come back. The woman answered him, 'I have no husband.' Jesus said to her, 'You are right in saying, "I have no husband"; for you have had five husbands, and the one you have now is not your husband. What you have said is true'* (vv. 16-18).

He did it skilfully and with infinite tact. He made no prior demand for confession. He did not even first explain why it had to be made. All that would have prolonged the agony. In his very accusation, he worded for her the confession she already wanted to make. One step in the revelation gently led into another. She was hurt badly as it all came out, and she felt it, even though by then she knew that he had already known it. Being deeply ashamed before him because of the very self-

71

respect he had already given her, she tried immediately if possible to change the subject. She began to talk theology (which is the best way at times to get off the most uncomfortable challenge of God himself) and with infinitely gracious understanding of her motives and feelings he let the whole matter drop, and allowed her to recover her composure.

What he did for her was thorough. The light he so suddenly and clearly shone on the festering sore that had caused her so much other misery, brought immediate relief and the promise of health. When she would later speak of what had happened to her that day she would always speak of the relief and joy that flooded into her life at the very moment he uncovered her sins through the light of his love and holiness. It takes us back to the message spoken so eloquently in the picturesque language of the thirty-second Psalm. The Psalmist first speaks of the misery of unconfessed sin: 'While I kept silence, my body wasted away through my groaning all day long.' Then he speaks of the great moment of release when 'I said, "I will confess my transgressions to the LORD."' The rest of the poem dwells with joy on the blessedness and confidence of those whose sin has now been so completely and simply dealt with. Having been exposed it is now gone for ever! 'Be glad in the LORD... and shout for joy, all you upright in heart.'

Preparation for witness

He knows she will want to become a witness to what has happened and, like the Psalmist, she will want to speak of this new and decisive experience: *'Come and see a man who told me everything I have ever done! He cannot be the Messiah, can he?'* (v. 29).

His concern is to give her more to speak about than simply what has happened to herself, and to anchor her faith on more than one sudden experience, even though it had brought such joy and liberation. Therefore he keeps her talking there in order to teach her about himself and God the Father. She herself is encouraged to lead the discussion on. She had felt that, by exposing her sin as he had done, he must at least be a prophet.

From this idea her mind rambled on to one of the chief concerns of the prophets—that of worship. She asked his opinion on where one could find the best form of worship. He answered her, speaking to her the famous words: *'God is spirit, and those who worship him must worship in spirit and truth'* (v. 24). One of his chief concerns now was to help her to understand the source of the seeking love that had led him to the well that day to find her. It was because the Father seeks such worship that he himself had come into the world to win it from men and women, and here he was now seeking it from her!

Following such an appeal she is led to talk about the Messiah who, she believed, *'will proclaim all things to us'* (v. 25). It was a simple matter for Jesus who had already shown her so much, to bring everything to a climax: *'I am he, the one who is speaking to you'* (v. 26). She was certain now that he was no other than the Christ.

It was free, open, intelligent dialogue. Jesus encouraged her to express herself on her own level and sought then to lift the conversation to his level. He even seized an opportunity to defend his race against the anti-semitism she had previously shown: *salvation is from the Jews* (v. 22), he reminded her.

We do not wonder that, thrilled with her new discoveries, as well as liberated from her burden, she left her water-jar, and went away into the city with her message. That she left the jar was a sign of radical change in the whole course of her life. She was now free from what it stood for. She had left the man for whom she had filled it. She had left her sin and her bondage.

The woman of Samaria (2)

John 4:27-42

4 Just then his disciples came. They were astonished that he was speaking with a woman, but no one said, 'What do you want?' or, 'Why are you speaking with her?' [28]Then the woman left her water-jar and went back to the city. She said to the people, [29]'Come and see a man who told me everything I have ever done. He cannot be the Messiah, can he?' [30]They left the city and were on their way to him.

31 Meanwhile the disciples were urging him, 'Rabbi, eat something.' [32]But he said to them, 'I have food to eat that you do not know about.' [33]So the disciples said to one another, 'Surely no one has brought him something to eat?' [34]Jesus said to them, 'My food is to do the will of him who sent me and to complete his work. [35]Do you not

say, "Four months more, then comes the harvest"? But I tell you, look around you, and see how the fields are ripe for harvesting. [36]The reaper is already receiving wages and is gathering fruit for eternal life, so that sower and reaper may rejoice together. [37]For here the saying holds true, "One sows and another reaps." [38]I sent you to reap that for which you did not labour. Others have laboured, and you have entered into their labour.'

39 Many Samaritans from that city believed in him because of the woman's testimony, 'He told me everything I have ever done.' [40]So when the Samaritans came to him, they asked him to stay with them; and he stayed there for two days. [41]And many more believed because of his word. [42]They said to the woman, 'It is no longer because of what you said that we believe, for we have heard for ourselves, and we know that this is truly the Saviour of the world.'

A shared joy

The woman was thrilled and radiant. Talking with Jesus had changed everything. She had met the Christ, the Saviour of the world. He had broken into her isolation and self-centredness, and had given her inward liberation and joy. He had led her into touch with the seeking love of God the Father.

The experience of the day had also filled Jesus with joy. In Jerusalem recently he had found himself in alien surroundings engaged in a work that to some must have seemed fruitless. Even amongst the crowds which had come round with enthusiasm he had found too many who only wanted to see miracles, rather than to hear and respond to his message. In the midst of so much uncertainty about the ultimate worthwhileness of some of his ministry, however, here before him now was clear evidence that a work that promised to be more fruitful was beginning to take place. He himself had been given the task of bringing it to perfection. He was thrilled to be here, as he said, to *complete* a work of God (v. 34).

His was the privilege of reaping where *others have laboured*. Possibly a local priest or some godly community leaders had spent years in patient teaching, in prayer and pastoral care amongst this people, and after years of nurture and waiting everything was now ready for a great community renewal. Here they were coming across the fields towards him, thirsty and searching souls ready to open their lives to his influence as the woman had already done. He looked forward to greater works than those that had already astonished Galilee and Jerusalem. He was going to reap the kind of harvest rejoiced in by the angels in heaven. Men and women were going to find God for now and for eternity.

He was looking forward especially to the joy and satisfaction of dealing intimately with individuals. He had come to found a kingdom and to build a church. He had a message for nations and governments about their social structures. But he never lost sight of the one among the many. Groups, congregations, cities were made up of individuals each designed for a special place within a community; each with his or her own name, each with his or her own background, desires and needs; each made for a special place within God's heart and mind and purpose.

What had brought Jesus into the world was not only the desire to restore a fallen universe and to acclaim a universal triumph over evil, but also what a great preacher of a former generation described as a 'passion for souls'. Those around him had become lost, each following his or her own way. Each had to be sought and found in his or her own place, and won as this woman had been, through personal understanding and love.

A revealing intrusion

He must therefore have been disappointed by the attitude which his disciples took up when they arrived on the scene. Of course his purpose had always been to involve them in this work. He had hoped to be able to teach them how to face, in their own future work, other situations of the same kind as this city presented. He had looked forward eagerly to their arrival, but they appeared to fail to respond either to the situation or to his own personal feelings. What had thrilled him they found strange. They soon revealed how much they were out of sympathy, perhaps embarrassed at least, if not a little shocked: *They were astonished that he was speaking with a woman...* (v. 27). Did he not clearly see the kind of woman she was—alone there and so inappropriately forward?

The story suggests that, out of a desire to save him from his mistake, their first instinct was to go and immediately interrupt him, but no one was able to pluck up the courage to do it: *but no one said, 'What do you want?' or, 'Why are you speaking with her?'* (Some preachers have sarcastically suggested that when they overheard bits of the theological conversation, and discovered the brilliance of the woman's mind, they became too ashamed to expose their own ignorance!)

Finally their insensitivity to Jesus' feelings came out clearly when they pressed him to eat. It was he who had sent them to buy food because he had been so hungry. But now the joy he felt in his heart and soul had made him forget his hunger and had indeed banished all thought of his physical needs. He could not be bothered at the moment to return to such a mundane concern as lunch. Could they not understand that this thrilling experience of harvesting in the kingdom of God had simply taken away for the time being his earthly hunger and thirst? The disciples, however, could not even imagine any such transforming uplift of heart and mind to be possible, and they decided that someone else had given him something to eat (v. 33).

Of course we are intended to notice the contrast between the woman and the disciples shown so skilfully by the narrator in telling the story. She forgets her water-jar because she has found so much else to satisfy her soul. They, unaware of what there is to thrill anyone, can think of nothing else but lunch!

The reproach

Jesus immediately reproached them for their short-sightedness. He questioned their outlook and attitude, and showed them where they had gone wrong. He accused them of forgetting some of his instructions to them when he had originally sent them out to serve him, and also of neglecting an important aspect of the task he had given them in the world.

They had come to regard that task primarily as the diligent sowing of the good seed of the gospel in the world around them as far and wide as possible wherever they could find people listening. They had taken to heart Jesus' teaching in the parables about planting the seed of the word in good soil and its growth where it was received. They had retold his stories. They had spoken about his miracles. They had shown how new and different were his moral standards from those accepted by the world or the Pharisees. They had repeated his calls to repent and had underlined the moral and social challenge of his message. They had believed that through such hard work eventually the

76

harvest would come. But it seems they had not thought too much about the reaping that had to follow the sowing if the crop was finally to be gathered. They had coined a slogan: *Four months more, then comes the harvest* (v. 35). They would leave all that to others and to the future. Perhaps the harvest would look after itself!

It was on this very point that Jesus challenged them. He rebuked them for their continual repetition of the *'four months more'* slogan. He reminded them that when he had sent them out he had spoken to them explicitly about the need to reap the harvest as well as to sow the seed: *'I sent you to reap...'* (v. 38). His concern was therefore now to recall them to this whole neglected dimension of their ministry. He had not sent them out as pioneers of a new faith. All round them wherever they went they could have discovered that *others have laboured* in the fields to which they were being sent. Here and there some seed had already taken deep root and the fruit was ripe, questions were being asked that called for an immediate answer, and urgent desires had been stirred. If they had only looked they would have discovered around them *the fields are ripe for harvesting* (v. 35). There was some reproach in his tone. Around them there had been men and women with an awakened hunger for a word about the grace of God here and now, for the promise of the forgiveness that could transform their whole destiny without a moment's delay; an assuring word could have brought them into the kingdom of God, but his disciples had failed even to notice the opportunity.

No doubt as he spoke to them in this way, Jesus had the hope in his mind that by coming to know and listen to the woman, and by the close fellowship they would find with himself in the work ahead, he would be able to kindle in their own hearts something of his own pastoral concern for the human situation, *his* 'passion for souls', and that they would begin to know what it meant to rejoice before God 'as with joy at the harvest' (Isa. 9:3).

A word in season

It is the fashion today within the church to concentrate the energy of our ministry especially on those aspects which involve its direct influence on community life and lead it towards politics. We are at pains to avoid the accusation that we are concerned only with the response of the individual to the gospel, and with the saving of souls. The results of much 'evangelism' seem to many to come too quickly and easily to be genuine. The preaching 'crusade' is suspected of being too one-sidedly triumphalist in its approach and expectations. Moreover there is the feeling often expressed that we have in our day entered a 'post-Christian era' when we face around us nearly everywhere an alien culture unresponsive and unmoved by the appeals that brought religious revival and renewal to churches in past generations.

Certainly today we must not underestimate the need for the quiet and steady work that so naturally absorbed the disciples of Jesus. There is much in his teaching that is meant simply to be disseminated, and as it is gradually absorbed by the human mind it will become powerful in its effects. It will act like leaven in the dough gradually penetrating and influencing personality and society too, even at times fermenting revolution.

Therefore we must not underestimate the need to sow and wait, and even perhaps to suffer as we wait. The example of Jesus' own life encourages us to zeal in such a ministry, for it was only after he gave himself up patiently to his death that the glorious harvest of Easter and Pentecost began to take place. 'Unless a grain of wheat falls into the earth and dies, it remains just a single grain; but if it dies, it bears much fruit' (12:24). We have to learn to our own cost that *one sows and another reaps*. We are given many words in the New Testament about our need for patience: 'So let us not grow weary in doing what is right, for we will reap at harvest time, if we do not give up' (Gal. 6:9).

Yet the gospel Jesus left us to proclaim still lends itself equally to reaping as well as sowing. He described the kingdom not simply as being like a seed to be sown, or like yeast to be inserted in the flour, but also as being like a great supper with 'everything... ready now' (Luke 14:17), where the host ordered his messengers to 'compel' the hungry, the poor and the desperate to enter and feast freely in order to enjoy liberty, wealth and satisfaction.

As we read through the New Testament epistles we find the apostles bringing before us in their preaching two distinct and important aspects of what Christ came to do for us, and of what he offers us in this life. They call on us to receive the gift of sanctification, thus yielding ourselves through the powerful influence of the Holy Spirit to a growing process of change which will be completed only in the world to come.

Yet alongside this gift of sanctification there is the offer of a quite distinct gift of free justification. As we receive Christ we are given a new status before God, the whole past guilt of our sin is completely blotted out, and we receive joyful assurances about our eternal destiny. Too many of us, by our short-sightedness, deprive ourselves of the enjoyment of the whole wealth which Christ seeks to share with us. Moreover, in our service of him we become like the disciples whom Jesus had to reproach so keenly. We allow a one-sided zeal for only one main aspect of the task of the gospel to absorb all our energies.

We become victims of our own planned routine of ministry, making ourselves sensitive only to certain aspects of human life around us. We miss great opportunities and become in some measure insensitive to the deepest emotional and psychological needs, and to the most fundamental questions of the people we are meant to serve—needs and questions which call for a different emphasis and approach.

We need therefore today to lift up our eyes and *see how the fields are ripe*. This incident before us teaches us that it is not always obvious where and when we might find ourselves challenged to seek and pray for a harvest. How unlikely it seemed that this woman that morning was so prepared for his word. How unlikely it was that Zacchaeus, who had hidden himself in a tree as Jesus passed, was so ready to respond to the least encouragement. In the autobiography of J. B. Gough, who was at one time a well-known American actor, he tells of the misery of his youth when every day he became hopelessly drunk. People despised him, and yet took no heed. 'It seems to me now', he wrote, 'that if one word of kindness had been spoken to me then—one touch of a loving hand—one look of sympathy from any human being had been given to me—I could have been led anywhere. But no man cared for my soul.'

Jesus' reminder, *others have laboured, and you have entered into their labour* (v. 38b), is still relevant to us today. Seed sown in past generations is still ready to bear fruit today which can be harvested. The influence of centuries of Christian tradition has by no means been eradicated from the thought patterns and the basic desires of many people around us. The shape of the modern mind has not yet thoroughly hardened into such an alien mould that it cannot be even immediately impressed by the clear and simple presentation of Jesus Christ and the Christian faith in language using the same modes of expression as are used in the New Testament. Memories are there to be stirred, stored wisdom is ready to come to the surface, and young minds often find something that they can relate to in old poems, hymns and books. I had the experience of working with a young Christian in a Middle East country, strong and steadily growing in his faith. His conversion took place when he was studying seventeenth-century English literature in the English class in an Arab university—John Bunyan and John Milton were responsible.

The woman's testimony and the presence of Jesus

We are finally told of the remarkable happenings that took place in the city even before Jesus' visit, of the decisive part played by the woman, and of the word she spoke. Without any delay Jesus kept his promise that he would make her a *spring of water gushing up to eternal life.* That we hear no more of the disciples may indicate that in such renewal movements lay witness can be of first importance.

The woman's testimony was obviously quite spontaneous: *'Come and see a man who told me everything I have ever done! He cannot be the Messiah, can he?'* (v. 29). She spoke of the new thoughts, hopes and experiences that had come to her. She spoke of what she knew of him as a person completely human in his touch and understanding. When she spoke of her belief that he was *the Messiah*, would she not have told how he led her to this discovery in that unforgettable talk that they had had together about worship and the seeking Father?

The evidence of the change of her life, her words about her experience and her confession of faith created at first such an impression in her community that many people claimed to have believed simply because of her word. But the woman herself knew there had to be much more. She said *'Come and see.'* We remember that Jesus said this to his two first disciples as they began to follow him (1:39). Philip said this when he was trying to win Nathanael (1:46). Our witness must lead people always towards personal encounter with himself.

She believed that Jesus would not allow her effort to be in vain. He would be there waiting for them to come, as she tried to point and lead them to him. He himself would answer their prayers, as they pled with him to come amongst them. It was because of his own presence and word that they came to believe that *this is truly the Saviour of the world* (v. 42).

The healing of the royal official's son
(The 2nd Sign)

At this time in his ministry Jesus, according to John, had already done many miracles in Jerusalem. Moreover, according to the other Gospels, he was healing many people miraculously in Galilee. John has already selected for us two examples of the kind of pastoral conversation into which Jesus must have entered with many around him. John now describes for us two examples of the miracles of healing which he regarded as being fit to take their place among the series of signs he has selected in order to share with us his impression of the glory of Jesus. In the first of these, his account of the healing of the royal official's son at Capernaum, he illustrates how Jesus draws out, inspires, trains and rewards our human faith, and how through such inspiration to believe and pray he opens up before us great new possibilities for breaking out of our tragic human bondage.

John 4:43–54

4 When the two days were over, he went from that place to Galilee ⁴⁴(for Jesus himself had testified that a prophet has no honour in the prophet's own country). ⁴⁵When he came to Galilee, the Galileans welcomed him, since they had seen all that he had done in Jerusalem at the festival; for they too had gone to the festival.

46 Then he came again to Cana in Galilee where he had changed the water into wine. Now there was a royal official whose son lay ill in Capernaum. ⁴⁷When he heard that Jesus had come from Judea to Galilee, he went and begged him to come down and heal his son, for he was at the point of death. ⁴⁸Then Jesus said to him, 'Unless you see signs and wonders you will not believe.' ⁴⁹The official said to him,

'Sir, come down before my little boy dies.' [50]Jesus said to him, 'Go; your son will live.' The man believed the word that Jesus spoke to him and started on his way. [51]As he was going down, his slaves met him and told him that his child was alive. [52]So he asked them the hour when he began to recover, and they said to him, 'Yesterday at one in the afternoon the fever left him.' [53]The father realized that this was the hour when Jesus had said to him, 'Your son will live.' So he himself believed, along with his whole household. [54]Now this was the second sign that Jesus did after coming from Judea to Galilee.

The faith that rebels

Now there was a royal official whose son lay ill in Capernaum. Indeed, as far as the doctors were concerned, the child was *at the point of death*, and there was no hope. No doubt the neighbours were showing their sympathy, for many of them already knew by personal experience how hard it was to wait by such a death bed, and to watch the strength of a little one ebbing away so relentlessly day by day. Some of them will have found comfort simply in resignation. Life was hard in those days and people had learned to say, 'The LORD gave, and the LORD has taken away...' (Job 1:21). They were therefore ready to help each other overcome sorrow with fortitude in the face of what they believed to be God's will.

Yet in this one home something had happened to a father which made him refuse to accept such an outlook. He knew the Word of God. It did not always teach such resignation. He knew promises made by God that inspired prayer and hope in such desperate situations. He knew stories of prophets to whom anxious parents had turned in prayer for their dying children, and God had heard them (1 Kgs 17:23; 2 Kgs 4:18-37). He could remember words about a God who could interfere powerfully in life, who in feeding his flock would 'gather the lambs in his arms, and carry them in his bosom' (Isa. 40:11). But above all he knew that Jesus was moving around the country teaching about God and his kingdom. He was possibly not too far away. Perhaps this man had already seen and heard him. Might he not be the Messiah sent by God to save? Had he not at times laid his healing hands on the dying, and spoken words that brought blessing to little ones even at the point of death? Possessed and compelled by such words which he believed to be from God, he made his own decision. He could not possibly resign his child to death. He must seek first the fulfilment of all these promises. He must above all seek the help of Jesus.

Such was the background to the faith of this official whose approach to Jesus finally brought about one of the remarkable signs recorded for us in this Gospel. Even though Jesus could also work equally powerfully without such faith being evident, it is important for us to know how eagerly he searched for such faith among the people who came to him, and how inspired he was when he found evidence of it.

Pioneer and example

We can regard the official of Capernaum as a pioneer and example in a very important field of human life and thought. The arguments which the story compels us to attribute to him found their echo in a popular religious book published in the 1920s.[2] It reminded us that while many in Jesus' day accepted disease, paralysis, blindness, leprosy and death as part of life, Jesus himself did not do so. He rejected these and set out to banish and destroy them. His was a faith that rebelled where others were resigned. The author pled with us to seek and cultivate such faith. Even though circumstances might force us to accept at times the inevitable sufferings and limitations that life brings to us, we must accept them not with resignation to what we suppose to be the 'will of God', but with a faith which resolutely and positively says, 'This is not what God meant life to be when he planned it.'

Such a faith, the author insisted, must inevitably affect our approach and attitude as we face life's most difficult challenges and problems. The claim was also made in this book (as in much of the Christian literature of the same period) that we owed the will to progress in medical science and the success which had so far been achieved in overcoming diseases, to this new and outstanding inspiration to faith given to us by the presence and example of Jesus in this world. Moreover, it was also held that progress in social and personal morals, and the attainment of humane and healthy standards in public entertainments and sports, were also due to the growing influence of the same Christian faith which impelled people continually to refuse to

---

2 *The Faith that Rebels*, David Cairns, London, SCM, 1927.

accept what was debasing and cruel, or to settle down at ease with what offends the Christian conscience.

Not long ago I expressed in general terms to a younger colleague in the ministry my regret that even within church circles our moral standards in many aspects of personal life were slipping so badly. The reply was chiefly a shrug of the shoulder, as I was told that today I must learn more readily to accept life as it is, and to live in and with the real world around me. My response was the simple argument that Christ lived, taught, died and rose again to prove that nothing contrary to his word and teaching can ever now be accepted as if it were just a part of life. We must see such things as tragedy, indeed as the work of an enemy of life.

Does our Christian faith not know Jesus today just as this official did—present in the world around us, telling us about a God with whom nothing is impossible (Matt. 17:20; 19:26) and inspiring us with such hope in face of even the desperate problems of our life, that we can never allow our minds to slip back into despair, fatalism or pessimism on any great issue?

Difficult journey and testing encounter

Rumour had it that Jesus was at Cana, possibly a day's journey away. Yet the journey might have been longer, for he was prone to move on quickly from place to place.

We must not therefore underestimate the difficulties the official had to overcome and the apparent risks he had to take in making his journey to Jesus. Seldom indeed in any of the Gospels do we read of anyone being forced to put so much at stake in order to gain the attention of Jesus. Dare he leave his wife and family at such a time to face a long period of tense anxiety with the child helpless in such a critical state? His venture could he criticized as callous and foolhardy. Indeed the faith he was able to summon in order to make the journey was as marvellous as the very miracle he was going to seek from Jesus. Whatever circumstances arose, whatever the outcome of his desperate venture, he believed Jesus would not fail to honour the trust and hope that he had inspired.

On his arrival in Cana, there took place a tense and dramatic first encounter. Jesus was at this time beginning to face the acute problem which continually dogged his ministry. In his recent visit to Jerusalem he had acquired a great reputation for his signs and miracles. News had spread, and now even in Galilee he was finding himself acclaimed and sought after by many people as a modern wonder-worker, a sensation (v. 45). They admired his success and his technique, and of course they wanted him to keep on demonstrating miracles.

But their attitude was, in his view, perverse. The more familiar they became with the kind of work he was doing, the more it was being proved that a prophet has no honour in his own country (v. 44). They were prepared in his presence to marvel, but never to worship, or to give him their whole personal trust. They were not listening seriously to what he said about the kingdom of God. Nor were they seeking to enter it, and experience God's forgiving and transforming love. They preferred excitement to salvation. It was a sign of Jesus' humanity that he felt baffled, lonely and troubled in heart as he found such people coming round him in droves. We are not surprised therefore that when this man finally reached Jesus he experienced momentarily a reaction arising from these troubled feelings. Was this rather wealthy-looking man from Capernaum not just another of them—drawn not by his word, his converting message, but only by his miracles; seeking not to enter into his kingdom or friendship, but just to see some sign of his astonishing power?

The word which Jesus spoke to him, *'Unless you see signs and wonders you will not believe'*, was a question about his motive rather than an accusation. The man knew that Jesus was not trying to turn him away but was simply testing him.

In the man's impassioned cry, *'Sir, come down before my little boy dies'*, Jesus heard more than a request for a physical miracle. He heard an affirmation of genuine personal faith, a cry of recognition, a commitment to complete surrender, a promise of trust whatever his decision, be it 'Yes' or 'No': 'Lord I want You. I want your kingdom and glory as well as your power. I want your God as my God, your thoughts as my thoughts, your ways as my ways. I want my home to be yours too, my children to be your servants. Come down into our midst and transform everything.'

His sincerity, his prayer, the tone of his voice in these few pleading words drew Jesus into immediate response.

'Sir, come down before my little boy dies'

Jesus spoke the word, *'Your son will live.'* The boy, we know from John's record, was healed the moment Jesus spoke it. Nothing else was needed. Even when he was amongst us in the flesh, distance made no difference to his divine power to heal or bless where he willed. Exalted as he now is, he has the same compassion, and is no less powerful in the word he is able to speak.

This venture in prayer for a child in critical need takes its place alongside other stories recorded in the Gospels about the readiness of Jesus to hear the prayers of distracted parents and to restore family relationships that have been tragically broken. They remind us again that he is the Messiah who comes to turn the hearts of fathers to their children, and the hearts of children to their fathers (Mal. 4:6). Such stories are all meant to encourage those of us who have the same kind of family problems to take them to Christ today with persistent faith. They are not there to delude us with false hope.

Today, however, it should not be only our own personal and family need that drives us to Jesus on behalf of the child in our midst. When we think even of one, we cannot avoid allowing our mind to turn to the dangers that threaten all. In the world environment and cultural climate in which we live, we will inevitably find ourselves re-echoing the prayer of the nobleman in its plural form: 'Sir, come down before our children die'. Every day our news media present us with harrowing stories of the suffering of children, both internationally and within our own country. We have therefore to pray for the whole world today as we pray for our children. It is even more difficult to persevere in offering such prayer, than in naming one particular child and seeking a particular answer. The obstacles to the large-scale progress we seek are truly so enormous, so political and so complicated. We seem to be asking for the reversal of years of social, industrial and moral habit. Indeed we seem to be praying for the removal of mountains.

Yet the prayer as it is worded for us here is simple. It is a prayer for Christ to come into our world's life and control the decisions of rulers and people where all these important issues are at stake. It echoes the prayer of Moses facing what for him were equally daunting difficulties: 'If your presence will not go, do not carry us up from here' (Exod. 33:15). As we pray it, we address one who has already proved his love for the world by sending his own Son to save us from perishing. Has he not put so much into it already that he cannot possibly forsake it? By coming once, has he not shown us that he can come again?

We must therefore persist. It was Jesus' own purpose to call us to this prayer when he taught us to say 'Your kingdom come. Your will be done, on earth as it is in heaven' (Matt. 6:10). Jesus himself once or twice showed us that the obstacles before us, in the way of the progress of his kingdom, would appear to us like a great mountain impossible to dislodge. He was reminding us of the prayer of the Old Testament prophet to whom in his day the difficulties were no less formidable. But he knew how they could be overcome. 'O that you would tear open the heavens and come down, so that the mountains would quake at your presence...' (Isa. 64:1). 'What is impossible for mortals', said Jesus, 'is possible for God' (Luke 18:27).

The word for the way ahead

The word which Jesus spoke was brief, *'Go; your son will live.'* Yet he put into it everything he had to give to the man himself. It immediately brought him new life and hope. He had been given no proof, no sign, yet a miracle happened in his own mind. His anxiety was gone. *The man believed the word that Jesus spoke to him and started on his way* (v. 50). Everything was changed, everything was done, because the word had been spoken!

Hannah in the Temple at Shiloh one day had come to the end of her tether. For years she had carried a heavy burden of vexation and sorrow. It suddenly came to a climax in uncontrollable weeping and a desperate prayer. Then a word was given her by the priest which she felt able to take for certain as the word of God. He had granted her petition. In due time she would have the child she had longed for. There was no proof, no other pledge than a mere word—from God. Yet it was as if everything had already happened. She went her way and 'her countenance was sad no longer' (1 Sam. 1:13-18). A whole future assured in a mere word!

As it happened to Hannah or to the official in this story, so it can to ourselves. It can happen as we read Scripture or hear it read. It can happen in other ways—for example through the word of a friend inspired to meet a need. A word comes to us—as if from God himself. It holds us and we hold on to it. It can alter our mood and our outlook. It can sustain our hope and courage day after day. Elijah, after the word of the angel, 'went in the strength of that food for forty days and forty nights...' (1 Kgs 19:8).

Commentators on this incident have often likened this royal official's journey home to our own journey through life. He had to spend the night in Cana. Did doubts begin to assail him? On the journey others came to him and gave their news and their witness (v. 51). The apostle Paul, having become depressed on his journey to Rome, met some Christians who had come to meet and talk with him; then 'Paul thanked God and took courage' (Acts 28:15). How much it helps us to compare notes with our fellow-Christians on our journey; their testimony helps confirm our faith and protect us from the attacks of doubt.

CHAPTER 5

AT THE POOL OF BETHZATHA

(The 3rd Sign)

John 5:1-18

5 After this there was a festival of the Jews, and Jesus went up to Jerusalem.

2 Now in Jerusalem by the Sheep Gate there is a pool, called in Hebrew Bethzatha, which has five porticoes. ³In these lay many invalids—blind, lame, and paralysed. ⁵One man was there who had been ill for thirty-eight years. ⁶When Jesus saw him lying there and knew that he had been there a long time, he said to him, 'Do you want to be made well?' ⁷The sick man answered him, 'Sir, I have no one to put me into the pool when the water is stirred up; and while I am making my way, someone else steps down ahead of me.' ⁸Jesus said to him, 'Stand up, take your mat and walk.' ⁹At once the man was made well, and he took up his mat and began to walk.

Now that day was a sabbath. ¹⁰So the Jews said to the man who had been cured, 'It is the sabbath; it is not lawful for you to carry your mat.' ¹¹But he answered them, 'The man who made me well said to me, "Take up your mat and walk."' ¹²They asked him, 'Who is the man who said to you, "Take it up and walk"?' ¹³Now the man who had been healed did not know who it was, for Jesus had disappeared in the crowd that was there. ¹⁴Later Jesus found him in the temple and said to him, 'See, you have been made well! Do not sin any more, so that nothing worse happens to you.' ¹⁵The man went away and told the Jews that it was Jesus who had made him well. ¹⁶Therefore the Jews started persecuting Jesus, because he was doing such things on the sabbath. ¹⁷But Jesus answered them, 'My Father is still working, and I also am working.' ¹⁸For this reason the Jews were seeking all the more to kill him, because he was not only breaking the sabbath, but was also calling God his own Father, thereby making himself equal to God.

The place

Jesus could not have personally approved of the strange happenings or superstitious ideas associated with the pool of Bethzatha. When there was a disturbance of the waters people gathered around the pool because they believed that the first person who managed to immerse in the waters immediately after each disturbance would experience a cure from his disease.[1] Since the disturbances were irregular, always one had to be on the alert, and great excitement was momentarily generated as the scramble into the water took place. Possibly several times a day they happened. They were numerous enough to keep the place popular, with large crowds gathering. Stories circulated through Jerusalem about remarkable cures. Nobody had ever checked up on their genuineness. Of course the legends attached to the place grew, and it acquired an established tradition. No doubt, with smart business people around, it had become commercialized by those who sold snacks and perhaps hired out mattresses or seats.

We can think, however, of reasons why Jesus might have been attracted to visit such a place. Certainly one of them was to be found in the varied make-up of the crowd—onlookers, helpers, patients. Nothing human was alien to Jesus and he must have loved being there watching now one, now another, finding them interesting to look at simply as individuals, or recognizable as families. It must have been a keen disappointment to him later in his ministry to find that the crowds, to whom he had loved to preach, showed so much hostility.

Jesus was all the more attracted to this crowd because so many of them were in such a wretched condition: *many invalids—blind, lame, and paralyzed* (v. 3). He once said, 'When you give a luncheon or a dinner, do not invite your friends... or rich neighbours, in case they may invite you in return, and you would be repaid. But when you give a banquet, invite the poor, the crippled, the lame, and the blind. And you will be blessed...' (Luke 14:12-14). He went on to tell a parable in which the servants were

---

[1] See the marginal note in the biblical text for verse 4 which is derived from certain ancient authorities but is not in the best attested manuscripts. That the water was occasionally disturbed is clear from verse 7. The water in Bethzatha came from Solomon's pool which acted as a reservoir, but may also occasionally have been fed by an intermittent spring thus causing the rippling or disturbance of the waters which had given rise to the popular belief expressed in verse 4.

sent out to 'the streets and lanes of the town' to 'bring in the poor, the crippled, the blind, and the lame' (Luke 14:21). Here was the company amongst which, before God, he wanted to be found.

It is possible, too, that he found this place and crowd attractive because the prevailing atmosphere was one of expectancy. Certainly, as we shall see, there were exceptions, but many were there even as casual onlookers because they expected to see signs that here in this place miracles could happen. In spite of all the strange superstition attached to their hope, they at least clung to the belief, so clearly encouraged by the Word of God, that ordinary men and women in trouble and distress need not resign themselves to sheer hopelessness. People on earth can experience angelic visitation, for life in this world is open to another world, and the sick can at times by the mercy of God experience divine healing.

It is noticeable today that in the midst of Christian communities, alongside our temples of orthodoxy there can appear quite often a 'pool of Bethzatha'. Those of us who belong to 'mainstream' Christian denominations are being more and more forced to take notice of what we are tempted to call 'fringe' groups which give support and fellowship to people who find us too rigid in our adherence to our traditional liturgy and practice, and lacking in enthusiasm. Sometimes in their own enthusiasm we find them verging on what seems to us superstition.

We have to be careful in our criticism, remembering that Jesus was not ashamed to pay his visit to Bethzatha. I have often felt how helpful it would be if we shared something of their expectancy—especially at that point in the service when the Scriptures have been read and the sermon begins. How good it would be if, even in the midst of our orderly routine, we would recognize our close kinship with those at Bethzatha who lay there waiting for the disturbance of the waters. If only we could realize that what interrupts the ritual is at times better than the ritual itself! (cf. 1 Sam. 3).

The man

When Jesus arrived at the pool on this particular occasion he found himself attracted by pure divine compassion to one lonely soul who in the midst of all the expectant hubbub had actually lost every vestige of faith and hope. He went straight to him and put a question which exposed the whole extent of his plight, *'Do you want to be made well?'* The only answer he could give to Jesus' challenge was merely a pitiful and evasive complaint: *'Sir, I have no one to put me into the pool when the water is stirred up; and while I am making my way, someone else steps down ahead of me'* (v. 7).

There must have been a time when such a straight question from Jesus would have received the immediately straightforward and positive response, 'I do.' But that was almost thirty-eight years ago. That whole length of time had passed with nothing ever happening to himself—always to others. All personal hope in his own case had gone with the years, and deep in his mind he had settled with himself that he would never make it. Habit had taken over.

The pool had become to him personally what the temple next door had become to many of its zealous attenders, or what a church today can become to some of its 'pillars'—a place of uneventful and unbroken ritual. The place itself had imposed its routine and taken over his life. He was there that day because he was there every day, and every day was the same. What kept him going in this way of life was the staying power of thoughtless habit.

The answer he gave to Jesus reveals another aspect of the sad plight which must have attracted Jesus to this man. In his moment of need he finds himself in complete isolation from all others. He confesses himself as lonely as he knows himself helpless: 'At the moment I most need help I find no one to turn to.' We thus discover that even amongst the invalids so pitied by Jesus, when there was something to be gained, the competitive instinct took over, and at the crucial moment all proved to be out for themselves.

We marvel therefore at what the coming of Jesus meant to this lonely heart. To the person who says 'I have nobody', Jesus in effect says 'I myself am here now at your side.' The poor invalid did not know that it was Jesus, the Christ, the Son of God, who spoke these words, but he had now found the friend who had already by his sympathetic question begun to help him to overcome his troubles. Can we not read this as a sign of the care that Jesus desires to give, and to be given, to those who are beginning to lose hope in the course of our present ruthless, materialistic, competitive society?

The word of healing

Since his question, and its answer, had clearly demonstrated the man's hopeless lack of faith and will-power, Jesus could now therefore use the occasion not only to exercise his compassion in healing the man, but also deliberately to stage a remarkable demonstration of his otherwise hidden divine power and majesty. The whole account of this incident and its aftermath makes it clear that Jesus is here giving a unique sign, to any who will receive it, of who he is. He made the miracle happen as he made creation happen in the beginning—by a word of omnipotent creative power: *Jesus said to him, 'Stand up, take your mat and walk.' At once the man was made well, and he took up his mat and began to walk.* Those who witnessed it were reminded of the description in Psalm 33:9 of how God made heaven and earth: 'For he spoke, and it came to be; he commanded, and it stood firm.'

Immediately after we read of how the miracle took place we begin to discover how closely people had been watching Jesus. We are told that *that day was a sabbath.* The command to the man to take up his mat and walk was therefore a deliberate command to break the accepted man-made rules of sabbath behaviour. Jesus' intention was deliberately to provoke the Jews into a confrontation for which he already in his mind had a well-thought-out answer. They fell into his trap and challenged the man. They obtained a description of who had healed him, and they came and accused Jesus of wrong-doing.

The reply Jesus gave was uttered not in defence or defiance but in the sheer majesty that had characterized every aspect of the miracle: *'My Father is still working, and I also am working'* (v. 17). They immediately understood what he was saying. It followed from their own teaching. Their theory was that God himself could be exempted from his own sabbath law. Indeed God was forced to work on the sabbath because he was God. He had to put out whatever effort was required to keep the universe going. The sun had to shine and the rain had to come even on the sabbath. Jesus here claims that he himself enjoys the same exception to the human rule as his Father himself. The Jews could not fail to realize now the equality with God not only in power but in privilege that he was claiming as they stood before him. He had driven his point home, and they had no excuse for ignorance as they determined more firmly than before that they must put him to death (v. 18).

Pastoral appeal and pastoral warning

The miracle which was to bring Jesus closer to his death also involved the healed man in trouble with the Jewish authorities. Jesus of course was concerned for him and followed him up closely as he went to the temple. We are not told everything that was said when he found him and spoke to him. We interpret the report we have here as simply a short summary of what was said as Jesus expressed his pastoral concern. The recorded words reveal what was in the mind of Jesus at that moment, and give us insight into the message he sometimes gave to those he healed: *'See, you have been made well! Do not sin any more, so that nothing worse happens to you'* (v. 14).

We must read this as an appeal as well as a warning. In the first place, it is the same kind of appeal for gratitude and goodness that we find echoed everywhere in the New Testament. Of course the appeal is positive. We must sin no more, simply because he has made us whole. He has set us completely free from the bondage and degradation of our past life, and made us new creatures. We do not need to return to our former slavery or yield again to the sin that has held us down (8:34). We have to consider ourselves now 'dead to sin and alive to God', and in sheer love and gratitude we have to make this the glorious dominant fact of our daily lives (cf. Rom. 6:1-18). The apostles learned such teaching from Jesus himself.

Why did Jesus on this particular occasion add also a pastoral threat—a clear and solemn warning: *'Do not sin any more, so that nothing worse happens to you'*? It is possible that in the case of this man there was a unique need to hear such a word at this time. Jesus knows the heart and mind of each individual. Many of us, if we know ourselves well, will recognize that at times we have benefited from the stark warnings offered by Jesus himself about the 'unquenchable fire' of hell (Mark 9:43 ff.).

We have seen that as he spoke this word of warning Jesus was anticipating his coming death on the cross. Because he had brought such healing to humanity, he was now facing the worst thing that can befall any member of the human race. Shrinking as he was even now from the unspeakable and incomparable horror of it, can we not think of him, knowing the weakness of this poor man before him, as pleading with him all the more urgently to turn away completely from the paths that lead humankind into such devastation and bitterness?

If there was occasion for such an utterance in the ministry of Jesus, there is still occasion for its being repeated to us today, in case for our own sakes we need to re-hear it. We must not become careless in a world where our salvation cost the death of Jesus himself. We dare not trifle with the sin that sent him to the cross.

Jesus as Prophet, Priest, and King

At this point a brief note is appropriate on one feature of Jesus' ministry which from now on is given some prominence in John's Gospel. It has been pointed out that Jesus here seems to have made this man's healing the occasion for demonstrating his divinity and authority. He used it to reinforce his claim to be who he was. Yet there has been no doubt throughout the exposition that the whole incident is an act of pure divine compassion .

I can remember speaking to a group of students on Jesus' miracle of the healing of the paralytic in the second chapter of Mark. I suggested that while Jesus healed this man out of compassion, nevertheless at the same time he demonstrated certain truths about himself and his ministry. 'How disgusting!' remarked one woman student. She pointed out that if we ourselves when we did some kindness to others were at the same time consciously trying to teach them, through our supposed act of love, some edifying lesson about who and what we are, then everything we did would be vitiated. When I listened to her I remembered how our teachers in divinity school used to warn us never to regard Jesus' miracles as proofs of his divinity. The warning would be deserved, and the argument valid in the case of any one of us other than Jesus. But with Jesus, it does not hold. As Augustine pointed out, Jesus himself is the Word of God. Therefore every act of Jesus the Word must itself be a word.

Jesus in everything he does is always Prophet, Priest, and King. As our Priest he is all compassion, showing us a pity and love that is always genuine and pure. As our King he acts with majestic and miraculous power. As Prophet he inevitably teaches as he sets his love and power in motion. Everything he does in his work is inevitably significant of who he is and of the redeeming purpose that has brought him into the world. We must rid ourselves of the idea that he could self-consciously switch about, playing different roles one apart from the other.

The works of Jesus and the blindness of the Jews

John 5:19-47

Jesus provokes controversy

Having drawn the attention of his enemies away from the healed man to himself, Jesus spoke in his own defence, delivering a discourse full of stinging accusations and warnings. This is the first of a series of lengthy utterances through which he provoked his enemies, and finally roused them into open controversy with himself not only in the temple and streets of Jerusalem, but also even in Galilee. These public discourses are an important part of John's Gospel.

Whatever his circumstances Jesus had so much to say and give that he never spared himself. Even in his self-defence there was always a new self-revelation. At this stage in his ministry many in the crowd around him were still uncommitted, and his disciples also were there listening. Therefore the appeals and claims which he made even in addressing his enemies are as significant, eloquent and convincing as any he ever uttered.

It is not the purpose of this exposition of the Gospel to make any detailed analysis of the sentence structure, or of the meaning of the words used by Jesus. Nor within the available space can the reader's attention be drawn closely to everything said. This exposition aims to provide guidelines through the text so that the reader can have an understanding of the general drift of Jesus' thought, some illumination of his most important and outstanding sayings in their primary setting, and thus comprehend better his witness to himself.

Chapter 5

John 5:19-20a

5 Jesus said to them, 'Very truly, I tell you, the Son can do nothing on his own, but only what he sees the Father doing; for whatever the Father does, the Son does likewise. [20]The Father loves the Son and shows him all that he himself is doing;

The reflection of the Father in the work of the Son

One of Jesus' most memorable sayings was to Philip: 'Whoever has seen me has seen the Father' (John 14:9). When we first reflect on these words we tend of course to make them refer to the moral and spiritual qualities which Jesus showed as a human being—his love, his patience, his righteous anger, his wisdom, his complete trustworthiness as a person, his trust in the Father as he underwent his passion. Here in this passage, however, Jesus urges us also to see a likeness to the Father's work displayed in his own miraculous work. In that work he always knew himself to be closely under the Father's direct inspiration and guidance. Maybe here he is likening himself to a son apprenticed to a father in a trade: the father demonstrates and the son copies. Certainly the mysterious and continuous bond between Father and Son throughout his entire ministry is referred to in these words. We wonder all the more at that cry of dereliction on the cross, 'My God, my God, why have you forsaken me?' (Matt. 27:46; cf. Luke 23:46).

Jesus must have been discouraged when people followed him because they saw his 'signs and wonders', took up a superstitious attitude to his miracles, and neglected the more important aspects of his message. Yet here in this discourse he affirms decisively that if people would show reverence rather than superstition, then *the very works that I am doing... testify on my behalf that the Father has sent me* (v. 36).

John 5:20b-29

5 and he will show him greater works than these, so that you will be astonished. [21]Indeed, just as the Father raises the dead and gives them life, so also the Son gives life to whomsoever he wishes. [22]The Father judges no one but has given all judgement to the Son, [23]so that all may honour the Son just as they honour the Father. Anyone who does not honour the Son does not honour the Father who sent him. [24]Very truly, I tell you, anyone who hears my word and believes him who sent me has

97

eternal life, and does not come under judgement, but has passed from death to life.

25 'Very truly, I tell you, the hour is coming, and is now here, when the dead will hear the voice of the Son of God, and those who hear will live. [26]For just as the Father has life in himself, so he has granted the Son also to have life in himself; [27]and he has given him authority to execute judgement, because he is the Son of Man. [28]Do not be astonished at this; for the hour is coming when all who are in their graves will hear his voice [29]and will come out—those who have done good, to the resurrection of life, and those who have done evil, to the resurrection of condemnation.

The Son of God and human destiny

His enemies, Jesus said, may have rejected the evidence of God's hand in the miracles they have already witnessed, but they are going ultimately to be forced to marvel as they become involved with the Son of God in *greater works than these* (v. 20b).

As this age comes to a close, two great final events will determine the future and place of each individual in the world to come—the raising of the dead and the last judgement. Jesus here claims that he himself has been given the power and responsibility to do these *greater works*. This section of the discourse therefore comes to its climax in a description of how, in the words of the Apostles' Creed, 'he will come again to judge the living and the dead' at the last day (vv. 28, 29).

Before Jesus finally describes what will take place at this second coming, he reminds us that none of us need wait before we ourselves are in a position to know our own personal destiny when the last day comes. He speaks of how any one of us, if we will, can even here and now experience already eternal life and resurrection from the dead as we hear his voice today: *'Very truly, I tell you, anyone who hears my word and believes him who sent me has eternal life, and does not come under judgement, but has passed from death to life. Very truly, I tell you, the hour is coming, and is now here, when the dead will hear the voice of the Son of God, and those who hear will live'* (vv. 24, 25).

In this remarkable declaration he speaks clearly of the greatest and most miraculous work which God has given him to accomplish as long as this world lasts. The Father has put it into the power of

Jesus to bring about for all of us who will hear his word and enter a believing relationship with him, a resurrection which exists now. It transforms the life we are at present living on earth. It is the experience of a great inward liberation, or rebirth, from spiritual death to eternal life, from blindness to sight, from slavery to freedom, from guilt to forgiveness. It happens when we hear the word of Jesus and put our trust in him. Such an inward resurrection also brings with it a great assurance about what will happen to us when we are brought face to face with Jesus the Judge at the last day, for it is the first installment of what will then take place, a preliminary foretaste of what will then be finally given.

Jesus completes his description of these *greater works* in a brief and dramatic picture of the final resurrection and judgement: *'for the hour is coming when all who are in their graves will hear his voice and will come out—those who have done good, to the resurrection of life, and those who have done evil, to the resurrection of condemnation'* (vv. 28, 29). He later added more detail to his description of this event in the parable in which he pictured all nations gathered before his throne, the separation of the sheep and the goats, and the judgement then pronounced on those who saw him hungry, thirsty, impoverished or imprisoned and who neglected their duty to him, and of the blessing pronounced on those who responded with compassion (Matt. 25:31–46).

Belief in these vivid New Testament descriptions is a vital part of the faith we confess when we repeat the Apostles' Creed. Although, of course, it is impossible for us to conceive or imagine how these descriptions can be literal fact—living as we do in a finite, material and transient world—nevertheless we are meant to hold before our minds the events they point to and allow our expectation to motivate us to shape and to transform the way we live. We are not to become perplexed or despairing. We are reminded that it is those *who have done good* who are resurrected to eternal life, and those *who have done evil* who are damned. These words are there to encourage us to live in love, fear and trembling as we wait in confidence and gratitude for Christ's coming. The one who gives us such confidence in waiting and serving is the one who comes in the end to put all things right.

John 5:30-40

5 'I can do nothing on my own. As I hear, I judge; and my judgement is just, because I seek to do not my own will but the will of him who sent me.

31 'If I testify about myself, my testimony is not true. [32]There is another who testifies on my behalf, and I know that his testimony to me is true. [33]You sent messengers to John, and he testified to the truth. [34]Not that I accept such human testimony, but I say these things so that you may be saved. [35]He was a burning and shining lamp, and you were willing to rejoice for a while in his light. [36]But I have a testimony greater than John's. The works that the Father has given me to complete, the very works that I am doing, testify on my behalf that the Father has sent me. [37]And the Father who sent me has himself testified on my behalf. You have never heard his voice or seen his form, [38]and you do not have his word abiding in you, because you do not believe him whom he has sent.

39 'You search the scriptures because you think that in them you have eternal life; and it is they that testify on my behalf. [40]Yet you refuse to come to me to have life.'

The inner darkness of unbelievers

Jesus now charges his hearers with the guilt of remaining blind and deaf in the midst of clear evidence of the truth they had decided to crush. They had stubbornly and deliberately closed their minds to the powerful revelation of God he had brought into their midst. They had complained that the witness he gave could not be truth because it was not corroborated by another person. In reply Jesus made a list of the supporting witnesses they were choosing to ignore. He mentions the Baptist whom in the early days of his ministry they had regarded as a shining light (vv. 33-35). He mentions again his own works which were a convincing proof to those who care to heed them (v. 36). He also mentioned the Scriptures: *'it is they that testify on my behalf'* (v. 39).

The most damning accusation of all was spoken in these striking words: *'the Father who sent me has himself testified on my behalf. You have never heard his voice or seen his form...'* (v. 37). They are an expression both of reproach and encouragement. Jesus here sums up his entire gospel in a few words. He had come so that if any around him were willing to listen they could at last hear the voice of God; so that if they were willing to look at the life he was living in their midst, they could see the form of God. And yet they had rejected it all. He also refers here to an inner witness which Jesus believed to have been given by the Father in the minds and hearts of those present around him as he went about his ministry—a witness which theologians have sometimes called 'the inner testimony of the Holy Spirit'. This, too, they were rejecting.

John 5:41-47

5 I do not accept glory from human beings. [42]But I know that you do not have the love of God in you. [43]I have come in my Father's name, and you do not accept me; if another comes in his own name, you will accept him. [44]How can you believe when you accept glory from one another and do not seek the glory that comes from the one who alone is God? [45]Do not think that I will accuse you before the Father; your accuser is Moses, on whom you have set your hope. [46]If you believed Moses, you would believe me, for he wrote about me. [47]But if you do not believe what he wrote, how will you believe what I say?'

The corruption of social values

In the Sermon on the Mount, Jesus pointed out that what determines whether our mind is full of either light or darkness depends on the orientation of the desire of the heart. The inner blindness which affected the Jews of his day was therefore due to the fact that, contrary to their profession, their inner motives and aims were debased and impure. 'The eye is the lamp of the body. So, if your eye is healthy, your whole body will be full of light; but if your eye is unhealthy, your whole body will be full of darkness. If then the light in you is darkness, how great is the darkness!' (Matt. 6:22, 23). Here in this passage Jesus develops the same theme, and applies it to his hearers. He warns them that we can see and receive the true light of God only if our hearts are oriented entirely towards God, seeking his honour and praise alone. This is when our eye is 'healthy'. He probes the inner darkness of their minds, the darkness which has led them to reject him: *'How can you believe,'* he says, *'when you accept glory from one another and do not seek the glory that comes from the one who alone is God?'* (v. 44).

In accusing them he draws a contrast between himself and them. He pointed out that he himself never for one moment sought any kind of honour from the world around him. Had he done so he could never have served God with complete singleness of purpose, or spoken the truth which the world requires to hear if it is to be brought to repentance. As for Jesus, here was the central rule of his life: '*I do not look to men for honour*' (v. 41, NEB). Here also was the point where the deepest difference between himself and all others most clearly reveals itself: '*How can you have faith so long as you receive honour one from another, and care nothing for the honour that comes from him who alone is God?*' (v. 44, NEB).

Here is the most devastating effect of the darkness in which they had allowed their minds to become engulfed. It had destroyed their sense of values and they had thus lost the power to discern clearly between what was genuine and what was false, what was worthy and what was unworthy. '*I have come in my Father's name, and you do not accept me; if another comes in his own name, you will accept him*' (v. 43). Their inner blindness had given rise to a corrupting and deceptive social system in which honour was continually bestowed where none was due. Jesus had seen through it from the time he was a growing child: 'Woe to you Pharisees! For you love to have the seat of honour in the synagogues and to be greeted with respect in the market-places' (Luke 11:43). Pride of place and love of earthly glory had bred self-centred personal ambition, competition for rank and lust for precedence. Hypocrisy had flourished: 'So you also on the outside look righteous to others, but inside you are full of hypocrisy and lawlessness' (Matt. 23:28). They were thus caught up in a vicious circle. So corrupting was the system that it inevitably prevented the recovery of a true sense of God.

The words of Jesus in this passage have to be interpreted strictly within the circumstances in which they were spoken. They refer to the particular set-up before him then. It need not always happen that people's praise is corrupting. It is obvious that within a healthy society there must be some place for bestowing honour on people. We are urged in the New Testament to give honour to whom honour is due, and to recognize and thank God for goodness and worth where these show themselves. Jesus himself could remind his contemporaries that 'the scribes and the Pharisees sit on Moses' seat', therefore they were to be listened to with deference (Matt. 23:2).

Yet in our humanistic, elitist, market-oriented society, there is truth in the accusation that, leaving God out, we have again set up a value-system that in his sight encourages us to seek vain-glory one from another, and to give glory to what is worthless. Human pride and selfish ambition are nourished, and the achievement of personal glory is held out as one of our chief ends in life. In more recent years the attainment of excellence in athletics and sport has tended to become debased by its being linked up with vast financial rewards, and media fame. A radio commentator, on the subject of a recent popular film, made the remark: 'We have turned our villains into heroes.'

I can remember Archbishop Temple, in an address to students, describing what had gone wrong with all of us. He said that our minds had become like a shop window into which overnight someone had broken. The intruder had re-ordered the price tags so that what was of true worth was now marked cheaply, and the things that were of no value had the expensive labels attached. The archbishop continued that for us to get things right again meant undergoing a complete revaluation in our standards of value.

We need to be continually recalled to a true sense of what is worthy of honour. In recalling us to the truth in this matter, Jesus offers himself as the example of a Man whose personal life demonstrates where glory should be sought and where it should be given. All the aims, values and ambitions of the world which crucified him are called in question by his consistent facing of the cross. His resurrection declares that God bestows honour on those who honour him as he was honoured by Jesus. No society can ever be healthy where its standards of value are not basically determined by what shines out as worthwhile in Jesus. The first task of the church is to help the world to see this, through seeing him.

CHAPTER 6

THE FEEDING OF THE FIVE THOUSAND
(The 4th Sign)

John 6:1-15, 22-27

6 After this Jesus went to the other side of the Sea of Galilee, also called the Sea of Tiberias. ²A large crowd kept following him, because they saw the signs that he was doing for the sick. ³Jesus went up the mountain and sat down there with his disciples. ⁴Now the Passover, the festival of the Jews, was near. ⁵When he looked up and saw a large crowd coming towards him, Jesus said to Philip, 'Where are we to buy bread for these people to eat?' ⁶He said this to test him, for he himself knew what he was going to do. ⁷Philip answered him, 'Six months' wages would not buy enough bread for each of them to get a little.' ⁸One of his disciples, Andrew, Simon Peter's brother, said to him, ⁹'There is a boy here who has five barley loaves and two fish. But what are they among so many people?' ¹⁰Jesus said, 'Make the people sit down.' Now there was a great deal of grass in the place; so they sat down, about five thousand in all. ¹¹ Then Jesus took the loaves, and when he had given thanks, he distributed them to those who were seated; so also the fish, as much as they wanted. ¹²When they were satisfied, he told his disciples, 'Gather up the fragments left over, so that nothing may be lost.' ¹³So they gathered them up, and from the fragments from the five barley loaves, left by those who had eaten, they filled twelve baskets. ¹⁴When the people saw the sign that he had done, they began to say, 'This is indeed the prophet who is to come into the world.'

15 When Jesus realized that they were about to come and take him by force to make him king, he withdrew again to the mountain by himself.

22 The next day the crowd that had stayed on the other side of the lake saw that there had been only one boat there. They also saw that Jesus had not got into the boat with his disciples, but that his disciples

had gone away alone. ^{23}Then some boats from Tiberias came near the place where they had eaten the bread after the Lord had given thanks. ^{24}So when the crowd saw that neither Jesus nor his disciples were there, they themselves got into the boats and went to Capernaum looking for Jesus.

25 When they found him on the other side of the lake, they said to him, 'Rabbi, when did you come here?' ^{26}Jesus answered them, 'Very truly, I tell you, you are looking for me, not because you saw signs, but because you ate your fill of the loaves. ^{27}Do not work for the food that perishes, but for the food that endures for eternal life, which the Son of Man will give you. For it is on him that God the Father has set his seal.'

A planned crisis in Galilee

Jesus was now in Galilee where he was still immensely popular. Many of his hearers believed that no prophet before him had ever spoken in such a challenging and liberating way. Yet others of them were attracted only by the more obvious aspects of his work and message, especially by his miracles. There was need for the issues to be clarified, for Jesus shunned popularity in the midst of pretence. He had made it as clear to those in Galilee, as he had already done in Jerusalem, where they were being led through his leadership and message, what he offered and who he claimed to be.

His line of approach to the problem was carefully thought out. Everyone knew the story of Moses, regarded as the greatest of all the prophets. Moses had taught that the Messiah would be a prophet like himself (cf. Deut. 18:15). One of the greatest miracles God had worked through Moses had been to feed the people with manna in the wilderness. Therefore there had developed a tradition that when the Messiah came he too would provide a marvellous feast for his people. They linked up this belief with the description of a feast which the Lord would provide for his people in a mountain place, at the time when he would clear up all the tragic mysteries of human life, 'swallow up death for ever' and 'wipe away the tears from all faces' (cf. Isa. 25:6-8; 49:9, 10).

Jesus therefore may have consciously gathered the Galilean crowd round him in the kind of place which would fit in to the common expectations of the people. He would feed them. As well as giving them bread, however, he would there and then share with them his message of the kingdom. As the Messiah, prophet and leader foreshadowed by Moses and foretold by the prophets, he had come not only to relieve the pressing earthly troubles of the people of God, but also to rid all creation of sin, death and our human darkness. In this way he would face his hearers with the issues before them, and challenge them to consider whether or not they understood and believed his claims and promises.

The miracle

Knowing that the crowds would eventually gather, Jesus carefully chose the place that would give the best setting for his sign—up among the hills in what one of the Gospels calls a 'deserted place'. It had enough room for all the people he expected. They had gathered quickly as the news spread that he was in the area. Some had followed him here and there as he went round the countryside, some may have come even from Jerusalem, but most were apparently from local hamlets.

Many of them were bound to be hungry even before they arrived. The other Gospel accounts emphasise more than does John that in revealing his Messiahship Jesus also inevitably acted with spontaneous compassion (cf. Mark 6:34f.). We can imagine his feelings as he faced the crowd before him—their intent faces looking at him, the obvious signs of prevailing poverty, the couples, the children, the tired, haggard and lonely ones. Of course he wanted to assure them that their Father who fed the sparrows understood and cared very much about their earthly needs. He had to offer them food. Yet his very compassion made him all the more anxious to tell them that they could not live by bread alone. They were made for God himself, for a greater freedom and destiny than this world can offer. He wanted them to know that he had come to lead them out of every form of earthly bondage to their final inheritance in the presence of God himself. He wanted to assure them that, through the fellowship he would offer them, they could begin to know the blessedness of a purity of heart that could see God, and that those who had a hunger and thirst for true righteousness would find satisfaction.

How majestically it was all done! It was organised as carefully as it was planned. Jesus *knew what he was going to do* (v. 6). Yet his consultation of the disciples was not a sham. He was genuinely open to their help and suggestions. Perhaps he was seeking their prayers and faith to support him in such a miracle! He was willing to let them do their part. Philip completely failed to read his mind or seize his opportunity. How gracious Jesus was to take up Andrew's tentative suggestion that he might use some of the resources that were already to hand. Looking back on his conversation with them the disciples felt he was testing them, and that they failed to grasp what he was going to do.

Yet even though they were not able to enter fully into his mind, they nevertheless cooperated loyally in the part he actually gave them. Their obedient help embellished what was done. It matters always to Jesus today that he has servants who do his bidding even though they might not always be perfectly in tune with his intention and will. Here where grace is so bountiful and free there must be order, reverence and a careful stewardship of what is given. The church always needs pastors and office-bearers who follow faithfully Paul's precept 'all things should be done decently and in order' (1 Cor. 14:40).

Failure and withdrawal

Jesus longed that the people would listen to him, and that through the sign they might see beyond the sign. His plan had been to lift their minds, at least for a decisive moment or two, to what he had come to do for them and give them. His purpose was to gain their confidence so that he could begin to speak about himself as the true bread of life, the Word of God. The majority of them were not interested, however, in anything but the earthly and the immediate. They wanted not the 'bread of life' but political bread there and then in their hands! They believed they knew their real problems better than any prophet of God could tell them. They thought they knew before he told them what 'blessedness' meant. Before he could speak they came to take him over, to make him their leader in all the revolutionary plans they had already dreamed up in their worldly thinking (v. 14f.).

We can understand why they thought this way. They believed that Jesus was the one of whom Moses had spoken: *'This is indeed the prophet who is to come into the world'* (v. 14). There was irony in the situation in that the extraordinary nature of the miracle had roused their excitement, actually contributing to their misunderstanding.

Certainly they wanted a religious Messiah but the religion was to be incidental and the righteousness merely external. He was to be the warrior judge and king who would defend them from their enemies, restore the land and lead them into earthly prosperity. The miracle he had done proved to them that he was their man—powerful, down-to-earth, sensitive to the needs of ordinary humanity. How efficient and well-organised everything had been, how calm his bearing, how convincing the way he could manage a crowd of people! How gracious, too, his encouragement of the kind little lad whose lunch he had taken so as not to disappoint him! They decided to *take him by force to make him king* (v. 15). The situation, they felt, was urgent. John the Baptist had just been executed in prison to satisfy the whim of Herod's adulterous consort. There were rumours that the powers-that-be in Jerusalem were determined to kill Jesus himself.

We can therefore understand Jesus' problem. His thoughts were not their thoughts (cf. Isa. 55:8). He had come into the world to set the pattern of a different kind of leadership. He was to reveal himself as the leader who had been pictured by Isaiah as the Suffering Servant of God, who won his authority over his generation by being willing to suffer rejection by his unflinching adherence to the whole truth, even though his rejection would lead him as a lamb to the slaughter in order to win recognition.

Some commentators suggest that Jesus at this point was faced again with the temptation he had already rejected in his refusal to turn the stones of the desert into bread. It was the temptation to convert his mission 'into an instrument for the cleansing and re-ordering of humanity's political structures'. It is also suggested this was undoubtedly a desirable end in a stricken world and oppressed society and was therefore so close to the real desire of Jesus as to present him with something of an inner crisis.

He did not dare even to show a sign of sympathy with his would-be followers. There was danger in this situation. The least compromise and he would soon have been identified with the most vicious aspects of their sometimes wild talk. He had to act with wisdom. He had to avoid the least suspicion of inciting revolt. They were in no mood to be reasoned with. Only one way was possible and he took it. He withdrew to the hills by himself. He felt he must withdraw his disciples too. We are told in one of the other Gospels that he sent his disciples into a boat to go before him, while he went to the mountain to pray (Mark 6:45f.). It was on this journey (of which a separate exposition is given later in this chapter under verses 16-21) that he gave to them the unique and unforgettable vision of his majesty and power as he came to them on the waters of the sea at night.

Accusation' warnings and appeal

The extraordinary miracle had such an effect on the crowd that they did not allow him to shake them off. Guessing the direction in which he had gone they found him next morning in Capernaum. They wanted to discuss the situation. It is possible that they were beginning to have second thoughts. Perhaps they felt now that they should have allowed him a chance to speak his mind before they tried to proclaim him as their leader. Perhaps he had something helpful to say about the political goals they cherished so dearly. Perhaps even in his own distinctive view of life and God, they might find inspiration for their social and political struggle. Perhaps they hoped that if they accepted some of his terms there could be a compromise.

At this new encounter Jesus must have suspected the crowd's continuing militancy. He was aware from the beginning that the discussion might end disappointingly. Yet he welcomed the opportunity to talk in order to make clear what he had meant by the sign he had given. His approach showed respect for their zeal and activism. After all, their night journey had cost them effort and sacrifice, and they seemed prepared to commit themselves one way or another.

He lost no time in useless words of introduction. He was blunt in his opening accusation. Their reaction to his miracle had clearly revealed the low level of their desires, and their tragic blindness to the whole new world he had come to open up to them: *'you are looking for me, not because you saw signs, but because you ate your fill of the loaves'* (v. 26). They had refused to look and think in order to see what the sign meant! They had missed his message about the kingdom of God and had gained only the temporary satisfaction of one good meal!

Since their thoughts were moving on such an earthly level, his opening argument was on a very earthly level. He was as blunt in his warnings as in his accusation: *'Do not work for the food that perishes, but for the food that endures for eternal life'* (v. 27). His words echo the wisdom in the Word of God which for generations had been taught them as a people. They echo verse 1 of Psalm 127: 'Unless the LORD builds the house, those who build it labour in vain. Unless the LORD guards the city, the guard keeps watch in vain.'

They are a reminder that no matter how ardent the effort, how noble the sacrifice and the heroism, how immense the amount of labour put into the building of the house or the defence of the city, the whole great endeavour can prove in the end to be utterly in vain unless it is indeed a house of God that is being built, or a city of God that is being defended. His words also echo the searching question of the prophet in Babylon to his contemporaries in exile. The exiles were evading God's call to return to Jerusalem to rebuild their own city because they were fatally attracted to the profit and comfort which they imagined to be offered them by settling down where they were in doomed Babylon: 'Why do you spend your money for that which is not bread, and your labour for that which does not satisfy?' (Isa. 55:2). We can indeed spend all the resources and devote the energies of our whole life to win in the end only false, short-lived and empty satisfaction.

As we read through the account of what happened, we can sense that, beginning on such familiar ground, Jesus did make a deep first impression on his hearers that day. They knew enough about human wisdom and about life itself to know that there was truth in these sayings. Therefore in this context he can begin to speak about the *'food that endures for eternal life'* and to make his claims to be able to give it to them.

We shall see, as we read on, that Jesus was not heeded on this second day, as had happened on the first—not because his words were ineffective or misdirected, but because his hearers made their decision in the face of the clear truth and went their own way. Let us not listen to the words we have just now heard from him merely as belonging to the record of an appeal that was once ignored. Rather let his words be a reminder of one of his constantly reiterated warnings: 'what will it profit them if they gain the whole world but forfeit their life? Or what will they give in return for their life?' (Matt. 16:26).

Chapter 6

A day of decision in Capernaum

John 6:28-63

6 Then they said to him, 'What must we do to perform the works of God?' [29]Jesus answered them, 'This is the work of God, that you believe in him whom he has sent.' [30]So they said to him, 'What sign are you going to give us then, so that we may see it and believe you? What work are you performing? [31]Our ancestors ate the manna in the wilderness; as it is written, "He gave them bread from heaven to eat."' [32]Then Jesus said to them, 'Very truly, I tell you, it was not Moses who gave you the bread from heaven, but it is my Father who gives you the true bread from heaven. [33]For the bread of God is that which comes down from heaven and gives life to the world.' [34]They said to him, 'Sir, give us this bread always.'

35 Jesus said to them, 'I am the bread of life. Whoever comes to me will never be hungry, and whoever believes in me will never be thirsty. [36]But I said to you that you have seen me and yet do not believe. [37]Everything that the Father gives me will come to me, and anyone who comes to me I will never drive away; [38]for I have come down from heaven, not to do my own will, but the will of him who sent me. [39]And this is the will of him who sent me, that I should lose nothing of all that he has given me, but raise it up on the last day. [40]This is indeed the will of my Father, that all who see the Son and believe in him may have eternal life; and I will raise them up on the last day.'

41 Then the Jews began to complain about him because he said, 'I am the bread that came down from heaven.' [42]They were saying, 'Is not this Jesus, the son of Joseph, whose father and mother we know? How can he now say, "I have come down from heaven"?' [43]Jesus answered them, 'Do not complain among yourselves. [44]No one can come to me unless drawn by the Father who sent me; and I will raise that person up on the last day. [45]It is written in the prophets, "And they shall all be taught by God." Everyone who has heard and learned from the Father comes to me. [46]Not that anyone has seen the Father except the one who is from God; he has seen the Father. [47]Very truly, I tell you, whoever believes has eternal life. [48]I am the bread of life. [49]Your ancestors ate the manna in the wilderness, and they died. [50]This is the bread that comes

111

down from heaven, so that one may eat of it and not die. [51]I am the living bread that came down from heaven. Whoever eats of this bread will live for ever; and the bread that I will give for the life of the world is my flesh.'

52 The Jews then disputed among themselves, saying, 'How can this man give us his flesh to eat?' [53]So Jesus said to them, 'Very truly, I tell you, unless you eat the flesh of the Son of Man and drink his blood, you have no life in you. [54]Those who eat my flesh and drink my blood have eternal life, and I will raise them up on the last day; [55]for my flesh is true food and my blood is true drink. [56]Those who eat my flesh and drink my blood abide in me, and I in them. [57]Just as the living Father sent me, and I live because of the Father, so whoever eats me will live because of me. [58]This is the bread which came down from heaven, not like that which your ancestors ate, and they died. But the one who eats this bread will live for ever.' [59]He said these things while he was teaching in the synagogue at Capernaum.

60 When many of his disciples heard it, they said, 'This teaching is difficult; who can accept it?" [61]But Jesus, being aware that his disciples were complaining about it, said to them, 'Does this offend you? [62]Then what if you were to see the Son of Man ascending to where he was before? [63]It is the spirit that gives life; the flesh is useless. The words that I have spoken to you are spirit and life.'

'I am the bread of life'

There are in this Gospel seven sayings of Jesus which begin with the words 'I am' (cf. also 8:12; 10:7-9, 11, 14; 11:25; 15:1-5). Commentators who believe the number seven to have some significance to the writer of the Gospel point out that he also selected seven of Jesus' miracles to use as illustrations of the revelation of the glory of Jesus. Of more importance than the enumeration of such sayings or signs, however, is the frequent use which now occurs of the phrase 'I am' in referring to himself. The use of this phrase can be regarded as a deliberate echo on his own lips of the name by which the God of Israel chose to make himself known to the people of Israel when he sent Moses to be their deliverer. 'God said to Moses, "I AM WHO I AM." He said further, "Thus you shall say to the Israelites, 'I AM has sent me to you.'"' (Exod. 3:14).

The saying *'l am the bread of life'* has always been given a central place among the texts which have inspired the devotion and worship of the church. It seems to be a word given to us especially for our liturgy when we celebrate the Lord's Supper. Spoken to us in this setting, it helps us to realize that the Supper is not merely a memorial service for one who lived and died centuries ago, but an occasion for communion with the one who has also risen again for us. It assures us that Christ is here and now in the midst, so near and real that we can enter into life-giving fellowship with him. Spoken along with the giving of the bread and wine, it is a pledge to us that receiving him by faith we will find ourselves strengthened, enabled to grow in grace and in vision, and to become more deeply rooted and grounded in the love we must have both for our fellow men and women and for himself.

Apart from the Lord's Supper, how much these words bring as we allow them to come home to us in the midst of a day-to-day life. They remind us that at the heart of our Christian faith, rather than a creed or an ethical code, there is a *Person* who meets and speaks to us, whose friendship is always open to us, and who is able to give us comfort in our deepest inward needs. Moreover, as he offers us himself, he also offers us everything most worth having in life not only for time but for eternity.

We should hear, along with the repeated saying, the assuring words that almost immediately follow: *'Everything that the Father gives me will come to me, and anyone who comes to me I will never drive away.'* That he himself could ever act in the brutal way those words *'drive away'* literally imply, is so impossible to conceive that we know for certain that we are safe as we yield to the least instinct to come to him. Moreover, the twice repeated promise which soon follows: *'I will raise them up on the last day'* underlines the affirmation that in our present communion with him we already have the foretaste of eternal life to come.

Jesus provokes offence

The very words which have brought so much illumination and strength to Christians from age to age brought deep offence to their hearers when they were first spoken. Their utterance indeed provoked a decisive reaction in the attitude of the crowd to Jesus just at a time when he had seemed to be impressing them with his wisdom and recovering their confidence.

Jesus had appeared to have his hearers in his hands. They were eager to ask him questions and to receive his answers. They expressed to him their desire to *perform the works of God* (v. 28), and they did not object when he suggested that this first of all meant believing in himself as God's messenger. They even accepted his claim that it was he himself, coming from the Father, rather than Moses, who could give them the *bread of God* which came *down from heaven*. *'Sir'*, they said, *'give us this bread always'* (v. 34). It is obvious that they would have been prepared to accept an offer from him to give them the *bread of life* if he had been prepared to make that simple offer.

When any teacher in those days referred to himself as giving bread to his hearers to eat, he was referring to the satisfaction that the truth he presented could bring to the human mind. The Old Testament spoke of God as 'feeding' his people, when he inspired the prophets to speak his word to them. The revelation of God given through the word is thus regarded as heavenly bread in contrast to earthly food. Even today we speak of the preacher as there in the pulpit to 'feed the flock' (cf. Acts 20:28).

If Jesus, therefore, in Capernaum that day had contented himself by saying merely: 'I have come to give you the bread of life', they might have accepted his saying, and respected his claim. He could have been understood to offer simply a revealed teaching which brought satisfaction to the longing heart and searching mind.

Jesus, however, did not merely claim to have come to give the bread of life; he said *'I am the bread of life'*. It was as astonishing a claim and as challenging a decision to faith in himself as he had ever given this Galilean crowd. It was the affirmation that those who willed to pursue his invitation to discipleship could find in his own personal presence and friendship the communion with God for which they were made. Moreover, it was the assertion that those who found what he had to give would never think of turning away from him to any other source of light or life.

It was at this point that the shock came to many even of his own so-called disciples among the crowd. They were enraged that this man seemed to he putting himself at the centre of everything good in the universe. He seemed to place himself at the gate of the kingdom of heaven, with power to decide whom he would receive and whom he would reject. He spoke as if he had this gift of eternal life in his own hands to give or withhold. They complained, saying, *'Is not this Jesus, the son of Joseph, whose father and mother we know? How can he now say, "I have come down from heaven"?'* (v. 42).

There was not the slightest attempt on the part of Jesus to tone down the point which had raised antagonism—the very point where his teaching was most challenging, and where there was a need to press on with it. Therefore the words he used became more and more provocative as he responded to the tension between himself and them. He said, *'the bread that I will give for the life of the world is my flesh'* (v. 51), and solemnly added, *'Very truly, I tell you, unless you eat the flesh of the Son of Man and drink his blood, you have no life in you'* (v. 53), insisting that only such eating and drinking of his flesh and blood would assure them of eternal life and resurrection at the last day. He further affirmed that he himself, having come *down from heaven* (v. 58), would ascend to where *he was before* because he was the *Son of Man* (v. 62).

Of course a long controversy developed of which we here have only an outline of its essence. As the day wore on, they moved from the streets into the synagogue. At the end of the day they expressed their bitterness and disillusionment and many of his disciples drew back and no longer went about with him (v. 66). The day's happenings marked the beginning of Jesus' alienation from the Galilean community.

The search for an explanation

It is possible for us to find historical and psychological reasons why Jesus at this stage of his earthly career should have been so deliberately blunt as he faced this crowd from which he had possibly hoped to win some disciples. He hated the pretence of a superficial popularity based on a misunderstanding of who he was, and what his claims really were. He did not want it to continue. He was certain that the time had come for the issues to be clarified. He once remarked: 'blessed is anyone who takes no offence at me' (Matt. 11:6). He knew that many around him in that crowd were living with beliefs that had to be challenged to the point of their being offended, if they were ever to be brought to faith in himself. Therefore he was prepared at this important point in his ministry to use this testing and provocative language.

We find, however, that a number of commentators on the Gospel find it impossible to believe that Jesus could have spoken in this way at Capernaum.

They affirm that the reported words of Jesus can be understood only if they are taken to refer to the Lord's Supper, and they raise doubts as to whether he would at this time have made such a reference. They object especially to the crude language used. They doubt whether Jesus himself would have spoken of our eating the flesh and drinking the blood of the Son of Man. Some writers have suggested that these words contain later reflections by the church on the Last Supper; others have suggested that they contain a view of the sacrament developed in the church under the influence of the surrounding pagan mystery religions. There has also been the suggestion that such words were actually spoken by Jesus himself at the first celebration of the sacrament in the upper room, and, since John decided to avoid useless repetition in his Gospel with another full account of the Last Supper, he inserted them here.[1]

Our 'mystical union' with Christ

It is possible, however, to regard Jesus' words as having no direct or exclusive reference to the sacrament. John Calvin, for example, whose judgement on the New Testament is always to be respected, said that 'it would be inept and unseasonable' for Jesus to preach about the Lord's Supper before he had instituted it. Therefore he wrote of our being called to enter a 'mystical union' with Christ. His argument can best be understood if we grasp the purpose Jesus had especially in mind when he spoke to this crowd at this particular time.

From the beginning of the Prologue and throughout the whole Gospel of John, it is stressed that Jesus' work is both light-bearing and life-giving. He came into the world not only to reveal God to us but also to bring us into living communion with the life of God, not only to displace our darkness of mind with what he reveals in his life and teaching, but also to replace the prevailing human corruption and death that mark all our existence on this earth, with the gift of eternal life. Throughout this present discourse Jesus was speaking almost exclusively about the latter life-giving aspect of

---

[1] The suggestion has also been made that as this Gospel was most probably written during intense persecution of the early church when allegations of cannibalism were being made against followers of Jesus Christ—they met in secret to eat flesh and drink blood of one 'Chrestus'—John deliberately omits from his Gospel any account of the Last Supper in the actual Passion narrative but makes oblique reference to it here where the enemies of the church would not expect to find it.

his ministry among us. This is why he referred several times to himself as having become incarnate (i.e. as having *come down from heaven*) in order to give life to the world.

There were however two conditions which had to be fulfilled if perishing men and women were to be able to benefit from his coming, and receive the life he gives. In the first place he himself had to die. When he spoke of giving his flesh *for the life of the world* (v. 51) he was referring to the fact that only through his cross could the world receive new life from him.

In the second place he insists in this discourse not only that he himself should be sacrificed, but also that each of us whom he calls to believe in him should enter a close, intimate and indissoluble union with him. It is only through such a union that the renewing power of the eternal life which he has come to give us can become effective within each of us.

It is this life-giving union between Jesus and ourselves that formed the central theme of the *bread of life* discourse when Jesus spoke that day at Capernaum. He insists that within this union we are both intimately close to him, and yet personally quite distinct from him. He is trying to convey to our minds its close and life-giving nature when he calls himself *bread* which he urges us to receive into ourselves by eating. Yet he is also trying to impress on us its spiritual and personal nature when he stresses that the relationship between us and himself is always one of faith in his own person and word, and when he insists that his words are not to be interpreted literally but are *spirit and life* (v. 63).

At the heart of the relationship between himself and us therefore, he wants there to be always trust, friendship, understanding and obedience. Yet at the same time he wants something even deeper. He does not want to influence us simply by remaining outside of us as in an earthly friendship. When he speaks about his *flesh* and *blood* we can understand that he is referring not necessarily to the Lord's Supper, but simply to himself in the humanity he assumed to save us. His challenge to us to *eat the flesh of the Son of Man and drink his blood* (v. 53) is a challenge to cultivate this union he is seeking to have with us through his humanity, and thus to allow an open entrance into our lives for the renewing power of his Spirit. It involves our seeking with our whole mind and heart to absorb into our lives the whole Christ in the humanity in which he is presented to us in the Word of God, in his birth, life, teaching, death and resurrection. Is he not here seeking to discourage us from cultivating simply a mere 'spirituality' which does not centre on, or orient itself towards the person he was, and the work he did for us as a human being? Might he not be warning us against the dangers of yielding uncritically to the promptings of any inspiration, however spiritual, that do not arise out of the Word of God as it witnesses to himself as the Word incarnate?

Jesus and the disciples (1)

(The 5th Sign)

John 6:16-21

[16]When evening came, his disciples went down to the lake, [17]got into a boat, and started across the lake to Capernaum. It was now dark, and Jesus had not yet come to them. [18]The lake became rough because a strong wind was blowing. [19]When they had rowed about three or four miles, they saw Jesus walking on the lake and coming near the boat, and they were terrified. [20]But he said to them, 'It is I; do not be afraid.' [21]Then they wanted to take him into the boat, and immediately the boat reached the land towards which they were going.

A night remembered

In three of the Gospels we hear slightly different accounts of what happened that night. It is obvious that each one who went through the experience remembered it vividly, with different details in the foreground of their memory. The apostle John never forgot the stress, the emotions, the strange thoughts and fears that arose, the relief that finally and suddenly came, and the lessons they then learned about life with Jesus.

They found themselves plunged suddenly into it. It was one of those dark and threatening nights on which they would normally not have chosen to venture out in a boat, but Jesus had given them the order without consulting them. John describes vividly how one thing seemed to follow another as soon as they were away from the land—the darkness growing more and more deep, the harsh contrary wind, the strange feeling of depression, a slight uncanny fear, and the loss of morale among the whole group. The worst thing of all was the strange questioning about Jesus. The expectations that morning had been great. The miracle of the bread had been so wonderful—and in the end it had all seemed to come to nothing! He had suddenly retreated when everything had seemed to be going his way. Had they ever before seen him so perplexed? Why had he abruptly dismissed them when they had so many questions to ask, and wanted reassurance? Why had he chosen this way for them to go on such a night? John's description of the situation seems to have a mysterious symbolic touch about it: *It was now dark, and Jesus had not yet come to them.* They had such a keen sense of his absence as they longed for his presence! So haunted had their minds become, so great their depression, that when they saw him coming over the waters, and drawing near them, *they were terrified.*

It was when they heard his voice that they knew that it was Jesus. With the word he spoke came the assurance that completely banished all their doubts and fears; there was no need at the time to ask their questions or tell him what they had felt: *'It is I; do not be afraid.'* His words reminded them of the name of the Lord of the exodus who had so marvellously manifested his control of the fire at the bush and of the waves of the sea, when he led his people out of Egypt. And then miraculously they found that *immediately the boat reached the land towards which they were going* (v. 21). They remembered one of the great Psalms which perfectly expressed their thanksgiving: 'He made the storm be still, and the waves of the sea were hushed. Then they were glad because they had quiet, and he brought them to their desired haven.' (Ps. 107:29, 30)

An Easter experience before Easter!

Of course the disciples were used to Jesus taking them apart from the crowds after the business of the day, sometimes to explain any difficult things he had been trying to teach, and to review with them what had been happening. They could ask him questions and he would teach them privately. He had always shown as much concern to train them as a group as he had to preach to the crowds. Indeed, as time passed, the less he found he could rely on the crowds, and the more he realized he must depend for the future of his work and his church on these few. The church of the future would have a solid foundation only if this core of disciples had an adequate store of wisdom, strong faith, unflinching loyalty and deep conviction. It was they who were to be sent out into the world under the inspiration of the Holy Spirit to continue his work.

He was concerned therefore during his ministry on earth to be with them as much as he could, to win their complete trust, to help them towards a clearer and deeper vision of who he was and of what the future held. He had on occasion taken them into special 'retreat' so that he could concentrate on teaching them. The disciples never forgot how thrilled he was on one of these occasions to discover that their faith in him had at last become like a 'rock' on which he could confidently build his church (Matt. 16:17, 18). They were always full of gratitude that before he gave himself up to death he took them all apart into the upper room for those last unforgettable hours of fellowship, cleansing and communion.

That strange night's retreat in Galilee came eventually to occupy a prominent place in their memory of these special times with Jesus, but it was only some time after Jesus died and rose again that they understood its full significance and meaning. Indeed it was only after they set out on their mission to proclaim the crucified and risen Lord to the surrounding world that the message he was presently teaching them came fully home to their minds. The spread of the early church under their ministry (as we read of it in the book of Acts) was of course miraculous, and in the long run a vibrant core of believers was established within the pagan world.

But the full story of their conquest was not always one of continuous and spectacular growth everywhere. As they tried to serve him, to do his will and to go the way he wanted in different places and in different times under different circumstances, they discovered that the experiences of that night on the lake seemed occasionally to repeat themselves. They felt themselves being put through the whole cycle of it all again—the uncertainty about direction, the depression, the nervous perplexity, the temptation to lose morale and to be edgy with one another, the irrational fears—and then he, the risen One, had come to them. They had recognized his presence by his voice (he had said that his sheep would know his voice), they had received him into their midst, Thus they had managed to attain almost immediately what, under their depression and difficulties, they had thought impossible. Here then was their clue to the revelation Jesus had given them of himself and his power on that memorable night on the lake. It had been an Easter experience before Easter, it had been a rehearsal of an act that was going to be repeated within his church again and yet again as time moved on.

Therefore, as they recalled these Galilean days with Jesus, this incident on the lake took a prominent place in the preaching and teaching to others, especially to those who were to follow them in the leadership of the church. No doubt they found the way that Christ was leading them at times truly expressed in one of the great Psalms which they often remembered: 'Your way was through the sea, your path, through the mighty waters; yet your footprints were unseen. You led your people like a flock...' (Ps. 77:19, 20).

Our way in the sea

At the beginning of the 20th century many of our large city churches (and many more that have been pulled down since then) were full to the back of the gallery Sunday after Sunday. The word of the church was seriously listened to in the nation's councils. The influence of the Christian faith was strongly felt in family and community life. Even in the thirties, when I began my ministry, its influence was still powerful. We still had many listening to the Word of God, and crowds of children and young folk around our doors. It did not occur to us then that this was not a 'Christian' country. To be a pastor in a congregation was like being up there on the mountainside with many around us, and Jesus in full command. We could think of ourselves as feeding the multitude under his direction, and in spite of our own deficiencies, at least there were few who questioned the authority of Christ's teaching.

Is there not a clue to what is now happening to us, here in this story of the disciples on the lake? We now have to set our face against an 'encircling gloom', and threatening contrary winds, in a world where life in general seems to be growing more harsh (yes, 'harsh', in spite of increasing affluence) for everyone, and more pagan. Public opinion and the 'spirit of the age' are no longer allies we can trust to be on our side. Alongside that of Jesus, many other names are being called upon to bring us inspiration and salvation. Many of our own ardent and sincere efforts at our own renewal and recovery have proved fruitless. There are uncertainties and questionings in too many of our own minds about our message, and even among those who adhere most faithfully to it, there can come at times that strange sense of the absence of Jesus, which is reflected in John's revealing confession of his own momentary desolation of spirit: *It was now dark, and Jesus had not yet come to them* (v. 17).

John Mark in his account of this incident, has added a detail absent from this Gospel. He reminds us that having sent them out on this journey, Jesus himself went up to the hills to pray, from where 'he saw that they were straining at the oars' (Mark 6:46-48). He was praying for them and watching with care and concern for every detail. They were those whose welfare the Father had entrusted to him. He could not dare risk even letting them out of his sight in the midst of any possible danger. He knew what they could bear, and he was ready to go to them if things ever reached breaking-point. He was praying that their faith might grow and that they would learn what it meant to trust and obey him when the way was hard and they did not understand.

So with us, even though we do not see him, he is there at the right hand of God making intercession for us. 'Christ loved the church and gave himself up for her' (Eph. 5:25). How much he cares for us! He wants us to learn to walk by faith and not by sight; to endure when things are hard and there is no sign of success; to believe and go forward when there is no apparent way open before us; to obey simply because we hear his voice, even when we do not understand. Like the disciples, everything depends on our recognizing him by his voice. Our doubts disappear when we hear him speak again to us in his own unmistakable words that assure us of his presence.

Then they wanted to take him into the boat (v. 21), says the original story. Even if nothing else in our circumstances seems to change, what a difference it immediately makes when we are assured that he is present in our midst as our companion on the difficult journey. Mark's account says that immediately their circumstances did change and 'the wind ceased'. But John does not mention this. As it happened, it seems he hardly noticed it. The one thing he did remember was how soon they got through. It had all seemed so nearly impossible, but they were there: *immediately the boat reached the land towards which they were going* (v. 21).

No doubt for some of us this way across the sea becomes a very personal story. The good Shepherd does not treat us simply as units of a flock under his care, but plans or leads us each in the way we have to go as individuals, calling his own sheep by name. The way he chooses can sometimes be through the dark and threatening valley, under strain and stress. Life grows hard, our personal situation seems to be hemmed around with darkness, and our hold on it grows weaker. From this incident we too can learn not to let go in despair. He will come. We will hear his voice. Nothing around us will prevent his taking us to the very destination we have sought and he has planned.

Encounter in apartness

This remarkable manifestation of the presence and power of Christ, which was finally to prove itself so inspiring and memorable, presents to us one feature which we must not overlook. It was given to the disciples by Jesus after he had completely withdrawn them from the multitude amongst whom they had been busily at work. Indeed, he could not have conveyed to them either the sign or the message he felt they needed so much, had he not brought them to this secret rendezvous. It is significant that during the hours he spent with them apart in the upper room, he made a promise that the intimacy he had established with them during such time of retreat would continue in the days ahead. He promised that he would come back especially to manifest himself to them and strengthen them through the Holy Spirit in apartness from the world. 'I will not leave you orphaned...' he said. 'In a little while the world will no longer see me, but you will see me' (14:18, 19). This promise of encounter in apartness was fulfilled during his Easter appearances. During these memorable forty days it was always quite apart from the world that the disciples knew him present and were strengthened, taught and encouraged.

After his ascension they continued to find themselves especially conscious of his presence with them as they gathered apart devoting themselves 'to the apostles' teaching and fellowship, to the breaking of bread and the prayers' (Acts 2:42). Of course he had sent them out with the great promise, 'I am with you always' (Matt. 28:20). They knew well what it meant to find themselves, by his present help, victorious in the struggles they had to face as they obeyed his command to go into all the world and serve him. But his last great command and promise did not cancel out their continuing need to come apart so that he could come to meet them.

The exalted Christ by his ascension has taken himself apart from the world into which he has sent us to evangelize and to engage in his service. He has gone to his own realm, from which he is prepared to come to us again and again to enter intimate, enriching and empowering dealings with us. Certainly he has not forsaken the present realm of this world and its history. It is under his providence. It is protected and preserved by his prayer. Its future is his deepest concern because he has died for its salvation and he is coming again to claim it for himself and to judge all. But it sees him no more, as we who are his own can do when we lift up our eyes, our faith and our hearts to seek him in the realm to which he has gone. Even as we rely on his promise to come and be with us always, we have to learn the discipline of turning aside from our busy lives to allow him to meet us.

Jesus and the disciples (2)

John 6:64-71

6 'But among you there are some who do not believe.' For Jesus knew from the first who were the ones that did not believe, and who was the one that would betray him. [65]And he said, 'For this reason I have told you that no one can come to me unless it is granted by the Father.'

66 Because of this many of his disciples turned back and no longer went about with him. [67]So Jesus asked the twelve, 'Do you also wish to go away?' [68]Simon Peter answered him, 'Lord, to whom can we go? You have the words of eternal life. [69]We have come to believe and know that you are the Holy One of God.' [70]Jesus answered them, 'Did I not choose you, the twelve? Yet one of you is a devil.' [71]He was speaking of Judas son of Simon Iscariot, for he, though one of the twelve, was going to betray him.

Jesus triumphant and tense

In a few verses in the middle of his discourse on the bread of life, Jesus had given some indication of his own thoughts as he reflected on both the successes and the difficulties he was having in his ministry. He affirmed his faith that everything of any final significance that was taking place was what was decreed by the Father (v. 37). He expressed his own confidence that he had in no way failed God's purpose (vv. 38, 39). He was certain that everything he had done would be vindicated in the last great day of judgement (v. 40). Neither the power of evil nor the human will could in any way prevent the salvation of one of those whom God the Father had chosen (v. 39).

At the end of the discourse the evangelist himself returns to this theme. Jesus, he assures us, knew from the beginning the failure he was going to have to face on that particular day, yet he was confident all the time that God's hand was there triumphantly at work. Then he gives us an account of how Jesus' serene confidence found its final expression in the challenge he uttered as he turned to the twelve and said *'Do you also wish to go away?'* (v. 67). This is not to be interpreted as an appeal to his disciples for their help in bringing in his kingdom. It is an expression of personal triumph. It is the elated utterance of one who, while he moves on to assured victory, needs nobody, but who nevertheless desires to share his kingdom with those he loves.

Amidst such expressions of supreme confidence, however, there is evidence that Jesus saw clearly the grim and tragic consequences of the rejection of his good news by so many around him. We cannot help noticing the urgency with which he made his appeal to them to respond to him, promising that he will not reject any (v. 37). He expressed amazement at the perversity that kept people back when they could have easily decided otherwise. The comment, *'But among you there are some who do not believe'* (v. 64), was a reproach for their stubbornness. He felt the tension all the more deeply because he was trying so hard to win them, and his heart was open. Satanic powers, too, were at work here frustrating the will of his Father. *'Yet one of you is a devil'* (v. 70), was his final comment as he looked at the twelve. Such powers had to be resisted even to death, and here they were, apparently triumphant, even amongst those he had chosen as his own, because he had not doubted their loyalty. He seemed to feel himself in the midst of an ongoing conflict between God and the devil.

In the end, of course, in one of his last recorded prayers to the Father as he looks back and sums up what has happened, it is the note of triumph that he sounds most clearly: 'I protected them in your name that you have given me. I guarded them, and not one of them was lost except the one destined to be lost, so that the scripture might be fulfilled' (17:12). God was certainly working his purpose out, even in the midst of what had caused him so much trouble. Yet the tension was real even to the end. Simon Peter undoubtedly belonged to Jesus, and yet the Lord kept hold of Peter only by intense prayer: 'Simon, Simon, listen! Satan has demanded to sift all of you like wheat, but I have prayed for you that your own faith may not fail' (Luke 22:31).

We can recognize as we read the New Testament that the first followers of Jesus, after he rose again, shared the same triumphant certainty that he was Lord of all and that in the end all things would be put under his feet. They emphasized the sovereignty of God so much that they attributed every work of salvation to his grace and power alone. People were saved because he had predestined them to be saved. Moreover, behind the deliberate obstinacy of those who rejected the gospel they tended also to see the hand of God hardening the wicked in their unbelief, and they could warn people about a hell prepared for the devil and his angels. Yet they were reluctant to give anyone up to such a fate. They too lived in tension. If Christ's kingdom was ever to come, they had to work for it, long for it and pray for it continually and earnestly. The more they discovered of the glory of the light of Christ, the more intolerable the darkness that seemed to prevail over so much of the world's life. It was to them sheer tragedy that so many seemed to be perishing in a world where Christ had died for all. Woe to them if they did not preach the gospel. They pled with people passionately to avoid destroying themselves.

The word we have heard in the cross and resurrection of Jesus enables us to share the New Testament mood of triumphant certainty. However much evil may seem to triumph, in the end it will be exposed, good will be vindicated, justice will be done, and those whom God has predestined for himself will be his for ever. Though we rejoice in such hope, however, we cannot avoid the tension that must come with it. The powers of evil have been decisively defeated, and are on their way out, but they are not already so disabled that they cannot threaten goodness and God's will. We ourselves have been placed in this world to watch, pray and resist.

The fact that Christ has died for all (1 John 2:2) must keep alive in our hearts the same desire for the salvation of individuals as Christ himself felt. Certainly Jesus finally called Judas 'the one destined to be lost' and in the end took control of his actions in a final demonstration of his sovereignty over evil, whatever it might try to do (13:27). Yet can we not sense in these final dealings with Judas a trace of reluctance at what was taking place? Was he not giving expression to a sense of tragedy when he said that it would have been better if the wretch had never been born? (Matt. 26:24).

A confession of experience and devotion

When Jesus abruptly challenged the twelve disciples, *'Do you also wish to go away?'*, it was a test of the strength of their faith and staying power. The question came as a shock to Peter. He had begun to feel that somehow his true destiny as a human being lay in his future with this man. His life had begun to be controlled only by the desire to serve him and win his approval. His commitment to Jesus had been so whole-hearted that the thought of leaving him had never entered his mind. Even the faint suggestion of it seemed to threaten the loss of everything that had made life worthwhile. So much had he found in this man's friendship and fellowship that now without him life would be dark, empty and hopeless indeed: *'Lord, to whom can we go? You have the words of eternal life. We have come to believe and know that you are the Holy One of God'* (v. 68).

Throughout the Gospels there are several notable confessions of faith: affirmations of belief which seemed to rise out of a sudden illumination of mind, or some deep immediate impression which certain people received, as they met and talked to Jesus. We can put in this category, for example, the confessions made by John the Baptist and other disciples during the early days of their encounter with Jesus, and that made by Peter himself at Caesarea Philippi (cf. 1:34, 41, 49; Matt. 16:16).

We must however notice that Peter's confession here (vv. 68, 69) can be described even more aptly as a confession of experience and devotion. It is an expression not simply of what he has seen in Jesus in any one momentary exchange or encounter, but of the conviction that has developed within his mind and heart through continuous experience over weeks and months.

The form in which he words his confession is to be noted: *'We have come to believe and know that you are the Holy One of God.'* 'Knowledge', observes Hoskyns at this point, 'is intensified and permanent belief that has not yet passed into sight.' Here we have from Peter indeed the kind of confession given by Polycarp, the aged bishop of Smyrna, who when he was being dragged into the arena and ordered to blaspheme Christ, said, 'Eighty and six years have I served him nor hath he ever done me wrong. How can I blaspheme my King and Saviour?'

Possibly the evangelist means us to notice a connection between the experience undergone by the disciples in their previous night's adventure at sea, and this confession of their faith and devotion. After all, that incident was marked by both a 'seeing' of Jesus (when they were confronted by the sudden theophany on the waters) and an experience of his power to deliver them from, and see them through, life's difficulties. Jesus' question and Peter's answer, seen in this light, bring out the lesson that such experiences and trials as they went through that night can serve to strengthen both our vision and our devotion.

Peter in his confession affirms the incomparability and finality of what Jesus brings to us in his person and his teaching. Nowhere else is it imaginable that anyone can find what is to be found in him! He stands unsurpassable, inspiring the awe, reverence and adoration that belong to God alone, utterly different and apart from all of us even though he is undoubtedly one of us — the Holy One of God!

How did Peter know, and what right had he to make such an affirmation? Certainly he had not worked it out on a demonstrable basis. In his small corner of the world he would have had no contact with what the other religious faiths or philosophies of the wider world brought to their adherents. In his affirmation of the incomparability of Jesus he was simply re-echoing what Jesus was continually saying about himself. He was giving genuine expression to a conviction that he believed inevitable.

Peter did not attribute his exalted belief about Jesus to any remarkable traits of human character or qualities of heart, mind and soul, but rather to the fact that Jesus had and spoke *'the words of eternal life'*. He did not just give information about eternal life; rather his speaking actually conveyed it. Jesus himself had lived that eternal life with God before the foundation of the world. He had now brought it with him to earth, and he shared it with his disciples when he spoke his words, imparted forgiveness, and gave them the knowledge of God: 'And this is eternal life, that they may know you, the only true God, and Jesus Christ whom you have sent' (17:3).

Do we ourselves not have the same opportunity as Peter and the other disciples of hearing these *'words of eternal life'*? When Peter wrote his epistle he invited his readers to listen for them. He spoke of our being born again by the resurrection of Christ from the dead, and then he explained how this new life came: 'You have been born anew, not of perishable but of imperishable seed, through the living and enduring word of God.... That word is the good news that was announced to you' (1 Pet. 1:23, 25). We hear them today when, hungry in our hearts for more than this world can give us, we sit and listen to the words of the preacher offering us Christ and his forgiveness, thus revealing the kingdom of God, and opening up to us heaven where Jesus himself is with the Father. He is the only Son of God who is there, the only Holy One of God—to whom else can we go?

CHAPTER 7

JESUS UNDER CONSTRAINT

John 7:1-10

7 After this Jesus went about in Galilee. He did not wish to go about in Judea because the Jews were looking for an opportunity to kill him. [2]Now the Jewish festival of Booths was near. [3]So his brothers said to him, 'Leave here and go to Judea so that your disciples also may see the works you are doing; [4]for no one who wants to be widely known acts in secret. If you do these things, show yourself to the world.' [5](For not even his brothers believed in him.) [6]Jesus said to them, 'My time has not yet come, but your time is always here. [7]The world cannot hate you, but it hates me because I testify against it that its works are evil. [8]Go to the festival yourselves. I am not going to this festival, for my time has not yet fully come.' [9]After saying this, he remained in Galilee.

10 But after his brothers had gone to the festival, then he also went, not publicly but as it were in secret.

People were now talking about Jesus everywhere and wondering—what next? Some still admired him; many had doubts and suspicions. In Judea, where it had become dangerous to express open support for him, the authorities were waiting to trap him.

Since not even his brothers believed in him (v. 5) we can understand how acute the situation was for him at home. No doubt his family hated the local gossip, and the questions they had at times to face. They were beginning to feel that his crusade had gone on too long without results. They thought it a sign of weakness and fear that he now seemed to be avoiding open confrontation. Possibly they fatalistically wished a quick end to the whole sad affair. The approaching festival of Booths seemed to offer a good opportunity of bringing everything to a head. He could now either prove himself, or face what they suspected to be the truth. *'Leave here'*, they challenged him, *'and go to Judea so that your disciples also may see the works you are doing; for no one who wants to be widely known acts in secret'* (vv. 3, 4).

In accusing him of such procrastination and fear, his brothers had shown complete misunderstanding. Jesus at this time was alert, praying, and indeed longing, for the hour to come in which he would be able to enter finally into the last stage of his life on earth, to show himself to the world as his brothers were demanding, to incur its bitter hatred, and to yield himself to death at its hands. In trying to answer their accusation he sought to justify himself with a remark that was deliberately enigmatic. Though his brothers would not understand immediately, he knew they would later remember what he said and then see the truth to which they had been so blind. *'My time has not yet come'*, he said, *'but your time is always here. The world cannot hate you, but it hates me because I testify against it that its works are evil'* (vv. 6, 7).

In the light of our knowledge of how events unfolded we can understand what he meant by these words. When he was baptized in the Jordan he had deliberately chosen to narrow his life down to one restricted path as he moved towards what the cross would bring him at the time chosen by the Father. He had then at the Jordan made an appointment with the loneliness, humiliation and suffering which would come to fulfilment in his death when the world would express its hatred of him. Now at this stage in his life he felt himself driven on by a slow, relentless pressure towards that time: 'what stress I am under until it is completed!' he had said (Luke 12:50), as he gave expression to the inner constraint that now dominated his life.

Jesus now compares the narrow way he has to travel with the way of freedom that was open to his brothers in their choice of path. Within the life of humanity he recognized that God had made 'a time for every matter under heaven' and 'everything suitable for its time' (Eccl. 3:1, 11). How varied were these 'times' selected by God in working out the lives of ordinary men and women on this earth! He looked around him at other people who could find simple and satisfying pleasure in daily work, healthy recreation, simple cultural pursuits and family life, and he thought about the contrast between them and himself. How much they could often themselves plan and choose within all those possibilities open to them! Had he himself not wished at times for freedom from the one dominating constraint that had so hemmed him in? *'My time has not yet come'*, he said to his brothers, *'but your time is always here.'*

The New Testament often underlines the contrast, here brought out by Jesus himself, between what he took on himself for our sakes when he went to the cross, and what he gives us in exchange. He was made 'sin' for us that we might be given his righteousness (2 Cor. 5:21). He became poor that we might be made rich (2 Cor. 8:9). He took our chastisement that we might have peace, our sickness that we might have health (Matt. 8:17). Here, from his own lips, we have another of these contrasts between the narrow restriction of the way he has to choose for himself, and the breadth of inheritance he offers up for those for whom he dies. Paul in one place tries to give full expression to this breadth: 'For all things are yours, whether... the world or life or death or the present or the future—all belong to you' (1 Cor. 3:21, 22).

His sense of isolation seemed completely to take him over at this point. We are meant to notice how concerned he was to detach himself publicly from any suspicion of yielding to family pressure in deciding the course of his public ministry. His gentle word of caution to his mother at the wedding at Cana had already revealed his desire to work free from such pressure. Now, much more bluntly, he resists the anxiety of his brothers to push him their way: *'Go to the festival yourselves. I am not going....'*

Yet the constraint under which the will of God had placed him later took him to the festival *not publicly but as it were in secret* (v. 10). There can be little doubt that after their recent dramatic confession of inseparable loyalty to him, his disciples were then with him in the background. The sight of them there also willingly sharing something of his isolation from the world of their day and of the constraint that was driving him towards his cross is a reminder to us that our own discipleship can at times demand the sacrifice of the very liberty he has died to win us. Paul, who repeatedly insists in his letters to the Corinthians 'All things are lawful' (1 Cor. 10:23), also sets before us in himself the perfect example of how to deny ourselves this very freedom: 'For the love of Christ urges us on, because we are convinced that one has died for all; therefore all have died. And he died for all, so that those who live might live no longer for themselves, but for him who died and was raised for them' (2 Cor. 5:14, 15).

Chapter 7

The great controversy
John 7:11 – 8:59

There are many details within the account of the long controversy
in the temple at the festival of 'Booths' (or Tabernacles in the NIV)
which cannot be brought within the scope and purpose of this
present exposition. The account has therefore been divided into
four sections, the first of which illustrates the mood and
development of the whole controversy, using the part as an
example of the whole. Selected for more detailed treatment, and
each within its own context, are three important words of Jesus,
which appear consecutively, and which are outstanding in the midst
of the whole discussion. The text is printed in continuity so that
the reader can read it through and note the connections.

Jesus on the attack

John 7:11-36

7 The Jews were looking for him at the festival and saying, 'Where
is he?' [12]And there was considerable complaining about him among the
crowds. While some were saying, 'He is a good man', others were
saying, 'No, he is deceiving the crowd.' [13]Yet no one would speak
openly about him for fear of the Jews.

14 About the middle of the festival Jesus went up into the temple and
began to teach. [15]The Jews were astonished at it, saying, 'How does this
man have such learning, when he has never been taught?' [16]Then Jesus
answered them, 'My teaching is not mine but his who sent me. [17]
Anyone who resolves to do the will of God will know whether the
teaching is from God or whether I am speaking on my own. [18]Those
who speak on their own seek their own glory; but the one who seeks the
glory of him who sent him is true, and there is nothing false in him.

19 'Did not Moses give you the law? Yet none of you keeps the law.
Why are you looking for an opportunity to kill me?' [20]The crowd
answered, 'You have a demon! Who is trying to kill you?' [21]Jesus
answered them, 'I performed one work, and all of you are astonished.
[22]Moses gave you circumcision (it is, of course, not from Moses, but
from the patriarchs), and you circumcise a man on the sabbath. [23]If a

133

man receives circumcision on the sabbath in order that the law of Moses may not be broken, are you angry with me because I healed a man's whole body on the sabbath? [24]Do not judge by appearances, but judge with right judgement.'

25 Now some of the people of Jerusalem were saying, 'Is not this the man whom they are trying to kill? [26]And here he is, speaking openly, but they say nothing to him! Can it be that the authorities really know that this is the Messiah? [27]Yet we know where this man is from; but when the Messiah comes, no one will know where he is from.' [28]Then Jesus cried out as he was teaching in the temple, 'You know me, and you know where I am from. I have not come on my own. But the one who sent me is true, and you do not know him. [29]I know him, because I am from him, and he sent me.' [30]Then they tried to arrest him, but no one laid hands on him, because his hour had not yet come. [31]Yet many in the crowd believed in him and were saying, 'When the Messiah comes, will he do more signs than this man has done?'

32 The Pharisees heard the crowd muttering such things about him, and the chief priests and Pharisees sent temple police to arrest him. [33]Jesus then said, 'I will be with you a little while longer, and then I am going to him who sent me. [34]You will search for me, but you will not find me; and where I am, you cannot come.' [35]The Jews said to one another, 'Where does this man intend to go that we will not find him? Does he intend to go to the Dispersion among the Greeks and teach the Greeks? [36]What does he mean by saying, "You will search for me and you will not find me" and, "Where I am, you cannot come"?'

'My teaching is… his who sent me'

The discussion began immediately Jesus arrived and it went on day after day. We find him moving around, confronting different groups here and there. Sometimes he lifts up his voice and addresses the whole assembly around him. The mood of his hearers varies. People around him at the beginning are anxious, questioning and suspicious. As the days pass the atmosphere grows more tense and hostile.

He sets the discussion in motion with a supremely confident affirmation of the undeniable truth of his teaching and the convincing authority with which it was always being given. It came from God. *My teaching is not mine but his who sent me'* (v. 16).

He was always certain that as he spoke, God the Father spoke too (cf. 8:14; 5:34ff.).

He believed that, whether or not it produced any immediate response, his voice would be always resonant with the same power that could heal the sick, open blind eyes and raise the dead. He was convinced, therefore, that his ministry among this crowd before him was going to reveal whether people were for or against God. If heart and mind were open and inclined to the truth, any hearer would respond and learn from him: *'Anyone who resolves to do the will of God will know...'* (v. 17). Any who responded otherwise would inevitably become perplexed, mystified and hardened into an attitude of deadly enmity.

He warned them about the hatred he had already discerned in their reaction to the healing of the invalud man at the pool on the sabbath day. He challenged them to be honest about the desire that was in their hearts to kill him. As if to save them from their folly he tried to show them that they could find no real support in the law of Moses for their attitude. A notable pause in their increasing hostility seems to take place towards the end of the festival when Jesus finds himself surrounded by a group of people who seem ready to believe in him; however, these very people soon find his attempt to help them towards true faith insulting, they react with open abuse and then take up stones in an attempt to kill him on the spot (8:48, 59).

The reader of the whole discourse will notice that much of the discussion is about Jesus' own personal origin. His attackers had objected to his claim to be the Christ because they knew where he came from, yet *'when the Messiah comes, no one will know where he is from'* (v. 27; cf. 6:41ff.). Jesus insists that his personal origin must remain a mystery about which in their present state of mind they can know nothing. Moreover, ironically, he provokes and puzzles them by warning them that in their present state of mind his future destiny will remain as unknown to them as his origin. Where he goes, they *cannot come.* They will die in their sin (7:34; 8:14, 21). Referring to their own origins, his conclusion is that since they do not recognize the Father from whom he has come, they have forsaken the fatherhood of God, and made the devil their father (8:42-4).

We are meant to notice the decisive part this controversy plays within John's Gospel, in bringing Jesus to his death. During these several days of teaching the whole climate of public opinion in

Jerusalem is being altered; people are beginning to think themselves disillusioned with him, and are wondering whether their leaders have had some justification for the judgement they have made. The Pharisees have become much more confident that possibly before the coming Passover they will have him in their power. Yet it is Jesus himself who brings about this movement of events. Throughout the festival, as everywhere else in the Gospel of John, he shows himself regally in control of everything that happens around him as he moves towards the cross. He lays down his own life. No one takes it from him (10:17, 18). He initiates the controversy, controls it at every juncture, decides the theme and the course of the discussion, increases or moderates the tension and provokes reaction.

It is to be noted that he exercises his complete command and control of the events around him by his word. He does no miracle during this momentous week. He makes no political manoeuvre, organizes no protest of any kind. It is simply by his speaking, pleading, teaching, warning, inviting and proclaiming, that he plays his decisive part in moving public affairs on to the course God has destined them to take. Here is the perfect illustration of how God's word goes forth from his mouth into human history to accomplish his will (cf. Isa. 55:10, 11). Moreover the theme of his teaching in this decisive week is, as usual in this Gospel, almost entirely himself. He speaks of who he is, where he has come from, what he has come to do and where he is going. This is how he fulfils the challenge laid down by his brothers to 'show himself to the world' so that it could make its final decision about him. The teaching he gives here is not consciously directed in any way towards public affairs or the details of personal ethics. There is no prophetic call for social justice, nothing directly 'anti-establishment'. These two chapters are difficult to fit into any theory that what brought Jesus to the cross was primarily his revolutionary teaching about our moral standards, his devastating criticism of our earthly social structures or his radical views about the distribution of wealth. What stirred the anger of his enemies, provoked their madness, and made them determined to crucify him was simply—himself.

In taking note of Jesus' attacking initiative we must not, however, fail to remember that here he was confronting the city over which at this very time he wept. These were the people he continually yearned to win for himself (cf. Luke 19:41). We must not therefore underestimate in any way the genuineness of the appeals with which this controversy is punctuated, nor the suffering he felt under the continual rejection which he had to face.

The offer of life

John 7:37-52

7   On the last day of the festival, the great day, while Jesus was standing there, he cried out, 'Let anyone who is thirsty come to me, ³⁸and let the one who believes in me drink. As the scripture has said, "Out of the believer's heart shall flow rivers of living water."' ³⁹Now he said this about the Spirit, which believers in him were to receive; for as yet there was no Spirit, because Jesus was not yet glorified.

40   When they heard these words, some in the crowd said, 'This is really the prophet.' ⁴¹Others said, 'This is the Messiah.' But some asked, 'Surely the Messiah does not come from Galilee, does he? ⁴²Has not the scripture said that the Messiah is descended from David and comes from Bethlehem, the village where David lived?' ⁴³So there was a division in the crowd because of him. ⁴⁴Some of them wanted to arrest him, but no one laid hands on him.

45   Then the temple police went back to the chief priests and Pharisees, who asked them, 'Why did you not arrest him?' ⁴⁶The police answered, 'Never has anyone spoken like this!' ⁴⁷Then the Pharisees replied, 'Surely you have not been deceived too, have you? ⁴⁸Has any one of the authorities or of the Pharisees believed in him? ⁴⁹But this crowd, which does not know the law—they are accursed.' ⁵⁰Nicodemus, who had gone to Jesus before, and who was one of them, asked, ⁵¹'Our law does not judge people without first giving them a hearing to find out what they are doing, does it?' ⁵²They replied, 'Surely you are not also from Galilee, are you? Search and you will see that no prophet is to arise from Galilee.'

The setting was picturesque and the occasion dramatic. Throughout much of the festival, the thought of those present was directed to the desert wanderings of the children of Israel, and to incidents on their way, such as Moses' striking of the rock to bring them water. The worshippers were reminded too, of certain prophetic texts which promised that in the days of the Messiah such refreshing waters would marvellously flow again. Zechariah, for example, had made the promise that one day 'living waters shall flow out from Jerusalem', and Ezekiel had seen a river flow from the rock underneath the altar of the Temple (cf. Zech. 14:8; Ezek. 47:1ff.). On each of the seven days of the feast the people went in procession from the Temple down to the fountain which supplied the pool of Siloam, where the priest filled a golden vase from the running water, and the choir sang verses from the twelfth chapter of Isaiah. They carried the vase back to the Temple through the Watergate, proceeded round the altar singing prayers from the end of Psalm 118, then they poured the water over the altar.

The eighth day, *the last day of the festival*, however, was a day of waiting. The crowd gathered in the Temple courts and there was silence. The devout worshippers there then prayed for the great day to come when all the hope of Israel would be fulfilled. Some indeed expected to see the promised miracle of a fountain of running water burst open in the Temple courts. It was this solemn moment that Jesus chose for one of his great acts of self-proclamation, raising his voice so that all could hear: *'Let anyone who is thirsty come to me, and let the one who believes in me drink. As the scripture has said, "Out of the believer's heart shall flow rivers of living water"'* (v. 37f.). As Moses had brought forth rivers of living water from the rock, here was their Messiah offering himself as the true river of life (Rev. 22:1), the source from which his people can from now on draw, and give to the whole world.

The disciples who reported this incident to us explained that Jesus spoke these words chiefly as a promise referring to the Holy Spirit who was poured out on the church when Jesus was later glorified (v. 39). His dramatic call, however, at the time of its utterance was as eloquent and emphatic a claim as he could have made to be the Messiah in whom his people were meant to find and enjoy their true destiny.

It is today, therefore, now that the Holy Spirit has been given in his fullness, that these words can be heard by us with even more challenging force than they had when first spoken. We can hear them as an appeal to us to re-assess what life has brought to us. We note that it was on the *'last... the great day'* —at the climax and crisis of their ancient festival—that Israel, year after year expecting so much, found their earthly hopes still unfulfilled. So we, too, have our own crises of disappointment and disillusionment, when we begin to know how unsatisfying the routine of life has been, and how much we really *thirst*. Earthly pleasure, wealth or success can suddenly expose what seems a basic emptiness. Life's inevitable changes, chances and bereavements can suddenly seem to rob us of what has been truly good and worthy. What comes to us through our religious devotion and worship, however magnificent the ritual, however fervent the enthusiasm, can leave us still with a longing for something more real and satisfying. It is especially at these times that we can hear this voice assuring us that in place of all the 'cracked cisterns that can hold no water', the 'fountain of living water' (Jer. 2:13) is full and marvellously refreshing if we will only come to him, drink and share what we have been given with a needy and perishing world.

If anything Jesus ever did was deliberately calculated to be sensational it was to make his public call at this time. It was carefully prepared for, and must have been deeply and genuinely impressive. No one could have escaped either the meaning of the action or the strength of the claim. No doubt he expected some sign that his words had gone home. Certainly some were moved to voice their opinions: *'This is really the prophet.... This is the Messiah'* (v. 40f.). Yet what finally happened proved in the end simply to be the beginning of a further controversy: *So there was a division in the crowd because of him* (v. 43).

THE GREAT CONTROVERSY (*cont.*)

The offer of light

John 8:12-30

8 Again Jesus spoke to them, saying, 'I am the light of the world. Whoever follows me will never walk in darkness but will have the light of life.' [13]Then the Pharisees said to him, 'You are testifying on your own behalf; your testimony is not valid.' [14]Jesus answered, 'Even if I testify on my own behalf, my testimony is valid, because I know where I have come from and where I am going, but you do not know where I come from or where I am going. [15]You judge by human standards; I judge no one. [16]Yet even if I do judge, my judgement is valid; for it is not I alone who judge, but I and the Father who sent me. [17]In your law it is written that the testimony of two witnesses is valid. [18]I testify on my own behalf, and the Father who sent me testifies on my behalf.' [19]Then they said to him, 'Where is your Father?' Jesus answered, 'You know neither me nor my Father. If you knew me, you would know my Father also.' [20]He spoke these words while he was teaching in the treasury of the temple, but no one arrested him, because his hour had not yet come.

21 Again he said to them, 'I am going away, and you will search for me, but you will die in your sin. Where I am going, you cannot come.' [22]Then the Jews said, 'Is he going to kill himself? Is that what he means by saying, "Where I am going, you cannot come"?' [23]He said to them, 'You are from below, l am from above; you are of this world, I am not of this world. [24]I told you that you would die in your sins, for you will die in your sins unless you believe that I am he.' [25]They said to him, 'Who are you?' Jesus said to them, 'Why do I speak to you at all? [26]I have much to say about you and much to condemn; but the one who sent me is true, and I declare to the world what I have heard from him.' [27]They did not understand that he was speaking to them about the Father. [28]So Jesus said, 'When you have lifted up the Son of Man, then

you will realize that I am he, and that I do nothing on my own, but I speak these things as the Father instructed me. [29]And the one who sent me is with me; he has not left me alone, for I always do what is pleasing to him.' [30]As he was saying these things, many believed in him.

Alongside the celebration involving the drawing of water there was also a festival of lights, involving the lighting of the golden candlestick in the 'Court of the Women' at the Temple. The Jews thus remembered that during their wanderings in the wilderness there was the miraculous pillar of fire to lead them, as well as the flow of water to refresh them. They always thought of God as one who gives light alongside of life: 'For with you is the fountain of life; in your light we see light' (Ps. 36:9; cf. John 1:4). A second dramatic appeal was therefore made by Jesus in the course of the celebration: *'I am the light of the world. Whoever follows me will never walk in darkness but will have the light of life'* (v. 12).

If we read the many lamentations, dirges and psalms of complaint scattered throughout the literature of the Old Testament we will be given a trustworthy impression of what men and women in that ancient world felt as they faced the darkness that surrounds our human life. They often felt hemmed in by it, and they feared the cruel and hostile nature of much that it enshrouded. We hear them crying and questioning out of a perplexity and pain that they felt at times to be unbearable and incurable. Why these ghastly horrors of war, terrorism and natural disaster—death entering the windows of their homes, dead bodies fallen 'like dung upon the open field, like sheaves behind the reaper'? It all sounds so modern, but in their case there was no one to gather up the corpses (cf. Jer. 9:21, 22). Why the unfairness and injustice of it all? Where is the meaning of life to be found in the midst of all its vanities, corruption and uncertainties? How and when is God going to put everything right, and show that everything *has* been put right? Of course they were able to endure and overcome, often with triumphant and indeed radiant faith, for even when they felt they had no direct answer to their questionings, the Word of God was a light to their path and a lamp to their feet. (Ps. 119:105). How much praise for triumph, deliverance and revelation there is in the same literature that so frankly faces up to the darkness!

It is in this context that we are to assess and understand the promise of Jesus. We *will never walk in darkness* (v. 12). Of course the darkness is still there around us, sinister and impenetrable in places, but the balance has swung entirely in favour of the light. We still have a few short dirges, lamentations and complaints in the New Testament—especially in the Book of Revelation—but they are brief and limited. The writer to the Hebrews puts it in perspective. He *almost* complains: 'we do not yet see everything in subjection.' There are many disasters and wars, many prayers and questions still unanswered, many longings still to be stifled. 'But', he adds, 'we do see Jesus, who for a little while was made lower than the angels, now crowned with glory and honour...' (Heb. 2:8f.). Here is true light, far-reaching, promising and clear. It is *the light of life*. Though it does not offer a quick solution to our intellectual problems, nor make it easy to indulge in continual triumphalism, it enables us to see enough of the purpose and meaning of life to have a wide-open field of opportunity and personal responsibility in the service of God, of whose guidance and friendship we can be sure.

It is a light that gives itself to those who obey it. It is *whoever follows me* who has the light. The gift which was celebrated in the festival of Booths was that of a light which went on the move, choosing the direction ahead and the way for God's people. To live in it they had to keep up with it. It was those who failed to follow who were left in darkness. We cannot control or refract this light, bending its rays in our self-chosen directions. We have to go where it is to be found. As Jesus himself later said: *'Whoever serves me must follow me, and where I am, there will my servant be also'* (12:26).

We are meant to take notice of the sweeping universality and unqualified breadth of his claim. He speaks of only One who claims to be *the light of the world*. He is not one among others. If others before him had some light, it must have been *his* light they saw. He was and is the One towards whom in their own darkness they were all moving. Whatever beams of wisdom and truth they possessed were derived from him. All is darkness that does not acknowledge him. Whoever looks to him shall see everything that matters in the realm of ultimate truth.

The light shines in the darkness

John 7:53 – 8:11

8 Then each of them went home, [1]while Jesus went to the Mount of Olives. [2]Early in the morning he came again to the temple. All the people came to him and he sat down and began to teach them. [3]The scribes and the Pharisees brought a woman who had been caught in adultery; and making her stand before all of them, [4]they said to him, 'Teacher, this woman was caught in the very act of committing adultery. [5]Now in the law Moses commanded us to stone such women. Now what do you say?' [6]They said this to test him, so that they might have some charge to bring against him. Jesus bent down and wrote with his finger on the ground. [7] When they kept on questioning him, he straightened up and said to them, 'Let anyone among you who is without sin be the first to throw a stone at her.' [8]And once again he bent down and wrote on the ground. [9]When they heard it, they went away, one by one, beginning with the elders; and Jesus was left alone with the woman standing before him. [10]Jesus straightened up and said to her, 'Woman, where are they? Has no one condemned you?' [11]She said, 'No one, sir.' And Jesus said, 'Neither do I condemn you. Go your way, and from now on do not sin again.'

A test case in the fight against Jesus

The scribes and Pharisees had not a shadow of doubt nor a qualm of conscience in their minds when they brought this woman to Jesus for his judgement. She had been caught in the act, and it was an anti-social act of the most serious nature. In the Ten Commandments it is listed along with murder and stealing as a sin which society must not tolerate, and in this case the prescribed punishment ordered by Moses was death. *'Moses commanded us to stone such women.'* No doubt they themselves hated the task of executing the sentence in cold blood, but they were the responsible guardians of public decency and order, and they were prepared to do it. They cared that their children around them should grow up in a healthy society where marriage was held in honour.

The thought, however, came to them: Why not make this a test case in their fight against Jesus? They had no doubt about the verdict they themselves had passed, but they were in real doubt about Jesus' loyalty to this law. He had once said something about lustful thoughts being as bad as adultery (Matt. 5:27f.).

Did this mean that the outward behaviour of people did not matter, and that adulterers were to be tolerated as being no more dangerous than people who sinned only with the mind? He had made suggestions about the possibility of tax-collectors and prostitutes entering the kingdom of God—and there were stories of him having dealings with women of bad repute. They would use this opportunity of putting him to the test in public: *'Teacher, this woman was caught in the very act of committing adultery.... Now what do you say?'* (v. 4). They had the stones in their hands, and they were confident of the outcome.

They had hoped that their sudden intrusion would bring about a dramatic and devastating public exposure of Jesus in the eyes of the public around him. Instead, they were completely taken aback at what happened. It was they who, in the sudden publicity they had brought on themselves, began to feel stupidly awkward just when they had hoped to be so triumphant. Jesus, instead, was calm, confident and silent for a while. No doubt to prolong the silence he bent down and wrote with his finger in the sand. When they had begun to grow even more uneasy with the situation they had so unwittingly created, *he straightened up and said to them, 'Let anyone among you who is without sin be the first to throw a stone at her'*, and he again bent down and wrote on the ground.

It is the complete collapse of their self-confidence in the presence of Jesus that we are meant to notice. Undoubtedly when they took the woman so boldly before him they thought they knew enough about themselves, about life and about Jesus, to see this whole case through. But then when they entered his presence the light of his truth began to penetrate their consciences, and when they heard his challenge to face what each of them now saw himself to be, *they went away, one by one, beginning with the elders*. All their sham self-certainty gone! They had no moral self-defence left. They found themselves unable to tolerate the light of his truth. To save their pride and protect their false self-image which had been their comfortable disguise, they felt they had to get away from him as quickly as possible—back to the darkness from which they had come. It is significant that the darkness to which they return is the very darkness under cover of which they will now join in the plot to quench the light that has so exposed them to themselves.

'Neither do I condemn you… do not sin again'

And now the world of difference between them and the woman
they had brought with them becomes clear. Of course the public
exhibition of her guilt had been at first like a torture to her, and
possibly they may have had to drag her along with them. But
something happened to her as well as to them during that strange
silence in the presence of Jesus, as he stooped down to write on the
ground. In contrast to the men, the woman seems to have found
herself accepted and at home with him. She made no attempt to
leave him, until *Jesus straightened up and said to her, 'Woman,
where are they? Has no one condemned you?' She said, 'No one,
sir.' And Jesus said, 'Neither do I condemn you. Go your way, and
from now on do not sin again'* (vv. 10, 11).

We need not imagine that his word, *'Neither do I condemn you'*
was Jesus condoning her sin. She herself had already, without any
attempt at self-defence, had her sin fully exposed and condemned
in his presence. There was no need for anything more to be said
about it. Moreover, the fact that she alone made no attempt to
leave his presence means that she accepted the condemnation, that
she no longer wanted to return to that darkness which she has now
given up for ever. A prominent biblical scholar of a former
generation once published an eloquent and persuasive sermon
suggesting that the word *'Go your way, and from now on do not sin
again'* was an expression of trust rather than a stern threat. She
went, knowing that he trusted her. The contrast between herself
and those who hauled her before him is complete. Our human
destiny is determined by how each one of us reacts when his light
falls upon us.

The offer of freedom

John 8:30-59

8 As he was saying these things, many believed in him.

31 Then Jesus said to the Jews who had believed in him, 'If you
continue in my word, you are truly my disciples; [32]and you will know
the truth, and the truth will make you free.' [33]They answered him, 'We

are descendants of Abraham and have never been slaves to anyone. What do you mean by saying, "You will be made free"?'

34 Jesus answered them, 'Very truly, I tell you, everyone who commits sin is a slave to sin. [35]The slave does not have a permanent place in the household; the son has a place there for ever. [36]So if the Son makes you free, you will be free indeed. [37]I know that you are descendants of Abraham; yet you look for an opportunity to kill me, because there is no place in you for my word. [38]I declare what I have seen in the Father's presence; as for you, you should do what you have heard from the Father.'

39 They answered him, 'Abraham is our father.' Jesus said to them, 'If you were Abraham's children, you would be doing what Abraham did, [40]but now you are trying to kill me, a man who has told you the truth that I heard from God. This is not what Abraham did. [41]You are indeed doing what your father does.' They said to him, 'We are not illegitimate children; we have one father, God himself.' [42]Jesus said to them, 'If God were your Father, you would love me, for I came from God and now I am here. I did not come on my own, but he sent me. [43]Why do you not understand what I say? It is because you cannot accept my word. [44]You are from your father the devil, and you choose to do your father's desires. He was a murderer from the beginning and does not stand in the truth, because there is no truth in him. When he lies, he speaks according to his own nature, for he is a liar and the father of lies. [45]But because I tell the truth, you do not believe me. [46]Which of you convicts me of sin? If I tell the truth, why do you not believe me? [47]Whoever is from God hears the words of God. The reason you do not hear them is that you are not from God.'

48 The Jews answered him, 'Are we not right in saying that you are a Samaritan and have a demon?' [49]Jesus answered, 'I do not have a demon; but I honour my Father, and you dishonour me. [50]Yet I do not seek my own glory; there is one who seeks it and he is the judge. [51]Very truly, I tell you, whoever keeps my word will never see death.' [52]The Jews said to him, 'Now we know that you have a demon. Abraham died, and so did the prophets; yet you say, "Whoever keeps my word will never taste death." [53]Are you greater than our father Abraham, who died? The prophets also died. Who do you claim to be?' [54]Jesus answered, 'If I glorify myself, my glory is nothing. It is my Father who

glorifies me, he of whom you say, "He is our God", [55]though you do not know him. But I know him; if I were to say that I do not know him, I would be a liar like you. But I do know him and I keep his word. [56]Your ancestor Abraham rejoiced that he would see my day; he saw it and was glad.' [57]Then the Jews said to him, 'You are not yet fifty years old, and have you seen Abraham?' [58]Jesus said to them, 'Very truly, I tell you, before Abraham was, I am.' [59]So they picked up stones to throw at him, but Jesus hid himself and went out of the temple.

The need for perseverance

Suddenly the tone of the debate in the Temple seemed to change for a short time. The mood of confrontation gave way to a wave of what seemed to be genuine interest. The evangelist describing the situation says that *many believed in him* (v. 30). It is obvious that their hold on what he was giving them was very tentative and slender. Calvin calls their change of attitude simply a 'preparation for faith'. But Jesus felt it was worthwhile trying to strengthen it. With pastoral concern and his never-slackening desire to win people over, he treated those who approached him as genuine inquirers.

He had already given warnings about those who endure for a while but when tribulation and persecution arise on account of the word immediately fall away (Matt. 13:18ff.). He knew only too well therefore that the wave of interest they were experiencing would soon subside unless he could persuade them to become more open in mind to all his teaching and bring them more fully under his influence. He made it clear to them what entering such commitment would involve: *'If you continue in my word, you are truly my disciples; and you will know the truth, and the truth will make you free.'*

The challenge to *continue in my word* of course involves us in a study of his teaching with the same ardent devotion as the Psalmist had for the Law when he made it his 'meditation all day long' (Ps. 119:97). It involves a persevering effort to know and understand the whole of it, refusing to be content with only a partial knowledge of a few selected passages that have caught our approval and imagination, and including those passages that tend to offend and condemn us. We must work out as fully as we can all the implications of obedience for our own lives. Moreover, we must bring before our minds in this way not only the words of

Jesus but his person, and of course the works in which we find him presenting himself to us. The New English Bible brings out this aspect of his exhortation in its translation of v. 31f.: *'If you dwell within the revelation I have brought... you shall know the truth...'.* After all, Jesus himself, in what he does, is the truth, and the truth, as Hoskyns remarks, 'cannot be detached from the figure of flesh and blood which was Jesus'.

Bondage to sin

There can be little doubt that this first piece of advice with its inevitable orientation to himself, would cause some annoyance among his hearers. The assertion that immediately followed was deliberately even more provocative, when Jesus claimed that the truth he brought them would make them free. It was an accusation that they were all in bondage, and they were angered.

Jesus, of course, was referring to our inner bondage to evil and self-centred ways of thought and behaviour, our bondage to sin. This was the one evil in life which gave him most concern: 'But what comes out of the mouth proceeds from the heart, and this is what defiles' (Matt. 15:18). His hearers on their own part should have understood what he was referring to. It was the teaching of their Scriptures, and they prided themselves in their faithfulness to the traditions of their fathers. But their minds had drifted from such truth and had become almost completely oriented to what was only of immediate secular and social relevance. They interpreted his reference to 'freedom' politically. He seemed to be implying that they were at present in bondage to Rome. They reacted immediately to what they took as an insult to their national pride. *'We are descendants of Abraham and have never been slaves to anyone. What do you mean by saying, "You will be made free"?'* (v. 33).

Jesus seized the invitation to give them an elementary lesson in the truth they had been unwilling to face. His argument is easy to follow. The original source of everything that has blighted our human life is our sin, our deep inward alienation from God. Unless we find true inward freedom, it takes over each one of us, working like an inner power within us, forcing us against our own better will into attitudes and habits that degrade us. Nothing in any aspect of our personal or social life can go right while we remain in such bondage to our self-will and inner weaknesses.

There is a warning here especially about the insecurity and transitoriness of the political freedom about which they were boasting: *'The slave does not have a permanent place in the household; the son has a place there forever'* (v. 35). Political stability is the privilege only of those who have inwardly accepted the liberation Jesus has offered and thus become themselves children of God. We can affirm that even a healthy social freedom can be enjoyed only by a people who give full and free place in their midst to the gospel which produces in the inward heart the liberty of the children of God to which Jesus is here referring. When our country was facing the Second World War, one of our church leaders published a little book about the foundations of the freedom we professed to be fighting for. He uttered a plea for the cultivation of the virtues of restraint and discipline that are peculiarly the fruit of the Spirit of Christ, and added the warning, 'You cannot grow an oak in a flower pot.' Only if the Son makes us free can we find true freedom.

'Before Abraham was, I am'

With a final rejoinder, Jesus thrust home his point and entered the attack again. These men who had professed themselves so deeply hurt at his accusation, were proving its truth by their very thoughts and attitude. They could not free themselves from the deceiving effects of their inward pride, nor from their completely irrational desire to kill him. The break in the controversy therefore simply opens it up again. The accusations of the Jews grow more insulting, and Jesus himself becomes less and less restrained in his replies. The discussion revolves around Abraham and what it means to be truly his offspring. In the end Jesus who had claimed that Abraham rejoiced to see his day, uttered one of his most majestic and memorable sayings: *'before Abraham was, I am.'* The One who revealed himself to Moses at the burning bush when he made all his greatest promises and claims to his people, used the same simple and majestic word to describe his incomparable self (cf. Exod. 3:14; Deut. 32:39; Isa. 43:10).

CHAPTER 9

THE MAN BORN BLIND

(The 6ᵗʰ Sign)

John 9:1-41

9 As he walked along, he saw a man blind from birth. ²His disciples asked him, 'Rabbi, who sinned, this man or his parents, that he was born blind?' ³Jesus answered, 'Neither this man nor his parents sinned; he was born blind so that God's works might be revealed in him. ⁴We must work the works of him who sent me while it is day; night is coming when no one can work. ⁵As long as I am in the world, I am the light of the world.' ⁶When he had said this, he spat on the ground and made mud with the saliva and spread the mud on the man's eyes, ⁷saying to him, 'Go, wash in the pool of Siloam' (which means Sent). Then he went and washed and came back able to see. ⁸The neighbours and those who had seen him before as a beggar began to ask, 'Is this not the man who used to sit and beg?' ⁹Some were saying, 'It is he.' Others were saying, 'No, but it is someone like him.' He kept saying, 'I am the man.' ¹⁰But they kept asking him, 'Then how were your eyes opened?' ¹¹He answered, 'The man called Jesus made mud, spread it on my eyes, and said to me, "Go to Siloam and wash." Then I went and washed and received my sight.' ¹²They said to him, 'Where is he?' He said, 'I do not know.'

13 They brought to the Pharisees the man who had formerly been blind. ¹⁴Now it was a sabbath day when Jesus made the mud and opened his eyes. ¹⁵Then the Pharisees also began to ask him how he had received his sight. He said to them, 'He put mud on my eyes. Then I washed, and now I see.' ¹⁶Some of the Pharisees said, 'This man is not from God, for he does not observe the sabbath.' But others said, 'How can a man who is a sinner perform such signs?' And they were divided.

¹⁷So they said again to the blind man, 'What do you say about him? It was your eyes he opened.' He said, 'He is a prophet.'

18 The Jews did not believe that he had been blind and had received his sight until they called the parents of the man who had received his sight ¹⁹and asked them, 'Is this your son, who you say was born blind? How then does he now see?' ²⁰His parents answered, 'We know that this is our son, and that he was born blind; ²¹but we do not know how it is that now he sees, nor do we know who opened his eyes. Ask him; he is of age. He will speak for himself.' ²²His parents said this because they were afraid of the Jews; for the Jews had already agreed that anyone who confessed Jesus to be the Messiah would be put out of the synagogue. ²³Therefore his parents said, 'He is of age; ask him.'

24 So for the second time they called the man who had been blind, and they said to him, 'Give glory to God! We know that this man is a sinner.' ²⁵He answered, 'I do not know whether he is a sinner. One thing I do know, that though I was blind, now I see.' ²⁶They said to him, 'What did he do to you? How did he open your eyes?' ²⁷He answered them, 'I have told you already, and you would not listen. Why do you want to hear it again? Do you also want to become his disciples?' ²⁸Then they reviled him, saying, 'You are his disciple, but we are disciples of Moses. ²⁹We know that God has spoken to Moses, but as for this man, we do not know where he comes from.' ³⁰The man answered, 'Here is an astonishing thing! You do not know where he comes from, and yet he opened my eyes. ³¹We know that God does not listen to sinners, but he does listen to one who worships him and obeys his will. ³²Never since the world began has it been heard that anyone opened the eyes of a person born blind. ³³If this man were not from God, he could do nothing.' ³⁴They answered him, 'You were born entirely in sins, and are you trying to teach us?' And they drove him out.

35 Jesus heard that they had driven him out, and when he found him, he said, 'Do you believe in the Son of Man?' ³⁶He answered, 'And who is he, sir? Tell me, so that I may believe in him.' ³⁷Jesus said to him, 'You have seen him, and the one speaking with you is he.' ³⁸He said, 'Lord, I believe.' And he worshipped him. ³⁹Jesus said, 'I came into this world for judgement so that those who do not see may see, and those who do see may become blind.' ⁴⁰Some of the Pharisees near him heard this and said to him, 'Surely we are not blind, are we?' ⁴¹Jesus said to them, 'If you were blind, you would not have sin. But now that you say, "We see", your sin remains.'

A plea for fresh vision and action

It is said of Queen Marie Antoinette that on one of her important royal processions through Paris, she gave orders that wherever she was going, the streets should be cleared of all the poor or deformed beggars who usually frequented that area. She did not want to be made to feel uncomfortable or sorrowful on a great occasion. In the days of Jesus, however, people passing through the streets on their way to market, temple, place of work or political assembly could not escape being confronted, sometimes dramatically and rudely, by the contents of their impoverished slum hovels laid out before them—helpless people with paralysis, ugly deformities, and wasting sicknesses that were sometimes due to poverty, sometimes to neglect and ignorance, sometimes to their birth, but all reminders of an immense amount of human suffering.

Of course the sight continually plagued the minds of sensitive people and formed a large, persistent, dark shadow in the background of their thought as they tried to figure out what life was all about. They gave alms no doubt generously, but they were at times disturbed by inner questioning—especially if they knew some of the intimate details and tragic circumstances of some of the cases around them. The disciples were this day discussing the obvious poverty and the pathetic misery of this *man blind from birth* whom Jesus himself had noticed. They felt certain that his suffering was due to sin. Was it possible that he was suffering for the sins of his parents? Or was it possible that the man himself in a previous life could have committed a grievous, damaging sin? They took the problem to Jesus: *'Rabbi, who sinned...?'*

The final answer that Jesus gave to their question was of course to heal the man before them and change the whole human situation, but before he did so he rebuked them. Their well-intentioned but fruitless discussion, their hopeless acceptance of things as they are, revealed the shortness of vision, the callous despair and darkness of mind that he had come to abolish. He pled with them to take a new look at the situation before them, to see that with his own presence now in their midst a new age had dawned on the world, transforming our ways of looking at life and our response to all the problems presented to us by its evils and injustices. He therefore lifted up the whole discussion to this entirely new level: *'Neither this man nor his parents sinned; he was born blind so that God's works might be revealed in him. We must work the works of him who sent me while it is day; night is coming when no one can work. As long as I am in the world, I am the light of the world'* (vv. 3-5).

There is urgency in his appeal. At this time in his life he had not long to live—perhaps only a week or two. His death had been plotted. His supporters were falling away. He likens himself here to someone approaching the evening of life with only a short span of daylight left. Therefore it was urgent that he should do his work before the night finally closed in. As he looked at his disciples with this thought in his mind he said, however, *'We must work...'* (v. 4). He was trying to communicate to them not only the same vision and the same deep concern as he himself had, but also the same sense of urgency.

We can assess the influence which Jesus' words had on the disciples if we turn to the book of Acts and watch them in the leadership of the early church. They now face the same kind of world, posing the same problems before which they had proved themselves so inept in their thought and so fatalistic in their attitude, but they are now transformed. They see everything differently. Christ, crucified and risen, is now to them the light of the world, shining in a darkness that is continually in retreat. Their eyes have seen the glory of his coming, the power of his kingdom, and the final total surrender of evil to his name. They have neither time nor inclination to indulge in any kind of analysis of the human situation or to think out its past causes. They want to know only how and where they must resist and attack. They are no longer on the sidelines. They have raised their banner and they are at the centre of the battle.

What about ourselves? We have (largely) cleared away from our streets the beggars and the sick. The front line at which we have to face the need of our human situation with its tragedies and injustices has shifted. It is now on our television screens that most of us see it. There the horror of it all presents itself to us no less vividly than it presented itself to the early disciples in Jerusalem, and on a much larger scale—earthquakes, wars, famines, brutalities, human diseases and deformities. And still today even on the closer and more personal home front, the same perplexing questions as plagued the disciples can also address themselves acutely to our own minds. Why did it all happen to us and ours? We, too, are being tested as to how we react in mind, emotion and will. We may not be tempted, of course, to indulge in the same kind of Rabbinic speculation about possible hereditary guilt as did the disciples of Jesus, yet we ourselves can slip back sometimes into the same fatalistic acceptance of the darkness around, out of which Jesus tried to deliver them, and we tend at times to add a measure of more modern cynicism and bitterness to our condition.

It is in this situation, above all, that we must allow Jesus' words to convict and inspire us, to enlarge our vision and to deliver us from all sloth and despair. We must avoid becoming over-concerned with analyzing the situation, assessing the blame and raising questions impossible to answer. 'Our first concern', as P. T. Forsyth once put it 'is not with the riddle of the universe, but with the tragedy of the universe.' Instead of complaining or cursing the darkness we must light our candle, recognizing the shortness of the time allotted to us. The night can come when no one can work.

The demonstration

Jesus healed the physical blindness in an unusually elaborate way. He took clay, mixed it with his spittle, anointed the man's eyes with the mixture, and told him to go and wash in the pool of Siloam. *Then he went and washed and came back able to see* (v. 7). When Jesus had healed so many, so often, with a mere word or a simple touch, why in this case these strange additions?

Some commentators think that Jesus was here making a concession to a superstition strongly held by the blind man that such a mixture of clay with the spittle of a holy man would have magical properties. The clay, the spittle and the washing can be interpreted, however, as signs deliberately given even more for the sake of the onlookers, including his own disciples, than for the sake of the man. He was giving them all a message about himself and his work.

Was this case before him not that of a man who from the beginning of his earthly life had never had eyes to see? If he were to be given sight would it not require a miracle, not simply of ordinary healing, but of the same creative power as had been exercised by God when he was originally made? Moreover, in the beginning when God made Adam, did he not form him from the dust of the earth and breathe into his nostrils the breath of life? Therefore it may well be that Jesus took the dust of the earth and mixed it with something intimately from himself to demonstrate that in this miracle he was exercising the very power by which God created Adam at the beginning, and was doing it in much the same

154

way. If this is so, then the act of healing was thus 'clothed in allegory', and was meant to be understood in this way by the onlookers.

The sign, of course, sets the seal on the word Jesus had spoken to his disciples. It is a clear demonstration that where he brings his influence to bear we can always expect the impossible.   No situation on earth is ever so chaotic, degenerate or perverted that his touch and word today cannot transform it. Where he is active, 'everything old has passed away; see, everything has become new!' (2 Cor. 5:17).

The preparation for rebirth

As we follow through the story, our attention is suddenly switched from what Jesus said to the disciples in word and sign. We now find ourselves in the midst of the quite mundane and yet fascinating details of what happened, possibly over a prolonged period, to the man who had received his physical sight. Like that of the woman at the well, it is an intimate story of the search of a soul for rebirth and renewal.

We have a key to understanding the whole incident if we notice that very soon after he begins to enjoy the marvellous social and physical freedom Jesus has now given him, one great question begins to dominate his mind: What is he to think of Jesus, and how is he to speak of him? Moreover, he has become gripped by the belief that this man Jesus has more to give him than he has already received simply on the physical level.

With his own ears he had heard Jesus claiming to be *the light of the world* (v. 5) and though he has now seen the beauty of the earth and the glorious light of an ordinary day, he wants to be able to see the full radiance of that other light too. The story of his pilgrimage therefore becomes not only that of a mind searching after the truth about Jesus, but also that of a heart more and more gripped by a desire to meet him again and receive from him more of his gifts in their fullness.

We can clearly trace the development in his thinking about Jesus, as he meets other people and is encouraged to talk about what has happened to himself. First of all he has to tell his former neighbours that *the man called Jesus* has healed him. He never forgot the kindness of that touch and the wonderfully sympathetic words he had overheard as Jesus has spoken about him to his disciples as a man destined for the glory of God (v. 3). No other person had ever made him feel that way!

The next factor in his development is his astonishment in hearing the controversy among the Pharisees when they first considered his case. Some of them tried to warn him against Jesus—a sinner who had deliberately and in public broken the sabbath! But others of them, on hearing him, shared his own wonderment. They challenged him to give his own thoughts, and in an inspired moment he moved towards the truth: *'He is a prophet'* (v. 17). Then he makes a decisive discovery—that where opposition to Jesus is found, it is always accompanied by a fear and hatred of him that excludes respect for his obvious truth and goodness.

The Pharisees reveal first their obstinate reluctance to face unwanted facts. They have to call his parents to prove that the miracle had really taken place. They then reveal their deviousness, suggesting to his mind that the miracle was to be attributed to a sheer unique act of God himself, and that Jesus had somehow cunningly managed to cash in on it and take the credit to himself. They continue to insist that a man who is such a sinner could not possibly have done such a thing. In a long drawn-out final conversation the man finds himself with surprising boldness entering the controversy between Jesus and his enemies decidedly on the side of Jesus, and in a moment of suddenly inspired 'obstinacy' on his part (cf. Mark 13:11), he affirms that Jesus must have come uniquely *from God* and that *'Never since the world began...'* (v. 32) was there such a man as this!

As his thinking thus develops so his devotion and desire for Jesus himself also increase. The shock of his parents' disloyalty may even have brought him a measure of shame, loneliness and suffering, and finally under the hatred of those whose authority he had challenged he finds himself cruelly excommunicated and cast out of the social life of his community.

It is at this very moment that Jesus comes to seek him out. We are meant to understand that all through his mental perplexity and searching, Jesus had been there in the background inspiring his very seeking so that he might find (Matt. 7:7). We are meant also to understand that the feeling of isolation brought upon him by the desertion of his parents and the cruel final persecution had their part to play in bringing him towards the glorious light that now comes to him with the presence of Jesus. 'It was in the school of affliction,' it is said of Oliver Cromwell, 'that he was kept till he had learned the lesson of the Cross, till his will was broken into submission to the Will of God. Religion was thus "laid into his soul with hammer and fire"; it did not come in only as light into his understanding.'

Yet it is what Jesus revealed and brought to this man quite suddenly during this final decisive encounter that made everything that had so far happened to him worthwhile. Otherwise the great miracle of his cure at the pool, his brave search for the truth and his defence of Jesus against his enemies would have been fruitless. It is as if Jesus, when he comes to this man, brings with him an open door into an entirely new world of thought and experience. His longing to believe is suddenly transformed into radiant faith. He seeks to know from Jesus alone what he must now think about Jesus himself. How futile his former thoughts have been! Could he possibly have escaped a sense of his own sinfulness as, yielding to Jesus' grace and love, *he worshipped him* (v. 38).

This is indeed the worship 'in spirit' (4:23) of which Jesus spoke to the woman at the well, and which he sought from her. We must not underestimate the worth of the orderly and liturgical worship 'in truth' which we regularly offer to God within his church week by week. Unless our liturgical worship, however, is often punctuated by such living encounters with Jesus himself (cf. Rev. 1:10-13) there will be unreality both in our church services and in our confessions of our faith. The truest worship is given spontaneously from the heart when the Holy Spirit enables us to see who Jesus is. This man is not yet able to express his faith and devotion in the biblical or philosophical language that we incorporate in our great creeds or liturgical services. But his eyes have indeed been opened to see what Peter saw when in his fishing boat he felt compelled to fall at Jesus' feet (Luke 5:8).

Signs of present judgement

Many commentators on this passage call our attention to what happened simultaneously to the Pharisees in contrast to the formerly blind man. On the one hand, he has moved from interest in and gratitude to Jesus, on to inner rebirth, gradually increasing illumination and adoring worship. On the other hand, the Pharisees who have been questioning him have in the same process plunged themselves gradually into a darkness, expressed in their increasingly angry reviling and the final act of gross cruelty towards a perfectly innocent man who had done them no harm. Jesus claimed that he himself had been instrumental in setting this process in motion. He often declared that after his second coming there would take place a day of judgement when he would bring about a final complete separation between those who were for him and those who were against him. Here he points out that much that will be revealed and sealed in this final judgement is already taking place in history here and now.

Many of the Pharisees then around Jesus seemed to have been so blind that they were unaware of what was happening to them. Yet one or two of them took the hint that Jesus might have been referring to them. *'Surely we are not blind, are we?'*, they said. His reply with its urgent appeal and warning, must be allowed to come through to ourselves today, with its full original force and meaning: *'If you were blind, you would not have sin. But now that you say, "We see", your sin remains'* (v. 41).

One of the most important discoveries Jesus wants us to make is that of our own blindness to what he has come to reveal to us—a blindness both natural and cultivated. One of the great prophets simply and profoundly describes our state:

> For my thoughts are not your thoughts, nor are your ways my ways, says the LORD. For as the heavens are higher than the earth, so are my ways higher than your ways and my thoughts than your thoughts.
>
> (Isa. 55:8, 9)

On the most crucial matters of life and destiny we have to allow his truth to displace even the fondest ideas of our own minds, and we have to conform in our ways to the light that has shone into our darkness. Jesus described the knowledge of God and of himself as a mystery which God had 'hidden... from the wise and the intelligent and... revealed... to infants' (Matt. 11:25). Here he refers to it as revealed to the 'blind' and hidden from those who think they see.

A note on a parenthesis (v. 7)

This story was circulated in the New Testament church with a short parenthesis referring to the pool of Siloam, and indicating an interpretation of the washing incident which circulated with the story. We are informed that Siloam *means Sent*.

Those who were spoken of as the 'Sent' in the New Testament were the apostles, and there was verbal similarity between *'Siloam'* and *'Sent'* in the original languages. The narrator in re-telling the story could have intended us to notice the similarity between what happened to this man through washing in Siloam, and what can happen when Christians who enter the church are washed in baptism, which is indeed the pool of the apostles who were sent to preach, teach and baptize (Matt. 28:19, 20). Baptism was seen as a sign of rebirth and renewal that could bring the same kind of illumination as had come through the ministry of John the Baptist at the Jordan. The story of this man's pilgrimage from baptism towards faith and illumination, therefore, could be taken as an example of what could happen to those whom the apostles themselves washed in their own special pool of baptism. Indeed, often when people were baptized in the early church, this chapter of John's Gospel was read in the service.

Certainly it is true that often in the New Testament people were baptized after they came to faith in Jesus. Yet this order of experience was not invariable. Many of us today who were baptized in childhood will be able to recognize in this story elements of our personal pilgrimage from baptism to illumination and rebirth.

CHAPTER 10

THE GOOD SHEPHERD

John 10:1-18

10 'Very truly, I tell you, anyone who does not enter the sheepfold by the gate but climbs in by another way is a thief and a bandit. ²The one who enters by the gate is the shepherd of the sheep. ³The gatekeeper opens the gate for him, and the sheep hear his voice. He calls his own sheep by name and leads them out. ⁴When he has brought out all his own, he goes ahead of them, and the sheep follow him because they know his voice. ⁵They will not follow a stranger, but they will run from him because they do not know the voice of strangers.' ⁶Jesus used this figure of speech with them, but they did not understand what he was saying to them.

7 So again Jesus said to them, 'Very truly, I tell you, I am the gate for the sheep. ⁸All who came before me are thieves and bandits; but the sheep did not listen to them. ⁹I am the gate. Whoever enters by me will be saved, and will come in and go out and find pasture. ¹⁰The thief comes only to steal and kill and destroy. I came that they may have life, and have it abundantly.

11 'I am the good shepherd. The good shepherd lays down his life for the sheep. ¹²The hired hand, who is not the shepherd and does not own the sheep, sees the wolf coming and leaves the sheep and runs away—and the wolf snatches them and scatters them. ¹³The hired hand runs away because a hired hand does not care for the sheep. ¹⁴I am the good shepherd. I know my own and my own know me, ¹⁵just as the Father knows me and I know the Father. And I lay down my life for the sheep. ¹⁶I have other sheep that do not belong to this fold. I must bring them also, and they will listen to my voice. So there will be one flock, one shepherd. ¹⁷For this reason the Father loves me, because I lay down my life in order to take it up again. ¹⁸No one takes it from me, but I lay it down of my own accord. I have power to lay it down, and I have

power to take it up again. I have received this command from my Father.'

An offer of leadership

We are told that it was at the *festival of the Dedication... in Jerusalem* (v. 22) that Jesus made this claim to be *the good shepherd*. This festival was held annually in winter to commemorate the rededication of the temple after its cleansing and restoration under Judas Maccabeus[1]. During that festival there was read in the liturgy the passage in Ezekiel 34 in which God expresses his anger at those whom he calls the 'shepherds' of his flock. 'Shepherd' was the name he gave then to those to whom he had entrusted the political, moral and spiritual leadership of his people. But the leaders to whom he had entrusted so much had abused their power and privileges: 'you clothe yourselves with the wool, you slaughter the fatlings; but you do not feed the sheep. You have not strengthened the weak, you have not healed the sick... my sheep were scattered over all the face of the earth, with no one to search or seek for them.' It is in this passage that God promises that he himself will come to be the good shepherd of Israel: 'I myself will be the shepherd of my sheep, and I will make them lie down, says the Lord GOD. I will seek the lost... I will strengthen the weak, but the fat and the strong I will destroy. I will feed them with justice.'

Jesus took up this theme as he faced the crowd around him in the Temple. That old Scripture had come to life again! The false shepherds of his own day, the contemporary Jewish rulers, were all there listening to him. A day or two previously he had seen some of these very Pharisees cast out of their fellowship the man he himself had cured. Their treatment of him had been callous. He had been there in their midst blind and poor from his birth. Certainly they could not have cured his blindness, but they had not cared about his poverty. They had owed him welfare, wise

---

[1] In the mid 2nd Century BC, Antiochus, the mad, bad, dangerous successor of part of the empire of Alexander the Great, initiated degrading persecution on the Jews. He was opposed by a movement known as the Hasidim (men of the covenant), led by Judas Maccabeus, a warrior high priest, who by brilliantly using guerrilla warfare, defeated the occupying Syrian forces and cleansed the Temple in Jerusalem in 165BC. This event was commemorated by the annual Feast of Hanukkah or Dedication. (See Apocrypha, 2 Macc. 6 – 10.)

guidance, encouragement in goodness and true piety. Instead, for years they had neglected him. They had not known he existed, until Jesus had himself found him. Moreover, when he had come to their notice they had tried merely to bully him into mental submission and to tie him up in unhelpful discussion. Finally when he had refused to respond they had made him an outcast.

There facing Jesus were many of the common people of the day. They were completely and culpably blind to the scandal of what was happening around them. Like the parents of the man he had cured, they were unable even to see that in Jesus God himself had come to be their leader and they were meekly accepting the ruthless tyranny of those who had proved themselves more like wolves and thieves than shepherds. In what he said to his hearers Jesus exposed the abuses that they were so meekly accepting from those above them. He offered himself as their good Shepherd, even though they had already rejected him when he had offered himself as the 'bread of life' and as the 'light of the world'. He already knew that soon they were going to give their final verdict on him: 'We do not want this man to rule over us' (Luke 19:14).

'My sheep hear my voice'

As he faced what was certain rejection by his generation Jesus knew that the very death to which they were going to subject him would give him all the more right to lay claim to leadership not only of the Jewish nation, but of the whole human race. He therefore spoke as if he were addressing every generation. We can listen to these words he spoke in the Temple courts at the festival of Dedication just as if they were addressed to us in our present circumstances. He is offering himself to us today as our leader. He is warning us, too, against the faithless leaders around us, against the powers, principles, parties and personalities, which seek within our modern world to gain from us the kind of loyalty which he who alone has died for us has the right to demand.

We cannot help hearing the repeated promise. In every age it will happen. The good Shepherd will speak, and the sheep will follow him, for they know his voice (v. 3). They *follow him because they know his voice* (v. 4). *'They will listen to my voice'* (v. 16). *'My sheep hear my voice. I know them, and they follow me'* (v. 27). This is the way Jesus is going to gain possession in every age of the minds and hearts of those he wants in his service. They will hear him calling, inviting, commanding, and thus they will find themselves subtly and impellingly brought under his personal influence and guidance. As they listen and respond, his word will become the dominant force in shaping their lives and destiny.

The early chapters of the book of Proverbs give us a vivid picture of life as it confronted the young man in that ancient world. As he grows up and walks the streets of his world, voice after voice comes to him. His father and mother speak: 'Hear, my child, your father's instruction, and do not reject your mother's teaching' (1:8). But there are also 'sinners' who 'entice'. There is the thug who says, 'Come with us, let us lie in wait for blood' (1:10-11); there is the 'scoundrel' and 'villain' with a 'perverted mind devising evil' (6:12-14); there is also the harlot: 'I have decked my couch with coverings, coloured spreads of Egyptian linen; I have perfumed my bed.... Come, let us take our fill of love until morning.... For my husband is not at home' (7:16-19). But in the background, always wanting to save from destruction, and seeking to control all human ways, there is one persistent voice which he can heed if he wills, an unerring guide—the voice of wisdom: 'Does not wisdom call, and does not understanding raise her voice? On the heights, beside the way, at the crossroads she takes her stand... "To you, O people, I call, and my cry is to all that live"' (8:1-4). What she says is 'righteous' and 'better than jewels'. It enables kings to reign and 'to decree what is just' (8:11, 15).

Is this not a description of modern life too, as many of us grow up in it? Is there not one voice after another, calling, advertising, tempting, offering pleasure, profit or purpose in various mixtures, to be found in new ways or old ways, in bad ways or good ways, in easy ways or hard ways? Yet in the midst of this 'babel' of voices we can hear the voice of Jesus if we will. It is he who is described in the figure of 'wisdom' in that Old Testament passage. It is he who comes to make his call heard today so that those who are willing to follow may come to know that they are his sheep, and that under his guidance and control human history itself has a purpose and a meaning.

A place and a purpose in the kingdom of God

Sometimes when I pass through the concourse of a great international airport on a busy day and see masses of people of different races, colours and backgrounds milling here and there with such differing business on hand and varied aims for life, I find myself asking one or two inter-related questions. Is there one all-embracing purpose really being worked out in the midst of this mass of people with its great turbulent clash of human interests? Do I as an individual have a place in that purpose, and a personal destiny that really matters? It is the fact that in the midst of such a world Christ's sheep hear his voice, that gives me a sufficient answer.

Centuries ago Abraham lived in a city that was at the centre of international trade and travel in one of the busiest regions of the world. Some scholars suggest that he was a transport agent with a thriving business. Perhaps he too had all these questions about himself and this thronging world to ask. But he heard the voice of God. Abraham was told that the God of all the earth had indeed a purpose for all nations to be worked out through generations to come, that there was a task he himself had to fulfil in its present working out, and a place for himself and his children in its future glory. To know this changed his religion and his way of life. Above all, two of the most important facts about life became clear to him: The God of all the earth was working out a great purpose within its history, and Abraham and his family after him had a place within that purpose.

God continued to fulfil the promise given to Abraham to bring blessing to all nations. The Bible is the story of how under changing circumstances and in varied ways God never failed from generation to generation to call individuals and to make the same great news known: 'I have a purpose for this world, and a place for you to fulfil in it.' God called Moses at the bush, Samuel in the sacred tent, all the great judges, kings and prophets of Israel, John the Baptist, and the disciples in Galilee. Now today we have the church where he speaks again and again with the same purpose to those who are given ears to hear. The fact that I hear his word today gives me the assurance that he is still in business, with the same plan encompassing all nations, still determined finally, as we move forward to the last day, to solve for us all the problems of human sin, suffering and destiny.

When I hear his voice I know that I myself am not lost in the crowd. I matter to him. God knows my name. He made me what I am. He understands my history from my birth. I begin myself to know, understand and accept my place in the working out of his purpose. I know that he wants obedience from me. He wants at times to give me a new direction. He seeks time and again to bring me back into line. He continually empowers and liberates. His voice may not be loud and dominant within the modern world, for when he speaks he does not necessarily push himself into the media. It often comes to us as the quietly spoken voice in the background of life. We remember how once Elijah heard it. It came in a quiet voice after the earthquake, wind and fire had proved with all their spectacular fury that they had nothing of any importance to convey (1 Kgs 19:11-13). A foreman on a factory floor can lift up a telephone and, in the midst of the continuous clash and din of machinery with workers shouting at each other across the floor, can put his ear close to the receiver and hear the voice that matters with the message that matters.

The credentials of the true Shepherd

We have to take note at this point of how Jesus dealt directly with his contemporary situation. In a series of vivid pictures and comparisons he brings out the contrast between himself and the false leaders of his own day, especially the Pharisees, underlining at the same time some unique features of his own leadership. As we follow this theme we find, as we have already pointed out, that his purpose widens. We find him giving us the pattern which he wished to be followed by those who had responsibility for leadership in the service of his own church and kingdom. We find also that his teaching has something to say to us about the leadership we cultivate within the secular world today.

Jesus first of all contrasts the approach of those he calls *thieves and bandits* (vv. 1, 8), who come to steal our support and loyalty by their own cunning, with the frank approach of the leader who has a genuine cause. In making this comparison, he takes us immediately to the heart of modern life. Often, because the ideas and aims of a movement do not stand up under searching examination, its leaders and sponsors resort to subterfuge as they seek to win adherents. Only the best few cards are put on the table. Only partial aspects of the programme are presented, and great emphasis is laid on the need for the creation of a 'public image', often significantly different from the reality, by advertising and effective media coverage, to disarm suspicion and lull the critical facilities. Jesus aptly describes the furtiveness and stealth of such an approach, as he warns us to beware of the leader *who does not enter the sheepfold by the gate but climbs in by another way* (v. 1).

Jesus describes his own attitude. The shepherd who is worthy of trust is *one who enters by the gate* (v. 2). From the start nothing is hidden. There is no 'small print'. He himself is transparent and his teaching is like himself. He makes no attempt to woo people with attractive promises and free gifts, before the difficulties and demands are made clear. From the very beginning we know that there is sin to be faced, guilt to be settled, a cross to be taken up daily, and a self to be denied as well as glorious liberty, a place within the family of God, and a heaven to be gained.

Jesus contrasts the kind of relationship that is set up through his manner of open approach, with that created by the leader who takes another way. The *thieves and bandits* may indeed gain some kind of admittance and achieve some kind of following by their stealth. But there can never be anything truly deep or finally effective in the movement they create or its achievements. The openness and trustworthiness of the good shepherd, however, creates true openness, trust and loyalty in his sheep. As he makes his approach, *'The gatekeeper opens the gate for him, and the sheep hear his voice. He calls his own sheep by name and leads them out... and the sheep follow him because they know his voice'* (vv. 3, 4).

Moreover, Jesus observes, as his followers respond to him, one of the first things they learn is the ability to distinguish the genuine from the sham. They learn to shun the superficial and the twisted. Jesus therefore pictures what will happen when anyone with any deep insincerity makes his approach: *'They will not follow a stranger, but they will run from him because they do not know the voice of strangers'* (v. 5).

This description by Jesus of his own approach to his future mission, and of the people he is aiming to gather under his leadership, gives us cause for reflection and examination of our own presentation of the faith and our aim in building up his church. If we are not entirely sure of the convincing power of a completely clear and direct approach to people with the unabridged truth itself, are we not at times apt to lay too much emphasis on the technique of impressive presentation? Do we not then overvalue what we think is the effectiveness of 'personality' and 'charisma'? Do we not tend, moreover, to select those aspects of Jesus and his teaching which we imagine to be especially attractive to our hearers, and to hide what we think might put people off, thus adding a touch of deceit to our whole approach?

Perhaps some do not respond to us wholeheartedly because they feel almost unconsciously that we are not entirely true to either Jesus, or to life as it really is. Paul shows us more clearly the way appealed for by Jesus: 'We have renounced the shameful things that one hides; we refuse to practice cunning or to falsify God's word; but by the open statement of the truth we commend ourselves to the conscience of everyone in the sight of God' (2 Cor. 4:2).

We find that with the mention of the word *stranger* and his description of his own intimacy with his sheep, Jesus has led our thoughts into another contrast—that between the distance which often prevails between the secular leader and those led, and the intimate closeness with himself into which he seeks to draw those who follow him. There is no doubt that in certain spheres of the world's life effective leadership and authority is often maintained by artificial means and sometimes by a superficial show of dignity. In the armed forces and judiciary, uniforms with insignia and 'robes' of office are worn. In bureaucracy and business, authority is sometimes maintained by an official manner behind an office desk. Rules, ceremonies and etiquette become barriers to real closeness. The distance is sacrosanct.

Yet Jesus himself is satisfied with nothing less than the warm intimacy that inspires love and a much greater loyalty. *'I know my own and my own know me'* (v. 14). The good shepherd must call *his own sheep by name* (v. 3).

Other characteristics of Jesus' pastoral leadership come to mind as we read through his words about himself. His intimacy with us of course involves humility. Moreover, he is always available. No need to make appointments, or to observe office hours with this kind of leader—we can take up the telephone anytime!

As Jesus brings his discourse to an end, he takes us to the heart of his own ministry as he warns us of the dangers against which the sheep have no defence unless the leader is watchful and utterly loyal. He envisages such dangers everywhere. There is the false leader, the thief who *comes only to steal and kill and destroy* (v. 10). There is also the 'wolf', the threat of whose coming is so terrible that it scares away every type of leader, except those who are prepared to lay down their lives for the sheep (vv. 11-13). It would be justifiable to imagine the *thief* here to be the teachers of false doctrine (always a danger as they intrude in the church) and the *wolf* to be the anti-Christian persecutors of those who profess loyalty to the gospel.

Rather than give encouragement to such detailed speculation, Jesus is more concerned here to bring before us his own personal example of true watchfulness and loyalty. Recalling his experience of Palestine in former days, George Adam Smith writes: 'I do not remember ever to have seen in the East a flock of sheep without a shepherd... on some high moor—across which at night the hyenas howl—when you meet him sleepless, far-sighted, weather-beaten, armed, leaning on his staff and looking out over his scattered sheep, everyone of them on his heart, you understand... why Christ took him as the type of self-sacrifice.'

It is the danger that we might become 'hired hands' that occupies Jesus' mind as he draws his discourse to an end. Under the trials and dangers involved in his service, such a person *runs away because a hired hand does not care for the sheep* (v. 13). It is our inward attitude of mind that is here in question. Most of us who have taken on the responsibility of leadership within our community are of course paid teachers, probation officers, doctors, nurses, welfare workers and pastors too. There is nothing wrong in this: 'the labourer deserves to be paid' (Luke 10:7). What matters especially in the ministry of the church is that we should never come under the suspicion of being a 'hired hand'—calculating, bargaining, demanding, setting limits, expecting exemplary response from the sheep, and giving way to slackness or depression when our expectations are not met. The motto of the greatest of the apostles is in place here: 'I will most gladly spend and be spent for you' (2 Cor. 12:15).

One flock' one Shepherd

Towards the end of the discourse Jesus gives us one important direct glimpse into a future development which he wished to see in his church: *'I have other sheep that do not belong to this fold. I must bring them also, and they will listen to my voice. So there will be one flock, one shepherd'* (v. 16). When he was speaking, of course, Israel was *this fold* from which he was seeking to gather his own sheep. Even in the midst of this task, however, he speaks of those *other sheep* which he will gather from elsewhere—from all nations. Here is the vision, which he communicated to the apostles, of the world mission of the church—one flock and one shepherd.

This single text is not the best place from which to make comments on his desire for unity in his church, or on the larger church structure which can best express this unity. The whole passage before us, however, does suggest that Jesus envisaged everywhere the development of local churches, each under the ministry of its own *one shepherd* or pastor, who would reflect in his care for his flock the characteristics of leadership which have been so carefully described here in his discourse.

In the fulfilment of this ministry one of the chief tasks of local pastors is to preach so that people can hear the voice of the good Shepherd himself. There is no doubt that the Word of God will often have to be delivered and heard through their ministry in much the same way as many of the oracles of the prophets were delivered and heard by their contemporaries. Preaching, according to the New Testament, is often the public proclamation of the good news of the gospel, to whomsoever will hear, by the herald and messenger of God. Peter's great sermon on the day of Pentecost, and many other sermons in the book of Acts, were stirring public addresses, and Jesus himself preached at times in this way to great multitudes. Preaching even by local pastors to their congregations can be a very 'public' affair.

Yet many of us who have found ourselves called to minister to local congregations will find in this present chapter further important insights into our task as preachers. All the Gospels show that, though Jesus loved to address the crowds around him, he loved more to speak when he was face to face with a solitary individual talking about deeply individual matters. It was often through this kind of conversation that he won personal trust and forgave people their sins. He spoke of how he loved to seek out the one among the many (cf. Luke 15:7, 10) and once, when a huge crowd of people was thronging round him, he showed how sensitive he was to the mere touch of one poor woman who was desperately seeking his help (Mark 5:31). 'Many thronged him', said Augustine of this occasion, 'one touched him'. It has been observed that Jesus' 'best sermons' were sometimes preached to one person.

When pastors become fully aware that Jesus seeks, through the ministry of the pulpit, to enter this kind of private and personal conversation with those who are listening to the preaching, it can affect the manner and style of their speaking, and the structure of their ministry. Even though there may be a comparatively 'large' congregation in front of them, they will tend not to be satisfied simply with addressing people *en masse* in the hope that somehow some relevant word may be overheard here and there. They will, rather, be concerned to express their message as a word personally directed to a particular individual. They may tend to feel that a low-key conversational approach to their hearers is best fitted to the task. They may discover a way of putting things so that they can often address the individual at the same time as speaking to the crowd.

It is, moreover, both fitting and inevitable that pastors who find themselves engaged in such a ministry in the pulpit will endeavour to follow it up by seeking entrance, as far as is humanly possible, into the same kind of personal relationship with each member of the flock as Christ himself is seeking. They cannot allow themselves to remain in any way remote from their people—strangers whom the sheep *will not follow*. Because they have accepted the call to be shepherds, then by this capacity they belong to their flock and the flock to them. They will not be able to regard their ministry in the pulpit as sound, unless as a continuation of it they seek out their people where they are to be found with their questions and needs, both in the routine and especially in the sufferings of their ordinary lives. Their visitation of the flock, even though it may sometimes appear to be the fulfilment of a routine duty, can become a symbol of the continuing care and concern of Christ for each and all. Indeed at special times it can become a sign that the good Shepherd himself has laid down his life for the sheep.

We must not in any way undervalue the tradition, which, inspired by this chapter of John's Gospel, has persisted throughout church history, within every Christian denomination, of local pastors who give their lives to the ministry of word and sacrament, and to pastoral visitation. Paul at Ephesus first gave the example and laid down the standard in his sermon to the pastors there when he spoke of how 'for three years I did not cease night or day to warn everyone with tears', teaching 'publicly and from house to house', pleading with them: 'Keep watch over yourselves and over all the flock, of which the Holy Spirit has made you overseers, to shepherd the church of God that he obtained with the blood of his own Son' (Acts 20:20, 28, 31).

Of course within the church each member of the body is called in the name of Christ to serve both others and the whole body. A rich variety of differing ministries represents various aspects of the one ministry of Christ to the church. It is, however, through what the local pastor is called to do that the ministry of Christ, the good Shepherd, is most fully represented and can be made most fully effective. Calvin went to the length of saying that the pastor was the one whom above all Christ had appointed to 'represent his own person', and the 'chief sinew by which believers are held together in one body'. We have to ask ourselves whether the large size of some modern congregations does not prevent the pastor who preaches from reflecting fully enough the picture given here by Jesus, and whether even a team of other assistant pastors can really make up for the defects both in the image and in the preaching.

The appeal to enter the 'gate'

Many of Jesus' parables encourage us to think of his kingdom as an influence that can enter us here and now when we hear and receive the Word of God. It is like seed sown within us. It grows within us, affecting the life of the world around us, and thus human history. At the final great consummation at the end of history, everything that has been achieved through its influence will be harvested for God's eternal glory and use.

There are other parables, however, that encourage us to think of the kingdom of God not only as if it were a powerful inner influence on personal and social life, but as if it were a new world already existing alongside this world. Jesus likens it to another realm, the door into which is open here and now to all whom he invites in. To enter offers joyful fellowship, enlargement of life and blessedness. He spoke in this way when he described the kingdom as a wedding banquet (Matt. 22:1-10) or as a great supper into which the needy and deprived were even to be compelled to enter so that they might enjoy what was lavishly prepared and freely given. There was no need to wait: 'Come; for everything is ready now' (Luke 14:17).

Jesus is further encouraging us in this latter kind of thought about the kingdom when he says of himself, *'I am the gate'* (v. 7). In our personal encounter with him as he comes to us in the midst of this world's life, there is opened to us a way of entry, an access, into that new world of which he spoke in these parables. The suggestion is that we should think of ourselves, even while living within this present world, as always on the border of another. Jesus himself, who invites us into that other world, also leads us across and back over the border between the two. *He calls his own sheep by name and leads them out* (v. 3). He also *goes ahead of them* when he has *brought out all his own* (v. 4). We ourselves thus *come in and go out* by him. Jesus here describes himself as especially at home within that other world to which he is the *gate*. At times he calls us in there to himself to find pasture, only then to lead us back refreshed to our life on earth under his guidance.

Such thoughts of our life with Christ as lived between two realms became more explicit in the minds of the apostles, and were given a prominent part in their message. When they saw Jesus lifted up from the earth and disappearing, they thought of him as having gone back to the realm from which he had come. They believed that he had opened a way for them to have fellowship with him in heaven. But they experienced also the coming of the Holy Spirit, and they knew that he was also here and now with them on earth guiding and helping them always even 'to the end of the age'. When they spoke of their experience of him, therefore, they spoke not only of his presence with them on earth, but also of their having been 'translated' to be in some way and measure with him in heaven. There they had their 'citizenship' and their hidden life. They were already 'raised... up with him' and made to sit in 'heavenly places' (Phil. 3:20; Col. 3:3; Eph. 2:6). Already they had indeed had a foretaste or 'guarantee' of things to come, of the full inheritance which would finally be given to them when this present world had passed away (Eph. 1:14; Rom. 8:23).

We will perhaps understand best the thrust of Jesus' words about his being the *gate* if we look on them as a sudden and spontaneous evangelistic appeal prompted by some whom he spotted among his hearers. Might it not be that he saw Nicodemus there listening to him? There may also have been others whom he had challenged already to seek birth from above into the kingdom of God.

Some scholars think that we have in this discourse the account of two very different parables spoken on different occasions and now brought together. However, there is no need for such a hypothesis. Jesus is not here switching his thought from one theme to another.

He continues throughout to describe himself as the Shepherd. At
the end of this discourse he offers himself as the Shepherd who will
lead his sheep finally through death when it comes. In these verses
he is the Shepherd who here and now can lead us into that other
realm, the kingdom of which he so often speaks.

Accepting his leadership in orienting ourselves towards the world
to come, Jesus promises that we *will be saved* (v. 9). He regarded it
as tragic indeed that any of us should live with our treasure and our
reward only in what is found in this present world (Matt. 6:19-21;
Luke 12:16-21).

He promises, too, that we *will come in and go out and find
pasture* (v. 9). These phrases suggest an offer of liberty, satisfaction
and enlargement of experience such as those who live in this one
world alone can never attain. As the hymn writer put it:

> Solid joys and lasting pleasures,
> none but Zion's children know.'

One of the important factors in bringing about the conversion of
John Bunyan was his hearing 'godly talk' by a few older women.
'They spoke as if joy did make them speak', and there was 'such an
appearance of grace' in all that they said, that they seemed to have
found a new world to which he was altogether a stranger. Bunyan
was humbled, and drawn again and again into their company,
before he himself found the *gate* into that new world.

The Hardening of the Reluctant

John 10:19-42

10 Again the Jews were divided because of these words. ²⁰Many of
them were saying, 'He has a demon and is out of his mind. Why listen
to him?' ²¹Others were saying, 'These are not the words of one who has
a demon. Can a demon open the eyes of the blind?'

22 At that time the festival of the Dedication took place in Jerusalem.
It was winter, ²³and Jesus was walking in the temple, in the portico of
Solomon. ²⁴So the Jews gathered around him and said to him, 'How
long will you keep us in suspense? If you are the Messiah, tell us

plainly.' ²⁵Jesus answered, 'I have told you, and you do not believe. The works that I do in my Father's name testify to me; ²⁶but you do not believe, because you do not belong to my sheep. ²⁷My sheep hear my voice. I know them, and they follow me. ²⁸I give them eternal life, and they will never perish. No one will snatch them out of my hand. ²⁹What my Father has given me is greater than all else, and no one can snatch it out of the Father's hand. ³⁰The Father and I are one.'

31 The Jews took up stones again to stone him. ³²Jesus replied, 'I have shown you many good works from the Father. For which of these are you going to stone me?' ³³The Jews answered, 'It is not for a good work that we are going to stone you, but for blasphemy, because you, though only a human being, are making yourself God.' ³⁴Jesus answered, 'Is it not written in your law, "I said, you are gods"? ³⁵If those to whom the word of God came were called "gods"—and the scripture cannot be annulled—³⁶can you say that the one whom the Father has sanctified and sent into the world is blaspheming because I said, "I am God's Son"? ³⁷If I am not doing the works of my Father, then do not believe me. ³⁸But if I do them, even though you do not believe me, believe the works, so that you may know and understand that the Father is in me and I am in the Father.' ³⁹Then they tried to arrest him again, but he escaped from their hands.

40 He went away again across the Jordan to the place where John had been baptizing earlier, and he remained there. ⁴¹Many came to him, and they were saying, 'John performed no sign, but everything that John said about this man was true.' ⁴²And many believed in him there.

A division

If Jesus was to be crucified there had to be a hard enough core of important people determined to take whatever risk might be involved in order to carry the whole affair to the end. We have already seen how during the controversy in the temple at the festival of Booths, one partly sympathetic section of the crowd became wholly alienated from him as, listening to him more carefully than before, they took offence at his claim to be uniquely related to God. This section of the narrative tells how another significant minority among the Jews, at first uncertain and hesitant to condemn him, finally threw in their lot with the majority.

After they had listened to his discourse on the good shepherd they were finding it difficult to resist the strength of his appeal to what was still left of honesty in their nature, and they may have been unhappy about the irrationality and bitterness their leadership was showing in the affair. They found it impossible to take seriously the accusation that he had a demon (v. 20), asking, *'Can a demon open the eyes of the blind?'* (v. 21). Yet they found aspects of his teaching disturbing and they were not able to define the reason.

They formed themselves as a group apart from those who had already made up their minds, and they went to Jesus hoping he would say something that would help them come to an independent decision. They stated clearly what they felt they had against him, *'How long will you keep us in suspense? If you are the Messiah, tell us plainly'* (v. 24). Listening to him they had become confused. Sometimes they had been thrilled with what he had said. At other times he said things they did not expect their kind of Christ to claim.

It must have taken Jesus by surprise to be accused of lack of clarity—the very fault he had always shunned, and for which he had so severely blamed the false teachers of his day. He immediately pointed out that the confusion lay entirely within their own minds: *'you do not believe, because you do not belong to my sheep'* (v. 26). Since the fault lay in themselves, the cure also lay in themselves. They must now allow his clear light to cast out the darkness of their own minds and in this way decide to belong to him. His word brings before us again the challenge we have heard at least twice before in this Gospel: the challenge to an obedience prior to understanding, to a response with our wills and minds so that we may have freedom from suspense and doubt (John 7:17; 8:31, 2).

Attracted' yet troubled

At the same time he gave them another chance to come to the very decision they had so far evaded. The point at which we are most likely to win people over to the faith is often the point which on first encounter tends to offend them. Jesus therefore had to challenge them again with some of the very words that had already attracted yet troubled them, involving them in controversy with their fellow Jews. He again made it clear that if they were to become his disciples they must indeed become like sheep before him, ready to be led, with minds open to his own personal influence; *'My sheep hear my voice. I know them, and they follow me'* (v. 27).

Having made his challenge and demands perfectly clear he added no less clear words of promise and assurance: *'I give them eternal life, and they will never perish. No one will snatch them out of my hand'* (v. 28). Of course, knowing his custom we expect the word that followed. He nearly always spoke about the Father when he spoke about his own place in the eternal world: *'What my Father has given me'*, he said, *'is greater than all else, and no one can snatch it out of the Father's hand. The Father and I are one'* (vv. 29, 30).

Did ever the light of truth and heaven shine as clearly into the darkness of the human mind as it did to those who first heard these words from Jesus? Through the centuries they have often become the chief source of comfort, assurance and strength to doubting and sincere souls, sometimes at the point of despair, sometimes at death. Yet at the time they were spoken, those at whom they were aimed heard only what shocked them: *'you, though only a human being, are making yourself God'*, they said and *'took up stones again to stone him'* (vv. 33, 31). It is to be noted that they took up the stones before they began any further discussion with him.

Jesus began his defence with a simple appeal to them to become reasonable, and to see how foolish and unjust they were becoming through the inner hatred that was unmasking itself: *'I have shown you many good works from the Father. For which of these are you going to stone me?'* (v. 32). It was the same kind of self-defence with which, when struck by the officer of the high priest, he made his reply: 'If I have spoken wrongly, testify to the wrong. But if I have spoken rightly, why do you strike me?' (18:23).

It is perhaps significant that they did not attempt to answer him. The question therefore still remains open and unanswered today in the midst of so much reactionary, confused and often irrational criticism of what traditional Christianity has done for us. It comes as a challenge to probe our motives and the facts of the case: 'Honestly, does anything I have done justify the stones you have in your hand?'

The argument from Scripture with which Jesus followed this protest is bound to seem strange to us. The Psalmist in one place had even used the term 'gods' to describe earthly rulers. Why then should they raise such strong objection to the language Jesus had used? It was the kind of argument they used with each other in their own theological discussion, and Jesus knew they were at home with it.

A place of retreat

We are now told about the place of retreat in which Jesus had been able to find safety, and indeed a place to work in, during the days in which he had to wait until he knew he had to appear again in Jerusalem to bring everything to a head. It was *across the Jordan to the place where John had been baptizing earlier* (v. 40). The Baptist's influence was there still powerful and lasting. It is at this point that we hear the final and perhaps the finest testimony to John's ministry: *John performed no sign, but everything that John said about this man was true* (v. 41).

CHAPTER 11

THE RAISING OF LAZARUS (1)

(The 7th Sign)

John 11:1-16

11 Now a certain man was ill, Lazarus of Bethany, the village of Mary and her sister Martha. ²Mary was the one who anointed the Lord with perfume and wiped his feet with her hair; her brother Lazarus was ill. ³So the sisters sent a message to Jesus, 'Lord, he whom you love is ill.' ⁴But when Jesus heard it, he said, 'This illness does not lead to death; rather it is for God's glory, so that the Son of God may be glorified through it.' ⁵Accordingly, though Jesus loved Martha and her sister and Lazarus, ⁶after having heard that Lazarus was ill, he stayed two days longer in the place where he was.

7 Then after this he said to the disciples, 'Let us go to Judea again.' ⁸The disciples said to him, 'Rabbi, the Jews were just now trying to stone you, and are you going there again?' ⁹Jesus answered, 'Are there not twelve hours of daylight? Those who walk during the day do not stumble, because they see the light of this world. ¹⁰But those who walk at night stumble, because the light is not in them.' ¹¹After saying this, he told them, 'Our friend Lazarus has fallen asleep, but I am going there to awaken him.' ¹²The disciples said to him, 'Lord, if he has fallen asleep, he will be all right.' ¹³Jesus, however, had been speaking about his death, but they thought that he was referring merely to sleep. ¹⁴Then Jesus told them plainly, 'Lazarus is dead. ¹⁵For your sake I am glad I was not there, so that you may believe. But let us go to him.' ¹⁶Thomas, who was called the Twin, said to his fellow-disciples, 'Let us also go, that we may die with him.'

Our human intimacies and eternal life

'I am convinced', wrote Paul, 'that neither death, nor life, nor angels, nor rulers, nor things present, nor things to come, nor powers, nor height, nor depth, nor anything else in all creation, will be able to separate us from the love of God in Christ Jesus our Lord' (Rom. 8:38, 39). These words are often read at funerals, because they give us all the assurance we need that there is a life after death for each individual with whom God has been able to establish a warm and close relationship. He will not allow death to deprive him of such a friend. As we have seen, Jesus himself expressed the same kind of argument for life after death when, having described the close earthly relationship between his sheep and himself, he said, '*I give them eternal life, and they will never perish*' (10:28).

After having heard Jesus state so clearly in the tenth chapter of John that not even death can separate him from his friends, we find him here in the eleventh chapter acting out in real life exactly what he has said. A crucial challenge and a divinely planned opportunity came to him to do so. Lazarus, a very special friend of his, has taken ill. His sisters sent Jesus an urgent message, hoping he would hurry to their home to cure their brother before he died. But Jesus was so far away that by the time the message reached him Lazarus was dead. Jesus knew it, and deliberately stayed a further two days in the town where he was at that time. Yet he felt immediately challenged by the message and recognized his opportunity. He had already spoken of the hour *when the dead will hear the voice of the Son of God, and those who hear will live* (5:25). He was now in a position to give a sign—it would probably be his last and greatest sign!—of how his friend Lazarus, even buried in his grave for four days, yet not separated from him, could hear his voice and come back to life.

This particular sign brings to us more than the mere assurance of our individual survival after death. It enables us to see beyond this life into something of the next. We sometimes ask what is it like—that life after death? The New Testament in its answer, in order to comfort us, sometimes resorts simply to negatives: 'Death will be no more; mourning and crying and pain will be no more' (Rev. 21:4; cf. 21:23, 27; 22:3–5). Here in this chapter, however, we are given a more positive and revealing hint about it: *Jesus loved Martha and her sister and Lazarus* (v. 5). This simple statement would be superfluous here, were it not meant by the writer to convey infinite meaning.

Is it not the case that very often the most precious characteristics that mark us out in human life as distinctive individuals are given their fullest expression, and can be appreciated most, within the closest ties which God enables us to form with each other? This can be true, not only within the life of a family, but also sometimes within ordinary friendship. Indeed what is of most value in our human nature can often unfold and develop best within such close relationships. Jesus enjoyed being in the midst of the circle of intimacy within this closely bound family at Bethany. Of course he had a distinctive place for each in his heart, but he valued them more fully and appreciated them best as he watched them together.

Jesus therefore made his journey that day to Bethany not only because he wanted to raise Lazarus but also because he wanted to restore what Martha, Mary and Lazarus together had given him. He hated even the thought of the break-up by death of those tender and true relationships in which his personal human life had found enrichment. The special mention here of this intention as being in his mind and heart surely encourages us to hope and believe that he has the same love today for what people are in their togetherness. He also has the same concern to restore in the life to come the precious relationships and friendships which have formed, because he led, guided and enriched the human life into which he found entrance.

Jesus cared, and still cares, about family life. His teaching shows how closely he was involved in every detail of it, in all its tensions, anxieties, sorrows and joys. It may be a significant feature of John's Gospel that both the first and the last of the miracles we are shown reveal his concern for the family. They tell us that we need him amongst us continually, both when we are in the midst of our happy home celebrations, and also our deepest family sorrows. They reveal that he hated everything that can destroy its health or break it up, and that he is willing to be in the midst whether it be in joy or sorrow to give his saving help.

An illness, for the glory of God

The request to go to Bethany meant much more to Jesus than simply a call from friends for help, for it was an opportunity, in the remaining days before his own death and resurrection, to stage the most remarkable sign of his whole ministry.

For weeks he had been waiting for a sign from his Father that the time had come for him to challenge his enemies in the Jewish community to do their worst, fulfil their plans and put him to death.

The Gospel story makes it clear that the exact day could not be decided by the Jews. They would have had it all over by now if it had been in their power to do so. Jesus, up till now, had felt that the time had not yet come, and had himself been hesitant. While he had continued to provoke the anger of his enemies, he had often withdrawn himself when the tension was mounting dangerously, and at this particular period had deliberately retreated to a safe distance. He had been waiting for the Father to decide and to let him know. Complete clarity about the way ahead came to him, however, immediately the message from the sisters arrived. He knew that the time had come, and that what had happened to Lazarus was God's way of setting in motion the whole final chain of events that was to bring salvation to the world he loved so much. He said, *'This illness does not lead to death; rather it is for God's glory, so that the Son of God may be glorified through it'* (v. 4).

John's Gospel, in its story of the last days of Jesus, makes it clear that the raising of Lazarus, witnessed by a large gathering of people, was a decisive factor in forcing the hand of the Jews. They were suddenly afraid of the possibility that he might again become popular, and were forced into desperate and speedy action. Indeed because the raised Lazarus was such a convincing proof of Jesus' power, they now planned to put him to death (11:45, 53; 12:9-10).

When Jesus realized how significant for himself and his purposes the hour was, *he stayed two days longer in the place where he was* (v. 6). Possibly he wanted to ensure that death would have such a firm hold over Lazarus that he could demonstrate all the more triumphantly that he had come indeed to release his people from its power.

Other reasons for the delay also come to our mind. He may have felt that at such a momentous turn of events he needed time to think things out, to collect himself, pray and plan. Though inwardly in sacrificial tension, it has to be made clear that he makes his way towards the cross with sovereign majesty. He is himself master of the whole situation. It was not fitting that he should appear now to be under compulsion or in haste. *'I lay down my life in order to take it up again. No one takes it from me, but I lay it down of my own accord'* (10:17, 18).

Twelve hours in a day

The writer of the narrative brings out the contrast between the majestic courage and calmness of Jesus and the fear that tended to invade the minds of his disciples. It had been haunting them at times since they finally left Galilee to go towards Jerusalem. At one juncture on that journey, as Jesus was walking ahead of them, 'they were amazed, and those who followed were afraid' (Mark 10:32). Now they expressed their fear also on his account: '*Rabbi, the Jews were just now trying to stone you, and are you going there again?*' (v. 8). Thomas had to rally them in their hesitancy: '*Let us also go, that we may die with him*' (v. 16).

Jesus at this moment expressed his mind and revealed the secret of his own majesty and peace in a word with which he tried both to encourage and warn them. It comes to us as one of these sayings with which his followers in every age are meant to live: '*Are there not twelve hours of daylight? Those who walk during the day do not stumble, because they see the light of this world. But those who walk at night stumble, because the light is not in them*' (vv. 9, 10).

Those who read and ponder the Old Testament will understand some of the thoughts that were on Jesus' mind as he faced this last phase of his life on earth. Waiting for his 'time' to come he may have had thoughts about the third chapter of Ecclesiastes: 'there is… a time for every matter under heaven… a time for war, and a time for peace' (Eccl. 3:1, 8). At the same time he may have been dwelling on the utterance of the Psalmist which occupied his mind during his hours on the cross:

> But I trust in you, O LORD;
> I say, 'You are my God.'
> My times are in your hand;
> deliver me from the hand of my enemies....
>
> (Ps. 31:14-15)

Undoubtedly before he spoke to his disciples he had in mind one of these eloquent and penetrating warnings uttered by Jeremiah to Israel:

> Give glory to the LORD your God
> before he brings darkness,
> and before your feet stumble
> on the mountains at twilight;
> while you look for light,

he turns it into gloom
and makes it deep darkness.

(Jer. 13:16)

He himself was taking this warning to heart: only if we live giving glory to God in perfect obedience can we walk in the daylight granted to us by God. Any attempt to evade that way involves us in the darkness and danger in which we will inevitably become lost.

We can understand from such inner thoughts the meaning of his own unforgettable word: each of us on our way has an exactly appointed day of life before us—a full twelve hours. Whether we live for 20 years or 50 years or 80 years, our days are all written in his book (Ps. 139:16). Duty is above everything, and duty, whether life be long or short, can make it full. And if it be full even though it has been but a breath on a glass, it has had its twelve hours. The pathos of life lies not in its shortness but in its misuse, whether long or short. For it is not quantity that counts but quality.

On the BBC overseas service I once heard an interview with a woman who had been told that she had only two or three weeks to live. She was about forty, had three teenage children, and had always been a committed Christian. She was being interviewed by her local pastor with his tape recorder. She began by saying how glad she was that her doctor had respected her enough to tell her the truth. She was asked if her values had changed now—and what did she regret most about the past? 'I wish I had played a little more with the children, and prayed more', she said. 'And what kind of thing do you want to do now?' she was asked. 'Well', she replied, 'just to go on doing what has to be done: living, loving, rejoicing.'

The Raising of Lazarus (2)

John 11:17-44

11 When Jesus arrived, he found that Lazarus had already been in the tomb for four days. [18]Now Bethany was near Jerusalem, some two miles away, [19]and many of the Jews had come to Martha and Mary to console them about their brother. [20]When Martha heard that Jesus was coming, she went and met him, while Mary stayed at home. [21]Martha said to Jesus, 'Lord, if you had been here, my brother would not have died. [22]But even now I know that God will give you whatever you ask of him.' [23]Jesus said to her, 'Your brother will rise again.' [24]Martha said to him, 'I know that he will rise again in the resurrection on the last day.' [25]Jesus said to her, 'I am the resurrection and the life. Those who believe in me, even though they die, will live, [26]and everyone who lives and believes in me will never die. Do you believe this?' [27]She said to him, 'Yes, Lord, I believe that you are the Messiah, the Son of God, the one coming into the world.'

28   When she had said this, she went back and called her sister Mary, and told her privately, 'The Teacher is here and is calling for you.' [29]And when she heard it, she got up quickly and went to him. [30]Now Jesus had not yet come to the village, but was still at the place where Martha had met him. [31]The Jews who were with her in the house, consoling her, saw Mary get up quickly and go out. They followed her because they thought that she was going to the tomb to weep there. [32]When Mary came where Jesus was and saw him, she knelt at his feet and said to him, 'Lord, if you had been here, my brother would not have died.' [33]When Jesus saw her weeping, and the Jews who came with her also weeping, he was greatly disturbed in spirit and deeply moved. [34]He said, 'Where have you laid him?' They said to him, 'Lord, come and see.' [35]Jesus began to weep. [36]So the Jews said, 'See how he loved him!' [37]But some of them said, 'Could not he who opened the eyes of the blind man have kept this man from dying?'

38   Then Jesus, again greatly disturbed, came to the tomb. It was a cave, and a stone was lying against it. [39]Jesus said, 'Take away the stone.' Martha, the sister of the dead man, said to him, 'Lord, already there is a stench because he has been dead for four days.' [40]Jesus said to her, 'Did I not tell you that if you believed, you would see the glory of God?' [41]So they took away the stone. And Jesus looked upwards and said, 'Father, I thank you for having heard me. [42]I knew that you always hear me, but I have said this for the sake of the crowd standing here, so that they may believe that you sent me.' [43]When he had said this, he cried with a loud voice, 'Lazarus, come out!' [44]The dead man came out, his hands and feet bound with strips of cloth, and his face wrapped in a cloth. Jesus said to them, 'Unbind him, and let him go.'

Bethany and Jerusalem

Bethany, we are told, was about *two miles away* from Jerusalem. It was far enough away to have a distinct community life of its own. It was no doubt one of the deliberate purposes of the evangelist to give us this pleasant glimpse of social life in Bethany in order to show us that life around the city could go on here and there with sanity and sweetness, even at the same time as the atmosphere at the centre of things was growing heavy with gross corruption and hatred of God, thus becoming void of goodness. The writer of this Gospel was not anti-Semitic. He wants us to know that *many of the Jews*, the local friends of Mary and Martha, were normal, kindly, good people. When Lazarus died they all rallied round their bereaved friends, shared with them their faith in the final resurrection of the dead, and brought them the comfort of their presence. They helped and encouraged them to weep, for this was the best therapy treatment they could give to each other in those days.

As the story proceeds, however, we are soon sharply to be reminded again of the contrast between these Jews and those within the city who were consumed by hatred of Jesus. There is an ominous note here in the mention that Bethany (though two miles away) was yet *near Jerusalem* (v. 18). It was too near! What was so tender and human in Bethany was all too easily soon to become infected and destroyed by the powers that be in Jerusalem. It was the usual tragic story of what happens to goodness and truth when a people allow themselves to be taken over by evil leaders and powers. It tormented a prophet like Jeremiah to see such a situation in his day, and to know so certainly that corruption and godlessness had taken a strong grip of the social and religious life of his people. Indeed, what still remained of true worth and simple human goodness would inevitably become crushed in the judgement he himself had finally to pronounce in the name of God upon the whole nation.

Jesus, Martha and Mary

When Jesus arrived he found that Martha and Mary were both troubled especially about the way this apparent tragedy had overtaken their family circle. Up to the end of his illness they had been praying fervently, watching and hoping that the Master would come before their brother died. They had all the more difficulty in accepting what had happened because their hope had been so strong. They were reproaching themselves for not realizing sooner how critical the illness really was, and for not sending the message earlier. And why had Jesus himself taken so long in arriving? Both of them unburdened their hearts and minds to him with the same words '*Lord, if you had been here, my brother would not have died*' (vv. 21, 32).

How human they were! So often after every kind of tragedy and break-up in a home, the same reproachful self-questioning can come to ourselves. We feel that so little on our part, and perhaps on the part of others, could have made such a difference to life—a little more alertness, care, wisdom, sensitivity to feelings that might be hurt, and the death or the alienation or the divorce might not have happened. And how human their relationship with Jesus was! They knew him well enough to voice all their self-regrets to him, as the Psalmists so often did in their prayers of complaint to God.

When he heard it from Mary, he wept with her (v. 35). He understood perfectly how she felt. He appreciated that she found her relief in simply weeping when he was there. When he heard it from Martha with whom he had a quite different relationship, he spoke to her the kind of word he knew would give her hope.

He did not try to apologize to either of them or to give any explanation of why it had happened. They at least had the comfort of his presence. With him there they were assured more than ever that God himself cared. As Martha began speaking to him she felt that all was well: '*But even now I know that God will give you whatever you ask of him*' (v. 22). They could not help trusting him as they had always done. After all, it was a proof of how much he cared that he had undertaken the journey in the face of the threats to his life that had been so recently rumoured. How much he had brought in bringing himself!

Though Jesus shows himself so much at one with them, the very conversation which follows Martha's sad, yet confident, greeting shows how unable they themselves are to be at one with him. It is sometimes pointed out that in none of the Gospels do we have any record of Jesus praying with his disciples. He prays for them, and teaches them to pray, but in his own praying he is shown always alone. In this incident, however, we see him at least expressing the desire for human help and fellowship in his own praying to the Father, but failing to find it.

What he wanted from them was that they, as well as he himself, might be expectantly prepared for the sign that was to happen, and even to pray for it. He was always sensitive to the conditions in which he had to work. Of course he had done mighty works even when the atmosphere around him gave no encouragement and there was no expectation of miracle. But he had often found it helpful and encouraging when people around him had themselves been hopeful and prayerful, and he had been at all times thrilled to find them persistent in their demands and great in their faith. Here at Bethany he knew himself challenged to an effort that was to tax his own faith, expectancy and self-giving as no other had ever done. He did not want to go to that grave-side entirely isolated and alone in mind and spirit, amongst such a huge crowd of mere onlookers. He therefore sought to find real support in the fellowship and faith of his two friends. In this case it was Martha he felt he must first approach. It was she who first met him. She was the key person who controlled everything that went on around the home. He knew, too, that he would ultimately need her practical co-operation, for if the stone of the tomb was to be rolled open, it was she who would have to give the order (v. 39f.).

He lost no time. When she started the conversation on his arrival, he broke in with the news: *'Your brother will rise again'* (v. 23). The confidence in his voice and the look in his eyes should have helped her to grasp that he meant, 'I have come to do it *here and now*'! But there was not a spark of kindled expectancy. She did not even pause to ask him what he meant, but rattled on as if he was merely repeating a dogmatic and pastoral platitude. They had discussed, time and again before, the subject of when the last day might come, and how the dead will all rise. *'I know'*, she said, *'that he will rise again in the resurrection on the last day'* (v. 24).

He made one last effort to switch her mind back from the distant future to the present day, and from dogma to reality. He did it in one of those eloquent and appealing words into which he had the habit of putting so much of himself, a word spoken as if he were addressing not simply the soul there before him, but every coming generation, each with its need to hear the same invitation and to listen for the same assurance. He said, *'I am the resurrection and the life. Those who believe in me, even though they die, will live, and everyone who lives and believes in me will never die'* (v. 25).

He pressed the challenge home: *'Do you believe this?'* He hoped that she would realize now that he had marvellous news to tell her about Lazarus, herself and her home, here and now. But he found her simply reiterating her agreement with what everyone in his small band of disciples was by now saying about him. *'Yes, Lord, I believe that you are the Messiah, the Son of God, the one coming into the world.'* It certainly was a glorious confession but he had wanted even more. He had no opportunity to test Mary herself in the same way. She was at the centre of a large crowd of mourners. He knew it was no use trying. It was undoubtedly with disappointment that, as so often before, having looked round for human understanding and help, he found it lacking. He had so much to give, and they would take only so little! So far they would go, and no further.

The sign, the agony and the prayer

In the spectacular procession of signs that we have witnessed as we have read through this Gospel, Jesus has shown himself able to meet whatever form of human need was brought before him, often dramatically majestic, always calm and in control even of the natural world around him. Yet never have we seen him so majestic as he is here. Never has his word been uttered in such a dramatic situation—the large crowd not knowing what is to happen, gathered to watch the tomb opened, the corpse in full view, the command loudly and deliberately given: *'Lazarus, come out!'* And it happened: *'The dead man came out, his hands and feet bound with strips of cloth, and his face wrapped in a cloth'* (v. 44). The word of God has the power to recall into his presence one who has passed through death, to reverse decay and corruption, and to bring the tied-up body out of its tomb.

There is one striking feature in the Christ who works so marvellously that we have not previously been allowed to glimpse in this Gospel. As he approaches the tomb, he is revealed as inwardly engaged in a deep struggle. When he allowed himself to be overcome at the sight of Mary and her friends in tears, we are told that *he was greatly disturbed in spirit and deeply moved* (v. 33). We further read that *Jesus, again greatly disturbed, came to the tomb* (v. 38). Commentators often translate these phrases in language more intense in its implications. One translates it: 'he shuddered, moved with the deepest emotion'. Others mention his

188

'groaning in spirit' and 'groaning within himself'. It is sometimes pointed out that John's Gospel gives us no account of Jesus' agony in the Garden of Gethsemane, and it is suggested that we are meant to think of this agony as the beginning of a long-drawn-out 'passion' that came to its full intensity as he went on his way to Calvary.

In the prayer of thanksgiving which he uttered when the stone was removed— *'Father, I thank you for having heard me'* —it becomes clear that, from the moment he knew that he had to raise Lazarus, he had been engaged in praying that it might be so. His intercession had been continuous throughout his journey to Bethany and had become more and more intense, finding its expression in his inward agony as the time came closer. Calvin understands the gaze he gave to heaven as a sign of the intensity of his prayer and as an example to us all: 'The fervour of prayer often affects the body in such a way that the body unwittingly follows the mind of its own accord. We certainly cannot doubt that when Christ raised his eyes to heaven he was carried thither with extraordinary vehemence.'

As he prayed thus, and as his prayer was being answered, he taught us something about the place such prayer had always played in his own life's ministry: *'I knew that you always hear me, but I have said this for the sake of the crowd standing here, so that they may believe that you sent me'* (v. 42). At Carmel Elijah drew attention to his prayer and its answer in order to let the Israelites know that there was a God in Israel and that he himself was his servant (1 Kgs 18:36). Jesus here wants his praying to be a public testimony to his own quite unique relationship to God. He wants it known that everything he has accomplished in his ministry on earth has been simply the answer of the Father to his praying: *I knew that you always hear me.* Though such praying on his part had never before been revealed with such visible and audible passion, it had always been there as a continuous inner orientation and exercise of mind and heart even during his busiest moments. Calvary itself was now to be his greatest act of prayer, and the resurrection was to be its final answer.

The final word to Martha

It is when we hear Jesus' final word to Martha, that the relevance of the whole incident for our situation today can come home most acutely to us. As Jesus approached the tomb, she demonstrated again her complete inability to understand what he had come to do, and to give him the faith and prayer support he had been seeking. He appealed for her help to have the stone removed, but she resisted and tried to prevent him from going further: *'Lord, already there is a stench because he has been dead for four days'* (v. 39). We can understand her anxiety—always she had been the wise and practical person who could foresee all the difficulties in the venturesome schemes that visionary people sometimes proposed. This one was too much for her. Perhaps, too, what had happened to her poor brother during his last days was so distressing and painful to her that she had been relieved when the stone had been set in place. She may indeed have tried there and then to bury with Lazarus the thoughts of what had been, and of what might have been. The tomb had become in her mind a closed book. She was trying now to write a new chapter and she did not want to go back over it all.

Jesus made a last attempt to overcome her resistance: *'Did I not tell you that if you believed, you would see the glory of God?'* (v. 40). It was certainly a reproach. She had failed to grasp what he had already patiently and clearly told her—how shameful that she should now stand there hindering rather than helping! But it was also an appeal to her. Was he himself not still waiting for her to be with him in heart and spirit? He was praying that even at this late hour she might submit to the inspiration of his own faith and fellowship, begin to share his vision of what was to be, join in the prayers he was making and give him a sign that, even though faintly, she understood something of the cost he was bearing. This final appeal to her was not in vain. Though we are not told how fully she was able there and then to respond in mind and heart, we know that they immediately received orders to remove the stone, and the glory of God was seen.

That Jesus dealt so persistently and patiently with Martha before he finally raised Lazarus can remind us today that he wants especially and personally to deal with us before he begins with our surroundings. We may be very acutely conscious of the great need there is in the human situation around us. Things may not be as they should in our home life, our church life, or amongst others we have to deal with from day to day. We have wished and prayed that it might be otherwise. We are certain that if only people could be won over to the faith, could learn to trust God and could open their situation to him, it would make all the difference. We may have in our praying sent a message to the Lord to come and help us all. Of course he wants to come and bring into our personal lives, and into the surroundings that we find so depressing and troublesome, everything that he brought into that home at Bethany. But he has got to start somewhere, and we are the first point of contact. He does not want to begin with the Lazarus situation at the tomb, but within ourselves, the key people, like Martha.

He is trying to be thorough with us. We may be sure that he himself has been even more urgently concerned than we have been about it all. He has been praying more earnestly and decisively for greater things to happen than we ourselves have thought about. He wants us to enter his praying and indeed his suffering over the situation. He wants us to have his vision of what is meant to happen. Therefore with a measure of both reproach and challenge he says to us today the very same words as he did then to Martha: *'Did I not tell you that if you believed, you would see the glory of God?'* (v. 40). They bring a challenge to us to review in the light of our situation what he has already said to us. Few of us who have already had dealings with him can have escaped hearing the words he is referring to: 'Ask, and it will be given to you....' 'For truly I tell you, if you have faith the size of a mustard seed, you will say to this mountain, "Move from here to there", and it will move; and nothing will be impossible for you' (Matt. 7:7; 17:20).

Perhaps he wants us to be more precise and less vague in our praying. He may want our minds to focus on certain definite things we should pray will happen to certain people, knowing that it is here that we find the centre of many of the problems around us. He once suggested that prayer might be seen to be effective when those who prayed could agree to focus on some definite request (cf. Matt. 18:19). Perhaps, also, he wants us to become more urgent in our request and more expectant of an immediate sign that we are heard, and that he is responding. Martha had failed badly in this respect at the beginning of his first interview with her. *'Your brother will rise again'*, he had said, when he told her he had come to raise Lazarus. 'Some day it will happen', she had replied, throwing the whole force of his word into the future when he had meant it here and now.

Might it not be that he is also seeking for himself a more open and deeper entrance into the emotional and psychological problems that might be hindering him from working as freely and fully with us as he would like? We have already raised the suggestion that Martha's resistance to the opening up of the tomb was inspired not only by the fear of the physical odour that might embarrass everyone, but also by an unwillingness to have opened up in her mind certain aspects of buried but nagging memory. Whether or not this may be a valid conjecture in the case of Martha, in seeking to deal with us today Jesus may want such a tomb opened: *'Where have you laid him?'* — 'I want to become involved with you at the exact place of your personal hurt and need. Even where the exposure might cause embarrassment both to yourself and others, give me an entrance into where there is any smothered bitterness or unsolved personal problems so that health and sweetness can be restored, and your commitment to my service can become complete.'

How exactly are we to interpret the promise that we will *see the glory of God*? The whole Gospel has been written to answer this question. In incident after incident, sign after sign, word after word we have been given hints of it. For example, we have seen Jesus manifesting the glory of God in saving a critical situation at a simple wedding ceremony, in answering the desperate cry of a father for a dying child, in the sudden transformation of a hopeless and wasted life, in his power to see a group of his own disciples triumphantly through strange and depressing difficulties. He wants our thought of what he can do for us today to be inspired by what we have read of himself in this book. Of course there are differences in how he manifests his glory today and how he did it then. He is not now here in the flesh to repeat the unique and miraculous signs that then marked him out as the Son of God. We have no need for any more of such signs. He has died, risen, given us the Holy Spirit and opened up for us a new way of prayer so that different, though even greater, works (cf. 14:12) can begin to happen in his name.

It can help us in thinking over the question of what we are to ask of him, if we pay heed to what he did say at the tomb: *'Father... I knew that you always hear me'* (vv. 41, 42). He himself is the one whose praying is certainly always heard and answered. The praying that arises out of our own will and wisdom is often too foolish and self-centred to be given this kind of status before God. Yet we are given the privilege of uniting with Christ in his own praying. When our prayers are inspired by his Spirit they are echoes of his intercession. Is this not why he went to the length of promising: *'If in my name you ask me for anything I will do it'* (14:14.) Does this 'anything' not mean whatever he himself has challenged us to ask by his approach, example and inspiration?

Of course he allows us to struggle with our own freedom before him, and warns us constantly to watchfulness and self-examination. The Word of God is not meant to deprive us of sanity and reason. Yet far too many of us, in this sphere of our Christian life, tend to bury our talent for fear of making mistakes (Matt. 25:24-25). We are not open enough to his invitation and promises. We tend to lay them on the shelf where they will not disturb us, and we content ourselves with the doctrine of prayer that regards it as having only the effect of tuning the mind to whatever must be, because things are as they are.

The Psalmist knew better. Though he always kept in reserve the ultimate hope that in the day when everything on earth collapsed God would then be his 'refuge and strength', he nevertheless made sure he prayed to him as a 'very present help in trouble' (Ps. 46:1).

After the Raising of Lazarus (1)

John 11:45-54

11 Many of the Jews therefore, who had come with Mary and had seen what Jesus did, believed in him. ⁴⁶But some of them went to the Pharisees and told them what he had done. ⁴⁷So the chief priests and the Pharisees called a meeting of the council, and said, 'What are we to do? This man is performing many signs. ⁴⁸If we let him go on like this, everyone will believe in him, and the Romans will come and destroy both our holy place and our nation.' ⁴⁹But one of them, Caiaphas, who was high priest that year, said to them, 'You know nothing at all! ⁵⁰You do not understand that it is better for you to have one man die for the people than to have the whole nation destroyed.' ⁵¹He did not say this on his own, but being high priest that year he prophesied that Jesus was about to die for the nation, [52]and not for the nation only, but to gather into one the dispersed children of God. [53]So from that day on they planned to put him to death.

54 Jesus therefore no longer walked about openly among the Jews, but went from there to a town called Ephraim in the region near the wilderness; and he remained there with his disciples.

Caiaphas, the prophet

Immediately after Jesus raised Lazarus from the dead an event took place which convinced him that from now on he must change the direction of all his efforts. The Jewish Sanhedrin held a hastily called meeting in which we are told that God himself, through Caiaphas the high priest, uttered the word which, entering and controlling history (cf. Isa. 55:10, 11), ensured the immediate and inevitable fulfilment of one of the most important Old Testament prophecies about the career God had for his Messiah. Caiaphas, presiding in gross ignorance and arrogance over a casually called meeting of the highest Jewish court, was taken over and controlled in his thoughts and utterance in a no less effective way than were the Old Testament prophets in their day taken over to utter their own divinely inspired and sometimes world-shaking pronouncements. 'Here', says Godet, 'was the central point of human history, the moment at which the most divine of mysteries was to be accomplished in the form of the greatest of crimes.' As we now read through the ensuing story, we are meant to note something special from this moment onwards in the life of our Lord: in a uniquely close and detailed way, God made every form of our human hatred that was there expressed against his Son, from the illegalities of the condemnation to the mockery, the smiting, the shouting and the indifference, all contribute their shame to the glory of Jesus' self-offering and add to its awful and wonderful significance. It was especially in John's mind, moreover, that we should notice at this point the irony of the fact that it was the word spoken by Caiaphas in his bout of extreme Jewish nationalism that set Jesus on the course of dying for all the nations of mankind so that he might *gather into one the dispersed children of God* (v. 52).

That *Jesus… no longer walked about openly among the Jews* alerts us to the change which was taking place in the nature of the service he felt God now wanted from him. Hitherto he had not deliberately avoided publicity. He had been tireless in presenting his claims and his message. He had constantly 'revealed his glory' in miracles so that his disciples might have their faith confirmed (2:11) and those in the world who would believe might take note. He himself as the trusted Son seems freely to have taken the initiative in the service of the Father, though always according to the Father's revealed mind and will. From now on, however, we can trace a growing passivity in the obedience he seems to offer to God. (We remember the theological distinction between his 'active' and 'passive' obedience.[1]) The way he finds himself being led becomes more and more contrary to his own sensitive human will. From this time on we find him turning his thoughts more and more towards the period of extraordinary suffering that he knew he would have to go through in order to fulfil his earthly mission. He had dedicated himself to such a mission when at the beginning of his ministry he gave himself to be immersed with sinners in the Jordan, and once he confessed that at times the very thought of having to go through with such a 'baptism' added great stress to his daily life, and affected its scope (cf. Luke 12:50). In the Gospel of John we will find both Jesus and the Evangelist referring to this coming period as his 'hour' (2:4; 7:30; 8:20; 12:23, 27; 13:1, etc.).

---

[1] An example of what theologians call Christ's 'active obedience' would be his voluntary subjection of himself to suffering and death. An example of his 'passive obedience' would consist in his paying the penalty of sin by his suffering and death. However, it is important to bear in mind that the distinction must not be pressed too far, for the two cannot be separated, but accompany Christ throughout his entire life and ministry, interpenetrating each other.

CHAPTER 12

AFTER THE RAISING OF LAZARUS (2)

John 11:55 – 12:8

11 Now the Passover of the Jews was near, and many went up from the country to Jerusalem before the Passover to purify themselves. ⁵⁶They were looking for Jesus and were asking one another as they stood in the temple, 'What do you think? Surely he will not come to the festival, will he?' ⁵⁷Now the chief priests and the Pharisees had given orders that anyone who knew where Jesus was should let them know, so that they might arrest him.

12 Six days before the Passover Jesus came to Bethany, the home of Lazarus, whom he had raised from the dead. ²There they gave a dinner for him. Martha served, and Lazarus was one of those at the table with him. ³Mary took a pound of costly perfume made of pure nard, anointed Jesus' feet, and wiped them with her hair. The house was filled with the fragrance of the perfume. ⁴But Judas Iscariot, one of his disciples (the one who was about to betray him), said, ⁵'Why was this perfume not sold for three hundred denarii and the money given to the poor?' ⁶(He said this not because he cared about the poor, but because he was a thief; he kept the common purse and used to steal what was put into it.) ⁷Jesus said, 'Leave her alone. She bought it so that she might keep it for the day of my burial. ⁸You always have the poor with you, but you do not always have me.'

The revealing incident at Bethany

We are here given a glimpse of the tense situation at the dinner. Jesus was aware that his enemies must here and now close in and arrest him and put him to death. He was deeply troubled at what he was being led into as, even under his Father's loving will, he yielded himself up to it. Yet he alone knew that even though he was losing some crowd support (there were those who now had doubts whether he would have the courage to show up!), there was still a strong enough public desire even for the sensation of letting him have his say openly, that the authorities had to resort to the furtive ways which finally brought about his arrest by night.

What took place at the dinner at Bethany is told with some detail in all the Gospels, because it illuminates an important aspect of the suffering to which he now felt he had to yield himself—his utter isolation of heart and spirit in a world that had despised and rejected him. In the midst of the cosy fellowship and confident triumphalism of the gathering in his honour, the very encouragement they offered him would make him feel all the more deeply the incongruity of his mood and presence in their midst. The Scriptures which he knew so well and studied so searchingly came home to him: 'I looked and there was no helper. I stared but there was no one to sustain me' (Isa. 63:5). The Messiah of Israel had to go his way and bear his lot alone! Would they not all forsake him as he went through his God-forsakenness (Mark 15:34)[1]? How untested they were and how feeble they could all become! How much they were out of touch with his own heart's purpose and the kingdom he sought first in life! He was possessed by such thoughts when suddenly, by an entirely spontaneous gesture of passionate devotion and deep understanding and without saying a word, Mary transformed the whole situation. Here was at least one who truly understood what his passion in life was all about! She had seen that the same love which had saved her so wonderfully from her sin was now yielding to the uttermost, and seeking to embrace each and all in the world. It was not just her gratitude that touched him but her recognition of the passion that was already deeply troubling him,

---

[1] Calvin comments on Mark 15:34: '[F]or Christ to make satisfaction for us he had to stand trial at God's tribunal. There is nothing more dreadful than to feel God as judge, whose wrath is worse than all deaths. When the trial came on Christ in this form, that he was now against God and doomed to ruin, he was overcome with dread (which would have been enough to swallow up all mankind a hundred times over) but he came out Victor, by the marvellous power of the Spirit. It is no fiction or play-acting that prompts his complaint, that he is forsaken by the Father…. We have noted a difference between natural sense and the intelligence of faith: so nothing prevents Christ, as far as ordinary sense dictated, taking thought of his estrangement from God, and at the same time, by faith, realizing that God was on his side.'

and her insight into its meaning. Here was the first-fruit of the church to which he was giving his life. Mark's account of what Jesus said of her brings all this out more fully than John himself does. 'She has performed a good service for me.... She has anointed my body beforehand for its burial. Truly I tell you, wherever the good news is proclaimed in the whole world, what she has done will be told in remembrance of her' (Mark 14:6-9). We might read that John adds symbolically, 'the whole church (lit., house)' will be 'filled with the fragrance of the perfume' (v. 3b). This story told and told again will not fail in its power to constrain us to true humility and devotion.

The story reveals to us how firmly at this time Jesus was in the hands of his heavenly Father. Even after he raised Lazarus, God continued to encourage Jesus by sign and word (cf. 12:23, 27, 28). The whole of this sudden event was a special sign to Jesus at the beginning of his passion that his heavenly Father and the inspiration of the Spirit were in control in all the circumstances around him. We can have little doubt, moreover, that the obtuse reaction of the disciples in this incident, and the further revelation here of the complete alienation of spirit shown by Judas made him realize how urgent it still was to strengthen his disciples to face their coming ordeal. It helps us to understand why he devoted so much of the remaining time of his life to their personal care and to ensuring that Judas was expelled from their midst.

Chapter 12

Jesus Among the crowds

John 12:9-26

12 When the great crowd of the Jews learned that he was there, they came not only because of Jesus but also to see Lazarus, whom he had raised from the dead. [10]So the chief priests planned to put Lazarus to death as well, [11]since it was on account of him that many of the Jews were deserting and were believing in Jesus.

12 The next day the great crowd that had come to the festival heard that Jesus was coming to Jerusalem. [13]So they took branches of palm trees and went out to meet him, shouting,

'Hosanna!

Blessed is the one who comes in the name of the Lord—

the King of Israel!'

[14]Jesus found a young donkey and sat on it; as it is written:

[15]   'Do not be afraid, daughter of Zion.

Look, your king is coming,

sitting on a donkey's colt!'

[16]His disciples did not understand these things at first; but when Jesus was glorified, then they remembered that these things had been written of him and had been done to him. [17]So the crowd that had been with him when he called Lazarus out of the tomb and raised him from the dead continued to testify. [18]It was also because they heard that he had performed this sign that the crowd went to meet him. [19]The Pharisees then said to one another, 'You see, you can do nothing. Look, the world has gone after him!'

20 Now among those who went up to worship at the festival were some Greeks. [21]They came to Philip, who was from Bethsaida in Galilee, and said to him, 'Sir, we wish to see Jesus.' [22]Philip went and told Andrew; then Andrew and Philip went and told Jesus. [23]Jesus answered them, 'The hour has come for the Son of Man to be glorified. [24]Very truly, I tell you, unless a grain of wheat falls into the earth and dies, it remains just a single grain; but if it dies, it bears much fruit. [25]Those who love their life lose it, and those who hate their life in this world will keep it for eternal life. [26]Whoever serves

me must follow me, and where I am, there will my servant be also. Whoever serves me, the Father will honour.'

His final self-declaration and the coming of the Greeks

John here gives a careful and detailed report of a brief but important ministry to the crowds during the last days Jesus was free to preach to them. He knew that as they began again to flock around him much of their fervour was superficial, and that in the end many of them would vote him to death. Yet his experience in the house of Bethany had proved that there might be among them some (who could know how many?), like Mary, there and then ready to yield their lives and hearts' devotion. He felt therefore constrained to invite their loyalty. He felt, moreover, that what he said in the remaining time he had on earth ('last words' recorded by John in chapters 14-17) would be most likely to be given a secure place in the tradition the disciples would eventually pass on within the church.

On the first morning of the feast he heard a considerable section of the crowd, still excited by the fact that he had raised Lazarus, coming his way. They were intent on forcing him to declare his hand, and expected him to declare himself the Messiah (in their materialistic misunderstanding of that prophet term). Their commonly held tradition taught that the entry of the Messianic King into Jerusalem was foretold in Psalm 118, and they welcomed him with its very words: 'Blessed is the one who comes in the name of the LORD.' According to such tradition they had also cut palm branches specially to mark the great occasion (v. 13)[2] Their leaders were expecting here and now, some visible manifestation of his power which would justify their hope. They were not motivated by personal faith in Jesus himself or by the words he had spoken and the promises he had

---

[2] Some have assumed the 'palm branches' must be a reference to the Feast of Tabernacles, or Festival of Booths, which came at the end of the Jewish year when the harvest had been gathered in (Lev. 23:34-36); it this Festival which is most probably referred to by John in 7:14-44. However, palm branches had already become a national (even a nationalistic) symbol and were associated with the hope of a messianic liberator. Every Jew knew the cry 'Hosanna' (lit. 'give salvation now') for Psalm 118 was part of the Hallel and was sung morning and evening by the Temple choir; it was also associated with the Feast of Tabernacles, the Feast of Dedication and the Passover (see Carson, p. 432).

given. Their hopes were politically oriented. The prophecy they had chiefly in mind as they welcomed him was that towards the end of the third chapter of Zephaniah (3:14-20) which begins:

'Sing aloud, O daughter Zion; shout, O Israel!...

The LORD has taken away the judgements against you....

The King of Israel, the LORD, is in your midst...'.

It goes on to tell of all Israel's enemies being destroyed and their national fortunes restored and was commonly interpreted in materialistic terms of an earthly kingdom rather than spiritually of that other 'kingdom' which 'is not of this world' (18:36).

It was indeed a lamentable and dangerous situation. We are meant to marvel at how Jesus acted in the critical situation. He deliberately disappointed the false hopes of the crowd by an action which would be easily understood by any who knew the Scriptures as deliberately aimed at shattering all perverted nationalistic enthusiasm.

The other Gospels tell how he searched for, before he found, the young donkey on which he sat while he then allowed the self-infatuated crowds to lead him in triumphal procession. He knew that eventually, after all the disillusionment that would come to them through his crucifixion, shattering all their false hopes, the message of Zechariah 9:9-10 might come to their minds:

'Rejoice greatly, O daughter Zion!

Shout aloud, O daughter Jerusalem!

Lo, your king comes to you;

triumphant and victorious is he,

humble and riding on a donkey...',

with its added promises that the chariots and the warhorses and the battle-bows would be 'cut off'. It was in his mind especially to purge from their minds the restricted and racist views that could be derived from a false interpretation of Zephaniah and replaced by the continuing promise of Zechariah that peace will be commanded for all nations, and the dominion of the Messiah shall be 'from the River to the ends of the earth' (9:10). What he did has since given to the church in every age, a message about his kingdom, its nature and power, which never fails from year to year to arrest, enrich and challenge those who give their minds to it. The church had indeed recognized the depth of the wisdom expressed in his quite spontaneous action. It has preserved a special time and place in its liturgical year for Palm Sunday alongside Good Friday and Easter, as it remembers the central events of salvation history.

We are intended to notice the gracious providence which enabled him to find the donkey there at the right time for his use, and we must interpret this as another of these signs given by his heavenly Father to encourage him on the way he had chosen. It was, moreover, of immense significance to him that at the very moment he was declaring himself the coming King of all nations (cf. Zech. 9:10) God inspired some Greeks to seek him out. Their coming not only brought him the certainty that his 'hour' had come but it also set God's seal on his hope and claim to universal dominion. He then gave expression to the sense of utter isolation which had now fully possessed him and he described himself as like a seed 'which falls into the earth' to die—alone! Yet in the thrill of the moment he knew himself on the way to being glorified by God, and he found himself inspired to utter one of his most memorable and commanding sayings and appeals, which we are meant to hear today as powerful in the relevance and as urgent in the issues they raise in our own minds and situation: *'Those who love their life lose it, and those who hate their life in this world will keep it for eternal life. Whoever serves me must follow me, and where I am, there will my servant be also. Whoever serves me, the Father will honour'* (vv. 25, 26). This saying is recorded elsewhere and was probably repeated often by him (e.g. Mark 8:34ff.; Matt. 10:38f.) and in our postmodern culture of 'pick 'n mix' challenges us all to that total commitment to Jesus without which there can be no true discipleship.

Chapter 12

The stress and the voice

John 12:27-30

12 'Now my soul is troubled. And what should I say–"Father, save me from this hour"? No, it is for this reason that I have come to this hour. [28]Father, glorify your name.' Then a voice came from heaven, 'I have glorified it, and I will glorify it again.' [29]The crowd standing there heard it and said that it was thunder. Others said, 'An angel has spoken to him.' [30]Jesus answered, 'This voice has come for your sake, not for mine....'

Suffering on behalf of struggling humanity

Here we have the account of an occasion when, as later in the Garden of Gethsemane, Jesus, facing the prospect of his impending agony, quite suddenly was so overcome by the approaching horror of it that he shrank from his commitment and prayed to his Father to save him from it (Mark 14:32-6). The 'trouble' of soul, as he called it, did not last. A word soon came from heaven which restored his poise and his peace, though, even after the heavenly messenger ministered to him and strengthened him, he prayed for a time even more earnestly (Luke 22:43, 44). Divine help in prayer may at first make us ready for even greater spiritual conflict before the calm assurance which follows from our obedience in 'reverent submission' (Heb. 5:7, 8).

His sudden utterance, and the agony with which he was obviously momentarily overtaken, obviously raise a most important question in our minds as we overhear him. What kind of *trouble* was it from which he was only *now* shrinking? He had already suffered all his days. The incarnation, it has been said, was not simply the cause but the beginning of his passion. This truth is given notable expression in the first verse of the Christmas carol:

> Child in the manger
> Infant of Mary
> Outcast and stranger
> Lord of all

As he grew up through childhood and early youth to manhood, his heart must inevitably have reached out to the humanity he had come to save, his brothers and sisters around him. Thus we are justified in imagining him to have experienced both a deep sympathy that awakened intense suffering on behalf of struggling humanity around him, and an intense abhorrence of the sordidness and vanity of the world in which they were all so deeply involved. Such human and imaginable sorrows and emotions would continue increasingly as his lot after his public ministry began. He was soon to find himself the victim of the arrogance and pride he had come to displace, of the perverse blindness of the crowds he tried to win and their final crowd-contempt, of his betrayal by one of his disciples, and of the hopeless weakness of the others in their failure to stand by him when he 'looked, but there was no helper' (Isa. 63:5).

We must, however, remember that when we venture to describe Christ's sufferings along the line we have so far followed, we fall far short. When Jesus entered Gethsemane and separated himself from his disciples it was a sign that an element was now beginning to enter his sufferings that cut him completely off from all human understanding and support. Not from our own experience nor from anywhere else in the realm of human tragedy can we gain any imagination of it. To begin to understand it we have to turn, as he himself did to those passages in the Old Testament which describe it for us. There are many hints of it in Isaiah 53. The full horror of it is especially brought out in Psalm 22 which clearly emphasizes the dreadful God-forsakenness[3] he would have to endure as he bore, for us and in our place, the curse of sin and the pangs of death, and entered the final and most bitter round of his conflict with the powers of evil.

The voice he heard, as the very anticipation of this horror began to trouble him, was the same as had come to him at his baptism (Matt. 3:17). He had then needed special help to enable him to launch out on his public vocation as the Suffering Servant described in Isaiah 53. It was the same as he had heard at the transfiguration—another moment, when the demands and dangers of his earthly ministry were at their peak (Matt. 17:5). Here it comes again at a crisis point. Jesus saw that God was enabling

---

[3] See p. 197, footnote 1.

the crowds also to hear the voice to bring to them a challenge to repent and believe and a last warning from heaven to beware of what they were going to do to him. *'This voice has come for your sake not for mine'*, he said, and he was encouraged there and then to make his final effort to win them to himself.[4]

A final self-affirmation and last warning

John 12:31-36

12 Now is the judgement of this world; now the ruler of this world will be driven out. [32]And I, when I am lifted up from the earth, will draw all people to myself.' [33]He said this to indicate the kind of death he was to die. [34]The crowd answered him, 'We have heard from the law that the Messiah remains for ever. How can you say that the Son of Man must be lifted up? Who is this Son of Man?' [35]Jesus said to them, 'The light is with you for a little longer. Walk while you have the light, so that the darkness may not overtake you. If you walk in the darkness, you do not know where you are going. [36]While you have the light, believe in the light, so that you may become children of light.'

After Jesus had said this he departed and hid from them.

A final self-affirmation and last warning

Realizing the humanly irretrievable nature of the situation before him, and under the certainty that God was about to glorify him, Jesus gave utterance to a word that must take its place amongst many outstanding personal claims and appeals that compellingly

---

[4] The question arises as to how the voice from heaven could have been for the benefit of those standing by if they could not understand what was said. Two points can be made. First, the fact of a thunder-like voice speaking to Jesus would have confirmed to the more spiritually sensitive that a major turning point in Jesus' ministry was about to take place. Second, after his resurrection and ascension, the faith of his disciples would be confirmed by the meaning of the words spoken (conveyed to them later by Jesus), and they would have realized more fully that the curse of his hanging on a tree was essential to the divine plan of redemption and had not been not a defeat, but a victory.

hold our minds as we read through this Gospel (cf. 6:35; 8:12; 10:11, etc.). *'Now is the judgement of this world; now the ruler of this world will be driven out. And I, when I am lifted up from the earth, will draw all people to myself.'* We are to interpret Jesus' words about *the judgement of this world* and about the *ruler of this world* being *driven out,* not simply as a hope-inspiring vision reserved for a future age, but also as a solemn announcement made by him on the way to the cross so that both the 'world's judgement' and the defeat of its 'ruler' were about to happen.

The world was about to bring judgement on itself when it finally refused to accept the One who had come to offer it salvation, and instead demanded his crucifixion. It had taken time for it to reach its verdict. Jesus had had to be born, welcomed and nurtured in its midst, till he began his short ministry proclaiming that the kingdom was at hand and calling for repentance. It had taken time for the authorities to evaluate his ministry among them as worthy of death. It also had taken time for the uncommitted crowd to arrive at the same verdict. At first the people had rejoiced in his preaching and healing. Yet it had gradually come home that what he finally offered was not what they truly in heart wanted; rather, that what he demanded was, deep down, not what they was willing to give; that what he manifested as light simply exposed the darkness in which they were determined to continue the old unrepentant ways of life and thought. Initially, the world hid its opposition by rating him as one more in the line of false messiahs. But finally, as he fully revealed himself on the way to the cross, the world said its 'No'.

As the world was finally brought to judgement through Jesus, Satan too, the *ruler of this world* was also being *driven out* by Jesus. Paul explains that it was in and through Christ's death on the cross that he 'disarmed the rulers and authorities and made a public example of them, triumphing over them in it' (Col. 2:15). After being defeated in his vain preliminary effort to subvert Jesus at the beginning of his ministry we are told that Satan retreated 'until an opportune time' (Luke 4:13; cf. NEB 'biding his time'). It was when he saw the world growing more alien to Jesus that he summoned his strength for the decisive encounter. How successful he was! He took full possession of Judas, and provoked and emboldened the Jewish authorities. It is to him alone that we can attribute the blindness and perversity that possessed the mob as Jesus' patience served to provoke insult, his love hatred, his humility spite, his peace mad frenzy. We are meant all the more to marvel at how God, through allowing Satan in his sheer folly to reveal himself, set him on the way to final self-destruction. Satan, though *driven out*, is not yet entirely destroyed. From now on he still has what God leaves him desperately to hold on to. We know only too well that he still has power to deceive and enslave. But it is a waning power which has become all the more vicious because its end is coming near.[5]

After such a brief yet comprehensive survey of what he was finally going to bring about through his coming death, Jesus goes on to speak about how, as time passes, all humankind, from generation to generation, will be brought under the life-giving and redeeming power of what he once-for-all, there and then, did to set them free: *'And I, when I am lifted up from the earth, will draw all people to myself'* (v. 32). He is referring to what will be at the heart of the soon-to-come victorious campaign over the broken power of his defeated enemy. Crucially defeated, Satan still has power to hurt and even destroy what is near to him and he exercises it all the more viciously because he knows his end is approaching. We all know to our cost his power to use the 'world' and the 'flesh' to seduce, distort and enslave. How calmly Jesus, referring to his coming ascension, assures us here that as all power will be given to him in heaven and earth we need have no fear if we refuse his enemies scope to work.

The context of the saying justifies us in taking Jesus' words about his being *lifted up* to refer, not only to his crucifixion, resurrection and ascension, but also to a healing and reforming ministry which he designed to take place within the church as it continually yields itself to do his will on earth. We are meant to remember how when he spoke to Nicodemus about his coming crucifixion he likened himself to the bronze serpent which was lifted up by Moses in the wilderness to bring healing to all who looked at it (3:14). It has always been accepted in the church as a valid deduction from Jesus' use of the phraseology and thought of both these sayings that it is as Christ crucified is lifted up before the congregation through the continuing proclamation of his

---

[5] In Revelation 20, the devil is depicted as being thoroughly defeated and bound at Calvary and then temporarily released (v. 7) until his final destruction (v. 10).

death, that the ascended Christ is continually enabled to fulfil his promise to draw all to himself. Where his cross is sincerely and clearly proclaimed in both word and sacrament, there he promises to be at work, laying hold of the hearts and affections of those who hear and will believe with consequently a greater power within them at a deeper spiritual level than that of any enslaving falsehood or evil lust.

He was speaking to a crowd who were soon going to want him crucified. Their minds were closing to what he might be seeking to say. They engaged him with contentious questions which he did not attempt to answer (v. 34f.). We are meant to overhear his warning. The darkness is always there seeking to overtake any of us through that inner hold which it already has on all of us. To give it room and scope is to yield ourselves to live without direction, meaning and hope. We are meant also to hear again the same promise as he had already made to us. Yielding to the light, and seeking to live in the light we become its children, 'born anew, not of perishable but of imperishable seed, through the living and enduring word of God' (1 Peter 1:23). We hold and are held, and are drawn on and on ever nearer to the One who has made us his own.

Reflections of the Evangelist

John 12:36b-50

12   After Jesus had said this, he departed and hid from them. [37]Although he had performed so many signs in their presence, they did not believe in him. [38]This was to fulfil the word spoken by the prophet Isaiah:

'Lord, who has believed our message,
and to whom has the arm of the Lord been revealed?'
[39]And so they could not believe, because Isaiah also said,
[40] 'He has blinded their eyes and hardened their heart,
so that they might not look with their eyes,
and understand with their heart and turn —
and I would heal them.'
[41]Isaiah said this because he saw his glory and spoke about him. [42]Nevertheless many, even of the authorities, believed in him. But

because of the Pharisees they did not confess it, for fear that they would be put out of the synagogue; [43]for they loved human glory more than the glory that comes from God.

44 Then Jesus cried aloud: 'Whoever believes in me believes not in me but in him who sent me. [45]And whoever sees me sees him who sent me. [46]I have come as light into the world, so that everyone who believes in me should not remain in the darkness. [47]I do not judge anyone who hears my words and does not keep them, for I came not to judge the world, but to save the world. [48]The one who rejects me and does not receive my word has a judge; on the last day the word that I have spoken will serve as judge, [49]for I have not spoken on my own, but the Father who sent me has himself given me a commandment about what to say and what to speak. [50]And I know that his commandment is eternal life. What I speak, therefore, I speak just as the Father has told me.'

Some remembered words

Jesus now ceased appealing to the scribes and *hid from them* (v. 36). 'The next time the crowd look on him', says Brown, 'they will look on a man suffering (19:5, 37) whom they have rejected.' The Evangelist, in a brief paragraph, recalls how appalled he became as it dawned on him what was taking place—the rejection of a true prophet. Jesus had done so many signs, even raising Lazarus! Yet they were wholly rejecting him and were preparing to brand him an impostor. As our writer pondered over it, he found it cast light on the whole of Israel's history he knew so well, and he seemed to draw light from it. He thought over the way God worked through his prophets towards the salvation of rebellious Israel. He was always in control even when they blinded themselves and hardened their hearts against his message and his truth; he had nevertheless continued his saving work. He saw that in Jesus a miracle even more wonderful was continuing to happen. God was working out his saving purpose for humanity by triumphing over and using the resistance of his chosen people. Their blindness to Jesus was God's way of bringing about this glory. It was because they were now going to lift up the Son of Man on his cross that, hanging between earth and heaven, he was going to draw all to himself. Although his own did not receive him, as many as received him were given eternal life (1:11, 12). Though uplifted by such hope he in no way excuses the cowardice displayed by many who had seen his glory and refused to commit themselves. They were afraid of persecution and *loved human glory more than the glory that comes from God* (v. 43; cf. 5:44).

It is at this point when his readers' attention has been temporarily detached from a definite historical context that the Evangelist inserts in his Gospel one or two of the Lord's sayings which may have been among the material before him but to which he had not assigned a definite place within the whole history. They are mainly about himself and the finality of his word. We do not know Jesus unless we experience him as leading us to God, and we can have no experience of God apart from that which Jesus brings to us. They remind us emphatically that he has come primarily to save rather than to judge. They stress the central importance of our receiving his sayings and words and keeping his commandments since in these he is passing on what he hears from the Father. They make clear, as Hoskyns puts it, 'that Christianity is not a "Jesus cult"'. We can truly know the Son only as One who is continually concerned that we should know the Father also.[6]

---

[6] More than once, Jesus insisted on the priority and centrality of his saving work: *'Indeed, God did not send the Son into the world to condemn the world, but in order that the world might be saved through him'* (3:17). Nevertheless, there is another perspective on judgement as indicated in this passage: *'on the last day the word that I have spoken will serve as judge'* (v. 48b). Elsewhere, Jesus indicates that he himself will be assigned by the Father the office of judging those who, in rejecting his word, have rejected the Father's word also (5:22, 27; 8:16, 26). During his earthly ministry, however, it is the Father alone who judges (8:50).

CHAPTER 13

THE CLEANSING OF THE DISCIPLES

The feet-washing

John 13:1-17

13 Now before the festival of the Passover, Jesus knew that his hour had come to depart from this world and go to the Father. Having loved his own who were in the world, he loved them to the end. [2]The devil had already put it into the heart of Judas son of Simon Iscariot to betray him. And during supper [3]Jesus, knowing that the Father had given all things into his hands, and that he had come from God and was going to God, [4]got up from the table, took off his outer robe, and tied a towel around himself. [5]Then he poured water into a basin and began to wash the disciples' feet and to wipe them with the towel that was tied around him. [6]He came to Simon Peter, who said to him, 'Lord, are you going to wash my feet?' [7]Jesus answered, 'You do not know now what I am doing, but later you will understand.' [8]Peter said to him, 'You will never wash my feet.' Jesus answered, 'Unless I wash you, you have no share with me.' [9]Simon Peter said to him, 'Lord, not my feet only but also my hands and my head!' [10]Jesus said to him, 'One who has bathed does not need to wash, except for the feet, but is entirely clean. And you are clean, though not all of you.' [11]For he knew who was to betray him; for this reason he said, 'Not all of you are clean.'

12 After he had washed their feet, had put on his robe, and had returned to the table, he said to them, 'Do you know what I have done to you? [13]You call me Teacher and Lord—and you are right, for that is what I am. [14]So if I, your Lord and Teacher, have washed your feet, you also ought to wash one another's feet. [15]For I have set you an example, that you also should do as I have done to you. [16]Very truly, I tell you, servants are not greater than their master, nor are messengers

greater than the one who sent them. [17]If you know these things, you are blessed if you do them.'

-Emptied himself of all but love-

The translation in the NEB (cf. NIV) at the end of verse 1 helps to bring out a meaning which the NRSV has failed to do: *He had always loved his own who were in the world, and now he was to show the full extent of his love.* He has already begun to draw us to himself as we grasp that he 'emptied himself of all but love' when he came among us at his birth. And he has continued throughout his whole life and ministry to make us marvel at his patient self-giving to us in all our needs. Yet here and now as he faces the kind of death he is to die, even more is demanded of him and even more is revealed as he freely gives his all.

There were already in circulation within the church several accounts of what happened that evening in the upper room. They tell how Jesus took bread and wine and celebrated with the disciples the first Lord's Supper. It was not necessary therefore for John to repeat these.[1] There was however one event which seems not to have gripped the other disciples as forcibly as it did John and he made sure that it was given a place of prominence in his witness to that evening. This was the quite extraordinary way in which Jesus, even after they were seated at table and everything had been done in order, himself deliberately interrupted the proceedings by stooping before each to wash their feet. John vividly remembered the conversation between Jesus and Peter, in which he had insisted that each disciple should think over the meaning of his actions, simply accepting the implications and yielding to the prompting of the example he was giving.

In washing their feet Jesus was adopting the kind of communication sometimes engaged in by the Old Testament prophets when they felt they could express what they wanted to

---

[1] It has been suggested that when John wrote his Gospel, already the young Christian church was undergoing fierce persecution; one of the charges being brought against believers was that they held secret feasts when they engaged in cannibalism, eating the flesh and drinking the blood of their leader. Therefore John, to avoid giving the church's enemies further evidence to prosecute their opposition, tactfully avoids giving an account of the Last Supper and simply concentrates on the washing of the disciples' feet by Jesus. He has already slipped in an indirect reference to the sacrament of the Last Supper where it might go unnoticed by the uninitiated (6:53-55).

say more fully and clearly in an action rather than in words (cf. Ezek. 3:22 – 5:4). Jesus did not expect his disciples to understand all that it was in his mind to say to them then and there: *You do not know now what I am doing, but later you will understand* (v. 7). Therefore he shaped what he did so that it had a richness of meaning (cf. Eph. 3:10; Ps. 104:24) which would gradually unfold itself to the disciples and later to the church as it was thought about prayerfully and patiently. Brown is certainly correct in what he calls the 'simplest explanation of the event grasped as a whole'. Jesus performed this servile task to prophesy symbolically that he was about to be humiliated in death. Yet Jesus also intended us to find a wealth of meaning in the gestures and details with which his action was staged. Our imagination is appealed to as he solemnly *took off his outer robe,*[2] *and tied a towel around himself* to remind us of the heavenly glory that he laid aside as if it were nothing, in order to be with us in such loneliness, pain and shame. He also sets us a personal example of the servile and humble kind of service that will sometimes be demanded of us as we too face the often unspectacular and sometimes sordid need presented to us by others. We are meant to take note of how Peter actually tried to hinder rather than to accept and encourage Jesus as he stooped in this way before him. Indeed he deeply grieved him by reacting at first with embarrassment and failing to show any appreciation of what was behind the gracious gesture.

Washing before eating

We must not, however, overlook another important aspect of what Jesus intended to bring home to his disciples through his feet-washing. He was about to institute the sacrament of the Lord's Supper, He intended the Supper, which he was teaching the disciples to celebrate, to dominate their future understanding of how he was going always to remain at the centre of their life and work. At the central point of the Supper he gave them bread,

---

[2] The Greek word is plural and while it is possible the reference is only to the outer robe, it is more likely we are intended to understand that Jesus stripped off down to a loin cloth which would have been the dress of the most menial slave. John uses the singular for one outer garment in 19:2, 5 and the plural for all garments in 19:23, 24. The symbolism implied in NIV's 'laid aside his garments' therefore may be the same as Paul's use of the phrase 'he emptied himself' (Phil. 2:7ff.).

signifying, he said, 'my body' (or 'myself') and made them eat it. By such an illustration he was bringing home to them how intimately close and life-giving his future relationship with each and all of them was to become. We find it therefore of great significance that, quite deliberately, Jesus himself washed the disciples' feet before he introduced them to the Supper. He is telling them clearly that they must allow themselves to be continually cleansed by him if they wish to be continually kept united to him in the close and powerful way illustrated in the Supper. His direct word to Peter on this matter: *'Unless I wash you, you have no share with me'* must be continually heard by us today. It is a warning that unless we are continually and consciously submitting our lives to the judgement of his word as it seeks to make us abhor what is evil in the life of this world and 'hold fast to what is good' (Rom. 12:9), it is vain for us to imagine that we can enjoy anything of the truth and genuine fullness of life that the New Testament offers.

The ensuing conversation with Peter enabled Jesus to elaborate more fully on the same theme. Peter reacted from Jesus' slight rebuke with his usual impetuosity. He reminded Jesus of his own teaching that head and hands lead us astray even more than our feet (cf. Matt. 5:29, 30), and raised the question of the adequacy of his choice of sign. Jesus in reply reminded him of the complete washing he had been given — now symbolized for us in baptism. Peter had indeed once-for-all in his whole person been thoroughly cleansed and liberated from the power of the world when Jesus had called, enlightened and converted him. Yet he must now concern himself that from day to day he needed fresh and continual cleansing from the stains and subtle influences that invariably arise casually through life's daily journey: all disciples' feet pick up dust and grime for all must travel through the wilderness of this world on their way to God.

A transformed way of life

I have set you an example, began Jesus when he had resumed his place at table. Certainly Jesus was giving the apostles there before him an example of how to bear and exercise true leadership and authority in the church he was going to found. In ruling the church they must always take as their pattern the deference and humility which he, the Master, had just shown. We must not, however, fail to notice how Jesus by his persistent use here of the word 'wash', quite deliberately refers to one important aspect of the help each could be to the other in the New Testament church. The early church, remembering Jesus' teaching and living by the power of his word and Spirit, both set for itself and expected from its members a new and transformed way of life that no one of them could have aspired to or thought possible on his or her own. Each had to depend continually on the fellowship of the community for the strength and courage needed to resist falling back into the seductive paganism of the local culture from which Christ had rescued them. It is to this cleansing influence continually at work within their fellowship that Jesus is pointing when he urges them to wash each other's feet. Christ was there at the heart of the community seeking to cleanse it by the word he continually gave them (15:3; Eph. 5:25ff.). In doing so he used the influence of the whole community on each, and of one individual member on another, to enable especially those who were weaker in their faith and resolve to keep running the race set before them. The stronger members of the community in the early church were conscious of being called by Christ to maintain the godly standards of the community. 'No true Christian', writes Joseph Hall, 'is his own man, so he freely lays out himself, by example, by admonition, by consolation, by prayer, for the universal benefit of all his fellow Christians.'

Jesus and Judas

John 13:18-30

13 'I am not speaking of all of you; I know whom I have chosen. But it is to fulfil the scripture, "The one who ate my bread has lifted his heel against me." [19]I tell you this now, before it occurs, so that when it does occur, you may believe that I am he. [20]Very truly, I tell you, whoever receives one whom I send receives me; and whoever receives me receives him who sent me.'

21 After saying this Jesus was troubled in spirit, and declared, 'Very truly, I tell you, one of you will betray me.' [22]The disciples looked at one another, uncertain of whom he was speaking. [23]One of his

disciples—the one whom Jesus loved—was reclining next to him; [24]Simon Peter therefore motioned to him to ask Jesus of whom he was speaking. [25]So while reclining next to Jesus, he asked him, 'Lord, who is it?' [26]Jesus answered, 'It is the one to whom I give this piece of bread when I have dipped it in the dish.' So when he had dipped the piece of bread, he gave it to Judas son of Simon Iscariot. [27]After he received the piece of bread, Satan entered into him. Jesus said to him, 'Do quickly what you are going to do.' [28]Now no one at the table knew why he said this to him. [29]Some thought that, because Judas had the common purse, Jesus was telling him, 'Buy what we need for the festival'; or, that he should give something to the poor. [30]So, after receiving the piece of bread, he immediately went out. And it was night.

Human responsibility and divine sovereignty

We are told how deeply Jesus was again *troubled* (cf. 12:27) in view of having to face the actual fulfilment of a particular prophecy which he took to refer to his coming passion—the words in Psalm 55:12-14 about Judas. The absurdity and tragedy of it came home to him especially when he was about to tell them how closely into his fellowship he was soon going to draw them all. One of his great concerns therefore, when he took his disciples apart, was to forewarn them of his coming betrayal so that they might not be too dismayed or too resistant when the Roman soldiers came into the secret garden hiding place to arrest him.

After forewarning them, his chief concern was to expel the traitor from the fellowship. It becomes apparent that Judas must have consistently refused at any point in their relationship to allow Jesus to cleanse him. Jesus could not possibly have handed him the sign of his personal self-giving and expected him to receive it with any sincerity (cf. 13:8b; 1 Cor. 11:27, 28). More-over, with Judas there, always critical and increasingly hostile (12:4-6), he had probably never been completely free spontaneously to share himself with all his disciples as he spoke to them as a group. Here in this last night together, his desire was to reveal himself to them in a closer and more intimate way than ever before. He wanted to speak to them of how he was going to

216

come back to them in the Person of his Spirit; he wanted them to share in his prayer for their unity. Judas had to be dismissed.

We are told in the other Gospels that when Jesus announced his coming betrayal the disciples began each to be disturbed by the question whether they might be the one referred to. 'Surely not I', each said to Jesus (Matt. 26:22). Jesus is here deliberately shown not to have sought to relieve them of their anxiety by any public exposure of the culprit. It was a well-known custom at a feast for the host to give to a favoured guest, as a token of affection, a 'sop' dipped in wine,[3] and Jesus permitted the disciples to assume it was such a sign of favour that he had given to Judas. Instead of suspecting him, they were kept in suspense about themselves. It was not morbid or unhealthy for the disciples to have feelings of deep unease as they began to become aware of the cost to be paid by Jesus for their pardon and liberty—nor is it for us today as we contemplate the immeasurable, unfathomable love of Jesus for poor sinners.

In introducing the whole subject of Judas, Jesus took to himself as elsewhere sometimes he did (6:51; 8:58; 18:4-8) the sovereign name that God had given himself in his revelation to Moses at the bush (cf. Exod. 3:14), *'I am he'* (v.19). It was as he dismissed Judas that he most fully and closely demonstrated his right to such a title. He gave him the sop and took complete command of the situation: *'Do quickly what you are going to do'* (v. 27b) He acted as if he were in complete control—as indeed he was—even of the evil Judas hatefully intended. He thus displayed God's complete sovereignty over all that was intended to lead to his own death (cf. Acts 2:23; 3:18).

There is no suggestion that Judas was not completely responsible for his treachery. There is no suggestion that God was not entirely sovereign in predestinating what took place. We are meant to allow our minds to dwell on the darkness of the 'night' which Judas, now freed from all saving restraint by Jesus,

---

[3] The word translated 'piece of bread' (lit. 'morsel') is used only here in the NT. It could refer to a tasty piece of meat as well as to a piece of bread. The action may refer to an early point in the Passover meal when 'bitter herbs' were dipped into a bowl of fruit puree and passed on. The custom had developed of the host handing such a 'sop' to a guest sitting in an honoured place near to him, possibly next to him.

finally courted as his destiny. The same 'night' is still here all around us to be shunned with horror.[4]

The exultant 'now' and the careless word

John 13:31-38

13 When he had gone out, Jesus said, 'Now the Son of Man has been glorified, and God has been glorified in him. [32]If God has been glorified in him, God will also glorify him in himself and will glorify him at once. [33]Little children, I am with you only a little longer. You will look for me; and as I said to the Jews so now I say to you, "Where I am going, you cannot come." [34]I give you a new commandment, that you love one another. Just as I have loved you, you also should love one another. [35]By this everyone will know that you are my disciples, if you have love for one another.'

36 Simon Peter said to him, 'Lord, where are you going?' Jesus answered, 'Where I am going, you cannot follow me now; but you will follow afterwards.' [37]Peter said to him, 'Lord, why can I not follow you now? I will lay down my life for you.' [38]Jesus answered, 'Will you lay down your life for me? Very truly, I tell you, before the cock crows, you will have denied me three times.'

Eternal fellowship with his Father

John's Gospel tells us that immediately Judas departed Jesus began a long discourse to his disciples, the report of which extends through chapters 14 to 16. It is obvious that the words, *Now the Son of Man has been glorified...* indicate Jesus is on the verge of what he still dreaded, though he finds himself also powerfully possessed by a sense of the glory of the mission with which he had been entrusted, and which was about to be

---

[4] '*And it was night.* Doubtless this is historical reminiscence, but it is also profound theology. Even though the paschal moon was shining at the full, Judas was swallowed up by the most awful darkness, indeed by outer darkness (Matt. 8:12; 22:13; 25:30). Judas was heading to his own place.... But in another way it was also the night time for Jesus: it was the hour of the power of darkness (Luke 22:53).' Carson, p. 476.

accomplished. He was upheld by his present eternal fellowship with his Father who, having sent him, would surely vindicate him. He can even speak of his future glory with his Father as if it were here and now. Moreover, it is obvious, that his intention during this whole evening's talk with his disciples was to concentrate their thoughts mainly on how they too will become sharers in that future redemptive glory. He expected to find already within their community life the new and wonderful evidences of the burden-bearing love and intimate personal concern one for another that prevailed in the New Testament community, and he confidently commanded them to begin to show it.

We are intended to notice that when he refers to the suffering he is facing, he chooses his language carefully. He speaks enigmatically yet profoundly. His, *'Where I am going. you cannot come'*, is one of the most profound statements implying substitutionary atonement in the whole New Testament—only he, the 'Faithful and True', could tread the winepress of the wrath of God (Rev. 19:15). In addition, the assurance with which he caps it, *but you will follow afterwards*, can become to us a help towards a fuller understanding of the Christian life, for it was the Lord's intention that his apostles, looking back later, should understand his words. We too, in the light of the fullness of the revelation of his grace, are able to grasp his meaning. Moreover, the further question Peter asked to elucidate it must have encouraged him, as it gave him an opportunity to underline again the lonely severity of the suffering that was going to redeem us.

None but himself could bear what had to be borne, or could offer what alone was an acceptable offering. Jesus was therefore deeply shocked and provoked by Peter's blunt and arrogant boast—*'I will lay down my life for you'* (v. 37b)—which flatly contradicted what he himself had so solemnly affirmed. Here was the best and most trusted of all his disciples revealing once again (cf. Matt.16:22, 23) the human arrogance and vain self-confidence that in so many different forms constantly asserts itself and denies our human need to owe him completely everything worth having in life!

Rash self-confidence

Peter cannot have thought out beforehand the implications of what he allowed himself impetuously to say when he provoked Jesus' rebuke. Jesus once warned us of the significance of thoughts and even words which can suddenly come into our minds on occasional unguarded moments when we are not conventionally on the watch against them. He called them 'careless' (Matt. 12:36, AV has 'idle'), and he warned us of how important it is that they should not in any way be allowed control over us as we seek to re-set our minds on the truth and way of Christ. He warned us that to allow ourselves to be controlled by such inclinations would bring us under the judgement of God. Here was Peter in grave danger of such judgement. Jesus found it impossible to allow his empty boast to pass without the most severe and devastating rebuke he ever gave to a disciple—*before the cock crows, you will have denied me three times.* Peter had to be recalled to his former self-questioning (cf. Matt. 26:22). Nevertheless while issuing so severe a rebuke, the Lord's pastoral love for Peter remained constant as he told him that in the hour of his great failure, his prayers for him would both keep him and restore him to usefulness in God's service (Luke 22:31, 32).

It did not require any supernatural insight to foresee the collapse of the loyalty inspired by such thoughtless boastfulness. Yet Jesus in the word he uttered does not merely foretell such a collapse. He quite divinely and exactly decrees what will come to pass. The word he spoke will inevitably impel Peter's denial as the word he spoke to Judas impelled his betrayal. The fulfilment will be exact. Three times he will swear 'No'! Then the cock will crow! Peter in his shame is as wholly in God's hand as Judas in his unspeakably evil way was in God's hand. But Peter is in God's hand for salvation rather than for damnation. Might it not be that when finally 'he went out and wept bitterly' (Matt. 26:75) something happened to the basic attitude of his heart which was confirmed in that personal but unrecorded interview he had with the risen Jesus on the first Easter Sunday (cf. Mark 16:7; Luke 24:34). A friend once gave me a plaque on which she had embroidered a sailing ship in the wind, and the words were: 'One ship drives East, another West, by the self-same wind that blows. It's the set of the sails, and not the gales, that determines the way it goes.'

CHAPTER 14

THE FINAL DISCOURSE (1)

The Father's house

John 14:1-7

14 'Do not let your hearts be troubled. Believe in God, believe also in me. ²In my Father's house there are many dwelling-places. If it were not so, would I have told you that I go to prepare a place for you? ³And if I go and prepare a place for you, I will come again and will take you to myself, so that where I am, there you may be also. ⁴And you know the way to the place where I am going.' ⁵Thomas said to him, 'Lord, we do not know where you are going. How can we know the way?' ⁶Jesus said to him, 'I am the way, and the truth, and the life. No one comes to the Father except through me. ⁷If you know me, you will know my Father also. From now on you do know him and have seen him.'

The dwelling places and 'Myself'

They had good reason to be *troubled*. 'Their master', writes Luther, 'is no longer the Christ who raised the dead, cleansed the buyers and sellers out of the temple and performed miracles that startled everybody. They have been told that one of their company is a traitor. They have seen Judas go out into the night. They have heard Peter warned that he will deny his master.' To Jesus, the most serious aspect of what was troubling them was the uneasy question about the whole life-situation now facing the disciples as to the kind of world in which they, and Jesus too, were struggling with such difficulty. What real place in the universe around them did this spirit have that could so possess those who dominated human society that they had become determined not only to reject, but even to annihilate, the One in their midst who had so clearly stood for God and goodness, truth and love? Here in these verses is the word Jesus spoke to redeem the whole situation, to deliver them from the gloom that was settling in on their minds and to bring comfort even to subdued and silenced Peter. Luther memorably sums up the first verse: 'Even though everything else fails... you have God and Myself!' The emphasis here as everywhere else in Christ's teaching is on the 'Me'. 'Jesus', said James Denney, 'knew no more sacred duty than to point men to his own person.'

With another brief and continually haunting word about the world they were living in, and what lay before them, he rescued them from all possible gloomy thoughts and fears about their life-situation. 'The world you are living in', he said, 'is *my Father's house*', assuring them that there was no allotted corner of it not designed and furnished with their exact need in mind, and no way within it for one of his loved ones to drift beyond his love and care. The *many dwelling-places* (v. 2, translated in AV as 'many mansions', and sometimes as 'places of abode') is best translated as 'many resting places' and may be thought of as frequent stages on a journey that might be short or long.[1] The promise is that he will make a point of preparing a place for each of us at each stage of our journey, giving us his fellowship with strength for the way ahead.

There is no doubt that Jesus was seeking to occupy the minds of his disciples not only with a new and inspiring picture of their way through this present life, but was also concerned to orient their thoughts towards a final resting place in the world to come. His disciples would soon be put through a real and most bitter experience of bereavement and he wanted too to help them with a relevant word. Verse 3 can include a reference to such a final resting place and to a final 'coming again' of Christ. William Temple, in his comment, finds a hint here of our movement from glory to glory (2 Cor. 3:18) as we progress on the heavenly way.

Jesus was here assuring his disciples that in the life to come there awaits us not only the magnificent freedom and glory of the eternal city, new Jerusalem, but also the familiar restoration of all

---

[1] The Greek word used for 'dwelling places' (*monê*) can refer both to temporary and permanent resting places. If such a double meaning is intended here, then the *Father's house* would include both earth and heaven so that wherever we are, we are in the Father's house. But *many dwelling-places* appears most obviously to refer primarily to heaven itself, as Dr Wallace indicates in his comment in the next paragraph.

that has made 'home' home, and the blessed gift of it to those who have never really enjoyed such a privilege. In making such a promise he assures us that he never mocks us with empty words. He felt that, having spoken so firmly and clearly and having assured them again and again of his own trustworthiness, he had said enough to enable them, if they were 'wise', to build their house upon a rock (Matt. 7:24).

When Jesus said to the group, *you know the way to the place where I am going* (v. 4), he was challenging any uncertainty or perplexity that might be lurking in their minds about the direction and aim of their way ahead. They had his teaching, and he had trained them how to interpret and apply it. They had also his promise to be with them, guiding them as they talked together. He spoke as if he expected such clear, down-to-earth, ethical and practical guidance about the next step on the way to be enough. But Thomas with a sudden new desire to know more about the place, revealed that in spite of his outstanding courage (cf. 11:16), he was still far from understanding even the basic elements of finding the way. And Jesus seized his opportunity to re-direct his whole mind-set. He turned the conversation back to *himself.* Following *himself* through life as he led them personally, they would know the 'way'; understanding *himself* and, seeing what he was pointing to in his teaching, they would know the 'truth'. Living touch with *him* was indeed eternal 'life'. Thomas had to learn no longer to seek ultimate truth in a 'system of propositions grasped by perfect intelligence' (Temple). He had to realize that 'the truth was there before him in Jesus, present concretely in the incarnate Son of God' (Hoskyns). It was inevitable that having laid such emphasis on himself, he should speak of how he lived only to enable those who came to him to come to the Father also. Here, through himself, the Father is to be sought and found. Indeed the Father is to be sought and found, not as One taught about above or apart from Jesus but as One found in Jesus himself.

A cry for reality—
the reproach and the answer

John 14:8-14

14 Philip said to him, 'Lord, show us the Father, and we will be satisfied.' [9]Jesus said to him, 'Have I been with you all this time, Philip, and you still do not know me? Whoever has seen me has seen the Father. How can you say, "Show us the Father"? [10]Do you not believe that I am in the Father and the Father is in me? The words that I say to you I do not speak on my own; but the Father who dwells in me does his works. [11]Believe me that I am in the Father and the Father is in me; but if you do not, then believe me because of the works themselves. [12]Very truly, I tell you, the one who believes in me will also do the works that I do and, in fact, will do greater works than these, because I am going to the Father. [13]I will do whatever you ask in my name, so that the Father may be glorified in the Son. [14]If in my name you ask me for anything, I will do it.'

The search after the knowledge of God

Philip, in his ardent cry to Jesus, is certainly expressing perplexity with what his discipleship has so far brought in the realm of personal religious conviction. No doubt he remembered the joy with which, after his first encounter with Jesus, he had gone to Nathaniel to share what he believed would bring about a complete transformation in habit, experience and character. That it had not done so in his own life, he may have blamed himself. Had he failed to enter into what Jesus offered? Certainly he had found himself unable to keep pace with it and to live it out as it deserved. Now that Jesus seemed to be addressing in Thomas a failure like his own, Philip felt impelled to make his confession, and seek Jesus' help. *'Lord,'* he cried, *'show us the Father, and we will be satisfied.'*

His plea was not simply a deeply felt cry for reality but a carefully formed prayer of intense desire. His mind may have been on the Old Testament prophets. He certainly knew that it was because God, at the beginning of the prophets' service, and at other critical times in their lives, had made himself so real to them through heavenly visions that they had never lost their zeal for his cause. It was because they had seen him, 'high and lifted up' that they had been enabled to endure without growing faint (Isa. 6:1, AV; 40:31; Heb. 11:27). He knew that to Jesus himself at the beginning of his ministry the heavens had been opened. Might not an experience such as this offer himself and the other disciples the satisfaction and strength that all the prophets had found in his service?

Jesus' immediate answer to Philip can be read as a gently worded reproach (v. 9). He had only himself to blame! What he was so earnestly seeking was what Jesus had been patiently trying to put within his reach, and asking him to open up to, all these three years of glorious opportunity. It was he on his own side who had still failed to grasp what had been offered.[2] One of Jesus' most memorable self-affirmations was his claim to have brought within the reach of all around him greater opportunities of transforming encounter with the living God than was ever given to the greatest Old Testament servants. 'But blessed are your eyes, for they see, and your ears, for they hear. Truly I tell you, many prophets and righteous people longed to see what you see, but did not see it, and to hear what you hear, but did not hear it' (Matt. 13:16, 17).

In the Prologue to his Gospel, the evangelist himself, speaking of it as a fact of history, clearly re-affirmed the claim Jesus here made for himself. 'The Word became flesh and lived among us…'. God has not only spoken about himself. He has uttered himself, giving away the inmost secret of who he is. He has done this throughout a whole human life, punctuated by spectacular miracles and ending in the shameful yet glorious death sealed by his resurrection. In our search after the knowledge of God, we are to look here for what we can find nowhere else. When Paul spoke of our being able to see the 'light of the knowledge of the glory of God in the face of Jesus Christ' (2 Cor. 4:6) he was referring to the outstanding character of this Man as a person, his love, openness and continual responsiveness to all human need around him, his humility, even his 'meekness and gentleness' (2

---

[2] It is noteworthy that the three times Philip is mentioned in this Gospel (his name only occurs in the Synoptic Gospels in their lists of the apostles) he is apparently at a loss what to say or do. See 6:5-7; 12:20-22 and here.

Cor. 10:1), his attractiveness to all who care for whatever is just, pure, true and honourable (Phil. 4:8). When Paul wanted to affirm Christ's omnipotence he spoke of how by enticing all the powers of evil to enter into conflict with him in his weakness on the cross, the Lord broke their power for ever in his final triumph (Col. 2:15). It is obvious that at the very moment of speaking these words, Jesus was perfectly demonstrating their truth through the calm trust he was showing in his Father as he faced all the questions raised by that final journey towards the Cross—a trust that was going to be finally expressed by the prayers to his Father which he uttered as he was being crucified.

The 'seeing' to which Jesus was here referring—*Whoever has seen me has seen the Father*—involved some measure of what we sometimes call 'insight'. Elisha's servant, when he rose that morning, looked around and, seeing only the overwhelming Syrian host, was terrified until Elisha prayed for God to 'open his eyes that he may see' (2 Kgs 6:17) and then everything was different! This 'seeing' can certainly become at times a prominent and dramatic aspect of a sudden experience. To Peter, for instance, as he witnessed Jesus accomplishing the miracle of the shoal of fishes there obviously came a quite sudden apprehension of the divine majesty there before him in the person with whom a moment before he had been so familiar (Luke 5:8f.). Paul, in his preaching, referred often to one dramatic and quite spectacular experience of 'seeing' on the road to Damascus (Acts 22:6ff.; 26:12ff.). Yet most of us can grow in the ability to 'see' in this way as our faith and Christian experience deepens and increases. Calvin believed that this 'seeing' could be simply perfect faith[3]

'In my name'

The test of how firmly we have grasped, and trusted in, the fatherhood of God lies in the place played in our daily lives by prayer to the Father through the name and the sonship of Jesus. It does not surprise us therefore that having been involved by Philip in such an important discussion on knowing the Father, Jesus should launch out on a discussion of how we can prove the

---

[3] Calvin: 'Christ rightly reproves Philip that he has not the clear eyes of faith.' *Comm. in loc.*

fatherhood of God through the works God will do on our behalf if we will simply learn trustingly to pray to him. He tells his disciples here that when he ascends to be forever with the Father, they will then be enabled when they pray, to ask him to offer to God in his own name the prayers that they themselves make, and plead for them to be answered. He describes this new form of prayer as made 'in my name'.[4] Such praying, he affirms, is certain to be answered, and he promises that it will dominate the life of the church which the disciples are going to found. It will enable them even to repeat the marvellous works he himself had been able to accomplish through his own personal prayer to God when he was on earth. Indeed he promises the disciples that in the church they are going to found and establish they will be able to do greater works than any of his own simply *because I am going to the Father* (v. 12).

When Jesus spoke of the 'greater works' that the church would learn to do by its asking and working 'in his name', we can think of him as looking forward to the inauguration of the mission of the church to all nations, which he even then expected. As Newbigin puts it, 'Signs given on the narrow stage of Galilee and Judea will now be multiplied on a much larger stage!' Athanasius, still in the days of the early church, could describe how fornicators become chaste, and murderers no longer wield the sword: 'They turn from fighting to farming... and extend their hands in prayer.' It is a greater thing, observes Temple, 'to have founded hospitals all over the world than to have healed scores in Palestine'.

---

[4] Prayers truly 'in Christ's name' will not be uttered out of selfish motives or for self-glory. They will be spoken in faith, will be according to the will of God and will be only for God's glory. 'Christ's name' is a synedoche for his character, his revelation of the Father and his authority to inaugurate the Kingdom. Therefore prayers truly 'in his name' are bound to be answered because they will reflect the eternal purposes and grace of God himself.

The commandments and the offence

John 14:15-24

14 'If you love me, you will keep my commandments. ¹⁶And I will ask the Father, and he will give you another Advocate, to be with you for ever. ¹⁷This is the Spirit of truth, whom the world cannot receive, because it neither sees him nor knows him. You know him, because he abides with you, and he will be in you.

18 'I will not leave you orphaned; I am coming to you. ¹⁹In a little while the world will no longer see me, but you will see me; because I live, you also will live. ²⁰On that day you will know that I am in my Father, and you in me, and I in you. ²¹They who have my commandments and keep them are those who love me; and those who love me will be loved by my Father, and I will love them and reveal myself to them.' ²²Judas (not Iscariot) said to him, 'Lord, how is it that you will reveal yourself to us, and not to the world?' ²³Jesus answered him, 'Those who love me will keep my word, and my Father will love them, and we will come to them and make our home with them. ²⁴Whoever does not love me does not keep my words; and the word that you hear is not mine, but is from the Father who sent me.'

Love the context of obedience

In what he had said to both Thomas and Philip, Jesus stressed the prime importance of having at the heart of their discipleship a personal devotion to himself: *I am the way* (v. 6); *Whoever who has seen me has seen the Father* (v. 9). Now he tells us to be no less ardent about the more thought-provoking and demanding aspects of the relationship he opens up for us. He has spoken words which he asks us to believe. He has spoken commandments which he asks us to keep. Now we have to be brought to realize that what he is calling us into when he calls us to himself in personal trust is, as Hoskyns puts it so well, 'no mere passionate emotion of the heart'. It is a love whose reality is expressed by keeping his commandments (1 John 2:3-6; 3:23). 'Obedience is the test of love, and love is the context of obedience' (Newbigin). We have to take his words as seriously as we take Christ himself: *If you love me, you will keep my commandments.*

Jesus was well aware that his commandments taught what the world[5] was bound to regard as a 'narrow' and 'hard' way of life (Matt. 7:14), often quite contrary to the 'broad' way of self-fulfilment which the world (even then—how little has changed over 2000 years!) assumed it was simply natural to follow. Therefore he knew that in thrusting them into the forefront of the witness which the disciples were to give to the world both in their teaching and way of life, he would be involving them in tension with those they were sent to win. Even his commandments, if they preached them faithfully, would always present to the world an offensive cutting-edge put there to block the way to any form of self-centred pride. The word of Jesus, if they preached it faithfully and clearly, would create disturbance. While it would call those who believed to a radical conversion of views and a new way of life, it would also stir up such an opposition from those who felt their dearest convictions were being attacked that it might lead to conflict and even persecution (cf. Matt. 5:10, 11; 7:14; 10:14, 34-36; John 16:1ff., etc.).

It was therefore of great concern to Jesus that his disciples should in no way become ashamed and attempt to avoid the offence with which any aspect of his message would confront the world he had sent them to save. They must not seek to re-interpret the gospel so that it fitted neatly into the cherished natural beliefs, ways and ideals of the generation to which they belonged. He therefore encouraged them to faithfulness by lavish promises of his loving support and reward.

The 'Spirit of truth' he promises will become an inner 'Advocate' (v. 16, 17).[6] He will be 'with you' as you take your

---

[5] John's theology knows nothing of the eastern dualism so prevalent today. The world (*Gk., kosmos*) is that which was created through the agency of the Word—now made flesh—and indeed there is nothing within it which he did not create (1:3). Yet the world is in rebellion against him, refusing to acknowledge him (1:10f.). Here Jesus speaks of that same world which still remains in moral rebellion against its Creator's word and person.

[6] The word translated here as 'Advocate' has been variously rendered as 'Comforter' (AV) 'Counsellor' (RSV, NIV) and 'Helper' (NKJ, GNB). 'Comforter' was used in an age when 'to comfort' meant 'to strengthen, to encourage, to bring succour'; today the word has undertones of a friend sympathizing with a

stand with him. Through him you will become possessed inwardly by convincing certainty (v. 17).[7] He assures them that through the presence with them of the Advocate they will experience himself alive, leading them for ever now, exactly as he always did previously (v. 19; cf. Heb. 13:8), always there, even when he seemed briefly to have left them to struggle without him (v. 18; cf. 6:17-21).

When Judas (not Iscariot) expressed amazement verging on perplexity as to how such wonderful promises could be fulfilled (v. 22), Jesus simply added the further promise of a deeper and more powerful inward experience of being at home with himself as their Brother in the fatherly love of God (vv. 20, 23; cf. Heb. 2:11). They are indeed blessed who have refused to be offended in him or his word! (Matt. 11:6).

---

bereaved widow at her loss! 'Counsellor' is better but is also open to misunderstanding, being commonly used of marriage counsellors or amateur psychologists. 'Helper' is perhaps better but can sound patronizing as helpers tend to be inferiors. The original word, sometimes literally translated 'Paraclete' meant 'one called alongside' to help. It could refer to a legal assistant or a barrister, defending, witnessing or assisting a client or friend in court. However, John uses 'Advocate' not only to denote an 'encourager, defender, strengthener' but also to denote a 'prosecutor' (see 16:7-11). The context then must guide us as to the intended meaning. Here, the word 'Advocate' is in close conjunction with *the Spirit of truth* (see also 15:26; 16:13), apparently because his office is to communicate the truth as expressed by Jesus who has just declared himself to be 'the truth' (14:6). Therefore in this passage we may take it that 'Advocate' carries the (partly legal) meaning of 'witnessing to the truth'.

[7] It is important to note that although the noun 'spirit' in Greek is neuter, John invariably and deliberately uses masculine pronouns here and elsewhere, thus defying the normal rules of Greek grammar: 'This is the Spirit of truth, whom world cannot receive, because it neither sees *him* nor knows *him*. You know *him,* because *he* abides with you, and *he* will be in you' (v. 17). The reader concludes therefore that the Spirit is a Person, not an impersonal force.

Chapter 14

A special promise and a special gift

John 14:25-31

14 'I have said these things to you while I am still with you. [26]But the Advocate, the Holy Spirit, whom the Father will send in my name, will teach you everything, and remind you of all that I have said to you. [27]Peace I leave with you; my peace I give to you. I do not give to you as the world gives. Do not let your hearts be troubled, and do not let them be afraid. [28]You heard me say to you, "I am going away, and I am coming to you." If you loved me, you would rejoice that I am going to the Father, because the Father is greater than I. [29]And now I have told you this before it occurs, so that when it does occur, you may believe. [30]I will no longer talk much with you, for the ruler of this world is coming. He has no power over me; [31]but I do as the Father has commanded me, so that the world may know that I love the Father. Rise, let us be on our way.'

Facing the final task

Jesus knew himself about to face the final ordeal into which his career on earth would lead him. The *ruler of this world,* in his desperate bid to deceive and seduce humankind, unwilling to accept as final what happened in the wilderness (v. 30, cf. Luke 4:13) would soon be there to confront him. All that Jesus needed now to do was, by his complete trust and patient self-offering, to let the whole world *know that I love the Father* (v. 31). His work would then be done. God would raise him up and crown with glory the perfect human life he has presented as ours, and offered in sacrifice.

One supremely important task in ensuring the effectiveness of his life and death remained as the responsibility of his disciples. They had been chosen with earnest prayer and discerning care as men who would become completely devoted to the service of God. He had kept them close to himself all through his ministry. He had taught them who he was and what he had come to do, and given them special insight into the significance of many of his particularly important actions, sayings and stories. Now they were to be faced with the final task he had purposed for them

231

when he chose them. The work now before them was to ensure that everything that gave meaning and character to his whole self-offering should be faithfully passed on to the growing church. It must be preached on with reliable insight. It must finally be recorded in books so that the Jesus they had known so well could be truly represented to their own and all coming generations as the living and revealed Word of God in his power to heal and redeem all who trust in him. Now he promised the final miracle that would ensure the fruition of his purpose: *'the Holy Spirit, whom the Father will send in my name, will teach you everything, and remind you of all that I have said to you'* (v. 26).[8]

Of course much of the story of the things he said would have to be passed over (cf. 21:25). Yet the whole essential sum of his wisdom and teaching and all the situations which made it relevant would be remembered. The full significance of the wonderful works, which gave a full picture of his glory and bore testimony to the power and presence of his kingdom, would be told so that succeeding generations would be able to understand and believe. Moreover, the inspiration and help which the disciples are to be given would not deprive them of all human fallibility nor crush their individuality. It would not even prevent them, when re-telling, from inadvertently reproducing the divine utterance in their own style. Yet this account would be entirely sufficient and completely reliable. The Spirit would ensure that, so that those who read, and through reading hear the apostles' record of his speaking, would indeed be enabled to hear again the voice that spoke in Jerusalem and Galilee; indeed those who yielded to him as the first disciples had done would find him working in their midst now as he had done there and then—'Jesus Christ is the same yesterday and today and forever' (Heb. 13:8).

Having promised this, he was at peace. He had seen to everything. He could trust the Father. He could trust the power of the Spirit and he could trust those to whom he had been speaking. He knew he was on the way to final triumph. We are meant to think about, marvel at and receive for ourselves this 'peace' (v. 27). It is a sense of deep 'at home-ness' (cf. v. 23) in

---

[8] '[There is] a further point: if [the Spirit] is sent in Jesus' name, he is *Jesus'* emissary (not simply his substitute...). Just as Jesus came in his Father's name (5:43; 10:25), *i.e.,* as his Father's emissary, so the Spirit comes in Jesus' name.' Carson, p. 505.

a world still toiling under the threat of alien powers. It is the precious possession of those who, under the direst of circumstances, know they cannot drift beyond the love and care of 'the God of peace' (Phil. 4:9). Along with joy, hope and love, peace ('shalom')[9] is numbered among the great messianic blessings of the kingdom, both in the Old and New Testaments (Num. 6:26; Isa. 52:7; Zech. 9:10; Col. 1:20; Phil. 4:7). It can enable us to bear up victoriously with patience through all the shocks and long tensions of the battles we at times have to face as we wait for final vindication.

The secular world around us, following its own 'thoughts' and 'ways' (Isa. 55:8, 9) can help us with its wise counselling and medicines too, to bear up under life's stress and depression. We ourselves, moreover, through our own self-discipline can train our minds to a more peace-giving outlook on providence around us. Jesus here, however, explains to us that this 'peace' itself is uniquely his own, and that he imparts it to us in his own unique way. He speaks his word to us (cf. 20:19-23) putting himself into the very word he utters so that, receiving him, we are assured that what is his is also ours (cf. 20:26).

Additional Note on: *'Rise, let us be on our way.'*

Some explain this apparent instruction as simply an exhortation to the disciples to summon up courage to meet their troubles victoriously (let's keep at it!). Though we take the Gospel at face value and accept that the whole of what is related in chapters 13-17 took place continuously while Jesus remained within the upper room, we acknowledge there may have taken place some disarrangement of manuscript material which could have caused an original end section to be displaced.[10]

---

[9] 'Shalom' was 'the customary Jewish greeting and word of farewell. Here it is primarily farewell.' Carson, p. 505.
[10] For a full discussion of the various solutions to the seeming incongruity of 14:31 and 18:1, see Carson, pp. 476-9.

THE FINAL DISCOURSE (2)

The mystery at the heart of the church

John 15:1-8

15 'I am the true vine, and my Father is the vine-grower. [2]He removes every branch in me that bears no fruit. Every branch that bears fruit he prunes to make it bear more fruit. [3]You have already been cleansed by the word that I have spoken to you. [4]Abide in me as I abide in you. Just as the branch cannot bear fruit by itself unless it abides in the vine, neither can you unless you abide in me. [5]I am the vine, you are the branches. Those who abide in me and I in them bear much fruit, because apart from me you can do nothing. [6]Whoever does not abide in me is thrown away like a branch and withers; such branches are gathered, thrown into the fire, and burned. [7]If you abide in me, and my words abide in you, ask for whatever you wish, and it will be done for you. [8]My Father is glorified by this, that you bear much fruit and become my disciples.'

Our union with Christ

We are not misinterpreting this passage if we even at times forget the original context and listen to what it says as a talk given by Jesus himself directly to ourselves and designed to help us to live the Christian life today. He just as much had us in mind then as he has us in mind now.

At the beginning of the chapter he sets the stage for us to think of ourselves in his church, each as a branch of a vine in a vineyard tended by a heavenly vine-grower whose chief aim for us is that we should be fruitful. When he stresses the continual need in a vineyard for the vines to be pruned, sometimes very drastically so that they can be more fruitful, he is reminding us of the severe providential chastening which our heavenly Father must sometimes administer to subdue that tendency always within us to be slothful and forgetful of our calling and thus useless in the service of Christ. He warns us about the possibility of our being rejected, cut out of the vinestock and destroyed, if we refuse to yield to his treatment.

This is one of several passages within the Gospels in which Jesus refers to the intimately close personal communion between himself and his disciples which would be consummated only after his death, resurrection and ascension: as the branch abides in the vine, so he will abide in us and we will abide in him. He refers elsewhere to this life-giving intimacy he would eventually create between himself and his disciples. In the sixth chapter of John, after he fed the multitude, he urged his hearers to think of himself as the 'living bread that came down from heaven' and expressed a desire that we would 'eat' his flesh (cf. 6:48-53). Moreover in his institution of the Lord's Supper, in order to signify what would lie at the heart of his future relationship with his disciples he gave them each a broken piece of bread saying, 'Take, eat; this is my body' (Matt. 26:26). The apostle Paul was later to emphasize the central place this union between the ascended Christ and ourselves is intended to play in enabling us to live the Christian life. 'I have been crucified with Christ;' he wrote, 'and it is no longer I who live, but it is Christ who lives in me' (Gal. 2:19, 20).

It is important that we fully understand what Jesus is referring to when he mentions the fruit which the vine-grower is seeking from the vine. Jesus not only died his death for our sake, he also lived his life for our sake. Not only in his death on the cross did he make the one atoning offering that could take away the sin of the world, throughout his whole life of perfect obedience he also offered to God on our behalf the one human life that would perfectly please him. All of us are 'under the power of sin' (Rom. 3:9) and so without his help we can never please God—*apart from me you can do nothing.*[1]

---

[1] Calvin comments on the words, *apart from me you can do nothing*: 'This is the conclusion and application of the whole parable. So long as we are outside Him, we bear no fruit good and pleasing to God, for we are quite unfit to do anything good... Christ declares... that we can do nothing of ourselves. "The branch bears no fruit of itself," He says. Therefore, He does not merely extol the assistance of His grace in co-operating, but deprives us completely of all power except what He supplies.' *Comm. in. loc.*

Jesus' earthly ministry was punctuated on significant occasions by a voice from heaven proclaiming God's pleasure in him (Matt. 3:17; 17:5).[2] He alone was raised up because death could have no hold over him (Acts 2:24). This gives us a clue to the marvellous transformation that God means to take place through our becoming united to Christ as fruitful branches of the vine. The Holy Spirit coming to us from the ascended Jesus and uniting us to him is now able to reproduce within us the kind of life he lived out for us when he took our place in humanity; the Spirit is able even to reproduce within us the kind of virtue and inclination Jesus described when he gave us that account of his own self in the Sermon on the Mount.[3]

We can think of it as the most wonderful work of the Holy Spirit that he is able to link us up with Christ, that is, Christ with us in all his risen and ascended power, so that he reproduces within us the kind of response to the Father (cf. Rom. 8:15, 16) that the human Jesus offered him on our behalf when he lived his life on earth. We must continually remember that it is the Spirit who enables us not only to displace self but also to present to God the kind of life with which Jesus pleased him when he lived in our flesh.

The call to a disciplined life

The call to *abide in me* is a call to a disciplined life. God's purpose is that we should maintain and even cultivate the faith-relationship by which Christ is enabled to dwell and work within

---

[2] The Father's affirmation of the Son echoes the words of both Psalm 2:7 and Isaiah 42:1. It was not that the voice from heaven brought to Jesus for the first time an awareness of his divine relationship to the Father; rather was it a confirmation of his already existing filial consciousness. Calvin comments: 'Christ was presented to us by the Father... that we might rely on this pledge of our adoption and without fear call God Himself our Father.... So God, in introducing our Mediator with words that praise Him as the Son, declares Himself to be a Father to us all.... The best interpreter of this passage [Matt. 3:17] is Paul (Eph. 1:6), where he says we have obtained grace in the beloved, that we may be beloved by God.' *Harmony*, Vol.1, p. 132f.

[3] Dr Wallace most probably refers here to the fulfilment of the Law and Prophets which Jesus came to accomplish. So, for example, nine times over he states: *But I say to you* as he lays down for all time the Christlike spirituality invoked in believers by the right understanding of the *Torah* (Matt. 5:18, 20, 22, 26, 28, 32, 34, 39, 44), which spirituality will reflect his own person and work and act as both light and salt in the world.

us. Such faith 'comes from what is heard, and what is heard comes through the word of Christ' (Rom. 10:17). We determine its growth by whether or not we continually make a positive effort to hear, listen, study and absorb what the Word says to us in our personal devotion as well as in the fellowship of the church. Our circumstances are all so different that detailed guidance in this matter is not always relevant. Yet it can be helpful to review the way that the Old Testament people of God were encouraged to intense and persistent faithfulness in 'seeking his face' (Pss 24:6; 27:8). 'Happy is the one who listens to me, watching daily at my gates, waiting beside my doors' (Prov. 8:34). Even through the habit of reading about Christ as he has allowed himself to be remembered in the Gospels, we are setting the Lord before us (cf. Pss 16:8; 91:14, AV; see also Ps. 54:3) so that our devotedness to him may grow.

This call to discipline involves a call to self-denial (cf. Matt. 16:24). In the words *abide in me,* 'he again exhorts them to be diligent and careful in keeping the grace with which they were endowed. For the [false] security of the flesh can never be stirred up enough.'[4] If Christ is to be given space and freedom to do his own sanctifying work within us we may have to deny not only our obviously sinful, rebellious inclinations, but also sometimes the personal goodness and ideals we have hitherto cherished. To *'abide in me',* says Godet, 'expresses the continuous act by which the Christian lays aside all he might draw from his own wisdom, strength or merit to derive all from Christ'.

In the Old Testament the people of Israel who were chosen by God eventually to bring blessing to all nations through the coming of Christ and his Church are sometimes referred to as a 'vine' (e.g. in Ps. 80:8-11, 'brought... out of Egypt' and planted in the land of Israel to take deep root and fill the land; cf. Hos. 10:1, etc.). When Jesus here, remembering the continual failure of Israel in the service of God, calls himself the 'true' vine, he is reminding us that we ourselves in him are now to become the true means of bringing to all nations the blessing he promised through Abraham's seed. We ourselves as branches of the spreading vine have been caught up in the purposeful history which must now

---

[4] Calvin, *Comm. in loc.*

inevitably move on to its glorious consummation in Christ's final kingdom over all nations.

It is in this context that we find it best to interpret what Jesus says here about our praying. Naturally since we are united to him, we will be moved to continual prayer, for he himself ever lives to make intercession for us (Heb. 7:25). Our praying, moreover, will inevitably be concentrated on bearing much fruit so that our Father may be glorified. Jesus promises that whatever we ask in such God-centred and God-glorifying praying will be done for us. We will become certain that our prayers are not in vain, so certain that though we may not always be able to pin exact cases to exact prayer we will be able to confess sincerely that whatever we ask in his name is answered.[5]

Abiding in love

John 15:9-17

15 'As the Father has loved me, so have I loved you; abide in my love. [10]If you keep my commandments, you will abide in my love, just as I have kept my Father's commandments and abide in his love. [11]I have said these things to you so that my joy may be in you, and that your joy may be complete.

12 'This is my commandment that you love one another as I have loved you. [13]No one has greater love than this, to lay down one's life for one's friends. [14]You are my friends if you do what I command you. [15]I do not call you servants any longer, because the servant does not know what the master is doing; but I have called you friends,

---

[5] Commenting on 15:7 and the invitation of Christ to believers to ask for anything, Calvin writes: 'When He promises to grant whatever we wish, He does not permit us undisciplined asking. God would have a poor care for our salvation if He gave way so easily and indulgently; for we know how men wanton in foolish desires to the extreme. Here He limits His people's wishes to that principle of praying aright which subjects all our affections to the will of God. This is confirmed by the context, for He means that His own do not *will* riches or honours or the like, which the flesh foolishly desires, but the vital sap of the Holy Spirit, by which they bear fruit.' *Comm. in. loc.*

because I have made known to you everything that I have heard from my Father. ^{16}You did not choose me but I chose you. And I appointed you to go and bear fruit, fruit that will last, so that the Father will give you whatever you ask him in my name. ^{17}I am giving you these commands so that you may love one another.'

We can soon stray away from pure love for himself. At times we can so overstress our zeal for keeping his commandments that we crush out the love we should have kept for himself. We can turn his teaching either into an all-demanding duty, or else into an ideal that expresses what we foolishly regard as the best of ourselves, consequently losing all reference to Jesus. The vital personal dimension too easily becomes lost. Therefore we must take pains to ensure that keeping his commandments is, and always remains, an exercise in abiding in his love, and brings us the experience of full joy which he here promises. We must ever remember our chief end is to glorify him and *enjoy* him forever.

In order to give the disciples an example of the kind of love he wants us to cultivate for himself, he points to what they can see already taking place within the life of the fledgling church around them where such loyalty and friendship was emerging that his followers were showing themselves prepared to lay down their lives for him and possibly for each other in love. (The disciples' pledge to die for Jesus, spoken at this time (Mark 14:31), could well have been a response to Jesus' words in verses 12 and 13 of our passage.)

As we read the New Testament we should not fail to marvel, as even those who lived on the fringe of church life marvelled, at the way these early Christians felt bound to one another in one body in which all suffered if they knew one was suffering (Rom. 12:15). It became their priority to care for those easily led astray, the sick in body or in spirit, no matter what sacrifice it cost. Even the under-privileged within the neighbourhood around them were not forgotten because they had first learned from Jesus to lay down their lives for their friends within the church. In no other sphere of life, indeed, could such rich, sensitive and self-giving love possibly have been nurtured and expressed. Jesus Christ, said Philip Brooks, came to vindicate the rights of the weak against the strong as an aspect of the foundation of the universe.

From servants to friends

Jesus now urges his disciples to think of the relationship between himself and them as that of such friendship. We are certainly still his servants and we are to expect to be rewarded or chastened as we observe or neglect his commandments. But he wants us to learn to render obedience always as an expression of friendship, and to accept either our rewards or our chastening as given out of such love (cf. Heb. 12:5-11). We must realize that in submitting even to the commandments by which he is seeking to shape our way of life we are submitting to his friendship and we must note the loving tone in which he speaks them to us. Their breadth, covering every important aspect of our lives, is itself a sign of the breadth of his love and care for fellowship with every phase of our lives. We must increasingly learn to trust him so much as our friend that whether or not we have a clear explanation of his ways with us, our friendship will make us certain that he is working all things together for good (cf. Rom. 8:28ff.). He does not want to lead us on blindly, though it is true at times we may not understand all that he is seeking to do in our lives. Rather he seeks from us a 'yes' to the way he is leading us—a 'yes' that is our trustful recognition that his way always *is* the best and most sensible way to take.

Jesus then gives voice to the inescapable conclusion that it is he and he alone who initiated their relationship with himself (v. 16).[6] 'We love because he first loved us' (1 John 4:19). He has caught us up not only with his friendship but into the service of what his love is achieving in history—his kingdom that will last for ever. As we yield to that love and purpose we will be encouraged to pray for its fulfilment, and the desires of our heart will be known and answered even before they are consciously expressed. However, yielding to his love will have the inevitable outcome that we will express that love to others.

Finally, we should not ignore how important Jesus' teaching on love is in this passage. It is instructive to notice how John in his

---

[6] Calvin comments on verse 16: 'It is commonly thought that there is a certain mutual combination between the grace of God and the human will, but that contrast, "I chose you; I was not chosen by you," claims completely for Christ alone what is usually divided between Him and man. As if He had said that a man is not moved of his own accord to seek Christ until he has been sought by Him.' *Comm. in loc.*

first letter develops this principle of love more fully to the extent that he tells us one of the marks that must distinguish true disciples is the love of Jesus shown to others in his name; indeed, it is what might be termed the 'social test' of genuine discipleship.[7] Here Jesus calls it 'my command' (vv. 12, 17, NIV), whereas in his letter John calls it the 'new commandment' (1 John 2:8-10; 3:11-20). While we may too easily take Jesus' command for granted, it was 'new' in so far as his love for us is an expression of the Father's love for him and it is this divine love of the Father for the Son in which we are to remain: that is, the love in which we must abide is to be of the same essence as the Father's love for Jesus (v. 9). Perhaps it was these words about love and loving together along with the saying about laying down one's life for one's friends (v. 13) which inspired John's greatest statement of all that 'God is love' (1 John 4:16).

The self-exposure of the 'world'

John 15:18 – 16:4

15 'If the world hates you, be aware that it hated me before it hated you. [19]If you belonged to the world, the world would love you as its own. Because you do not belong to the world, but I have chosen you out of the world—therefore the world hates you. [20]Remember the word that I said to you, "Servants are not greater than their master." If they persecuted me, they will persecute you; if they kept my word, they will keep yours also. [21]But they will do all these things to you on account of my name, because they do not know him who sent me. [22]If I had not come and spoken to them, they would not have sin; but now

---

[7] The structure of John's First Letter revolves around three tests of genuine discipleship. First, there is obedience or the moral test which consists in obeying Christ's commands (2:3-6); second, there is love or the social test which consists in loving others as Christ has loved us: this is the 'new commandment' (2:7-11); third, there is the doctrinal test which consists in confessing Jesus is the Christ (2:18-27). John then applies the three tests more fully in the second section of the letter, 2:28 – 4:6. He repeats the threefold application for a final time in the section 4:7–5:5.

they have no excuse for their sin. [23]Whoever hates me hates my Father also. [24]If I had not done among them the works that no one else did, they would not have sin. But now they have seen and hated both me and my Father. [25]It was to fulfil the word that is written in their law, "They hated me without a cause."

26 'When the Advocate comes, whom I will send to you from the Father, the Spirit of truth who comes from the Father, he will testify on my behalf. [27]You also are to testify because you have been with me from the beginning.

16 'I have said these things to you to keep you from stumbling. [2]They will put you out of the synagogues. Indeed, an hour is coming when those who kill you will think that by doing so they are offering worship to God. [3]And they will do this because they have not known the Father or me. [4]But I have said these things to you so that when their hour comes you may remember that I told you about them.'

Jesus is here warning his disciples of things about to happen that cast new light on their whole world-situation, deeply affecting both their understanding of human nature and their message and mission in life. The world will soon crucify Jesus, expressing itself against him in a frenzy of virulent spite, brutality, pride and madness. Some whom they thought allies and even friends will join sides against him. The disciples themselves will fail in utter shame to stand by him. Though they will finally be brought through their agony into glorious, wonderful and redemptive freedom, the inevitable bias of the world against his kindness will have been revealed. It will now be known by them for what it truly is. They will be hated and persecuted as he was, and their lives may even be threatened. Jesus warns them of this beforehand in order to give them time to prepare themselves to stand the shock of being reckoned first as aliens and then as enemies by those to whom they once were close. He hopes they will be helped to regard the very hatred they have incurred as an encouraging sign that they must have been truly faithful to him. He prays that they will be comforted, emboldened and stirred up to continue the battle without compromise.

As he speaks in this way about the hatred which he believes the world will show for his church, Jesus himself seems suddenly to be overcome by the prospect of having to encounter its full violence at close hand as his own hour approaches. He shares his thoughts and feelings with the disciples. It brought him grief beyond measure and explanation as he discerned that men and women who had heard his teaching and witnessed his miraculous signs could then have hated both himself and his Father. It faced him with the inexplicable absurdity of the stark presence of sin in this godly, good creation (vv. 24, 25). There are echoes here, in the phraseology he uses, of the same astonishment, hurt and grief that were at times expressed in the Old Testament by the Lord over what he had to face as he dealt in love with Israel (e.g. Isa. 5:4; Jer. 2:13; Hos. 11:7). But even in all the hurt they did to their Lord, the people of Israel were never seen to manifest the enormity of the hatred which the world was now to show to Jesus who had proved himself worthy of true faith and adoration. Here was what must indeed be called 'sin' (vv. 22-24).[8] Jesus at this point was led to express his horror in the part he was having to play in provoking the very hatred that was to nail him on his cross. The enormity of the sin in rejecting him is in that those who hate him, hate his Father also. It is a most solemn indictment that those who refuse the gracious words of the gospel, are actually refusing God himself. How sobering it is to consider that there are many who reject the words of the gospel, but nevertheless want to be thought of as sincerely worshipping God; but, as Christ here plainly says, the truth is that within their hearts is nothing less than contempt for the Father (v. 23).

It was only for a moment or two that he unburdened himself in this way to the disciples. Lest he might have troubled them too greatly he now reassures them. As the situation before them develops and becomes more perplexing and dangerous, the Spirit

---

[8] 'It seems as if by these words [v. 22] Christ was suggesting that there is no other sin but unbelief—and indeed some think this... [But here] the word "sin" is not taken generally, but in respect of the subject now under consideration. [It is] as if Christ said that their ignorance is utterly inexcusable, because in [rejecting] Him, they maliciously rejected God... Christ's acquittal of them is confined to one kind of sin... despising and hating the Gospel.' Calvin, *Comm. in loc.*

of truth[9] whom he had earlier promised, would not only be with them to bring all things to their remembrance (14:26), but will also at the same time act as their Advocate.[10] His assurance here is the same as he already gave to them earlier (cf. Matt. 10:19-31) that what they were to say need not be thought of beforehand, for the Spirit would be there to give them the words they were to say, speaking through them even to their persecutors. The Spirit would testify about Christ so that they in turn could fulfil their task of testifying[11] to all they had seen and heard of him because they had been with him from the beginning (15:26bf.).

They are also assured that even the way they take their suffering and bear up under it will register powerfully for the very truth which is being rejected. 'Their life, words, deeds and suffering', writes Newbigin, 'will be the occasion, the place where the mighty Spirit has his own witness to the hearts and consciences of men and women so that they are brought to look again at the hated, rejected, crucified man and confess: Jesus is Lord.'

Additional note on: the 'world' and its hatred of Jesus

We are bound to discuss how far we must allow Jesus' exposure of the 'world' that crucified him to affect our attitude towards the culture of the world around us today. We accept the verdict of Brown that Jesus is here affirming that 'the "world's" hatred is not a passing phenomenon. Hate is as much the essence of the world as love is the essence of the Christian.' We note how often

---

[9] 'When he says that *he will send him from the Father* and again that *he proceeds from the Father*, He does so to increase the weight of His authority. For, unless we were convinced that He had proceeded from God, the testimony of the Spirit would not be sufficient against attacks so powerful and stratagems so many and fierce. Hence, it is Christ who sends the Spirit, but from the heavenly glory; that we may know that He is not a human gift but a sure pledge of divine grace.' Calvin, *Comm. in loc.* On the basis of this saying of Jesus, the Eastern Church has traditionally denied that the Spirit proceeds from the Son as well as from the Father. However, the Western Church has always accepted that the Spirit proceeds both from the Father and the Son. See Acts 2:33.

[10] See p. 229, footnote 6.

[11] 'Testifying' in the NT invariably refers to bearing witness to Jesus as the Christ, God's anointed One. It does not normally refer to 'faith-stories' in the sense in which 'giving testimony' is often used in many church circles today. Note that Paul's testifying before Agrippa focussed on the Person and Work of Jesus Christ (Acts 24:21; 26:22, 23).

the verdict of Jesus is re-echoed in the New Testament by John, James and Paul (1 John 2:15, 16; Jas 4:4; 2 Cor. 6:14-18). The world of Jesus' day crucified him because relentlessly, with persuasive confidence and irresistible power, he demanded from its leaders and people a way of life that seemed inevitably to threaten too many of the cherished ideals and ways that were at the heart of its culture. Other New Testament convictions, however, must be allowed their scope as we ourselves finally make up our minds about the contemporary 'world' we find around us. The society that crucified Jesus had been richly endowed by God with many features meant originally to be uplifting and even ennobling. Paul reminds us that there are things that are honourable, just and pleasing belonging to the world around us today, and we have to make it our wisdom to cherish them (cf. Phil. 4:8). He urges Christians to approach the 'world' with the positive intention of influencing it with the gospel (1 Cor. 3:21-23). Moreover, Jesus in his parable of the yeast (Matt. 13:33) and in his teaching about salt and light (Matt. 5:13, 14) suggested that as the gospel was preached, received and lived out there would occur a modifying and health-giving influence within the whole social community surrounding the growing church. Wherever throughout the course of history the gospel has been welcomed and allowed its full influence on social life we can trace such beneficial and uplifting effects. We have at times felt able to speak of a Christian culture.

It is precisely because what is so valuable in our culture has depended on such a transformation continuously taking place that the warnings given here by Jesus about the nature of the 'world' are relevant, and have to be kept in mind. What has been hard won, over centuries, by the positive influence of the gospel can too soon be lost if the Christians in society fail to be a leavening and stabilizing influence and their light becomes dim. The world has not been converted and will constantly tend to revert. Situations can arise in which what is current in our cultural life will inevitably become alien to the gospel, even to the extent of having itself to be 'hated' (cf. Rom. 12:9) by those who are willing to allow Christ to sanctify them.

CHAPTER 16

THE FINAL DISCOURSE (3)

The work of the Spirit

John 16:4b-15

16 'I did not say these things to you from the beginning, because I was with you. ⁵But now I am going to him who sent me; yet none of you asks me, "Where are you going?" ⁶But because I have said these things to you, sorrow has filled your hearts. ⁷Nevertheless, I tell you the truth: it is to your advantage that I go away, for if I do not go away, the Advocate will not come to you; but if I go, I will send him to you. ⁸And when he comes, he will prove the world wrong about sin and righteousness and judgement: ⁹about sin, because they do not believe in me; ¹⁰about righteousness, because I am going to the Father and you will see me no longer; ¹¹about judgement, because the ruler of this world has been condemned.

12 I still have many things to say to you, but you cannot bear them now. ¹³When the Spirit of truth comes, he will guide you into all the truth; for he will not speak on his own, but will speak whatever he hears, and he will declare to you the things that are to come. ¹⁴He will glorify me, because he will take what is mine and declare it to you. ¹⁵All that the Father has is mine. For this reason I said that he will take what is mine and declare it to you.'

Proving the 'world' wrong

Jesus is now alerting his disciples to expect soon his 'going' away.[1] They had only recently opened their minds to the thought

---

[1] There has been much discussion about the apparent contradiction between Thomas' question in 14:5, 'Lord, we do not know where you are going. How can we know the way?' and Jesus statement here in v. 5, 'none of you asks me, "Where are you going?"' The simplest solution may be that some little time earlier during the Supper, Thomas had asked not *where* Jesus was going but

that they could possibly at any time lose him. He is concerned to lift them out of the sorrow that has begun to possess them, and beyond the temptation to depression. *But now I am going....* They must rid themselves of all suspicion that he can be either hindered by or subject to any will other than his own or his Father's. He was completely in charge of his own destiny. 'I lay down my life in order to take it up again', he had already said. 'No one takes it from me' (10:17f.). He urges them to look forward with hope to his earthly departure. Only if he goes can the new era of the Spirit begin (14:16ff.).[2] He had already spoken about how the Spirit's coming would ensure that their memories of himself and his teaching would be trustworthy, comprehensive and strengthening (14:26; 15:26). He now goes on to speak of how the Spirit will be there always in their continually recurring need to reorient their thinking from falsehood to truth. It was his concern even then that the disciples and the church they would found (Eph. 2:20) should become aware of an ever-present, constant danger that would beset it throughout its history: it would be lured into allowing its thinking on central matters of the faith to be dominated by the constant drift of the world's attitudes into the kind of error that would breed again the self-righteousness and legalism that had so blatantly characterized the opposition of the Pharisees to himself. He speaks of three areas concerning which the Spirit should be allowed to expose[3] the perversity of the world's thinking. *'And when he comes, he will prove the world wrong about sin and righteousness and judgement'* (v. 8). Since we are so prone to share the world's errors and drift back into its thought-patterns, we must endeavour

---

which *route* he was taking—hence Jesus' answer that he was 'the way'; whereas at this point in time, none of them had yet asked him what his *destination* was to be.
[2] The kingdom could not be fully inaugurated until Christ had died, been raised and exalted to the Father's right hand. Not until then would he receive from the Father the Spirit to send him to make good his physical absence from the human world by the Spirit's unrestricted, ubiquitous presence. While Jesus was with the disciples, by the very nature of the self-imposed limitations of his earthly pre-resurrection body, he could only be present in one place at one time, whereas Pentecost transformed that temporary limitation.
[3] The Greek word in v. 8 translated by NRSV as '*prove* the world *wrong* about...' is here well paraphrased by Dr Wallace as 'expose perversity'. It is used eighteen times in the NT and generally means showing people the shame of their sin, convincing them of their guilt and summoning them to repentance.

to follow through the brief hints with which Jesus directs our thoughts on each of these three issues.

When we discuss 'sin' for instance, two closely related definitions will find easy acceptance in our minds. We tend naturally to think that sin is merely the breaking of a kind of shared and accepted code of rules, or even the falling short of some hallowed humanistic ideal of what is good for ourselves and all humankind. If we remember what Jesus himself had recently said (15:22-24) about the essentially absurd and devilishly hate-ridden nature of evil, and if we allow him to control our thinking, we are bound to dismiss such legalistic and idealistic views as quite inadequate, though perhaps containing an element of truth. Though there are many hints in Old Testament history of a more realistic and deeper view (cf. Ps. 51; Isa. 5:18, 20, 24, etc.), the true nature of sin, as he himself said in the agony of facing it, was only *then* given its full and unfettered expression in the reaction of the world to his claims. For us to sin is to give scope to the inclination innate within us, to reject and crucify our Lord, and therefore to reject the Father himself (15:23).

We are apt to think about 'righteousness', as does the world around us, as a praiseworthy virtue we can acquire in our personal character and even display in an aspect of our conduct before God. Righteousness in this worldly view often takes the form of strict adherence to a required and accepted code of moral conduct. Jesus here, however, asks us to accept as our model of it, his own trustworthy and perfectly obedient, sometimes passive, sometimes active, subjection to whatever he knew to be the will of God from stage to stage of his incarnation and earthly life, unflinching in the service of his Father (4:34; 5:19; 6:38). Righteousness[4] as unfolded by Jesus in John's careful record is the 'yes' of obedient self-offering in whatever situation and whatever way God asks. Abraham said that 'yes' when he

---

[4] There is an alternative view to that given by Dr Wallace as to the meaning of 'righteousness' here (the only occurrence of the word, incidentally, in John's Gospel). It is that it is in parallel with 'sin' and 'judgement' and refers to the 'self-righteousness' of legalistic religion (cf. Matt. 5:20). In any case, a study of Jesus' own use in the Synoptics of the 'righteousness' word group shows that while condemning a purely external self-righteousness, he commends, and in himself exemplifies, that inner righteousness of heart and soul (Luke 18:9-14) to which Dr Wallace refers in his comments. Because Jesus is going to the Father, the Spirit, in his absence, will 'prove the world wrong... about righteousness'.

'obeyed and went, even though he did not know where he was going' (Heb. 11:8, NIV); he simply obeyed God's word from day to day and trusted firmly in his promise. Tamar the Canaanite woman who was willing to act the harlot to maintain righteousness in the family of Abraham into which she had married, also spoke that 'yes' and in her obedience was counted righteous by God (Gen. 38:14ff., esp. v. 26).

We normally expect the word 'judgement' to define the process of searching out the criminal, issuing an indictment and using the law court. Here is a 'judgement' brought about in a way significantly different It is through what happened in history that Satan has been condemned and judged. By the coming of Jesus he was provoked to expose his true nature so that no further evidence was needed and, as Brown puts it, 'the very fact that Jesus stands justified before the Father means that Satan has been condemned and had lost his power over the world'.

The coming of the Spirit will not only prove the world wrong but at the same time will ensure that nothing of what Jesus has come to reveal is in vain. Even though the disciples were so close to him during his earthly ministry, and in spite of their whole-hearted desire to be loyal, they did not have at that time the capacity to grasp the full significance of what was taking place before their very eyes. They had been allowed only occasional glimpses of the glory of the One who had veiled himself in flesh in order to dwell with humankind. Jesus now assured them that when the Spirit came, their understanding would be opened to appreciate the full significance of what had been there and then before them in Galilee and Jerusalem. When the Spirit inspired them to remember words and deeds of Jesus he would enable them as they looked back to see and understand what previously they had been too blind to grasp fully.[5] They would therefore now be able even to record the full truth of the word God has spoken in Jesus. Moreover they were also promised that the Spirit would inspire their understanding and insight as they sought to write to the churches about the redeeming and

---

[5] The Spirit's role with regard to the truth is variously described by Jesus. In 14:26, his is a 'teaching' and 'reminding' role. Commentators, however, differ as to the role of the Spirit as described in 15:13-15, some opting for a revelatory role, and others for a role of illumination of what Jesus had already taught his disciples. Dr Wallace (probably rightly) opts for the latter.

sanctifying power of the exalted Christ, and as they outlined *the things that are to come* (v. 13) while they waited for the final day of his revelation in glory. The work of the Spirit would simply be to unveil what was already then and there in Jesus. *'He will glorify me, because he will take what is mine and declare it to you'* (v. 14). The word which the Spirit was to proclaim would be no more and no less than the word of Jesus. 'The Word of the Spirit', says Newbigin, 'does not lead past, or beyond, or away from Jesus.'

On that day

John 16:16-28

16 'A little while, and you will no longer see me, and again a little while, and you will see me.' [17]Then some of his disciples said to one another, 'What does he mean by saying to us, "A little while, and you will no longer see me, and again a little while, and you will see me"; and "Because I am going to the Father"?' [18]They said, 'What does he mean by this "a little while"? We do not know what he is talking about.' [19]Jesus knew that they wanted to ask him, so he said to them, 'Are you discussing among yourselves what I meant when I said, "A little while, and you will no longer see me, and again a little while, and you will see me"? [20]Very truly, I tell you, you will weep and mourn, but the world will rejoice; you will have pain, but your pain will turn into joy. [21]When a woman is in labour, she has pain, because her hour has come. But when her child is born, she no longer remembers the anguish because of the joy of having brought a human being into the world. [22]So you have pain now; but I will see you again, and your hearts will rejoice, and no one will take your joy from you. [23]On that day you will ask nothing of me. Very truly, I tell you, if you ask anything of the Father in my name, he will give it to you. [24]Until now you have not asked for anything in my name. Ask and you will receive, so that your joy may be complete.

25 'I have said these things to you in figures of speech. The hour is coming when I will no longer speak to you in figures, but will tell you plainly of the Father. [26]On that day you will ask in my name. I do not

say to you that I will ask the Father on your behalf; ^{27}for the Father himself loves you, because you have loved me and have believed that I came from God. ^{28}I came from the Father and have come into the world; again, I am leaving the world and am going to the Father.'

New birth to dying souls

Jesus prepared his disciples not only for the coming of the Spirit but also for the extremely significant experiences that they would go through as he now left the world and went to the Father (v. 17). *'You will no longer see me, and again a little while, and you will see me'* (v. 16). He possibly deliberately puzzled them with this remark because he wanted to ensure that they understood the crucial importance of the coming events, then when he had their anxiety and curiosity aroused he explained the riddle (v. 25, *figures of speech*; NKJ: 'figurative language'; NIV: 'this kind of language'; cf. v. 29).[6]   He was obviously referring to the devastation and shame they would go through as they witnessed his death and burial, and the glorious joy that would come to them during the forty days in which they witnessed him alive by many convincing proofs, and the subsequent outpouring of the Holy Spirit (Acts 1:3; 2:33).

As he elaborated on the meaning of these coming events, Jesus refers his disciples in thought back to several Old Testament passages (Isa. 13:6-8; 14:1; 54:1-3, 66:9-11) which speak especially of how Israel and the nations, even in spite of sinful resistance, are going to be put through suffering like that of a woman in labour (v. 21) as God moves history to its fulfilment. He dwells on the joy which will replace the sorrow and pain—the joy of taking part in events of world-transforming significance which will bring new birth to dying souls; it will be the joy of being able to see him again (v. 22) as he himself comes and goes in a never-ending fellowship—an 'indescribable and glorious joy' (1 Peter 1:8).   We can contrast the formality of the song and worship of the heavenly host in Revelation chapter 4 with the

---

[6] Calvin explains verse 25 thus: 'I seem to you to be speaking figuratively now and not simply and plainly; but I will soon speak to you more familiarly, that there may be nothing perplexing or difficult for you in My teaching.' *Comm. in loc.*

triumphant enthusiasm of chapter 5, following the ascendance to the throne of the 'Lamb that was slain' (AV).

One foretaste of that coming glory, he tells them, will be a new-found urge in their desire to pray and a new-found reality in their praying (v. 23, 24; see also 14:12-14; 15:7, 8). Their range of praying will be broadened and they will now have confidence that their prayers will be answered because they are asking in the name of One who, having ascended to the throne, is able to present their prayers to the Father. Indeed if they ask *anything* that they seriously believe will further the purposes he lived and died to achieve, they can allow themselves to persist in confident and expectant asking till they receive the answer.[7]   The experience of such answers to prayer will add even something more of stability and radiance to the joy they already know.

Even though they are conscious that it is Christ alone who opens the way and gives them free access to the Father, they will experience on that day an inspiring sense of closeness to and confidence in their Father in heaven and a new boldness in their praying born out of that very experience. They will have a new awareness that the Father himself loves them, and thus they will no longer need to depend entirely on Jesus' 'talk' about the Father. They will know they have the heart of the Father and they will feel themselves speaking directly to him.[8]   Here Jesus implicitly anticipates what Paul later says about the work of the Spirit: when we cry, 'Abba! Father!', it is the Spirit himself who bears witness that we are the children of God (Rom. 8:15, 16).

---

[7] See p. 227, footnote 4.

[8] Calvin comments on v. 26f.: 'Christ does not directly deny in this passage that He will be Intercessor, but only means the Father will be so inclined towards the disciples, that without any difficulty He will give freely whatever they ask. He says, "The Father will meet you, for His great love towards you will anticipate the Intercessor who otherwise would speak on your behalf." Again, when Christ is said to intercede with the Father for us [Heb. 7:25], let us not imagine anything fleshly about Him, as if He were on His knees before the Father offering humble supplications. But the power of His sacrifice, by which He once pacified God towards us, is always powerful and efficacious.... *because you have loved me....* These words tell us that the only bond of our union with God is union with Christ. To Him we are united by an unfeigned faith which springs from the sincere attitude which he describes by the name of love.' *Comm. in loc.*

Parting words

John 16:28-33

16 'I came from the Father and have come into the world; again, I am leaving the world and am going to the Father.'

29 His disciples said, 'Yes, now you are speaking plainly, not in any figure of speech! [30]Now we know that you know all things, and do not need to have anyone question you; by this we believe that you came from God.' [31]Jesus answered them, 'Do you now believe? [32]The hour is coming, indeed it has come, when you will be scattered, each one to his home, and you will leave me alone. Yet I am not alone because the Father is with me. [33]I have said this to you, so that in me you may have peace. In the world you face persecution. But take courage; I have conquered the world!'

Plain speaking

When Jesus made his remarks on the inability of the disciples during his earthly ministry fully to take in what he was saying to them (v. 12) he was touching on something about which they themselves felt sensitive. Time and again in his teaching he had said to them that he was pointing to things that, to be fully understood, would require more insight than they at present had. He kept them continually questioning him. They must have felt at times that it was humiliating to be faced, e.g. in his parabolic teaching, by so much that was at present confessedly mystery (Matt. 13:10-13). We recall how many of his disciples 'turned back' from him because they found his teaching difficult (6:60, 66). Yet the twelve felt themselves continually and compellingly drawn to follow and keep close to him. Moreover they were occasionally encouraged by being allowed sudden glimpses of his glory (e.g. Mark 9:2-8) and granted moments of God-given certainty that he spoke the divine word (cf. 6:69; 12:27-30). They had already begun to experience some measure of what would be finally and securely given them only when the cost of their salvation had been paid, Christ had been raised, had ascended and the Spirit had been sent.

Towards the close of his discourse, following a promise that when the Spirit comes he would speak plainly of the Father rather than in figures of speech, he gave them there and then a very satisfactory summary of the whole sweep of the gospel which they would come eventually to understand and glory in: *'I came from the Father and have come into the world; again, I am leaving the world and am going to the Father'* (v. 28). (Godet calls this 'a simple and exact recapitulation of all the mysteries of his existence, past, present and future'.) Immediately they heard it there came to the disciples another of the rare moments of preliminary insight into who he was and of felt confidence in a great future with him.

They felt themselves lifted up extraordinarily in mind and heart. There did not seem to be one anxious question in their minds that he had not fully answered or one need in the future that he could not fully meet, and they gave utterance to a confession of such faith (v. 30)! Jesus must have been thankful when he heard it. Possibly he took it as he took Simon's confession at Caesarea Philippi (Matt. 16:17) as being of truly divine inspiration. Yet he knew—as also in the case of Simon (cf. Mark 8:32-35)—that he had to warn them. They had to be made aware of the sheer self-ignorance that obscured to them the frailty of their very profession of loyalty. For them, not *now,* but only after 'the hour' of his death and their shame (v. 32) and re-birth could they begin to know and speak about him in sincerity and truth. To win his true place in heaven and in the hearts of men and women he had to die alone. The Scriptures were on his mind: 'I have trodden the wine press *alone,* and from the peoples no one was with me' (Isa. 63:3), and he quoted from them (Matt. 26:31; cf. Zech. 13:7).[9]

Having sought deliberately to shatter all their self-confidence, he rescued them from brooding over his rebuke by setting himself again and finally before them in all his loving mercy and majesty, assuring them of his peace: *'I am not alone because the Father is*

---

[9] Some have been inclined to argue that not all the disciples were 'scattered' (v. 32) at Jesus' arrest. Did not Peter and John follow him to the high priest's house (18:15), and was not John present at the foot of the cross (19:26)? But the point is easily answered for even though John did not deny Jesus as Peter did, neither disciple had the courage to identify himself as his follower. Jesus was left utterly alone.

with me.' His own faith will hold not only through what awaits him from friends and enemies, but through the God-forsakenness[10] in which he knows his Father will be there to support him.

He warns them of their own forthcoming conflict (v. 33). It is their bondage to the world that will be the cause of their defect and shame. Only by his power to give them victory will they be able to endure the intensified hatred of the world as they now give themselves to serve him who has defeated it. He answers them: *I have conquered the world*—all its enticements and entrapments, clever threats and plots. He is assuring them, 'There is no fascination from the hold of which I cannot draw its victims more powerfully to myself. There are no depths of degradation from which I cannot rescue those whom it has dragged down, no sin for which I will not abundantly give pardon.' In these words he sums up his whole life's achievement in the work entrusted to him by the Father. This is what he came to do—his offer is to all (Rev. 22:17)—and he has done it! Hearing such a word they must have taken courage. There can be traced to these words the source of all the New Testament texts that through the ages have given the victory to all who have trusted in him. The only ground for his disciples' (and our) perseverance in the faith is that victory.

---

[10] See p. 197, footnote 1.

CHAPTER 17

THE HIGH PRIESTLY PRAYER

John 17:1-8

17 After Jesus had spoken these words, he looked up to heaven and said, 'Father, the hour has come; glorify your Son so that the Son may glorify you, ²since you have given him authority over all people, to give eternal life to all whom you have given him. ³And this is eternal life, that they may know you, the only true God, and Jesus Christ whom you have sent. ⁴I glorified you on earth by finishing the work that you gave me to do. ⁵So now, Father, glorify me in your own presence with the glory that I had in your presence before the world existed.

6 'I have made your name known to those whom you gave me from the world. They were yours, and you gave them to me, and they have kept your word. ⁷Now they know that everything you have given me is from you; ⁸for the words that you gave to me I have given to them, and they have received them and know in truth that I came from you; and they have believed that you sent me.'

Jesus dedicates himself

The disciples were aware that Jesus during his earthly life was continually conscious of his Father's near presence. They knew that when he wanted to heal people, or when in perplexity or need, he prayed and was answered. They had asked him to teach them to pray. He had responded by giving them the kind of prayer they themselves should offer to God, had told them to pray unceasingly, and had encouraged them to ask (14:14; see also Luke 11:1-13). But he himself had apparently not asked them to join with him as he prayed, and only on one recorded occasion had they been allowed to overhear in a fleeting way the kind of prayer he uttered (cf. 11:41, 42).

We can only guess why he now so freely and fully allowed his disciples to overhear the very words he was speaking to his Father as he consecrated himself in preparation for his death, and made intercession for them and his future church.[1] We are intended to notice the sheer undisturbed peace and indeed the sublimity of the communion with his Father brought out in the confidence with which he utters this prayer. We know how readily his compassion could enter his praying and bring deep agony of soul as he pled with God for the forgiveness and healing of those who came around him. Here he seems to be beyond even the possibility of any such disturbance. Sometimes the comment is made on this prayer that the Jesus who utters it seems to be already ascended to heaven and in the Father's presence. We believe that Jesus is here deliberately allowing his disciples a clear glimpse of how near and close he had been continuously through all his earthly life to his Father so that both the mystery and the horror of what was soon to begin to happen in the Garden of Gethsemane might become the more clearly impressed on their minds. He wanted them to become all the more understanding and appreciative of the completely strange, gross and demonic obtrusiveness of what he allowed to envelope him as he yielded himself into the hands of God in his hour of dereliction.

As we read through the prayer, mindful of when and where it was uttered, we are meant to marvel at the way Jesus was enabled as he prayed to be carried in his thought and hope beyond what he had to go through on earth. He speaks of himself as if all his work was accomplished, all his agony and conflict over, as if he was already ascending into his Father's presence, and the victory was completely won. Indeed, he speaks of the coming 'hour' as one when he would be glorified and would thereby glorify his Father (v. 1).[2] The writer of the Epistle to the Hebrews (12:1-3)

---

[1] 'In some respects the prayer is a summary of the entire Fourth Gospel to this point. Its principal themes include Jesus' obedience to his Father, the glorification of his Father through his death/exaltation, the revelation of God in Jesus Christ, the choosing of the disciples out of the world, their unity modelled on the unity of the Father and the Son, and their final destiny in the presence of the Father and the Son.' Carson, p. 551.
[2] Calvin comments: 'He says the hour has come, because, although he has been manifested as the Son of God by miracles and every kind of work, yet His spiritual kingdom was still obscure, which soon after shone forth. If it be objected that nothing could be less glorious than Christ's death which was then

reminds us that it was the dominant habit of Jesus' life to keep in mind the 'joy that was set before him' so that he could even disregard the shame which he knew he had to endure. He indeed suggests that in orienting our minds through such hope we ourselves will be enabled to 'lay aside every weight'. Jesus here makes special mention in this prayer of what it was in his life-work that gave him most satisfaction as he offered it to his Father. He gives pride of place to having introduced men and women to eternal life (v. 2f.).[3] His aim in all his efforts to teach his disciples the knowledge of God and himself (17:2-3) had been simply that through hearing and believing they should receive and rejoice in such new life (17:3, 6). Even though he knows that for a moment or two they will fail and desert, he is certain that he can ultimately hold them together to experience Easter and the 40 days of wonder till the Spirit descended to make them more than conquerors through his love. This is his prime achievement—this *ecclesia* of God founded on the faith of his first disciples, that his word was the word of God and that he came uniquely from God and was God. Note that they had been given to him by the Father *from the world* (v. 6), the preposition 'from' or 'out of' implying a sense of separation from the world that had rejected Jesus. Soon they would be sent into the world as his witnesses (vv. 18, 23).

When we think of defining Christianity it is well to remember, as Hoskyns points out, that he did not think at this moment of mentioning his religious teaching about the Fatherhood of God, or of pointing to the great and growing social and international influence that would occur in the wake of his earthly effort. Rather he mentions simply the church which was his first love, which he continues to love and pray for, and which he died to create (cf. Eph. 5:25-27). It is also well that it should become

at hand, I reply that in that death we see a boundless glory.... For there we know that by the expiation of sins the world has been reconciled to God, the curse blotted out and Satan vanquished.' *Comm. in loc.*

[3] On verse 2 and the phrase 'authority over all people, to give eternal life to all whom you have given him', Calvin comments: 'Now, Christ does not say he has been placed in command of the whole world to bestow life indiscriminately. But He restricts this grace to those given to Him.... Only the elect belong to His own flock which He guards as a shepherd. Hence the kingdom of Christ extends to all men, but it is saving only to the elect who follow the Shepherd's voice with willing obedience.' *Comm. in loc.*

clear what it means for us to have been given eternal life: *since you have given* [the Son] *authority over all people, to give eternal life...* (v. 2). It must not be imagined that we should seek assurance of having received such a gift through the influx of a sudden feeling of well-being, nor that such a gift is reliably recognizable through any kind of ecstasy. To receive eternal life is to hear and believe his word (5:24) and to obey it (v. 6). It is to *know* him, that is, to have entered by faith into the closest of any personal relationship that we can imagine taking place in human life. He has given us an analogy of that relationship in a most verifiable sign when, in handing us the bread in his Supper, he says to us, 'This is my body that is for you', (1 Cor. 11:24) and asks us to participate ('share') in that body by eating: 'The bread that we break, is it not a sharing in the body of Christ?' (1 Cor. 10:16).

Additional note on: *'your name'* (v. 6).
In Scripture, the name embodies the character of a person (cf. footnotes: p. 227, note 4; p. 238, note 5). Here Jesus says that he has made known ('revealed', NIV) the Father's name, meaning he has made God's character known; the statement occurs again in verse 26. Some have seen a reference here to Exodus 3:13-15. Notice that John has already told us in his Gospel that Jesus has made the Father known: *No one has ever seen God. It is God the only Son, who is close to the Father's heart, who has made him known* (1:18). There 'made known' is the word from which we get our English word 'exegesis'; the same verb is used elsewhere in the NT with the meaning of 'narrate' (Luke 24:35; Acts 10:8, etc.) so that we might almost say that Jesus 'is the narration of God' (Carson, p. 135). In verse 11, Jesus prays the Father will *protect them in your name that you have given me*, and again in verse 12, he has *protected them in your name that you have given me*. The meaning would appear to be that 'the God he (i.e. Jesus) has revealed, may in that revealed character keep those who have that need of him' (Morris, p. 727). However there is probably another dimension to Jesus' saying that he had protected the apostles in *your name that you have given me*: he shows himself to be in the form of a Servant who does nothing except by the authority and power of the Father. *Ed.*

Prayer for his disciples

John 17:9-19

17 'I am asking on their behalf; I am not asking on behalf of the world, but on behalf of those whom you gave me, because they are yours. [10]All mine are yours, and yours are mine; and I have been glorified in them. [11]And now I am no longer in the world, but they are in the world, and I am coming to you. Holy Father, protect them in your name that you have given me, so that they may be one, as we are one. [12]While I was with them, I protected them in your name that you have given me. I guarded them, and not one of them was lost except the one destined to be lost, so that the scripture might be fulfilled. [13]But now I am coming to you, and I speak these things in the world so that they may have my joy made complete in themselves. [14]I have given them your word, and the world has hated them because they do not belong to the world, just as I do not belong to the world. [15]I am not asking you to take them out of the world, but I ask you to protect them from the evil one. [16]They do not belong to the world, just as I do not belong to the world. [17]Sanctify them in the truth; your word is truth. [18]As you have sent me into the world, so I have sent them into the world. [19]And for their sakes I sanctify myself, so that they also may be sanctified in truth.'

All one in Christ

What Jesus says in verse 9 about not praying for the world, must not be taken to mean that when he died on the cross he had in mind only the salvation of the elect. He died for 'all' (2 Cor. 5:14; 1 Tim. 2:6; 1 John 2:2; 2 Pet. 3:9) and therefore the offer of his grace is to all—*so that everyone who believes... may have eternal life* (3:16; cf. Rev. 22:17). He has already expressed his shock and grief that in his conflict with the powers of evil, the 'world', for which he was giving his life, was continuing to ally itself in hatred against himself and his disciples. However, what he says here about the burden of his prayer indicates that his mind is occupied with a special and exclusive concern at this moment over the danger and suffering to which his church is going to be exposed when he is no longer with them in the flesh. His prayer therefore moves naturally into a series of petitions, first on behalf of his chosen twelve (v. 9), then those who have already gathered round the twelve (v. 20; cf. Acts 1:15) and then on behalf of the church (vv. 20-26) which they will launch out into history, inspired by the apostles' word and teaching, to continue his mission.

His concern, therefore, is first for those who were then presently his disciples. Soon his physical presence would be withdrawn from them (v. 11a) so Jesus prays they may not think they are disadvantaged that he was no longer bodily with them. He knows that the evil one whose control of the world he had come to destroy, when faced with the certainty of eventual defeat and desperate because his time is now limited, will stir up against those who proclaim his name the same intensity of hatred as he himself encountered (cf. 15:20-25). They will not only be threatened and at times thwarted by persecution but will come under the same subtle temptation to preach another kind of gospel more pleasing to the natural thoughts and compromising ways of those around them (cf. Isa. 55:8, 9; Gal. 2:11-14). The burden of his prayer is that they may stand fast, united together as one[4] under their Father's protection (vv. 11, 15), that they may be sanctified (v. 17), and that they may remember that they have been sent by Jesus as he was sent by the Father (v. 18). They would all be kept safe by the Father's power; only Judas would desert (v. 12; cf. Ps. 109:8; Acts 1:20).[5] Jesus makes it clear that the purpose of this prayer within the hearing of the apostles is that they might be reassured and even filled with joy by the knowledge of God's loving concern for them (v. 13).[6]

---

[4] Verse 11b: [S]o that they may be one, as we are one. 'Our unity will be truly happy when it bears the image of God the Father and of Christ, as the wax takes the form of the seal impressed on it.' Calvin, Comm. in loc.

[5] 'Lest anyone should think that God's eternal election was overthrown by Judas' destruction, He immediately added that he was the son of perdition; meaning by these words that his ruin, which before men's eyes was a sudden occurrence, had long since been known to God.' Calvin, Comm. in loc.

[6] 'He calls it His joy, because the disciples had to receive it from Him; or if you want it more briefly, because He is its author, cause and pledge. For in us there is nothing but fear and disquiet; in Christ alone is there peace and joyousness.' Calvin, Comm. in loc.

We find it helpful to understand what Jesus said here about the effect of his self-sanctification on the life of his disciples (vv. 17, 19) if we follow the explanation of it given in the Epistle to the Hebrews. There it is brought out that the purpose of Jesus in becoming incarnate was to live a perfect human life and to offer himself in death on the cross so that he could become for our sake a 'merciful and faithful high priest in the service of God' (Heb. 2:17). Being sinless he had no need to offer anything to God for his own sake. Moreover the offering he made 'once for all' of his perfect life and obedient death was of such worth in the sight and plan of God that it could be spoken of as perfecting for all time all those who will avail themselves of it (Heb. 10:10, 14) and unite themselves to him. We have already spoken (see above on 15:1-8) of how, when Christ through the Spirit unites us to himself, he seeks to reproduce within us as the fruit of this union all the graces of the new sanctified humanity which was offered to God in him. If this holy life had not been first realized in Jesus, there would be no new humanity for the Spirit to impart to us. Through the Spirit we are thus both cleansed by the holiness of Christ and made partakers of it.

There can be no doubt that having heard this prayer, and keeping in mind Jesus' previous warnings about the 'world' they had then to face, the early disciples kept themselves aware of the subtlety and power of the temptations set before them in their pagan surroundings. The full extent of the world's folly and wickedness was being demonstrated in its refusal to repent even of its crucifixion of the Son of God. They clearly saw that the world indeed lay 'under the power of the evil one' (1 John 5:19). In their determination to obey the wise precept to 'hate what is evil, hold fast to what is good' (Rom. 12:9) they found themselves in need of much discernment and circumspection. They had no hesitation in making clear where they stood and where they could not possibly enter into its common pursuits and indulgences. God honoured their witness to his word. He gave them joy as they suffered criticism. He opened the doors of their prisons when they were persecuted (cf. Acts 2:37ff; 4:18-20; 12:6-11, etc.). We ourselves, while we recognize how greatly the world around us today has been influenced by the gospel (cf. p. 000), must not, in face of the instability of all such change, forget our need always to hold their example before us.

Prayer for the church

John 17:20-26

17 'I ask not only on behalf of these, but also on behalf of those who will believe in me through their word, [21]that they may all be one. As you, Father, are in me and I am in you, may they also be in us, so that the world may believe that you have sent me. [22]The glory that you have given me I have given them, so that they may be one, as we are one, [23]I in them and you in me, that they may be completely one, so that the world may know that you have sent me and have loved them even as you have loved me. [24]Father, I desire that those also, whom you have given me, may be with me where I am, to see my glory, which you have given me because you loved me before the foundation of the world.

25 'Righteous Father, the world does not know you, but I know you; and these know that you have sent me. [26]I made your name known to them, and I will make it known, so that the love with which you have loved me may be in them, and I in them.'

His love in his church

Jesus finally utters a prayer for the church[7] which is to be launched out into history through the witness of the twelve. One of his chief concerns for it was *that they may all be one*. As far as possible the church must present itself to the world as one united body of people with one clear aim and message. In the tenth chapter of this Gospel he had already given us a sketch of the organic structure into which any living and powerful church must allow itself basically to be formed. He there gives us the picture of a church consisting of many distinct congregational units, each being a flock with one shepherd whose ministry to his people

---

[7] In the Old Testament era, there was also a church, but it was based on the ethnic community of Israel and its theology was essentially one of *promise* enshrined in 'types' and 'shadows'. The New Testament church is now the spiritual Israel, an international community, composed of those from 'all nations' (Matt. 28:19; Rev. 7:9), and its theology is now one of *fulfilment* as Jesus Christ has become both the 'chief cornerstone' and the 'capstone' (Eph. 2:20; 1 Pet. 2:6, 7).

would be to preach the word, give leadership in its interpretation, and give his whole life, as Christ gave his, in pastoral care of each and all. Here now he expresses his anxiety that the witness of the church to the world at large will be impaired unless it also presents to the world clear evidence that it is one church which speaks one clear message with one united voice. The apostle Paul was later to repeat what was here and now in Jesus' mind, when he wrote to the Ephesians reminding then that there is 'one Lord, one faith, one baptism, one God and Father of all' (Eph. 4:5). In the same passage in Ephesians, stressing the need for manifest unity, Paul spoke also of the need to 'maintain the unity of the Spirit in the bond of peace' (Eph. 4:3). As we move through Jesus' prayer we find him expressing the same concern for the inner nurture of love one for another within the fellowship. Each must recognize how deeply and closely the Spirit binds one to another as life-sharing members of the one Body of Christ, each joined to the other in a unity comparable with that between the Father and his own dear Son.[8]

Those who have responsibility for leadership within the churches should recognize the importance of both aspects of what Jesus is praying for. The true church is universal. We must not be content with a Christianity that fits too comfortably within a small corner. As earnestly as we seek to manifest the righteousness and newness of the life he has given to us, so when we know Jesus we must also seek to manifest to the world the ecumenical unity with those who also know him and which we have in our hearts already through the same message received from him through the apostles (v. 20).

The prayer moves on to the request that they may *see my glory, which you have given me*. Many commentators find here a reference by Jesus to the promise later to be given in 1 John 3:2; they understand Jesus here to be referring to a glory visible to us

---

[8] The unity for which Jesus prays for the disciples will be characterized both by their love for one another (13:35) and their obedience to the revelation of the Father which they have been given through Jesus and have accepted (vv. 6-8). This unity will extend to those who also believe that same revelation entrusted to them (v. 20). Further, this unity will be modelled on the unity of the Father and the Son. The Son is distinct from the Father: in the beginning 'the Word was with God' (1:1); here the Son prays to the Father (v. 1) whom he obeys (v. 4), who sent him (v. 8) and who has given the apostles to him (v. 6). Though distinct, yet the Father and Son are one (v. 21).

only after death. We find ourselves, however, expecting more in answer to his prayer, especially as we remember Paul's suggestion that we already look at what cannot be seen (2 Cor. 4:17, 18) as we now are transformed from one degree of glory to another (2 Cor. 3:18). We certainly cannot expect to have experience of seeing the glory of Jesus such as came to the disciples during the transfiguration or the 40 days after Easter. However, during the routine of their service, once or twice they had sudden flashes of extraordinary insight into who he really was, which brought about thrilling confession and deep abasement (Matt. 13:17; 16:16, 17; Luke 5:8). These faith experiences of the disciples give us ground for believing that Jesus in this prayer might have had it in his mind that for his followers even here and now during this life there will occasionally be given such a sense of the power of God in Christ and insight into its significance as can be called a 'seeing' of his glory.[9] With such conviction and insight they are sent into the world as he was.

Jesus here outlines their message. They are to tell the world of the glory of the love which the Father and the Son have for each other, and which the Son has come from the Father to share with us in this world (vs. 23, 26). They must have allowed it to possess them. If the world is to know it, they must be ready to speak about it and even to proclaim it if they are given the opportunity. 'Faith comes from what is heard, and what is heard comes through the word of Christ' (Rom. 10:17). Whatever hate may linger on in an world which insists on a false independence from God, it must nonetheless know itself continually being challenged and condemned by such love.

---

[9] Carson agrees: 'Christians of every generation glimpse something of Jesus' glory even now...', p. 569. However, note that in verse 24 (cf. v. 5) there is unambiguous reference both to the pre-existence of Christ and the church's eschatological hope of the consummation of world history; then the glory of Christ in the here and now will be eclipsed by that unalloyed divine glory which is grounded upon the Father's love for the Son from all eternity.

CHAPTER 18

JESUS TAKEN, QUESTIONED AND DENIED

John 18:1-11

18 After Jesus had spoken these words, he went out with his disciples across the Kidron valley to a place where there was a garden, which he and his disciples entered. [2]Now Judas, who betrayed him, also knew the place, because Jesus often met there with this disciples. [3]So Judas brought a detachment of soldiers together with police from the chief priests and the Pharisees, and they came there with lanterns and torches[1] and weapons. [4]Then Jesus, knowing all that was to happen to him, came forward and asked them, 'For whom are you looking?' [5]They answered, 'Jesus of Nazareth.' Jesus replied, 'I am he.' Judas, who betrayed him, was standing with them. [6]When Jesus said to them, 'I am he', they stepped back and fell to the ground. [7]Again he asked them, 'For whom are you looking?' And they said, 'Jesus of Nazareth.' [8]Jesus answered, 'I told you that I am he. So if you are looking for me, let these men go.' [9]This was to fulfil the word that he had spoken, 'I did not lose a single one of those whom you gave me.' [10]Then Simon Peter, who had a sword, drew it, struck the high priest's slave, and cut off his right ear. The slave's name was Malchus. [11]Jesus said to Peter, 'Put your sword back into its sheath. Am I not to drink the cup that the Father has given me?'

---

[1] The lantern was a cylindrical terracotta container with a carrying handle and an open side into which an oil lamp could be inserted; the torch was made by binding together strips of resinous wood which burned with bright flames. The question arises why such means were required for light when at the Passover season there would be a full moon. The answer is probably that when the authorities knew they were going to a grove or garden to arrest Jesus, they expected their quarry would try and hide among the bushes and they were therefore taking no chances of him escaping into the garden's shadows.

Chapter 18

The arrest

There is the story of an English admiral who, realizing that his ship had no chance to survive in the face of the overwhelming force against him, sent out the message, 'I have sounded out the depth of the water, and when my keel rests on the bottom my flag will still be flying above sea level.' Jesus twice before, when they had wanted to arrest him, had escaped out of their hands (7:44; 8:59; 10:39). But now, certain that his hour had come and that such evasion was no longer his Father's will, he began to submit to the injustice, pain, silence and darkness, as these began to take him over. It is important that, as we read through the whole ensuing account from the moment of his arrest, we should recognize the freedom, indeed the lordliness, which he finds himself still able to maintain as he continues to give his witness through sign and word.

As we watch him leading his disciples into the Garden[2] where the arrest is to happen we are to remind ourselves how its important details — the timing and the place of the encounter — were all 'pre-arranged' by himself when he sent out Judas to betray him (v. 4; cf. 13:27b, 31). There is no doubt that, as they met, the Jewish authorities felt sure of themselves. Though they had wisely taken care so far not to move against him during the daily celebrations (Matt. 26:4, 5), they may have imagined that the public enthusiasm for him was on the wane, on account of the ease with which they had corrupted Judas; his promise of betrayal made them all the more certain as they proceeded with him to the Garden. Moreover they had persuaded the Roman authorities to lend them soldiers for the arrest of a 'dangerous' and important criminal to make sure that nothing could foil their success.[3]

---

[2] John says that Jesus 'entered' the Garden (v. 1) and then later says he (lit.) 'went out' (NRSV, 'came forward' v. 4). Thus the Greek clearly implies a walled garden. Gethsemane (Matt. 26:36) means an 'oil-press' which also suggests an enclosed grove, perhaps belonging to some wealthy supporter of Jesus with whose permission he was using this secluded place.

[3] The Greek translated 'detachment of soldiers' makes it clear these were Roman auxiliaries and not Jews. While the word John uses often refers to a 'maniple' of about 200 armed men, it is not necessary to assume as many as that had been detailed to accompany the Temple officials for the arrest. The Roman auxiliaries were not normally stationed in Jerusalem but were moved to billets in the fortress of Antonia during feast days to deal with any nationalist unrest that might arise among the huge throngs gathering in the capital. The popularity of

Yet it is Jesus who with ease and majesty dominates the whole situation as he hands himself over.[4]   Standing forward and directing all eyes upon himself, he set the stage for them to ask him twice verbally for the one they were seeking: *Jesus of Nazareth*, and twice in solemn reply he uttered the name God had first given for himself as he promised redemption for Israel in his encounter with Moses at the bush (cf. Exod. 3:13-15); *I am he* was the name which he knew his Father would honour for ever. When we read how, for a brief moment, his captors drew back in obvious awe and fell to the ground[5] (cf. Ps. 17:2, 8-12; 35:4) we are intended to realize that at the utterance of his name by Jesus, there took place the same verbal divine self-manifestation as was there when it was first so powerfully uttered at the burning bush, and heard with such awe by Moses. He had already demonstrated to his disciples the power that accompanied the utterance by himself of this solemn name when, walking on the waves, he had used it on their behalf to calm the sea (6:20, cf. 13:19) and now he repeats the sign. That the mere utterance of his name should render his enemies so suddenly powerless reminded Calvin of the prophecy in Isaiah 11:4 ('with the breath of his lips he shall kill the wicked'). For the disciples it was meant to be understood as one of his final signs of who he truly was and is for ever.

It was in the words that immediately followed the utterance of his name that this whole account comes to its climax: *'if you are looking for me, let these men go'* (v.8). What he is concerned about is not his own self-preservation. He is here indeed finally yielding himself up to the hands that will shackle him. His care is for the safety of those he has led so far into what seems

---

Jesus with the people would be sufficient reason for the authorities to accede to the request of the Temple police and chief priests for help in arresting Jesus whose presence might cause dangerous religious fervour.

[4]   The Greek word translated 'betray', 'hand over', is used of the betrayal of Jesus with the implicit nuance that it was God who was actually 'handing over' his Son to death. See Acts 2:23.

[5]   The meaning in the Greek seems to be that the front ranks of the posse drew back, creating confusion among those behind them and causing them in the darkness to stumble and fall about in total disarray. Dr Wallace suggests this 'drawing back' arose from the divine disclosure, *I am*, which could well have been the case with the Jews among the arresting party. The Roman soldiers, however, may have been disconcerted by finding that the 'country peasant' they believed they were coming to arrest, instead of hiding among the trees of the garden, stepped out of the shadows and calmly presented himself to them with dignified authority.

compromise and danger. We are meant to read his command for the freedom of his disciples as an assurance that he will never shirk his responsibility for our safety (Calvin) or leave us to find our own way out of the difficulties into which he has led us. We are to notice that here he is offering himself for the freedom he seeks to guarantee his disciples. For them he pleads liberty and peace. For himself he accepts bondage and the ensuing torment.

A central element in the burden which Jesus was evidently finding hard to bear was its loneliness. Jesus had already tried to make it clear to Peter especially that the suffering he was now on the point of accepting could not in any way under present circumstances be either eased or shared (13:36). No one could possibly stand with him as he went through that final 'hour'. Yet again Peter showed how far he was even now from understanding either the situation or the mind of Jesus. He simply wanted to prove that he had meant it when he had vowed himself ready to die for the sake of Jesus. We can sense a note of disappointment in the rebuke Jesus felt he had to give. Yet knowing that Peter would soon ultimately come to understand, he haunted Peter's mind with the memory of his experience in Gethsemane, and the searching question: *'Am I not to drink the cup that the Father has given me?'*

How typical of Jesus' continuing care for his disciples was his last earthly miracle! There was a scuffle when Peter brandished his sword, and cut off the ear of a slave of the high priest.[6] We can take the healing as a sign of his power to repair the damage done at times through our stupidity, and to bring even healing and liberty in its wake. That the slave could be referred to by the name of 'Malchus' most probably means that at the time this record was written, he was known as a member of the church.

---

[6] Some readers may be puzzled by Luke's record of the sayings (immediately prior to Gethsemane and the betrayal) about swords (Luke 22:36-38). The first saying about selling one's cloak to buy a sword is most probably intended to be a reference to the self-sacrifice that is going to be needed in the post-crucifixion days; a cloak was regarded as an absolute essential in these days, whereas a sword (though commonly worn) was not. The Lord's reply, 'It is enough!' to the disciples' volunteering that they have two swords between them, most probably should be interpreted as a rebuke: 'Enough of that!' For a full discussion of these verses, see Marshall, pp. 825-6.

Where only Jesus can stand, Peter falls

John 18:12-27

18 So the soldiers, their officer, and the Jewish police arrested Jesus and bound him. [13]First they took him to Annas, who was the father-in-law of Caiaphas, the high priest that year. [14]Caiaphas was the one who had advised the Jews that it was better to have one person die for the people.

15 Simon Peter and another disciple followed Jesus. Since that disciple was known to the high priest, he went with Jesus into the courtyard of the high priest, [16]but Peter was standing outside at the gate. So the other disciple, who was known to the high priest, went out, spoke to the woman who guarded the gate, and brought Peter in. [17]The woman said to Peter, 'You are not also one of this man's disciples, are you?' He said, 'I am not.' [18]Now the slaves and the police had made a charcoal fire because it was cold, and they were standing round it and warming themselves. Peter also was standing with them and warming himself.

19 Then the high priest questioned Jesus about his disciples and about his teaching. [20]Jesus answered, 'I have spoken openly to the world; I have always taught in synagogues and in the temple, where all the Jews come together. I have said nothing in secret. [21]Why do you ask me? Ask those who heard what I said to them; they know what I said.' [22]When he had said this, one of the police standing nearby struck Jesus on the face, saying, 'Is that how you answer the high priest?' [23]Jesus answered, 'If I have spoken wrongly, testify to the wrong. But if I have spoken rightly, why do you strike me?' [24]Then Annas sent him bound to Caiaphas the high priest.

25 Now Simon Peter was standing and warming himself. They asked him, 'You are not also one of his disciples, are you?' He denied it and said, 'I am not.' [26]One of the slaves of the high priest, a relative of the man whose ear Peter had cut off, asked, 'Did I not see you in the garden with him?' [27]Again Peter denied it, and at that moment the cock crowed.

Having successfully arrested Jesus, the Jewish authorities now had to define the offence with which he could be plausibly charged before he was condemned to death. Several interrogations took place before they managed such an outcome. The first was before Annas, a former high priest, the father-in-law of Caiaphas who was at present in that office. Annas was then highly respected and his opinion was greatly valued.[7]

It is now twice mentioned that Jesus was kept *bound* (vv. 12, 24) by his captors, and forcibly moved around. The humiliation which he had had to endure all through his life with us on earth thus becomes for a while more vexatious and tormenting. Hitherto when his opponents were becoming overwrought and were beginning to utter threatening insults, he had been able to withdraw himself (8:59) and escape 'from their hands' (10:39) so that the worst might not happen. Now without means of avoiding insults he was aware that eventually he would have to submit to whatever cruelty or humiliation came his way. He no doubt had in mind the portrait in Isaiah: 'I gave my back to those who struck me... I did not hide my face from insult and spitting' (50:6). Considering his prayer for forgiveness for the soldiers charged with the task of his execution (Luke 23:34) and his refusal to

---

[7] Only John and Luke mention Annas (Luke 3:2, 'during the high-priesthood of Annas and Caiaphas....'). Annas had served as high priest from AD 6–15 but had been deposed by the Roman procurator Gratus who had appointed Caiaphas, his son-in-law, in his place. Annas' deposition, however, was not recognized by the Jews. At this time, therefore, there were two high priests in Jerusalem though only Caiaphas had official recognition by the Romans. John is therefore correct to refer to Annas as the high priest (v. 19). Jesus' examination by Caiaphas (v. 24) is not reported on at all by John but all three Synoptics give the account which John omits. However, none of the Synoptics make mention of the preliminary questioning of Jesus by Annas, high priest emeritus, recording simply that Jesus was taken to Caiaphas' house (Matthew) or to the high priest's house (Mark and Luke) whose courtyard Peter entered. Thus Matthew appears to contradict John's account which implies that Peter's first denial took place within the courtyard of the house of Annas (vv. 13, 15-17). However, the problem is easily resolved if, as is highly likely, the houses of Annas and Caiaphas had a common courtyard. Some commentators regard John's account of the trial as incoherent and full of contradictions—they assume it has been rewritten by him to bring out points which he regarded as important (e.g. C. K.Barrett, p. 437f.). Other commentators find no difficulty in reconciling John's account of the trial with those given in the Synoptics (e.g. Carson). Carson suggests that John's mention of the unwitting prophecy of Caiaphas (v. 14; cf. 11:49-52) indicates that his main concern is to show the reader how all that is taking place is fulfilling the sovereign purposes of God; John therefore did not intend giving a full chronicle of the night's events—others (the Synoptics) have already done that and the story is apparently well known in the early church (Carson, p. 581).

drink the wine intended to lessen the pain (Matt. 27:34), many believe that when it came to his crucifixion he stretched out his arms and opened his hands to help them to nail him to the cross (see Chapter 19 below on 19:17ff.). We are meant to appreciate however that even as the insults heaped on him grew more spiteful and his humiliation deepened, for as long as was humanly possible he maintained a positive witness to his coming kingdom. Here, instead of submitting meekly to the arrogant and suggestive questioning of Annas and the brutal assault by his police guard, we find him vigorously asserting his innocence, counter-attacking those who insulted him and exposing their malice by searching questions (cf. vv. 21, 23).[8]

It is symbolic that these chains (cf. Mark 15:1) and this deepening personal abuse isolate him from his disciples.[9] He begins here and now deliberately to move towards the agony under the judgement of God which he has come ultimately to suffer entirely alone in our place in the final hour of his being actually crucified. He has already warned his disciples that where he was going they could not come with him (13:33) and had given a special warning to Peter, 'Where I am going, you cannot follow me now...' (13:36). At the same time, seeming to know that Peter would be so foolhardy as to risk it, he had even warned him of the danger of a downfall (13:38).

We must not underestimate Peter's courage, nor his ardent devotion to the person of Jesus. 'I will lay down my life for you', he had said, and he proved that he meant it when he took his sword into the Garden and showed himself ready to enter deadly conflict—though the wider context shows that drawing his sword was human folly. Yet, like many of us who come after Peter, he had a tendency at times to think he could improve on what Jesus proposed and planned (cf. Matt. 16:22; Acts 10:14). Here and now, therefore, he quite spontaneously poured out his courage

---

[8] The questioning of Jesus focussed on his followers and his teaching (v. 19). Annas' concern was probably to assess the strength of Jesus' following, the likely threat posed to priestly authority, the identity of Jesus and who he claimed to be (cf. 19:7; Matt. 26:63). However, the examination proved to be indecisive as Annas passed Jesus on to Caiaphas (v. 24) and the charge brought against him before Pilate was initially very hazy (v. 30).

[9] This isolation of Jesus from his disciples is further emphasized in the following verses by Peter's threefold denial. The significance of this symbolic isolation is undoubtedly to make clear the uniqueness of the suffering and death of Jesus.

and devotion in what he had made himself believe was the best
way that could be taken for the sake of both Jesus and himself. It
is one of the saddest features of his fall that he felt so good when
he was going so wrong. How it all tragically worked out is told
in a few verses. At the beginning it was providentially made
difficult for him.[10] The gates through which Jesus was taken
were firmly closed and he had to devise an entry (v.16).[11] When
he found himself unable to give a frank response to the query of
the woman at the gate (v. 17), he should have taken the warning
that his courage was not going to be able to cope. But his self-
confidence prevailed and he offered himself up, as an easy prey to
the falsehood that was everywhere prevailing. As Luthi puts it:
he 'does not hide behind pillars or shrubs'; instead he rashly
mixes with the people, joins their conversation, and sits down by
the bright light of the watch fire! Inevitably he openly denied the
Lord,[12] and *at that moment the cock crowed.*

The trial (1)

John 18:28-32

18   Then they took Jesus from Caiaphas to Pilate's headquarters.
It was early in the morning. They themselves did not enter the
headquarters, so as to avoid ritual defilement and to be able to eat the
Passover. [29]So Pilate went out to them and said, 'What accusation do
you bring against this man?' [30]They answered, 'If this man were not a

---

[10] Was this the 'way of escape' promised to us all in the hour of our temptation
and testing (1 Cor. 10:13)?
[11] The identity of 'the other disciple' has traditionally been taken to be John.
While some scholars have questioned this, the most recent evaluation of all the
evidence tentatively concludes that 'the other disciple' was indeed 'the beloved
disciple'. See note below.
[12] Only John records that the third denial was made to a relative of Malchus (v.
26; cf. v. 10). This seemingly insignificant detail suggests that 'the other
disciple' was indeed the writer of the account as only he among the disciples
apparently would have been familiar with the high priest's household servants
(v. 15). Notice also that John's restrained narrative omits any reference either to
Peter's cursing and swearing (Matt. 26:74; Mark 14:71) or to his bitter tears of
remorse (Matt. 26:75; Mark 14:72; Luke 22:62). John is directing his readers'
attention solely onto Jesus.

criminal, we would not have handed him over to you.' ³¹Pilate said to them, 'Take him yourselves and judge him according to your law.' The Jews replied, 'We are not permitted to put anyone to death.' ³²(This was to fulfil what Jesus had said when he indicated the kind of death he was to die.)

The kind of death he was to die

If earlier in their history his enemies had been allowed in the heat of their anger to rid themselves of Jesus they would have put him to death by stoning (cf. 8:59; 10:31). It is therefore all the more remarkable that when they finally determined to label him an imposter and reject his claims, they firmly made up their minds that he had to be put to death by crucifixion at the hands of the Roman authorities. This is why, after further questioning before the Sanhedrin in the house of Caiaphas,[13] he was so soon sent to the court of Pontius Pilate, then governor of Judea.[14] A sentence of death by crucifixion could be pronounced only by him, and he now increasingly becomes the key figure in the narrative leading to Jesus' crucifixion. The Jewish authorities[15] knew well that they had no clear case to plead before Pilate for his execution, but they had in previous issues put pressure on the governor in various underhand ways to do what they wanted, and they were certain that they had the political leverage over him to coerce

---

[13] Matthew's and Mark's accounts make it clear that Jesus was arraigned before the Sanhedrin (Matt. 26:57 = Mark 14:53). Only the Sanhedrin, convened by the officially recognized high priest, could demand the death sentence from the Roman governor. Normally, Roman governors were based in Caesarea in Herod the Great's palace, but during Jewish religious festivals, it was their practice to stay in Jerusalem in case of any untoward nationalistic disturbances.

[14] NRSV's translation 'to Pilate's headquarters' (v. 28, cf. 'to the palace of the Roman governor', NIV) renders what is literally 'into the praetorium'. 'Praetorium' could denote either the headquarters of the commanding officer of a military camp or else the headquarters of a Roman governor.

[15] Verse 28 states that the Jews (i.e. the members of the Sanhedrin) did not enter the praetorium to avoid ritual defilement so they could eat the Passover. This introduces the problem of John's dating in contrast with the dating of the Synoptics which clearly indicate that earlier that same day Jesus had already eaten the Passover with his disciples (e.g. Mark 14:2, 12-16). Recent commentators argue that there is in fact no contradiction between John's dating and that of the Synoptics. The suggestion regarding verse 28 is that by 'Passover' is meant the ongoing Festival of Unleavened Bread which continued for a further seven days (Lev. 23:4-8). Ritual defilement would debar the religious leaders from taking part in this important aspect of the Passover until they had been ceremonially cleansed.

him. Pilate was firmly determined at the beginning of his encounter with them over Jesus to give the case a fair hearing and issue a fair verdict, and at first he determined to set Jesus free.[16] It took him some time before he became aware of the strange intensity of the desire, even of the whole Jewish nation, to have this innocent man killed.[17]

If we are fully to understand, however, what was happening as Jesus was bound and taken to his cross, we must realize that God had not only Jesus closely and firmly in his hands, but also Pontius Pilate and the whole Jewish community. He was shaping every detail of the whole event of Jesus' sacrificial death so that there might ultimately come about a perfect fulfilment of the loving purpose of saving the world, towards which he had begun to work centuries before in the Old Testament era. The actual way that Christ's death occurred as he offered himself to be crucified helps us to see him as fulfilling the role of the slaughtered offering in the Old Testament ritual of sacrifice. There in the Old Testament the sacrificial innocent animal was accepted by God as bearing the condemnation and sin of the one who brought it to the altar. Here on the cross, the completely innocent one was to be legally condemned and slain as if he were guilty, so that all who plead his sacrifice may know themselves forgiven because he himself has borne their sin and guilt.

It was under the providence of God, and even foreshadowed in the Old Testament (cf. 3:14), that he should die 'lifted up' from the earth as he was, with his arms stretched out to signify his longing that we should come to him, and with the blood and water flowing from his wounds signifying that what he gives us through his death is able to cleanse us perfectly from all that defiles us. The New Testament also encourages us, when we preach about the death of Christ, to allow such physical aspects of

---

[16] The fact that Roman soldiers had been involved in the arrest of Jesus (v. 12) suggests that Pilate was already aware of impending charges against Jesus. Perhaps the members of the Sanhedrin expected an immediate verdict from the governor. If so, they were disappointed. His question, 'What accusation do you bring against this man?' (v. 29) indicates initially he was resolved to act justly and convene a fair hearing.

[17] The charges which John records were brought against Jesus were not of any particular interest to Pilate. Though not mentioned explicitly, John makes it clear that Pilate understood their accusation to be that Jesus claimed some kind of kingship (v. 33) and so Pilate's questioning of Jesus was to focus primarily on this (vv. 33, 36, 37, 39).

the spectacle of his crucifixion fully to register on our minds and in our imagination, so that we can be brought totally under the cleansing and renewing power which God means Jesus' death to bring to us (Gal. 6:14).

One most important feature of his having to die thus by crucifixion is that in this event the whole Gentile world is seen to stand solidly alongside the Jewish world in humanity's total rejection of his Lordship. It was not the Jews but the Gentiles, to whom we ourselves so closely belong, who took over the responsibility for the judicial sentencing, the fierce wounding, the long, painful ordeal of being hung up on that cross, the ridicule and the utter loneliness of his rejection by all humankind. His death thus had to be seen as at the hands of the world, for he died for the sins of the whole world (1 John 2:2).

Early in his ministry Jesus was deliberately imprecise about the exact form his death would finally take. He signified it by his baptism in the Jordan, and described it as a 'baptism' he would ultimately have to endure (Luke 12:50). It was only after some more exact reflection on what awaited him that he began to speak of it definitely as a crucifixion (cf. Matt. 20:19; earlier references only refer to him being killed: Matt. 16:21; cf. Mark 8:31; 9:12; 9:31 etc.). The evangelist here encourages us (v. 32) to think of earlier comments about his impending death as prophecy that brought it to pass in the way it actually occurred (cf. Isa. 55:10, 11). God was in control, not mere men.

The trial (2)

John 18:33 – 19:16a

Pilate faces Jesus

John 18:33-38a

18 Then Pilate entered the headquarters again, summoned Jesus, and asked him, 'Are you the King of the Jews?' [34]Jesus answered, 'Do you ask this on your own, or did others tell you about me?' [35]Pilate replied, 'I am not a Jew, am I? Your own nation and the chief priests have handed you over to me. What have you done?' [36]Jesus answered, 'My kingdom is not from this world. If my kingdom were from this world, my followers would be fighting to keep me from being handed over to the Jews. But as it is, my kingdom is not from here.' [37]Pilate asked him, 'So you are a king?' Jesus answered, 'You say that I am a king. For this I was born, and for this I came into the world, to testify to the truth. Everyone who belongs to the truth listens to my voice.' [38]Pilate asked him, 'What is truth?'

Confrontation, evasion and rejection

Here we have the first of several interviews which took place between Jesus and Pilate, the Roman governor, as events moved towards his being sentenced to death. Pilate had been in his place long enough to be aware of Jesus' massive popularity among the crowds. He may well have heard about his extraordinary miracles. Things he said about God and life may have reached his ears. His opening remark when he met Jesus for the first time may indicate that he knew of his claim to be 'king' of his nation, the king whom God had centuries ago promised to send through a descendent of the house of David. Perhaps in the actual first meeting here recorded, he had to suppress some astonishment that the man lacked the outstanding personal characteristics that his reputation seemed to suggest (cf. Isa. 53:2). It is of course also possible that Pilate had received some intimation of the possible charges that were to be brought against Jesus by the Sanhedrin.

When Pilate initially raised the question, *'Are you the King of the Jews?'*, he had hoped Jesus would respond with information that would help him towards making as fair a judgement as he could on the nature of the case before him. What he wanted from Jesus was talk—possibly information about past history, maybe about religion, even theology. Perhaps they could discuss even how worthwhile one human value was alongside another! However, such information and discussion never came. It becomes patent as we read through the opening interview that it was not Pilate but Jesus who quite decidedly took over the entire initiative and set the line of questioning. His first word to Pilate was a provocative question which challenged him to lift his mind off the whole line of current talk about the legal case that was absorbing him and to allow it to be taken up by what really mattered to himself (v. 34, *'Do you ask this on your own...?'* Cf. NIV) and his future personal destiny.[18]

Jesus, whenever he preached, or even conversed with people, was always deeply concerned that they should at the same time encounter the reality about which he loved to initiate conversation. He had brought the kingdom of God into the world, and he was concerned, wherever he went, to invite and challenge all who heard him to the re-birth without which the kingdom cannot be entered (3:3, 5). He had brought truth into the world (14:6) to shine everywhere untruth prevailed, as it did in the attitude and mind of Pilate. He wanted those who had the privilege of seeing and hearing him to enjoy a new and quite wonderful experience of being 'blessed' (cf. Matt. 13:16-17). In the brief time he was now given to be with this man before him,[19] his primary concern was, therefore, to engage him in the same kind of conversation as he had with Nicodemus or with the woman at the well with the same hope that he would hear, respond and live. Alas, Jesus was well warned of what was

---

[18] 'Jesus cannot possibly answer with a simple 'Yes' or 'No'.... He therefore asks Pilate if the question the governor has posed spontaneously springs from his own understanding and curiosity, or is simply a repetition of the Sanhedrin's charge. If the former, then perhaps Jesus can lead him to better or deeper understanding; if the latter, then Pilate is already so profoundly misled that major clarification will be necessary if Jesus is to answer truthfully at all. Jesus... has become the interrogator; the prisoner has become the judge.' Carson, p. 593.
[19] See the last sentence of note 18 above.

finally to come, when he heard Pilate, in response to his first challenging question, express his determination not to be moved in any way from the facts of the case before him: *'Your own nation and the chief priests have handed you over to me. What have you done?'* (v. 35).

As we follow through the ensuing conversation we find Pilate continuing thus perversely to refuse to hear what Jesus was saying, or to see what Jesus with such ardent love was bringing before him. It is possible that the report preserved by John for us here of what passed between them is to be read as simply a concise summary, indicating the main themes raised by Jesus in the conversation and recording Pilate's evasive responses and his final 'No' to the offer of grace.

Since Jesus realized how much Pilate's mind was continually occupied by the thought and exercise of political power, he opened the decisive conversation by talking about his kingdom.. He uttered a word that not only described its nature but proclaimed it as present in their midst with all its invasive power. *'My kingdom is not from this world. If my kingdom were from this world, my followers would be fighting to keep me from being handed over to the Jews. But as it is, my kingdom is not from here'* (v. 36). It is most likely that Pilate was meant at that moment to hear what Jesus was offering him with no less cogency and persuasive power than accompanies the same words when Jesus himself arrests us and changes us today. If Pilate had truly listened and heeded, how many questions of true life-importance would have been raised in his mind and how shaken would have been his complacent self-security! Yet all he took in when he heard the words was what he felt to be an important point in trying to work out a solution to the legal case before him: *So you are a king?*[20] Clearly he was baffled that Jesus had been brought before him at all. He has sarcastically asked, *I am not a Jew, am I?* (v. 35). It would appear that the reader is intended to understand him to be saying, 'Do you think you are *my* king?'

With Pilate having failed so badly in such a crucial test, Jesus, having come so far, made one last effort to win the man before

---

[20] *'You say that I am a king'* (v. 37). Some commentators have understood this reply to Pilate as meaning '"king" is *your* word, not mine.' But we are better to take the NIV's translation as a more accurate understanding of Jesus' response: 'You are right in saying I am a king.'

him. Let Pilate look again at him and listen! Certainly he was a king! He was the king of truth! All around him, those who had had any love of truth, had heard what they knew to be the final word about life and destiny when they had heard his voice. Let Pilate, then, simply open the mind he was closing, listen and believe![21] Pilate's *What is truth?* may have passed from his lips often before as a cynical remark about the vanity and stupidity that he felt to be behind much of the current philosophical discussion of the time. At this point, however, it signified much more: Jesus' kingdom was the kingdom of truth. Pilate, in decidedly rejecting Jesus, was now decidedly rejecting all truth and eternal life.

Pilate beyond his depth

John 18:38 – 19:5

18 After he had said this, he went out to the Jews again and told them, 'I find no case against him. [39]But you have a custom that I release someone for you at the Passover. Do you want me to release for you the King of the Jews?' [40]They shouted in reply, 'Not this man, but Barabbas!' Now Barabbas was a bandit.

19 Then Pilate took Jesus and had him flogged. [2]And the soldiers wove a crown of thorns and put it on his head, and they dressed him in a purple robe. [3]They kept coming up to him, saying, 'Hail, King of the Jews!' and striking him on the face. [4]Pilate went out again and said to them, 'Look, I am bringing him out to you to let you know that I find no case against him.' [5]So Jesus came out, wearing the crown of thorns and the purple robe. Pilate said to them, 'Here is the man!'

Behold the man!

Immediately Jesus allowed himself to be taken captive, he said to those who seized him, '[T]his is your hour, and the power of

---

[21] Jesus was born in order to *testify to the truth* (v. 37). Paul understands Jesus here to have inaugurated the early Christian practice of making 'the good confession' (1 Tim. 6:12, 13; cf. Rom. 10:9). Thus one day every tongue will 'confess that Jesus Christ is Lord, to the glory of God the Father' (Phil. 2:11). His testimony before Pilate becomes the paradigm for all his followers.

darkness!' (Luke 22:53). He knew at that very time that his own 'hour' of which he had spoken so often (2:4; 7:30; 12:23, 27, etc.) had now come. He had used the word 'hour' to refer to the time when he had to give himself up to the will of his enemies and be killed. He had known too that as this happened it would also be the time and occasion when he would enter his final conflict with the powers of darkness that from the beginning of history had held humankind down in bondage and death. He had already entered conflict in a preliminary way with those powers of darkness during, for example, his fierce temptation in the wilderness, his ministry of healing and his political conflict with the Jewish authorities. He had looked forward with expectation, mingled occasionally with dread, at this decisive final conflict to come. When he called on his disciples to be aware that they too would become involved with him in the hour and power of darkness, he at the same time also wanted them to 'stay awake and pray' (Matt. 26:41); thereby would they be able to overcome the uniquely powerful temptations that they would now be faced with, for they too, would find themselves caught up in the reverberations of the same conflict as was then taking place around himself. They would need special help to be able to resist the pervading influence of the darkness that was as never before exerting itself in the vain endeavour to extinguish the overcoming light of Jesus, and so to bring pain, shame and death in its wake.

We have to be aware of this prevailing hour and 'power of darkness' when we seek to interpret the account of what at this time happened around Jesus. This alone, for example, can explain the unusually vicious atmosphere Jesus encountered when he was interrogated by Annas and brutally assaulted by his servant, as he pointed out to them how without any grounds and beyond all reason had been their behaviour (18:21, 23). We should not be surprised that the fickle crowd so easily allowed itself to be caught up in the alien and irrational mood of the 'hour'. Though a few days before the people had gone out of their way to welcome him as their king, now, without even the exhortation of an upstart political leader, we find them ardently against him as they shout 'Crucify!' [22]

---

[22] The Greek word translated 'they shouted' (v. 6) carries the meaning 'they roared' or 'they screamed out'. There is no pronoun 'him' in Greek: the cry was simply 'Crucify! Crucify!' a slogan that would have quickly caught on.

No one was more shocked at the absurd and sudden change in the attitude and behaviour of the crowds than was Pilate. Though he had himself refused to believe in Jesus' claim to have brought in a kingdom with life-changing power, he had nevertheless been completely convinced that he was no criminal. He was certain that it was simply through the deadly spite and malice of the Jewish authorities that Jesus had been accused and handed over. Thus it was in an attempt to subvert them and obtain Jesus' release through an appeal to the crowds that he had made the surprise offer to release a prisoner, certain that their choice would be their popular 'king' Jesus. He was all the more shocked that it was the most notorious bandit of the day, Barabbas, whom they called for. The evangelist makes a brief interjection—*Now Barabbas was a bandit* (NIV, 'had taken part in a rebellion')—to underline the sheer absurdity of the choice and the shock it would cause to any decent person (18:40).

Differing explanations have been given as to why Pilate should now so radically change the whole routine of his treatment of Jesus. He suddenly decided to have him flogged, a punishment often meted out to base criminals who were to be executed. He seemed momentarily to allow himself to be caught up along with the Roman soldiers in the prevalent dark frenzy of spite and malice against the Lord. He permitted them to mock him,[23] and then exhibited him to the crowds in his robes[24] of mockery, shame and disgrace to whip up their contempt. Perhaps he thought that the sight of Jesus, bleeding and mocked, would arouse either pity from the crowds or else convince them that such a pathetic person could pose no threat to them: *Behold the man* (v. 5, AV). What else could have caused him to subject Jesus to such callous treatment when he professed to remain convinced of his innocence, and still anxious to gain his release—*I find no case against him* (v. 6)?

However, it is also suggested that Pilate's motive in submitting Jesus to such public treatment and then exhibiting him in this way was a desire to ingratiate himself with the crowds and to satiate as far as he could, short of execution, their strange desire for his

---

[23] The irony of the soldiers' mocking words, 'Hail, King of the Jews!' would not have been lost on John's early readers who worshipped Jesus as 'King of kings and Lord of lords' (Rev. 19:16; cf. Rev. 11:15).
[24] The purple robe would have been a chlamys, the garment worn by high-ranking officers and men in positions of importance.

chastisement. But such deviousness on Pilate's part could easily go hand-in-hand with his deliberate action in making an abject display of Jesus' weakness in the attempt to convince the crowds of his innocence. 'Look at the fellow!' is his appeal to them. How on earth could such a helpless person be taken seriously as a political threat to the social set-up either in Israel or Rome? Though such may have been his conscious intention, it seems obvious that Pilate, even though he tried to remain a detached observer of events, was himself unable to resist being caught up, as was everyone else, by the volatile mood of the situation. He himself in this hour and 'power of darkness' has been carried far beyond his depth.

As we reflect on the story, we realize that Jesus was being led no less closely and purposefully under the providence of God when he was being subjected to such cruel mockery as he was when he submitted himself finally on the cross to his utter God-forsakenness.[25] The picture we have of his suffering at the hands of Pilate and the soldiers brings to our minds in its many details what was prophesied to happen to him in, for example, the fifty-third chapter of Isaiah and the twenty-second Psalm. 'Yet it was the will of the LORD to crush him with pain', and thus to put him to grief when he made his life an offering for sin (Isa. 53:10). Moreover, he had even braced himself to face it (Mark 10:34) as he read of his future in the scroll of the book (Pss 22:16-18; 40:7).

We feel we can attach the significance of a special momentary inspiration to the impulse that led Pilate to make a public exhibition of him in his weakness and shame: *Here is the man!* We remember how earlier in the story God inspired Caiaphas, though he was unaware of it, to utter the word through which he accelerated and re-directed contemporary affairs in a fresh and decisive way towards the fulfilment of Christ's passion (cf. 11:49-53). In a similar way God inspired and used the gesture of Pilate. William Temple's comment is to the point: 'Here in this life of perfect obedience and love; here in this courage that views the worst that hate can do and is still unfalteringly calm; here in this love that is unquenched and undiminished by the desertion of friends; here in the blows and jeers of enemies—here we see man, fulfilling his true destiny and manifested as superior to circumstance.'

---

[25] See p. 197, note 1.

CHAPTER 19

PILATE AND JUDAISM SELF-EXPOSED

John 19:6-16a

19 When the chief priests and the police saw him, they shouted, 'Crucify him! Crucify him!' Pilate said to them, 'Take him yourselves and crucify him; I find no case against him.' [7]The Jews answered him, 'We have a law, and according to that law he ought to die because he has claimed to be the Son of God.'

8 Now when Pilate heard this, he was more afraid than ever. [9]He entered his headquarters again and asked Jesus, 'Where are you from?' But Jesus gave him no answer. [10]Pilate therefore said to him, 'Do you refuse to speak to me? Do you not know that I have power to release you, and power to crucify you?' [11]Jesus answered him, 'You would have no power over me unless it had been given you from above; therefore the one who handed me over to you is guilty of a greater sin.' [12]From then on Pilate tried to release him, but the Jews cried out, 'If you release this man, you are no friend of the emperor. Everyone who claims to be a king sets himself against the emperor.'

13 When Pilate heard these words, he brought Jesus outside and sat on the judge's bench at a place called The Stone Pavement, or in Hebrew Gabbatha. [14]Now it was the day of Preparation for the Passover; and it was about noon. He said to the Jews, 'Here is your King!' [15]They cried out, 'Away with him! Away with him! Crucify him!' Pilate asked them, 'Shall I crucify your King?' The chief priests answered, 'We have no king but the emperor.' [16]Then he handed him over to them to be crucified.

He claimed to be the Son of God

We here find Pilate, having rejected the truth, and finding himself beyond his depth, seeming to give way to a series of passing moods. At first in a moment of deeply frustrated anger he expressed himself ready, without any more ado, to throw the whole case over to the chief priests and to allow them to do what he knew to be quite beyond the law: *'Take him yourselves and crucify him'* (v. 6). It was when his adversaries began to demand the sentence of death on the grounds that he had blasphemed by claiming to be *the Son of God* (v. 7)[1] that for some moments Pilate became alert with fear. He had had nagging moments of unease as he had increasingly felt affairs moving beyond his control. Now he was *more afraid than ever* (v. 8). The Hellenistic world to which he belonged had firmly nurtured his growing mind with stories of gods who had come amongst us and married women, producing earthly sons endowed with occult powers. Pilate had just had Jesus flogged (v. 1) and living in a superstitious age, it is possible that he now feared he had whipped someone with supernatural powers.

It casts tragic light on the whole character and attitude of the man that, while he closed his mind as firmly and finally as we have seen him do to the truth and power of what Jesus had personally pressed on him, he now allowed himself to take Jesus seriously only when he was prompted by empty, superstitious fears to do so. Of course with such an approach (cf. 18:14) there would be no fitting response except silence, and Jesus had no alternative but to refuse any answer along the line of Pilate's pagan superstition.

Pilate, having regained his composure and perhaps in reaction to his deference, sought to re-assert himself. Was Jesus not aware of what was at stake if he dared to lose favour with his judge and governor—crucifixion or freedom? Silence before a Roman governor with his sweeping powers was equivalent to contempt of court. *I have power...* (v. 10), said he, with all the self-assertiveness and arrogance that so commonly corrupts governing status. It was at this point that Jesus uttered a clear rebuke and a solemn warning. No one in any authority anywhere held his position otherwise than responsibly to serve God. Pilate had already sinned by using his possession of it to be personally overbearing and to threaten. But let him take warning against the 'greater' sin. The Jewish authorities, with no just cause whatever,

---

[1] Verse 7: *'We have a law....'* The reference may be to Leviticus 24:16: 'One who blasphemes the name of the LORD shall be put to death....' By about two hundred years before the time of Jesus, blasphemy had become understood as actually articulating the all-holy name of God. This charge of blasphemy has been repeated several times by John in his Gospel. (See 5:18; 8:58; 10:33.)

as Pilate well knew, had now gone the length of charging him as a criminal and handing him over.[2]   Let Pilate beware!   It is to Pilate's credit that he did take heed of Jesus' warning, convinced of his innocence and seeking even more earnestly to release him.[3] It makes all the more tragic his sudden and complete collapse under the threat of a report to Rome that he had in this case tolerated the threat of treason. His tenure of power from Rome was slender. Everyone was aware that it was not because of personal ability but because he had curried favour from Rome that he held his office, and Caesar had a reputation of being hard on those who had failed to live up to his trust and friendship.

Even though he knew himself entrapped and defeated, he kept up appearances, taking his seat with all the pomp and in the place where the most solemn sentences of justice were pronounced.[4]   In sentencing Jesus he indulged in a sarcasm that ruthlessly exposed the complete insincerity of the Jewish establishment. *Here is your King!* (v. 14) was spoken with contempt and mockery, not of Jesus but of themselves and when, with even greater ferocity than ever before, they expressed their death-threat against Jesus, he deliberately manoeuvred them with a designedly pointed question into a confession of their complete apostasy: *We have no king but the emperor.*[5]   The evangelist significantly at this point in the

---

[2]   The passion narratives usually attribute the 'handing over' of Jesus to Judas. Acts 2:23 has often been taken to refer to Judas in the 'handing over' of Jesus to the Jewish authorities. However, in the context here, it is likely that the Sanhedrin in general, and the high priest Caiaphas in particular, are in the mind of Jesus when he says, *therefore the one who handed me over to you is guilty of a greater sin* (v. 11). The use of the singular (*the one*) is not surprising in the light of the common Jewish view of racial solidarity.

[3]   Though Pilate's authority was given *from above*, and therefore the crucifixion of Jesus was in the sovereign will and purpose of God, the Roman governor remained culpable (as did Judas) for his actions.   In Scripture, divine sovereignty never detracts from human responsibility.

[4]   Visitors to Jerusalem today are shown a paved area, identified as originally within the Fortress of Antonia, which (it is conjectured) may be the very place where the governor's judgement seat was placed. However, the irony of the situation John depicts would not have been lost on the early church which first read this account. Here was the Judge of all the earth, to whom the Father had committed all the ultimate decisions of the final, inexorable, divine justice (5:24-30), himself being 'judged' by a flawed Roman governor at the bidding of a corrupt religious establishment.

[5]   Pilate knew perfectly well that the Jews bitterly resented the Roman occupation and that their protestations of loyalty to Caesar were out of sheer

story reminds us (v. 14) that the time of the handing over of Jesus to his death was very close to the time at which the lambs were being slaughtered for the Passover Festival.[6]

Additional note on: *'power... from above'* (v. 11).

It may be helpful to consider more fully the word with which Jesus uttered his rebuke and last warning to Pilate (v. 11). Though given in the first place within such an engrossing conversation, Jesus spoke it intending that it be also treasured in the memory of his apostles as an important aspect of their Christian tradition. Paul repeats it in his Epistle to the Romans: 'those authorities that exist have been instituted by God' (Rom. 13:1), and he also points out that under God earthly rulers are meant not only to govern wisely but also to restrain and punish wrongdoers (Rom. 13:4). Jesus himself was always ready to pay such deference to his rulers (Matt. 17:24-27). However, being himself the true and living way, he was given to Israel to be nurtured with complete freedom to express himself fully and so to further his own personal kingdom in their midst. But instead of giving him that freedom and accepting him (1:11), they offered resistance and opposition and so ended up crucifying him. That the governor failed to support him in the freedom he required of all who encountered him made Pilate also a crucial adversary in spite of his own better judgement.

The risen Jesus still chooses today to present himself in the midst of every kind of community. Governments have to face the question of whether or not to give him the freedom he asks for as they make their decisions about the place and status of the church in their midst. It can happen that where his church is given true freedom, his teaching and ways will prevail and bring such health and blessing that he will be given not only freedom but even acknowledged established status though he does not ask in any

---

political expediency with a view to securing the condemnation of a just man of whom they were intensely jealous.

[6] John records that *it was the day of Preparation for the Passover....* If this was so, then John is saying that Jesus died at the precise moment the Passover lamb was being sacrificed (the ninth hour—3p.m.—on the day of Preparation, Matt. 27:45, 6). Carson argues that 'the day of Preparation' was simply Friday—the day of Preparation for the Sabbath—and that 'Passover' here simply refers to the Passover week. (Carson, p. 603-4.) See the commentaries for full discussions of John's dating compared to that of the Synoptics. See also p. 274, note 15.

magisterial way for such privilege. There is, however, a warning in the account that if full freedom is not granted to those whom he sends into a community to serve his name, the danger will also arise there of his being 'crucified' afresh, and where that happens, all that is best in life is crucified with him.

THE CRUCIFIXION AND BURIAL

John 19:16b-42

There they crucified him

John 19:16b-25a

19   So they took Jesus;   [17]and carrying the cross by himself, he went out to what is called The Place of the Skull, which in Hebrew is called Golgotha.   [18]There they crucified him, and with him two others, one on either side, with Jesus between them.   [19]Pilate also had an inscription written and put on the cross. It read, 'Jesus of Nazareth, the King of the Jews.'   [20]Many of the Jews read this inscription, because the place where Jesus was crucified was near the city; and it was written in Hebrew, in Latin, and in Greek.   [21]Then the chief priests of the Jews said to Pilate, 'Do not write, "The King of the Jews", but, "This man said, I am King of the Jews."'   [22]Pilate answered, 'What I have written I have written.'   [23]When the soldiers had crucified Jesus, they took his clothes and divided them into four parts, one for each soldier. They also took his tunic; now the tunic was seamless, woven in one piece from the top.   [24]So they said to one another, 'Let us not tear it, but cast lots for it to see who will get it.' This was to fulfil what the scripture says,

'They divided my clothes among themselves,
and for my clothing they cast lots.'
[25]And that is what the soldiers did.

Chapter 19

The passion of the Christ

Though *they took Jesus* (v. 16), it was not unwillingly that he
went with them and he did his best to make it as far as he could[7]
carrying the cross by himself (v. 17).[8] Not only was this the
living out of an example which he expected all his followers to
emulate when they too might have to bear a cross (cf. Luke 14:27,
1 Pet. 2:21), but it fitted best into his whole life's pattern. We
were his enemies, and not his friends and helpers, when he died to
save us. None of us could go through, even to the least extent,
the wrath and punishment that he bore for our sins. Therefore he
had to endure and bear it all alone with none alongside to help
and comfort. To make this point clear our evangelist omits the
story of how when Jesus collapsed physically under the sheer
weight he was carrying, they conscripted a passer-by to ensure he
could move on (Luke 23:26).

Of course the measure of all the earthly torture that he
underwent was exactly the same as the others with him or any
like victims also went through. In the actions of the soldiers who
handled him, pulling his limbs apart and hammering in the nails
there must have been the same callousness (and possibly
something of the same sadistic brutality) as usually characterized
such dirty work. It is a significant feature of the account that it
does not even hint that he went through such physical agony. We
have to turn to the Old Testament to find a muted description of
what he had physically to endure (cf. Pss 22:14-17; 60:3). That
the physical suffering is not dwelt on is a reminder to us of its
comparative insignificance in his vocation when compared with
the life-long humiliation and final anguish of soul under the

---

[7] The Roman practice was that the condemned man carried the crossbar to
which his hands would be nailed. At the place of execution, the upright stake to
which the crossbar would be fixed was already embedded in the ground.
[8] 'To prove that He is the sacrifice for our sins, He wished both to be led out of
the city and to be hanged on a tree. For, according to the command of the Law,
the custom was that the sacrifices whose blood was shed for sin should be
carried out of the camp; and the same law pronounces accursed whoever is
hanged on a tree (Lev. 6:30; 16:27; Deut. 21:23). Both were fulfilled in Christ,
that we might be fully assured that our sins have been expiated by the sacrifice
of His death, that He was made subject to the curse to redeem us from the curse
of the Law (Gal. 3:13), that He was made sin that we might be made the
righteousness of God in Him (2 Cor. 5:21).... To the same purpose is what
follows about the robbers....' Calvin, *Comm. in loc.*

judgement of God—the ultimate ordeal from which he prayed in Gethsemane that he might be spared (Matt. 26:39-44).

It is sometimes suggested that the evangelist avoided any reference to the physical torture in his presentation of the crucifixion because of his desire to present to our minds that Jesus' actual crucifixion was an aspect of his enthronement to kingship. It was Pilate who gave an unconscious but most eloquent witness to the kingship into which Jesus was uplifted on the cross. In the place where the description of the crime of the culprit was usually displayed, the Roman governor arranged for there to be nailed an inscription in three languages, most commonly used throughout the world: *Jesus of Nazareth, the King of the Jews.* If Pilate had really desired to proclaim the crucifixion as the enthronement of Jesus over all nations to 'draw all people to himself' (3:14f.; 12:32) he could not have devised a sign more apt. Certainly his intentions came far short of giving such glory to Christ. He may well have wanted simply to make a prominent public affirmation that Jesus was innocent of the charge of which he had been convicted. But we must, like Calvin, affirm that beyond all that he intended, God dictated to him his 'commendation of the Gospel, even though he did not understand what he wrote'.[9] He no doubt was delighted to anger the Jews with the implication of his action. It was the pleasure he found in their angry protest that stiffened his resolve to stand fast against them and to say, *'What I have written I have written'* (v. 22).

The evangelist hopes the story of what the soldiers did will impress us no less than what he has just told us about Pilate. Of course it was normal for executioners to divide among themselves

---

[9] 'Pilate's intention was to avenge himself indirectly on the Jews, who by their obstinacy had extorted from him the unjust execution of an innocent man.... But God's providence, which governed the pen of Pilate, looked far higher. It did not occur to Pilate to praise Christ as the author of salvation.... But God dictated to him this commendation of the Gospel, even though he did not understand what he wrote.' Calvin, *Comm. in loc.*

'The chief priests' demand that Pilate insert into the inscription, *"This man said, I am...."* would strip the governor of his last revenge. And so he stands firm. Thus Pilate's firmness is not motivated by principle and strength of character, but by the hurt obstinacy and bitter rage of a man who feels set upon. It is not... that Pilate refuses to change the truth into a lie, but that he is determined to humiliate those who *have* humiliated him' Carson, p. 611.

whatever was desirable from the discarded clothing[10] of the victim and there was nothing unusual in casting dice for special perquisites. What is meant to stand out here is the unusually deep concern that came to their minds in the case of Jesus' seamless tunic *woven in one piece from the top.* That God himself drew near them and at the time especially inspired them with such concern is clear from the fact that he had planned and foreordained the sanctity of that garment from the time the cross itself was planned and foreordained, and had it written down that it was to be observed (cf. Ps. 22:18; Exod. 28:32). Some commentators have found this whole incident of the presentation of the seamless garment of Jesus recalling to them the seamless robe which was worn by the high priest of Israel and have been content with the message that Jesus was crucified and exalted not only as King but also as our High Priest for ever (Heb. 4:14; 5:5; etc.). The church has found in the very special emphasis given by the evangelist to this concern, *Let us not tear it....* (v. 24), an eloquent plea above all things to avoid any careless tearing up of the unity of the church.[11] Certainly for the sake of the very survival of the church visible, divisions in its unity have at times to be tolerated, and it has to be remembered that Christ has continued to bless with his word and his presence those who from sincere conviction have found themselves forced to act as members of a branch of a divided church. Is this passage not

---

[10] There would probably have been five items of clothing. There were apparently four soldiers who each took his share: sandals, head-covering, belt and the outer garment. The seamless inner garment (NIV 'undergarment') was gambled for.

[11] 'I would not object to the comparison that, as Christ's garments were once divided by ungodly soldiers, so today there are perverse men who mutilate with their alien inventions the whole of Scripture, with which Christ is clothed to show Himself to us.... When [some] separate faith from Scripture, so that it may be attached to the Church alone, they not only despoil Christ by such a divorce but tear up His body in cruel sacrilege.... we grant them that the coat without seam is a symbol of the Church....' Calvin, *Comm. in loc.* Carson, p. 614, and Morris, p. 809, note 54, find the suggestion of the unity of the church represented by the seamless robe highly unlikely. Barrett cites etymological evidence (Lev. 16:4) to support the view that the undergarment is intended by John to refer symbolically to the high priesthood of Jesus; he also mentions with approval the view that the casting of lots for the seamless robe is probably intended to point to 'the death of Christ as bringing into one flock the scattered children of God'. Barrett, pp. 457-8.

here, with so many others that could be quoted, as a reminder of what he desires us to become again?

Words from the cross

John 19:25b-30

19   Meanwhile, standing near the cross of Jesus were his mother, and his mother's sister, Mary the wife of Clopas, and Mary Magdalene. [26]When Jesus saw his mother and the disciple whom he loved standing beside her, he said to his mother, 'Woman, here is your son.' [27]Then he said to the disciple, 'Here is your mother.' And from that hour the disciple took her into his own home.

28   After this, when Jesus knew that all was now finished, he said (in order to fulfil the scripture), 'I am thirsty.' [29]A jar full of sour wine was standing there. So they put a sponge full of the wine on a branch of hyssop and held it to his mouth. [30]When Jesus had received the wine, he said, 'It is finished.' Then he bowed his head and gave up his spirit.

Intensely human feelings

As I seek to set before my mind the situation in which the word of Jesus to his mother and John was spoken, studying the text, praying for light and reading the commentaries, I find meaning upon meaning thrusting themselves into my mind. I find myself dwelling on it as, on the part of Jesus, a word of quite spontaneous and heart-felt sympathy for Mary. Since he had left home he had been too busy to come back much to her and had found a new spiritual family among his disciples. She had longed at times to be closer to him and more active in his ministry but circumstances had not seemed to allow her, and he had not encouraged her (cf. 2:4, 5 which indicates that real faith was already born in Mary and therefore she was among the earliest of his true disciples). When his troubles became acute, however, she had followed his trial as closely as she could and there she was, supported by some friends[12] among the first of those few who gathered at the cross to watch and pray with him.

Her suffering was all the more intense because she could be of so little help. No doubt she longed to try to ease his pain and give him closer signs of her intense love for him than she was able. She was seeking all the time to hold on to the wonderful words she had heard from God about his birth. She knew that all would be well (2 Kgs 4:23b, 26b). She had known that he was destined for both suffering and greatness (Luke 2:28-35), but here now was a dark cloud over everything, and he was her son! Jesus saw her there, and John beside her, and committed her to John there and then to care for from that day on. Possibly he also had in mind the need for John to take her to his house in order to spare her the further agony she would endure if she stayed on there, of hearing and seeing him go through what was still to come; maybe she had already had enough.[13] The sword (Luke 2:35b) that was her lot for offering herself so purely and freely to be his mother had already pierced her soul and there was no more she need now take. Jesus' loving charge was willingly accepted. The group of them waited there with John in his house till they heard the end had nearly come and they began again 'looking on from a distance' (Mark 15:40). How wonderfully it casts light on what he feels for us in heaven today that, with the burden of the whole world's sin pressing so closely on him, in that moment he could have so keenly and intimately on his mind and heart what his mother was going through at the same time:

> He still remembers in the skies
> Her tears and agonies and cries!

Though it is impressive to dwell on the intensely human aspect of Jesus' word to his mother, the language he used to meet her need, *'Woman, here is your son.... Here is your mother'* (v. 26, 27), encourages us to lift our thoughts to the further meaning, on which the church, when it sought to interpret this incident, has

---

[12] For a comprehensive discussion of the women at the cross recorded by all four Gospels, see Carson, pp. 615-6.

[13] 'It was natural, perhaps inevitable, that during the long vigil some who loved him would venture closer, and revulsed by the suffering, drift away again — only to return.' Carson, p. 615.

more often dwelt because it is so profound and far-reaching. Jesus, indeed, seemed to see in the togetherness of Mary and John the nucleus of the great new family of God, his church.[14] It had been on his mind throughout his whole ministry to found and prepare it, and when he rose again it was his purpose to pour out his Spirit so that under his risen inspiration and guidance it could continue his mission and ministry, until his will for humanity was perfected. Mary was to play an important part in the example she would set within it. She more than any other had opened her life fully to him and had responded to him most closely. Now that the 'hour' of his passion, death and resurrection had at last come she was indeed being called to the central role in his ministry that his circumstances and plans earlier denied her (cf. John 2:4). As he looked at her now he saw her not only as his own mother but as typical of many other women within the leadership of the great new community, the new Israel through which the whole world was to be blessed. They would not only rejoice to live as she had done, united to him in one body, but they would especially continue her gracious role in the family in a ministry of mutual burden-bearing, of travailing prayer, personal concern and care for the erring (cf. Gal. 6:1-20), as they entered his conflict with the evil in the world.

John too had his distinct place in Jesus' vision. He was typical of and favourite amongst the apostles Jesus had trained to understand the full meaning of his life, teaching and death, and whom he sent out so that their tradition and decision might have supreme authority within the church which their word would create as they proclaimed the gospel everywhere.

We must remember that what we have here from Jesus is simply a vision of the coming church. He was not concerned either to give an outline of church structure or to allocate rigidly the ministry to which each sex should confine itself. His only

---

[14] While not endorsing the Roman Catholic traditional view of Mary as 'the new Eve', the antitype of the first woman who said, 'I have produced a man with the help of the LORD' (Gen. 4:1), it might appear to some readers that Dr Wallace in his discussion here tends towards a similar typology. Other readers may prefer the understanding of the verses which see Mary, now cared for by John according to Jesus' dying instruction, becoming a faithful member of the early church (Acts 1:14) without needing to attribute to her—in the absence of any scriptural evidence—a leading role in the apostolic hierarchy. However, Dr Wallace carefully avoids the various fanciful symbolic interpretations of this passage which certain commentators have suggested.

concern seems to have been that these two, Mary and John, should realize how much each could give by serving the other and receive by listening to the other. Neither sex must in any way separate from the other as it exercised its distinct ministry. In him there would be neither male nor female, neither slave nor free—all would be one in himself (Gal. 3:28).

The three hours passed and he knew he had come to the end of all he had to bear. There was nothing more of what he had so fearfully shrunk from in the cup that his Father had given him to drink (Luke 22:42; John 18:11). Did he turn his thoughts in his dying moments towards the triumphant words of the twenty-second Psalm, which had so occupied his mind at the height of his suffering (Ps. 22:25-31)? Even if he did, the physical distress was still intense, not least the maddening thirst. Thus breaking the restraint he had set on himself to bear the fearful physical torment in silence, he allowed himself now the relief of crying out, as if for help, *'I am thirsty'* (v. 28).[15]

We cannot be certain that he expected what then took place. Was he really pleading for pity or did one of the Roman soldiers mercifully try to help so that with his thirst momentarily allayed he could now utter the final cry: *It is finished,* as he yielded his spirit to the Father to whom he belonged? (See Luke 23:46.) His cry was not only a word of relief but also of achievement. It was the seal of the presence of his perfect kingdom in all its fullness in the midst of our world. It was the inauguration of what had been in his mind in that parabolic picture of the great banquet (Luke 14:15-24); the cry can now go out: 'Come; for everything is ready now!' 'For by a single offering he has perfected for all time those who are sanctified' (Heb. 10:14). It was above all a cry of victory. When he began his ministry, challenging the

---

[15] The drink Jesus is given at this point should not be confused with the wine mixed with myrrh which was offered to him on his way to the cross (Mark 15:23) and was intended to dull the physical agony of crucifixion; that drink he did not receive. Only John mentions that the wine he drank in his dying moments was presented to him on hyssop—probably a stalk of hyssop whose branches form a small 'cup' suitable to cradle the wine-soaked sponge. The hyssop fits in with John's constant references to OT passages which foretell the atonement accomplished on the cross: e.g. Exodus 12:22, 'Take a bunch of hyssop, dip it in the blood that is in the basin, and touch the lintel and the two doorposts....'; Numbers 19:18, 'take hyssop, dip it in the water, and sprinkle it....'; Psalm 51:7, 'Purge me with hyssop, and I shall be clean....' Cf. Hebrews 10:19.

tempter in the wilderness, he was entering his conflict with the devil, the enemy of all good. The success of his early ministry on earth had been to him a sign that Satan was already being 'thrown down' from his place of prominence in the heavenly realm (Luke 10:18; John 12:31; cf. Rev. 12:9, 10). Now his final conflict with all that caused 'darkness' to reign (Luke 22:53) had ended in his triumph.

Dead and buried

John 19:31-42

19 Since it was the day of Preparation, the Jews did not want the bodies left on the cross during the sabbath, especially because that sabbath was a day of great solemnity. So they asked Pilate to have the legs of the crucified men broken and the bodies removed. [32]Then the soldiers came and broke the legs of the first and of the other who had been crucified with him. [33]But when they came to Jesus and saw that he was already dead, they did not break his legs. [34]Instead, one of the soldiers pierced his side with a spear, and at once blood and water came out. [35](He who saw this has testified so that you also may believe. His testimony is true, and he knows that he tells the truth.) [36]These things occurred so that the scripture might be fulfilled, 'None of his bones shall be broken.' [37]And again another passage of scripture says, 'They will look on the one whom they have pierced.'

38 After these things, Joseph of Arimathea, who was a disciple of Jesus, though a secret one because of his fear of the Jews, asked Pilate to let him take away the body of Jesus. Pilate gave him permission; so he came and removed his body. [39]Nicodemus, who had at first come

of his bones shall be broken.' [37]And again another passage of scripture says, 'They will look on the one whom they have pierced.'

38 After these things, Joseph of Arimathea, who was a disciple of Jesus, though a secret one because of his fear of the Jews, asked Pilate to let him take away the body of Jesus. Pilate gave him permission; so he came and removed his body. [39]Nicodemus, who had at first come to Jesus by night, also came, bringing a mixture of myrrh and aloes,

weighing about a hundred pounds. [40]They took the body of Jesus and wrapped it with the spices in linen cloths, according to the burial custom of the Jews. [41]Now there was a garden in the place where he was crucified, and in the garden there was a new tomb in which no one had ever been laid. [42]And so, because it was the Jewish day of Preparation, and the tomb was nearby, they laid Jesus there.

Blood and water

Though it was regarded as important that the bodies of the crucified had to be removed in haste from public display before the Sabbath,[16] the body of Jesus was safeguarded from undesirable careless handling. Here we are told of sudden impulses that entered the minds of two of the soldiers in the hurried routine examination of the corpses. The one whose work it was to break the legs to hurry on the actual death[17] refrained from damaging him. The other, to make quite sure that he was already dead, pierced his side with a spear. We marvel at God's mysterious control over everything that took place. 'By a wonderful arrangement', says Calvin, 'Christ's body remained uninjured and blood and water flowed from his side.'

We can easily understand why God carefully preserved his bodily frame from being broken. We are meant to ponder why the evangelist regarded it as equally under the providence of God that blood and water together flowed from his side.[18]   He

---

[16] Deuteronomy 21:22-3: 'When someone is convicted of a crime punishable by death and is executed, and you hang him on a tree, his corpse must not remain all night upon the tree; you shall bury him that same day, for anyone hung on a tree is under God's curse. You must not defile the land....' The Roman practice was to leave the victims on the cross for a much longer period as a warning to others; death could take several days and the bodies were then eaten by vultures.

[17] There was usually a small platform nailed on the upright stake of the cross on which the victim could place his feet to relieve the agonizing pressure on his body. When his legs were broken, it was no longer possible to support the body's weight and so death occurred quickly through intense constriction of the chest.

[18] 'Tasker cites a paper by a medical man, J. L. Cameron, arguing that the passage indicates a flow of blood from the heart and great blood vessels adjacent, and water from the acutely dilated stomach.' Morris, p. 819, note 88. This detail is important to John who is bearing personal, eye-witness testimony to the fact that the Word who became *flesh* actually died; he may well have wanted to counter the early heresy of docetism which denied Jesus really became a man, but only *seemed* to be human. (Cf. 1 John 1:1; 2:18-23; 4:2, etc.)

obviously saw it also as a sign full of meaning. It was a sign that the one who now hung there dead—and he *was* truly dead—would become the source of new life. He who died crying out in pangs of thirst would now be able to fulfil his promise that those who come to him will never thirst (4:14). But there will be new life only because he died, and only to those who know themselves brought to that new life through his death. He had to go through death to make baptism in water truly cleansing. He 'came by water and blood..., not with the water only but with the water and the blood' (1 John 5:6). The church has always recognized in this simple event of the gush of blood and water from the pierced side of Jesus a sign also that new life is offered to us by Jesus not only through his word but also through two very special sacraments—baptism and the Lord's Supper.[19]

What the evangelist tells us here were to him happenings of so unlikely a nature that he felt he must assure us that he heard from a completely reliable eye-witness that they did take place (cf. 21:24). Moreover, in quoting to us the command that no bone of the paschal lamb was to be broken (Exod. 12:46), he confirmed that what may seem to be a merely incidental miracle was in God's mind to take place exactly as it did from the very time the future events of Jesus' life were being sketched in the Old Testament. John's mind also turned to the twelfth chapter of Zechariah. There we are given a picture of the people of Jerusalem in deep mourning and repentance over the unspeakable harshness of the treatment they have meted out to a leader they have rejected: 'when they look on the one whom they have pierced, they shall mourn for him...' (Zech. 12:10). He is reminding us of the healing change of mind and heart that will come to us as *we* look, and allow ourselves to be drawn to the One who is 'lifted up' (3:14).

Jesus had made a decisive impact on a rich man, Joseph of Arimathea, who had not yet followed him openly. Knowing that the authorities would be in haste to have the crosses stripped before the coming Sabbath, he went to Pilate and begged to be given the body of Jesus (Mark 15:42-6). The urge had come to

---

[19] Not all theologians agree that the two sacraments are symbolized here. However, there is general agreement that John wants us to understand the blood (i.e. the atoning death of Jesus) is the ground of our new life in Christ (6:53f.; 1 John 1:7), while the water speaks of washing away of sin (3:5), life (4:14) and the Holy Spirit (7:38f.).

him to lay it in the hewn rock tomb—a tomb fit for a king—which he had prepared for himself. Pilate was no doubt glad to be able to make amends for his former weakness in dealing with Jesus. Nicodemus who believingly had gone to Jesus by night also took courage and joined with Joseph in the entombment. Was Jesus truly beginning to draw all people to himself?

CHAPTER 20

THE RESURRECTION

The empty tomb

John 20:1-10

20 Early on the first day of the week, while it was still dark, Mary Magdalene came to the tomb and saw that the stone had been removed from the tomb. [2]So she ran and went to Simon Peter and the other disciple, the one whom Jesus loved, and said to them, 'They have taken the Lord out of the tomb, and we do not know where they have laid him.' [3]Then Peter and the other disciple set out and went toward, the tomb. [4]The two were running together, but the other disciple outran Peter and reached the tomb first. [5]He bent down to look in and saw the linen wrappings lying there, but he did not go in. [6]Then Simon Peter came, following him, and went into the tomb. He saw the linen wrappings lying there, [7]and the cloth that had been on Jesus' head, not lying with the linen wrappings but rolled up in a place by itself. [8]Then the other disciple, who reached the tomb first, also went in, and he saw and believed; [9]for as yet they did not understand the scripture, that he must rise from the dead. [10]Then the disciples returned to their homes.

The eloquence of the empty tomb

Some of the Gospel writers can tell from their own memory what was experienced on that first Easter. However, some scholars believe that all the accounts are dependent on what other sources, oral or written, had been available to the four Gospel writers. Obviously the longer the time gap became from the original event, the fainter the memory and the more freely the imagination might elaborate, without that promised inspiration of the Holy Spirit to bring everything to their remembrance (14:26; 15:26; 16:14). Even the sources re-told or re-written can be recounted from very different perspectives, not least when the writer has a particular purpose in view. Differences therefore appear in the Gospel accounts. Yet these very differences confirm the genuineness of the central facts 'that Christ died for our sins in accordance with the scriptures, and that he was buried, and that he was raised on the third day in accordance with the scriptures, and that he appeared to Cephas [Peter], then to the twelve' (1 Cor. 15:3-5).

The description here in John's Gospel of what happened on that first Easter morning 'reproduces the scene in all primitive freshness and vividness' (Godet). It impresses us as simply true to life and most free from imaginative intrusion or contrived invention. Mary Magdalene (the other Gospels record that other women were with her), impelled by love and longing devotion, had gone very early to the tomb.[1] The stone at its mouth was rolled back. She looked and saw it was empty. One thought entered her mind: the tomb robbers had taken the body! She hurried to call Peter and John.[2]

We are intended to notice the contrast in the approach to the tomb and the impression of each disciple when they entered and saw what was there. John, who reached it first, had hesitated at the entrance and was emboldened to enter only when Peter, rushing in without any restraint, encouraged him to follow. It must have dawned on both of them that the tomb could not have been robbed. The clothes that had wrapped the body of Jesus were still in an undisturbed position and the napkin that had been on his head was there aside, tidily folded.[3] The possible meaning

---

[1] 'But it may seem strange that he... starts with a woman.... The disciples certainly had no more earthly greatness than the women who followed Christ; but it pleased Christ to have them as the primary witnesses of His resurrection on the one ground that they are entitled to belief and are above any objections. ... John is content to name Magdalene alone, but without excluding the others [Mark 16:1]' Calvin, *Comm. in loc.*

[2] Luke only mentions Peter visiting the tomb (Luke 24:12) and therefore some commentators have cast doubts on John accompanying him. However we should note that Luke also records Cleopas saying, 'Some [plural] of those who were with us went to the tomb and found it just as the women had said; but they did not see him' (Luke 24:24). We may conclude Luke was not unaware that the beloved disciple had been with Peter that first Easter morning.

[3] Carson invites us to consider 'the contrast with the resurrection of Lazarus (11:44). Lazarus came from the tomb wearing his grave clothes, the additional burial cloth still wrapped round his head. Jesus' resurrection body apparently passed through his grave-clothes, spices and all, in much the same way that he

did not dawn on the mind or heart of Peter, who accepted the situation with bewilderment.[4] But for John it meant that the apparently impossible must really have happened. This affirmation means that John, there and then, by some intensely private intuition, believed Jesus had risen from the dead. No doubt his abiding sense of the love of the Father for his Son helped him to realize that Jesus could not have been left in the hands of death: *he saw and believed* (v. 8b). His conviction, however, did not come to him in such a way that he wanted to share it with others or to talk with others about this most strange possibility. He indeed felt it so extraordinary and unbelievable that he wanted to think about it before he talked: *For as yet they did not understand the scripture, that he must rise from the dead* (v. 9)

That the two disciples, after what they saw in that tomb, could go back home so casually, so untroubled, is put down by John himself to their lack of understanding of the message and purpose of the Old Testament revelation (v. 9).[5] They should have been able to think it through that the long history of such great promises from the call of Abraham to the birth of the Messiah—whom they had come to believe was Jesus—must be bound to come to fulfilment in glory. They should have been able when they saw it to recognize spontaneously and clearly that the empty tomb meant the defeat for ever of death and all its accompaniments that have blighted human life throughout the ages—disease, sorrow and meaninglessness.

Peter would soon rise to it when the Spirit opened his mind to the place where it is most obviously foretold in the Psalms. Recall how in his great sermon at Pentecost he put it so clearly:

---

later appeared in a locked room (vv.19, 26). The description of the burial cloth that had been round Jesus' head does not suggest that it still retained the shape of the corpse, but that it had been neatly rolled up and set to one side by the one who no longer had any use for it.' Carson, p. 637.

[4] 'Some seed of faith remained in their hearts, but smothered for a time, so that they were not aware of possessing what they did possess.' Calvin, *Comm. in loc.*

[5] Hoskyns comments: 'The pre-eminence of the faith of the beloved disciple is the climax of the narrative. His faith was not derived from ancient prophetic texts; the fact of the empty tomb illuminated the sense of Scripture.' Quoted by Morris, who further comments: 'Some have felt that the recording of the fact that he was the first to believe shows a certain pride. In view of v. 29 it is more likely to be humility. "He saw and believed"—and therefore did not attain to the blessing promised to those who believed without seeing.' Morris, p. 834.

'But God raised him up, having freed him from death, because it was impossible for him to be held in its power' (Acts 2:24; cf. Ps. 16:10; also e.g. Ps. 73:23, 24). Paul, given time to delve more deeply with a more acute and disciplined mind, was able to sum up all the implications of that long history in his glorious fifteenth chapter of 1 Corinthians, re-echoing at its end what was already said even as eloquently in the book of Isaiah (25:7, 8): 'Where, O death, is your victory? Where, O death, is your sting?' 'But thanks be to God, who gives us the victory through our Lord Jesus Christ' (1 Cor. 15:55, 57).

The appearance to Mary

John 20:11-18

20   But Mary stood weeping outside the tomb. As she wept, she bent over to look into the tomb; [12]and she saw two angels in white, sitting where the body of Jesus had been lying, one at the head and the other at the feet. [13]They said to her, 'Woman, why are you weeping?' She said to them, 'They have taken away my Lord, and I do not know where they have laid him.' [14]When she had said this, she turned round and saw Jesus standing there, but she did not know that it was Jesus. [15]Jesus said to her, 'Woman, why are you weeping? For whom are you looking?' Supposing him to be the gardener, she said to him, 'Sir, if you have carried him away, tell me where you have laid him, and I will take him away.' [16]Jesus said to her, 'Mary!' She turned and said to him in Hebrew, 'Rabbouni!' (which means Teacher). [17]Jesus said to her, 'Do not hold on to me, because I have not yet ascended to the Father. But go to my brothers and say to them, "I am ascending to my Father and your Father, to my God and your God."' [18]Mary Magdalene went and announced to the disciples, 'I have seen the Lord'; and she told them that he had said these things to her.

The 'gardener'
Mary lingered at the tomb[6] not knowing what more to do or where to go—so powerfully had she allowed her conviction to

---

6   The implication is that the other women, whom John chooses not to mention, had returned home, leaving Mary alone. We may ask why John did not share his

grip her that the tomb had been robbed. Even the vision of the angels[7] in white (or might they not truly have been real angels actually there, rather than only a vision?) did not move her out of her depression. Their position *sitting where the body of Jesus had been lying, one at the head and the other at the feet*—with the empty grave clothes between them—ought to have demonstrated to her clearly that Jesus must by himself have slipped out of them, and so challenged her about the supposed cause of her grief! Yet she did not 'see and believe' as John had done.

The risen Jesus, recognizing her plight, could not have left her there at the tomb, so alone and desolate. It gave him the opportunity of making her the first of the disciples to whom he appeared.[8] He stood beside her. He even spoke to her, challenging her tears with the very same words as the angels had spoken, and appealing to her to look at him rather than mourn (v. 15). But she thought he was the gardener and even the possible culprit! It was only when he suddenly called her by her name, *Mary!* (see 10:3, 4), that the situation was all at once transformed. She knew that it was he, her redeemer there to call her his own (cf. Isa. 43:1). Of course she instinctively tried to embrace him. How much he allowed her we are not told, but he made to disengage her as gently and as firmly as he could.[9] Then with a few unforgettable words intended to thrill and haunt her mind as she thought them over, he told her the good news she was to tell as she spoke of how he had come to her, risen from the dead.

---

new-found faith with her, but possibly they did not meet after John had seen and believed.

[7] It is interesting that all four Gospels mention the angels. Matthew records one angel whose appearance was like lightning and whose clothes were white as snow (28:2, 3); Mark records a young man in white sitting on the right in the tomb (16:5); Luke tells of two men in dazzling apparel whose presence so frightened the women that they bowed their faces to the ground (24:4, 5). In all four accounts, the message is the same whether the witnesses saw one or two angels: God is announcing through heavenly visitors that he is gloriously at work, as in all four Gospels the angels address the grief-stricken women.

[8] See note 1 above.

[9] Carson, p. 644, offers the following paraphrase of verse 17: 'Stop touching me (or, Stop holding on to me) for... I am not yet in the ascended state, so you do not have to hang on to me as if I were about to disappear permanently. This is a time for joy and sharing the good news, not for clutching me as if I were some jealously guarded dream-come-true. Stop clinging to me but go and tell my disciples that I am in process of ascending to my Father and your Father.' For a full discussion of the verse see Carson, pp. 641-5.

Here is the gist of it: 'My Father will be yours, in even a more wonderful and close way than ever before.' God was always, as Jesus said in his teaching, to be thought of and prayed to, as one who controlled and cared about every detail of our lives. But now, Mary is being told, he will soon take the very human nature he has assumed, to be his for ever in heaven. There at the right hand of God he will be for ever the One who has become deeply intimate with every aspect of our state and plight. Surely now we can think of the Father who gave us his Son as having an even greater tenderness of feeling towards us (Heb. 4:15) and a depth of understanding of what we are and what we need, so that we can pray to him with greater boldness, hope and confidence than ever before was thought possible.

We must notice the other piece of good news that Jesus was concerned to send by Mary. Now that he is about to ascend to the Father he calls his disciples *my brothers* (v. 17).[10] On one specially significant occasion he had encouraged his intimate disciples to think of themselves as no longer servants but friends (15:15). Now he encourages all who hear Mary's message to an even deeper understanding of their relationship with him. Commentators recall to us how in Psalm 22 the Messiah, having passed through all the horrors of his suffering, says, 'I will tell of your name to my brothers and sisters' (v. 22). How closely he has bound us to each other by his death and resurrection! We recall the vision he had of the church as the new family of God when, hanging on the cross in his dying moments, he sent off Mary and John together as fellow-disciples in the fledgling new community of faith. It is a vision we must continually seek to cultivate when we gather in our various congregations to sing, pray and listen together to his Word, echoing his own prayer, 'Abba! Father!' (Gal. 4:6). It should manifest itself also in a feeling of family responsibility that will constrain us to suffer and pray rather than criticize and condemn those who have strayed from our fellowship into disgrace or trouble (Gal. 6:1, 2). Moreover, as we look forward, it is also meant to bring to our minds, that being his brothers and sisters, even though adopted,

---

[10] '[T]he expressions *my Father and your Father* and *my God and your God* assume distance between Jesus and his followers, even as they establish links. But the emphasis here is on shared privileges (cf. Rom. 8:15, 16; Heb. 2:11, 12; Ps. 22:22).' Carson, p. 645.

we are also joint heirs (Gal. 4:7; cf. Rom. 8:15-17) with even a right to share in his glorious future.

Of course he intended the message itself would help her to understand his gently spoken word of disengagement: *Do not hold on to me*. He sensed that she was longing to experience again the same kind of familiar closeness that prevailed between them while he was with her on earth and had allowed her even to wash and caress his feet. She must realize that he had much more now to give her, if she would allow herself to go his way. He is seeking to assure her with the hope that as he ascends to the Father he will pour out his Spirit on the church to give those who receive him a much more enriching and fuller relationship with him that was ever possible even to those who were close to him as he was on earth. The Spirit's presence would abundantly compensate for his physical absence.

We must always remember that we have his presence within this new relationship only as the exalted Lord. We have to allow him to dictate the mould and the intensity of the experience we are granted, and in submission to him to keep our self-centred desires in restraint. If we are truly submissive we will find the pattern of it is described in the multitude of New Testament texts to which we must hold on if we are to keep close to him. There will be tension and difficulty punctuated by wonderful deliverance and vision as by faith we hold on to his overcoming power (2 Cor. 4:7-11). There can be no doubt of its basic warmth and intensity. Those who do not see him but believe can be described at times as experiencing for themselves 'indescribable and glorious joy' (1 Pet.1:8).

The appearance to the disciples

John 20:19–23

20 When it was evening on that day, the first day of the week, and the doors of the house where the disciples had met were locked for fear of the Jews, Jesus came and stood among them and said, 'Peace be with you.' ²⁰ After he said this, he showed them his hands and his side. Then the disciples rejoiced when they saw the Lord. [21]Jesus said to them again, 'Peace be with you. As the Father has sent me, so I send you.' [22]When he had said this, he breathed on them and said to them, 'Receive the Holy Spirit. [23]If you forgive the sins of any, they are forgiven them; if you retain the sins of any, they are retained.'

His hands and side

This is the second of further occasions in which he 'presented himself alive to them by many convincing proofs, appearing to them over the course of forty days' (Acts 1:3) until he visibly ascended. He described himself to Mary (20:17) as, during this interim period, being in a state of ascending though not yet fully ascended. During this transition he is described as appearing to his disciples both to prove that he had risen, and to convey some special message about its significance. During his appearances one of his concerns was always to urge his disciples to recognize that he was there with a human body (he is eternally one of us), but a body wonderfully transformed and endowed with new qualities adjusted to his future environment of the Father's right hand. While he was still 'the Lord', he was not always immediately recognizable. (See 20:14; 21:12; cf. Matt. 28:17; Luke 24:16, 31, 37). On this occasion when he *came and stood among them*, he showed them his hands and his feet and they knew it to be the Lord.[11]

The disciples were in fear that the freshly manifested hatred of their crucified master might continue to motivate some further attacks on themselves. The writer merely states the fact that they *rejoiced when they saw the Lord,* and wisely makes no attempt to describe the thrilling intensity of what came to their minds and hearts when beyond all doubt, and after such despair, they recognized him. Jesus, in his promise of it, had likened such joy to that of a woman who has gone through the agony of birth-pangs to receive her child (16:20-22). Archbishop Temple

---

[11] Paul indicates that although Jesus is eternally a Man, after his resurrection he was significantly different: he had become 'a life-giving spirit' with a resurrection body. His first human body had been sown perishable, but was now raised an imperishable human body; it had been sown in dishonour, but it had been raised in glory; it had been sown in weakness, but had been raised in power; sown a physical body, it had been raised a spiritual body (1 Cor. 15:42-45).

ventures to suggest that there must have been at least 'a few moments of silent rapture'. There he really was!

It is important to dwell on how in his greeting he showed them his hands and his side at the same time as he spoke the words, *Peace be with you*. It was all one gesture. He was enabling them to see it was only through the conflict and plight in which he had sustained these wounds, that he had won for them the peace which he has now come to offer in its stead. His gesture reminds us of the description of the Suffering Servant of God whom Isaiah described as having been 'wounded for our transgressions' and as having borne 'our chastisement' so that we might receive in their place the peace and healing that have been made available through his self-sacrifice (see Isa. 53:4-6). It was from this beginning in the upper room that the church, following the more developed thought of the New Testament writers (e.g. 2 Cor. 5:18-21) in its proclamation of the gospel, stressed what the Reformers called the 'wonderful exchange'. Christ was presented as the One who has come to take upon himself all that in our sinfulness belongs to us, so that we can now have in its place all the wealth of righteousness and truth that belongs to himself.

He again repeated, *'Peace be with you'* (v. 19, 21), as a summary of the message he was commissioning them to share with the world. They were well aware of the glory of the task they were meant to fulfil as they sought to publish the 'good news' of such peace (cf. Isa. 52:7). The kingdom of God had now come in its full reality. The forgiveness of sins which he had bought by his blood was freely there for all who would receive his constraining love. With prayer in his name[12] now possible, nothing was to be thought impossible. And here he was, urging each of them to think of themselves as enlisted to complete the same glorious task as he had been given to inaugurate when his Father sent him into the world!

That he breathed on them all and said, *Receive the Holy Spirit*, when he told them to go and proclaim forgiveness, was a sign and promise that whenever and however forgiveness was sincerely offered and received even fearful hearts would truly be given peace, lives would be changed and names would indeed be written in heaven. It was all soon to happen in a spectacular way when Peter preached on the day of Pentecost, and on a more

---

[12] See p. 227, note 4.

normal and modest level, it remains always what pastor and people are meant to hope for whenever the Word of God is preached within the gathered congregation. Yet alongside Peter, to hear the same commission and receive the same promise, were also Mary and others with her, such as the other Marys, Nicodemus and Simon of Cyrene.[13]   Forgiveness is to be effectively mediated and realized where no Peter is present. It can happen when the Scriptures are opened in a group, and one member speaks to another of what they see and hear through the passage before them. As the Lord washed the feet of the disciples, he urged them to seek to wash one another's feet. And in the New Testament church they believed they could restore even a seriously erring brother by the prayerful and loving concern that bears the burden of others (cf. Gal. 6:1, 2).

When Jesus commissioned and sent them, he warned that the light that brought salvation would at the same time bring judgement to those who, seeing it, would choose to remain in darkness (cf. 3:19): *'if you retain the sins of any, they are retained'* (v. 23).   When he himself experienced how the Pharisees had deliberately time and again refused to acknowledge what they already saw of his miraculous cure of the man born blind, he told them that the guilt of their pretence to see nothing would remain ever to condemn them (9:41). There will always be those around the witnessing church who, by their hatred of its goodness and rejection of its clear and powerful light, would harden and blind themselves in their opposition and thus be condemned by the genuineness of what they have rejected.

We are to think of everything that happened in that upper room as simply a quiet pre-enactment of what was later to be repeated in its fullness when the ascended Jesus poured out the Spirit upon the church. Yet the Spirit was truly given when Jesus breathed on

---

[13] 'How large a group is referred to by "the disciples" is not certain, but in the light of the circle at the last supper (made up of Jesus plus the Twelve, and then, after Judas left, the Eleven), and in the light of the fact that Thomas is singled out as not having been present (v. 24)—though doubtless there were countless other "disciples" less tightly connected with the Lord who were not also present—we should probably think of the Ten (*i.e.* the Twelve, less Judas and Thomas.' Carson, p. 646. It is a moot point whether, with Carson, we accept that by 'disciples' John here means apostles, or with Dr Wallace, a wider circle of Jesus' followers is referred to. However, the reformed churches have invariably agreed with Wallace that forgiveness is to be both 'mediated and realized where no Peter is present'.

them. It was a real inauguration, as Hoskyns put it, to a task that was not yet begun. I remember being impressed by an illustration I read likening the risen presence of Jesus there before his disciples to the chink of morning sunshine we sometimes have seen when we have awakened, having gone to sleep in a heavily curtained room. How much the encounter with the risen Jesus was meant to signify to the disciples as they thought through it and grasped its meaning! The kingdom of God was now more imminent than ever before, and ready at any time to break into this benighted world with invincible power and forgiving love—to change everything.[14]

Jesus and Thomas

John 20:24-31

20 But Thomas (who was called the Twin), one of the twelve, was not with them when Jesus came. [25]So the other disciples told him, 'We have seen the Lord.' But he said to them, 'Unless I see the mark of the nails in his hands, and put my finger in the mark of the nails and my hand in his side, I will not believe.'

26 A week later his disciples were again in the house, and Thomas was with them. Although the doors were shut, Jesus came and stood among them and said, 'Peace be with you.' [27]Then he said to Thomas, 'Put your finger here and see my hands. Reach out your hand and put

---

[14] Many explanations have been given in the attempt to harmonize John 20:22 with the outpouring of the Holy Spirit at Pentecost (Acts 2:1ff.). Perhaps the simplest and best is that hinted at by Dr Wallace. A helpful analogy is offered by Carson (see his discussion on pp. 649-655, esp. p. 655): At the foot-washing in John 13:1-17, Jesus states that unless Peter's feet are washed he has no part in Christ (v. 8). This by no means implies that the physical act of washing Peter's feet replaces the atonement accomplished by his death. Rather are the events at the Supper symbolic of what would be achieved a few hours later when he died for the sins of the world. Similarly, when Jesus breathed (literally, 'exhaled'—there is neither preposition nor pronoun in the Greek, and 'on them' is supplied by translators on the bold assumption that John intends us to understand he did actually breathe on the disciples), it was an acted parable of what would later take place when the Spirit proceeded from the Father and Son in an historic and epochal event in the formation of the NT church.

it in my side. Do not doubt but believe.' ²⁸Thomas answered him,
'My Lord and my God!' ²⁹Jesus said to him, 'Have you believed
because you have seen me? Blessed are those who have not seen and
yet have come to believe.'

30 Now Jesus did many other signs in the presence of his disciples,
which are not written in this book. ³¹But these are written so that you
may come to believe that Jesus is the Messiah, the Son of God, and
that through believing you may have life in his name.

'Let us learn to believe what we do not see'

That Thomas was absent when the others were drawn together for
mutual support, may indicate that he was a fringe person, tending
often to form and firm up too quickly his occasionally non-
conformist opinions. Of course there could well be another
perfectly understandable reason why he was unable to be present
that evening. However, he at times could express some doubt
about the way Jesus was going (cf. however, 11:16) and could
voice questioning about things he said (14:5). When the issues
were basic and he could see through things clearly he was
passionate in his loyalty, and under the immediate shadow of the
crucifixion he shared deeply in the distress they were all going
through.

Certainly he isolated himself when he heard the news that Jesus
had appeared among them that evening. Unfortunately the report
that he heard apparently gave too great prominence to the fact
that Jesus had proved that it was he, by showing them his hands
and his side. Maybe that did not seem to him to be an action fully
worthy of what he would have expected from Jesus. He was
deeply suspicious that the whole group had allowed themselves to
be carried beyond common sense by some strange corporate
illusion. He allowed himself an immediate (even scornful)
reaction to the sudden pressure of the news: *'Unless I see the
mark of the nails in his hands, and put my finger in the mark of
the nails and my hand in his side, I will not believe'* (v. 25).

'Such vigour of disbelief,' says Temple, 'plainly represents a
strong urge to believe.' Jesus understood Thomas' tendency to
self-esteem, and he certainly valued his loyalty. As anxious to
rescue Thomas as he had been to expel Judas, his was the chief
influence that drew him back to the group, and drew them all
together to meet in hope that his appearance might be repeated on

the corresponding night the following week. Jesus' quiet challenge to Thomas to touch him put him to shame over the crudity of the vow he had expressed, and he was reprimanded firmly but graciously for his doubt: *'be unbelieving no longer, but believe'* (v. 27, NEB). Jesus laid his hand gently on the state of mind that Thomas must henceforth deny as he seeks to rise to new life.

So powerful was the impact of Jesus' appearance and word on Thomas that it immediately drew from him a confession of faith far surpassing anything that even the other Apostles had ventured: *'My Lord and my God!'* Of course we take it for granted in our trinitarian thought today that nothing less than the title given to the Lord in the Old Testament can be ascribed to Jesus too. Yet it took time and thought for even Paul in his letters to voice clearly the conviction that such a title alone was adequate if the crucified, risen and exalted Jesus were to be given his true name.

That Thomas had believed continued the work of grace in one on whom Jesus had lavished so much care and prayer; Thomas also now knew the way. Yet even as the risen Christ confirmed a living faith in Thomas, he knew himself to be on the verge of his ascension and he could now announce for all of us yet to come a new and final beatitude: *Blessed are those who have not seen and yet have come to believe.* At this point it is hard to improve on Calvin: 'He calls blessed those eyes which spiritually behold in him what is heavenly and divine. For today we behold Christ in the Gospel no less than if he stood with us. In this sense Paul tells the Galatians that he was crucified before their eyes. Therefore if we desire to see in Christ what makes us happy and blessed, let us learn to believe what we do not see.'

At what seems to be a fitting climax to the Gospel we find now indeed a very short appendix. The evangelist believed that even the few signs he had carefully selected and arranged to preface Jesus' subsequent teaching of the apostles would adequately reveal to us not only who Jesus was when he lived among us — *the Messiah, the Son of God* — but also what he would do for us today from where he has ascended. We on our part will be enabled to *have life in his name.* We must absorb in our mind and heart all we read and hear of him, let the patterns shown in his whole history and teaching mould our way of life — especially his self-sacrifice. Thus opening ourselves to him we can be assured of receiving from him, even in the midst of our continuing human frailty, the pledge of eternal life.[15]

---

[15] 'When you look at these two verses [20:30, 31], the simple order is as follows: first evidence, then belief, and then life. So, life is the ultimate goal; John's is a Gospel of life. But the only goal to this life eternal is through faith in Jesus as God's only Son. And then the only way to genuine Christian belief is through the first hand testimony of the apostles to their Lord and Saviour recorded in the sacred writings, the Scriptures' (Lucas & Philip, p. 10).

CHAPTER 21

THE SAME YESTERDAY AND TODAY
AND FOR EVER

John 21:1

21 After these things Jesus showed himself again to the disciples by
the Sea of Tiberias; and he showed himself in this way.

An afterword

It seems to be confirmed by its last verse that the evangelist quite
deliberately brought his Gospel to a finish at the end of chapter
20. The 21st chapter is often supposed to have been added to an
already completed Gospel after some traditions, not recorded
elsewhere, came under the purview of the evangelist soon after he
had brought his Gospel to a finish. They are deemed to have been
Johannine in style and vocabulary and no copy has ever been
found of the first 20 chapters without this 21st chapter.

We ourselves, encouraged by Hoskyns, have taken the view
that the evangelist, when he was originally writing his Gospel,
had it in mind to reserve the record of what would have been a
third appearance in Galilee for a specially intended appendix.
This was to be added after he had drawn his Gospel to what
already was a full and quite satisfying conclusion. Such an
arrangement of material was intended to help the interpreter or
reader to understand that Jesus, as he then engaged his disciples
in this final protracted incident, had an entirely forward-looking
purpose. He was showing how Jesus was now going to set to
work on and with his disciples in his coming church. This final
incident shows what they could expect from him and what he
would expect from them. The subsequent questioning of Peter
then reveals what ideals he had for the ministry of those he was
from now on going to set to his work.

A further purpose of this appendix is obvious. A rumour was in
circulation about the beloved disciple of Jesus. It was held that

Jesus had been referring in particular to him when, appearing to speak of the time of his second coming, he had spoken of some around him not dying before the end had come. The evangelist in reporting what was before him as material for this afterword took the opportunity of negating this false impression (vv. 22, 3).

The appearance at the seashore

John 21:2-8

21 Gathered there together were Simon Peter, Thomas called the Twin, Nathanael of Cana in Galilee, the sons of Zebedee, and two others of his disciples. ³Simon Peter said to them, 'I am going fishing.' They said to him, 'We will go with you.' They went out and got into the boat, but that night they caught nothing.

4 Just after daybreak, Jesus stood on the beach; but the disciples did not know that it was Jesus. ⁵Jesus said to them, 'Children, you have no fish, have you?' They answered him, 'No.' ⁶He said to them, 'Cast the net to the right side of the boat, and you will find some.' So they cast it, and now they were not able to haul it in because there were so many fish. ⁷That disciple whom Jesus loved said to Peter, 'It is the Lord!' When Simon Peter heard that it was the Lord, he put on some clothes, for he was naked, and jumped into the lake ⁸But the other disciples came in the boat, dragging the net full of fish, for they were not far from the land, only about a hundred yards off.

An old miracle with a new significance

After the first Easter appearances, Jesus had left them greatly excited and in readiness for action in the service for which he had so carefully trained them. Their commissioning and the promise of the Spirit which they had experienced in his momentary presence, though it had been commanding and powerful, had none the less been prospective. It had put them on hold like soldiers who had been served notice of a final call-up at any moment. He had, moreover, sent them a message through Mary that he was on his way to a climactic ascension after which even the experience of God they had already enjoyed in his presence would be wonderfully transcended. The very remembrance of their past with him would remind them that though he had at times left them alone and even allowed them to experience deep trouble and tension previously, he had always come and more than fulfilled their greatest expectations at what he knew was the right time: 'I will not leave you orphaned; I am coming to you' (14:18).

We take it that Jesus had not yet forbidden them to depart from Jerusalem (cf. Acts 1:4) nor had he yet spoken of their coming baptism with the Holy Spirit. (Had they remembered John's foretelling of a baptism 'with [lit. 'in'] the Holy Spirit' which Jesus had come to administer (1:33)?) Therefore we cannot blame the group of seven for passing some of the time on a quite natural visit to the sea of Galilee. They had no real intention now of scattering each to his house as had happened when Jesus was being tried, sentenced and crucified. But we can blame them for their undisciplined failure to encourage each other in prayerful waiting. Something came over them. The zeal that seemed so firmly to have possessed them began to falter. The warmth went out of their expectancy. Most of us can easily understand it from our own experience when we fail to strengthen each other's hands in God and to wait on him continually for renewal. Therefore when Peter, in the lead again, proposed a night's fishing, they all fell in line.

It was Jesus who providentially ensured *that night they caught nothing* (v. 3). He wanted to appear to them in a situation which would forcibly bring to their minds the day when in the same place under exactly the same circumstances he had taught them through a miracle that none of them could have forgotten (Luke 5:4-11) that they had now been called to be 'fishers of men' and that he had the power to fill the nets they were soon to cast for this purpose, when he finally sent them out. It often happened that those to whom Jesus appeared and talked did not always immediately grasp who it was there encountering them (cf. Luke 24:16, 31, 37) and in this case it seemed at first to the disciples that he was simply a friendly by-passer, offering some sympathy. Somehow they were impelled to heed him and to cast their net at his suggestion. The old miracle again happened and memories flooded into their minds. They not only realized who it was but it also began to dawn on them what he was seeking to say.

They were meant to take what was happening as a sign,[1] and remember that their task was now to let down the net of the kingdom of God (cf. Matt. 13:47, 48) into the life of the world and believe that as they did so, he himself would not fail to honour their faith and obedience. The miracle assured them that as they proclaimed his love and power, he himself would be with them to draw all to himself (12:32) and the miracle of a growing church would far surpass even the glory of what happened around the earthly Jesus in Galilee. They must never imagine that though risen and on his way back to the Father, he could not still do among them what they had seen and rejoiced in when he was with them in the flesh. He was now to be thought of and trusted as 'the same yesterday and today and for ever' (Heb. 13:8).

How relevant this Easter gesture of Jesus can be to us today. The parishioners who live around the doors of our churches are everywhere becoming more disinclined to take what we must confine ourselves to offer them in the gospel, and we ourselves, so often seeking to devise new ways of contacting them, are often forced to admit that much of our toil is for nothing. Is there not a promise here even for us today that though his work in our midst might not be as spectacular as that with the apostles, we can pray to him with confidence, surely expecting his answer, to continue to gather in our generation within our own church a flock that will indeed glorify his name and prove an answer to our prayer? In an extremely downtown parish where there were few whom one could aim to contact in the immediately surrounding area, I always viewed enquirers who came, at times from a distance, as possibly there because drawn into my care by Christ himself to make a truly gathered congregation. This continuously miraculous experience of his work made me realize that I could expect to find him repeating in our midst today not only this one work but all the works he is described as wonderfully accomplishing during his days in the flesh. He is still opening

---

[1] The experience may also have arisen through financial straits. It is possible that since the death of Jesus, the material support the disciples had been receiving had appeared to dry up. The failure to secure a good catch (and therefore replenish their empty purses) until Jesus intervened must have been a powerful reminder that in obedience to him in the commission he had given, their material needs would be adequately supplied. Following on from that was the eloquent action parable of an abundant harvest of people for those called to be 'fishers of men'.

blind eyes, making the lame to walk, the deaf to hear, enabling those who have been dumb to witness to his glory. Indeed, the Gospels now appear to be not only about what he once did, but about what he wants to do in our midst today, especially through his word preached within our churches.

Things present—things to come

John 21:9-14

21   When they had gone ashore, they saw a charcoal fire there with fish on it, and bread. [10]Jesus said to them, 'Bring some of the fish that you have just caught.' [11]So Simon Peter went aboard and hauled the net ashore, full of large fish, a hundred and fifty-three of them; and though there were so many, the net was not torn. [12]Jesus said to them, 'Come and have breakfast.' Now none of the disciples dared to ask him, 'Who are you?' because they knew it was the Lord. [13]Jesus came and took the bread and gave it to them, and did the same with the fish. [14]This was now the third time that Jesus appeared to the disciples after he was raised from the dead.

The care of the divine Pastor

It certainly can be helpful and edifying when expounding this incident to dwell on what it reveals of Jesus' intense care for the disciples in the aftermath of their far too impulsive return to their old trade. As well as miserable after such an unprofitable night they were full of regret that they might have incurred Jesus' suspicion about their absolute loyalty to his kingdom alone. What was he really going to think of them? Even though they longed to be with him, they were worried about having to face up to him. They had by now realized that their whole fishing enterprise had been self-willed and stupid, and that his question from the shore, *you have no fish, have you?* had indeed been a reproach. Yet when they reached him they found not only that he had understood how hungry and wet they were but also how anxious they should know his mind about them. He made the utmost effort to make them feel at home again in his fellowship. He had catered wonderfully: *'Come and have breakfast'*, and his personal greetings were so warm that they knew he was not there to express displeasure at their return to the fishing nets. Rather was he concerned that they should be able to rid their minds completely of the self-reproach that might prevent them from fully remembering everything he had wanted to say to them in the miracle they had witnessed.

While we are dwelling on the human compassion and forgiving love which moved him to prepare their breakfast, we must also give due attention to some further obviously noticeable features which characterized his completion of the whole miracle. They were told to bring for the feast some of the fish (in v. 9 *fish* is singular—was it one large fish which was already being cooked on the fire?—but in v. 10 *fish* is plural) they had caught—not to be prepared for the market but to be used then and there as an object lesson! He wanted to give them a sign that the great multitude, which the miracle foretold they were soon to catch (the massive 153^2 in their net would soon become 3,000 at Pentecost) had to be given the same compassionate pastoral care as he himself had always shown, not only to themselves but also to the hungry crowds which he had once fed on the mountainside also with bread and fish to show that he himself is the true bread from heaven (6:11, 12).

Moreover, he knew that they would find themselves almost overwhelmed by the responsibility of coping with the follow-up at Pentecost—the organization into cell-groups, the selection of leaders, the maintenance of unity among this eager, needy and diverse multitude. He therefore gave them the sign that the frail net, even when it was hopelessly strained, did not break. With all their inexperience they would be given the ability to cope! He also, by the way, added a special touch to the breakfast meal to signify that he was offering them more than mere earthly victuals. He made it seem a uniquely solemn ceremony when he *took the bread and gave it to them* (v. 13). He wanted to intimate to them that he himself, even when he was ascended to the Father, would be with them to bless their own breaking of bread so that it would become indeed the true bread of life. It is noticeable that when the early church began to settle down to organize itself 'they devoted themselves to the apostles' teaching and fellowship, to

---

[2] For a full discussion of the many attempts to find spiritual symbolism in the number 153, see Carson, p. 672f.

the breaking of bread and the prayers' (Acts 2:42). Of course the 'breaking of bread' was the Lord's Supper which they now regarded not just as a continuation of the Last Supper in the upper room and a proclamation of the Lord's death but also as a continuation of their Easter meals with Jesus (Like 24:30,43). It is important that as we ourselves celebrate the supper, we seek not only communion with Christ in the power of his death but also realize that he comes to be the host who indeed breaks the bread we offer to make its reception by faith indeed a wonderful, self-giving of himself as the bread of life.[3]

Jesus, Peter and ourselves

John 21:15-19

21 When they had finished breakfast, Jesus said to Simon Peter, 'Simon son of John, do you love me more than these?' He said to him, 'Yes, Lord; you know that I love you.' Jesus said to him, 'Feed my lambs.' [16]A second time he said to him, 'Simon son of John, do you love me?' He said to him, 'Yes, Lord; you know that I love you.' Jesus said to him, 'Tend my sheep.' [17]He said to him the third time, 'Simon son of John, do you love me?' Peter felt hurt because he said to him the third time, 'Do you love me?' And he said to him, 'Lord, you know everything; you know that I love you.' Jesus said to him, 'Feed my sheep. [18]Very truly, I tell you, when you were younger, you used to fasten your own belt and to go wherever you wished. But when you grow old, you will stretch out your hands, and someone else will fasten a belt around you and take you where you do not wish to go.' [19](He said this to indicate the kind of death by which he would glorify God.) After this he said to him, 'Follow me.'

'Do you love me?'

Throughout the whole dramatic and prolonged encounter by the sea of Galilee, Jesus had been concerned primarily to give a clear

---

[3] The reference to this being *now the third time that Jesus appeared to the disciples after he was raised from the dead* (v. 14) probably only refers to those resurrection appearances which John has recorded in his Gospel and should not be taken as excluding other appearances such as those recorded in Luke 24.

message to his apostolic group. Yet he had on his mind
something quite particular to say to Peter and he took the
opportunity of doing so by engaging him in a searching
conversation immediately after breakfast. Peter knew already
that he had been forgiven.[4] He would not have been able to
continue amongst the apostles unless somehow it had been borne
in upon his mind that Jesus had not cast him off after his
shameful denial three times that he was a follower of the Lord.
Jesus, however, was concerned that the memory of the folly and
cheap bravado which had been exposed during Peter's denial, and
the sense of shame and guilt which it all had left on his mind and
soul, should not prevent him now from taking up the task to
which he had called him and for which he had trained him. The
time would soon come for the infant church to require
courageous, steady and far-seeing leadership. By his prolonged
three-fold dramatic repetition of the searching question about his
personal love and loyalty, Jesus in a deliberately forceful way
was recalling to Peter all the details of that night in which he
denied Jesus. He gave him ample time to go over it all in his
imagination and even brought back to his mind that foolish
original boast that, though all should fail Jesus, he himself would
never do so (cf. Matt. 26:33). His purpose in bringing it all back
to light was to ensure that Peter, knowing that everything was
exposed, might at the same time become fully assured that
everything was forgiven. Peter in the very event of his being thus
restored to leadership gives proof that he himself has undergone a
conversion. His confidence now rests not on what he finds in
himself but on what he knows that Jesus sees and finds in him.
Lord, …you know that I love you (vv. 16, 17). The one who is to
feed, tend and care for the sheep and the lambs has discovered
that he himself after all is a sheep which has every tendency to
become lost again and needs to be cared for and held by the
shepherd.

We can thus discover so much of interest and edification when
we seek to bring out what Jesus was aiming to say to Peter in this
interview. Yet we must also realize that the words with which he

---

[4] The message from the young man dressed in white who met the women at the
empty tomb had specifically been directed to the 'disciples and Peter' (Mark
16:7) and there had also been a resurrection appearance (unrecorded) to Simon
Peter alone (Luke 24:34).

questioned and constrained Peter were at the same time quite deliberately uttered by him with a much wider and far-seeing purpose. He well knew that what he said to Peter would find its place in the treasured and repeated tradition of the church, and he worded it so that it would become directly and closely relevant to every generation of its continuing life. Once, in my student days when I was extremely ill in hospital, on an Easter Sunday, I happened to hear on the radio this interview read, as it deserves, slowly and eloquently. I myself was not then in any way committed in service to the church. I knew little about the Bible and nothing much about Peter. Yet I felt myself quite strangely and deeply challenged as Jesus' three questions came home to me. They seemed to call me to realize and resolve that the way I continued to live my life really mattered. Of course when I now, as a church elder and pastor, overhear Jesus' questioning, I find myself even more pointedly challenged as to whether I can meet the requirement of love and faithfulness which he seeks from all to whom he entrusts such responsibility.

Here he demands from us an ever acute awareness of the intensity of his love for his church, and of the greatness of our responsibility of having it put in our care. He reminds us of what God said time and again to his beloved Israel: 'They shall be mine' (Mal. 3:17; cf. Isa. 14:1) and by that expression he meant 'my beloved is mine and I am his' (Song of Songs 2:16). The best analogy that we have is that found in a truly blessed marriage. The hymn paraphrases eloquently what the New Testament elsewhere teaches (cf. Eph. 5:25ff.):

> From heaven he came and sought her
> To be his holy bride;
> With his own blood he bought her,
> And for her life he died.

Here is what we must constantly keep before us in all our dealings with those committed to our care. Of course he knows our difficulties. He warned his apostles about the hindrances with which they would be confronted as they gave themselves to their leadership and pastorates. There would be tares among the wheat (Matt. 13:24-30). Their net would contain 'some good, some bad' (Matt. 13:44-49). Calvin in his comment on this passage felt that he had to warn us: 'Nothing is more difficult than to keep men under the yoke of God. Some are weak, others are light and unsteady, others are dull and sluggish and yet others hard and unteachable... and add to this the ingratitude of many.' We could also add to this the persistent tendency in all human nature to claim for ourselves some decisive place in achieving salvation (cf. Rom. 3:27, 8; 9:30-32, etc.).

It was because he knew it all so well that Jesus three times[5] and with such dramatic force brings home to us the one thing we must also become possessed by if we are to fight the good fight and win through: *do you love me...?*[6] We will be able to overcome and see our way through everything that daunts and hinders us in our task, only if we originally had and still maintain as our chief inducement and dominant motive the personal love and devotion for himself that he here demands. And we ourselves, as we allow ourselves to be questioned, can adequately reply only with the same kind of answer as he inspired Peter to give. We will

---

[5] The NRSV does not distinguish between the two different Greek verbs used in the three questions, 'do you love me...' and the three answers. Twice Jesus uses the Greek verb *agapaô* but in the third question uses the Greek verb *phileô*. In all three of Peter's answers, he uses *phileô* in his reply. Commentators differ in their understanding of the distinction between the two verbs. Some hold that *agapaô* has the meaning of a higher, self-giving love (which undoubtedly it has later on in NT writings) and that *phileô* has a less intense meaning of 'have affection for'. This would mean that in the Lord's third question, he deliberately descends to Peter's more modest affirmation, asking, 'But do you even have affection for me?' Other commentators hold the opposite view that in John's Gospel, *agapaô* has a weaker connotation than *phileô*. Yet others hold there is no intended distinction between the two verbs. However, as the two Greek verbs have been deliberately chosen by John to report a conversation which was originally in Aramaic, one must assume John is seeking to bring out subtle nuances in the Lord's exchange with Peter. See note 6 below.

[6] 'Simon son of John, do you love me *more than these*?' (v. 15). The question arises as to what Jesus meant by 'more than these'. There are clearly three options. First, was Jesus referring to the fishing boat and gear a few metres away on the shingle? Second, was Jesus referring to the affection Simon had for the other men and was he asking who came first in his life—his colleagues or the Lord? Third, was Jesus asking if Simon's love for himself was greater than that of the other men—as Simon Peter had earlier boasted (13:37). John is fond of ambiguous nuances in his writing, and it may be that we are to understand the Lord's reference to both the first and the third of the three options. How we interpret the question will probably have a bearing on our interpretation of the verbs used in the question and Simon's reply (see note 5 above). Finally, note there is likely to be significance in Jesus' use of Simon's 'pre-Christian' name (see 1:42) and an implicit challenge to him to turn his back forever on the old life.

discover as we search our hearts that our ability to give a positive answer lies with him alone. We have been and still are entirely in his hands. His love to us has been clearly and finally expressed in redemptive history, and our love to him can arise only out of the place he has given us (and is still willing to renew) in that history. We hold on to him because he still holds on to us.

As the conversation comes to its close we are brought back to Peter and are called to allow ourselves, like him, to listen afresh to the implications of his call to *Follow me*. When we first heard from him that call, it was through the echo of his word: 'If any want to be come my followers let them deny themselves and take up their cross and follow me' (Matt. 16:24). Responding to him, we gradually discovered that as he led us through life he always beckoned us on through his teaching and personal guidance in a direction contrary to our own self-will. We discovered, too, that he had allocated to us the kind of cross he wanted us to bear. He indeed planned and measured the nature and the weight of the burden of affliction or persecution which would conform our lives outwardly to the pattern he willed for us.

Now we are reminded through the example of Peter of the overwhelming nature of the cross some of us are called, and others forced, to bear. The chief element in self-denial, our personal choice, is allowed little place in what happens to us. The will and power of 'someone else' will fully decide the direction of our lives and carry us beyond our depth and ability to cope. How good it is to know that this 'someone else' who girds and carries us is indeed the Lord himself.

'Follow me'

John 21:20-25

21 Peter turned and saw the disciple whom Jesus loved following them; he was the one who had reclined next to Jesus at the supper and had said, 'Lord, who is it that is going to betray you?' [21]When Peter saw him, he said to Jesus, 'Lord, what about him?' [22]Jesus said to him, 'If it is my will that he remain until I come, what is that to you? Follow me!' [23]So the rumour spread in the community that this disciple would not die. Yet Jesus did not say to him that he would not die, but, 'If it is my will that he remain until I come, what is that to you?'

24 This is the disciple who is testifying to these things and has written them, and we know that his testimony is true. [25]But there are also many other things that Jesus did; if every one of them were written down, I suppose that the world itself could not contain the books that would be written.

The 'undivided heart'

We refer to what we have already said about the need there was at the time this Gospel was being compiled to scotch a current rumour in the church, that the beloved disciple would not die before the final return of Jesus. The record of the short conversation that conveys this information also brings before us an example of how Jesus in his discipling of Peter dealt with his most besetting faults. He once described one of the basic requirements of his followers as that of having an 'eye that was healthy'. They must be single-minded—that is, have 'undivided hearts' (cf. Ps. 86:11; Ezek. 11:19, NIV)—in their devotion to himself alone; otherwise they were in danger of having a heart and mind 'full of darkness', and of becoming unstable in all their ways (Matt. 6:22, 23; Jas 1:8; 4:8). It must, therefore, have deeply concerned Jesus when Peter, so soon after making his sincere profession of loyalty and love, looked round from the way he was being led, and questioned him with a quite unwarranted curiosity, perhaps even bordering on envy, about the privilege he appeared to continue to bestow on his obviously favourite disciple.

Jesus was gentle and understanding in his comment on Peter's reaction. He knows well how inadequate our very best can be (cf. Ps. 103:14). It is impossible for any of us always to maintain the undivided heart as it is to maintain the purity of heart that is never tempted by a lustful thought (cf. Matt. 5:27, 28). There is sympathy and understanding in his reproach to Peter for his fault: *'If it is my will that he remain until I come, what is that to you? Follow me!'* The exposure of Peter's weakness in no way destroyed his complete trust that his future would be as he had prophesied. He pledges himself again, as so often before, ready to lead, forgive and restore—a good Shepherd of his sheep, present always and going before, so that they can hear his voice and thus become enabled to follow.

We interpret the final comment as made by the editor of the book who was responsible for the final form and publication of the Gospel as we have it. He tells us that in editing the text he had the beloved disciple there with him as an eyewitness to the whole recorded history and that he was the actual author of much of it.[7] We are also confirmed here in our belief that the beloved disciple was the apostle John himself. Having restricted himself so rigidly to recording only reliable fact, he allows himself to indulge in his one exaggeration (hyperbole) in the whole book to express his conviction that as long as time lasts, from generation to generation, Jesus himself will triumphantly continue to bless with healing, salvation, new life and glorious hope, all who put their trust in him.

---

[7] There are many commentators who accept John himself is the author of the whole Gospel. Others assume that it was his recent death that precipitated the writing of chapter 21. Yet others hold that 'the beloved disciple' is an idealized 'believer'. As it stands, v. 24 would appear to be claiming Johannine authorship for the entire gospel. However, contrary to that view is the identity of the plural pronoun, 'we know that his testimony is true' (v. 24b). To whom does the 'we' refer? Some have suggested the elders at Ephesus are referred to. Others that this is a general term John uses from time to time (cf. 3:2, 11; 20:2). Whatever conclusion we come to, John's stamp on the entire Gospel can be accepted as being definitive and authentic.

Editor's Bibliography

Barrett, C. K., *The Gospel According to St John,* SPCK, London, 1955.

Calvin, J., *Harmony of the Gospels,* 3 Volumes, ed. David W. Torrance & Thomas F. Torrance, St Andrew Press, Edinburgh, 1972.

Calvin, J., *The Gospel According to St John,* 2 Volumes, ed. David W. Torrance & Thomas F. Torrance, Oliver & Boyd, Edinburgh, 1959.

Carson, D. A., *The Gospel According to St John,* PNTC, Apollos, Leicester, 1991.

Dick Lucas & William Philip, *Teaching John,* Christian Focus Publications, Fearn, Tain, 2002.

Marshall, I. H., *The Gospel of Luke,* NIGTC, Paternoster Press, Carlisle, 1978.

Morris, L., *The Gospel According to John,* NICNT, Eerdmans, Grand Rapids, 1971.

Tasker, R. V. G., *The Gospel According to St John,* Tyndale Press, London, 1960.

Notes

Notes

Notes